THE
MESSAGE REDISCOVERED

Original title: *Le Message Retrouvé ou l'Horloge de la Nuit et du Jour de Dieu*
Translation directed by J. d'Hooghvorst-Lohest
First French edition: ed. Denoël, Paris, 1956

© J. d'Hooghvorst-Lohest
© of this edition:
Éditions Philomène Alchimie
27 rue de Locquirec
29620 Lanmeur
FRANCE

All rights reserved, including the right to reproduce this book or any part thereof in any form.

ISBN: 9782493577986

www.editionsphilomenealchimie.com
contact@editionsphilomenealchimie.com

LOUIS CATTIAUX

THE MESSAGE REDISCOVERED
OR THE CLOCK OF GOD'S NIGHT AND DAY

Preface by Lanza del Vasto
Presentation by E. and C. d'Hooghvorst

Text revised and corrected 2024

Éditions Philomène Alchimie

TO THE READER

The Message Rediscovered is not a collection of thoughts produced by human wisdom; nor is it a literary work among the hundreds that appear every day in the publishing world. No, it is quite a different book. It is dedicated, as its inspired author states on the very first page,

> To the glory of God and at the service of men who shall read *with the eyes of the spirit and of the heart* the signs inscribed in the flesh of the world [...] This book is not for all, but only for those to whom it is given *to believe the unbelievable.*

E. d'Hooghvorst in reference to the origin of inspired word, wrote the following on Poetry:

> Of all forms of art, poetry certainly is the most worthy of admiration down here, for its material is the noblest of human functions: the Word. Poetry, true poetry, is the same thing as prophecy. The Ancients had no doubt that poets were possessed by a divine being: the Muse. Without muses there were no poets. The rhythmic terms of poetry were those of an incarnate god. The god of poetry was Apollo himself, head of the Muses' choir and source of all prophecy or mantic word.[1]

This is why the British translators, on rendering the text into English, have adhered strictly to the precise meaning of the French words and present a literal translation.

---

1. E. d'Hooghvorst, *Le Fil de Pénélope*, t. I, ed. La Table d'Émeraude, Paris, 1996, p. 98.

Thus, in verse 40 of book I: « He who is learned *(instruit)[...]* » becomes « He who has been instructed [...] » : the French *instruit* does not have to be understood in the sense of university teaching, but rather in the sense of a divine teaching, that is, instructed by divine Light, which hermetic philosophers call « The Light of Nature ». One of these philosophers, Thomas Vaughan, alias Eugenius Philalethes, wrote in the treatise *Lumen de Lumine*:

> I wrote only what God confirmed for my eyes alone, and that He can prove before the world in general. I have seen His secret Light, His candle is my teacher.

This is the true instruction to which *The Message Rediscovered* refers, for example, in book I, verse 2:

> Pure men reach God without the aid of clerics or scholars since they are already saints in the Lord, who instructs as he wants, when he wants and where he wants.

« Pure men »: it could be said, are those that have been made holy by divine initiation, but they are certainly very few in number.

Let us also consider verse 3' of book XIX:

> The Book speaks to intuition, to love and to deep memory, and not to men's intelligence, will and superficial reason. « What the Book says is great, but what it induces in each one of us is incommensurable. »

What we are concerned with here is revelation, rather than literature. The first twelve books represent the quintessence of Louis Cattiaux's *Message*. The verses are short and concentrated in the extreme, and this is why their hermetic meaning is more difficult to penetrate.

From book XIII onwards, the poetic aroma becomes more perceptible. Some extracts taken at random provide examples of this. Let us consider book XXVIII, verse 14, book XXXVIII, verses 24 to 34", or book XXXV, verses 74 to 79".

> Let us not break our head over the Book; instead, let us break our heart over it, so that our precious soul germinates and fructifies before God in the secret of the beginning and end of all things. (XVII, 53')

A first edition of *The Message Rediscovered* was published in 1946 at the author's expense, containing only the first twelve chapters, those that had been finished by then.

That first edition was received by the public with total indifference, and the literary critics scarcely gave it a mention, except a few ones, among them René Guénon.

The Message Rediscovered opens with two prayers in triangular form; one represents the sign of ascending fire, as the Father; the other, the sign of falling water, as the Mother. This work contains 40 books, or chapters, and is presented as a series of verses in two columns that should generally be read horizontally from left to right. Each chapter is preceded by epigraphs and followed by hypographs drawn from the holy Scriptures of all Nations.

> We speak a new language, but we repeat the ancient unique revelation, for nobody invents anything in the ART of God. (XXXIII, 42)

This is the affirmation of the universality of a single and identical revelation since the beginning through all the holy books.

The Message Rediscovered does not necessarily have to be read like an ordinary book, from beginning to end. A way of approaching it is to open it at random and to read the verses that your eyes fall upon. Or even better, one can consult it on a particular subject by inserting the point of a paper-knife into its closed pages and reading the response indicated by the point of it. For it is, in fact, a kind of magic book that replies to questions one puts to it with simplicity and without malice.

But to approach it is not to penetrate it. With regard to its profound content we read:

> The Book is like the ark that carries and transmits the secret of the Unique One. Many shall carry it, but few shall penetrate it. (XXIII, 61')

> Here there is more than a moral and more than an asceticism, more than a philosophy and more than a mysticism. Here is the key to the restitution of man and the world in God. (IX, 36')

> The Book teaches us how to come out of death and repose in life, but how many of the believers are passionate about this mystery? (XII, 5')

This is the true content of this *Message*, which has been called prophetic.

As the author says, this book addresses itself to intuition and profound memory, and not to speculative reason. Very few in number are those that have had the intelligence and the patience to read it and ponder over it, so as to penetrate it and discover the path that leads to the living secret of man, buried in the deepest depths of the nature of this world.

Has the murkiness of ignorance descended so thickly to that extent upon today's humanity to make it forget the trace of the holy science of the disciples of Hermes, transmitted from age to age through filiation?

At the time, even those who still believed in it and who practised alchemy did not recognize L. Cattiaux as one of their own.

« This book is all very fine », they say, leafing through *The Message*, « but it has nothing to do with our alchemy; it contains not a single practical formula like those taught by our masters. It is just one more mystical book among so many others ».

Did the learned masters not also repel the Book as being alien to their revelations, their traditions and their sciences? (XXXVIII, 13)

This verdict was almost unanimous.

In short, *The Message Rediscovered*, in an uncommon language, that is to say, in a language other than that normally used by masters of alchemy, a language with which Cattiaux was perfectly acquainted from having studied the works of the ancient masters, *The Message Rediscovered*, speaks nevertheless on every page of their famous matter, light of Nature, secret fire of the opus capable of dissolving vulgar gold without violence, of making it germinate, fructify and multiply, that is, of converting vulgar mercury into the Mercury of the Philosophers and maturing it, through the union of that which is most high with that which is most low.

Louis Cattiaux, in a good many of letters to his close friends Charles (1924-2004) and Emmanuel d'Hooghvorst (1914-1999), had expressed his heartfelt wish to see his major work translated into English. He even thought an English edition should appear before the first complete edition in French:

> [...] in any case, English seems to me more in keeping with *The Message Rediscovered*, because there is among the English-speaking peoples a quest for God, a serious-mindedness and a faith that is, you might say, totally lacking in the French.
>
> [...] I continue to believe that the English edition of *The Message Rediscovered* is the only reasonable solution, for French has become the classic language of the ungodly, it must be said.
>
> [...] I think an edition in English would be more successful than one in French, which has become the language of sceptics and atheists par excellence.
>
> [...] an edition in an English-speaking country would be of great importance for the circulation of the work.
>
> [...] English is better than French because circulation is better and quicker. America would be the best place at the moment. We need to find a black publisher, preferably. A French edition will be possible afterwards.

But this wish could not be fulfilled at the time, the first complete edition in French appeared in 1956, three years after his death.

Subsequently, *Le Message Retrouvé* has been republished seven times in French, the very latest version has been published by **Philomène Alchimie** in January 2024. The same publisher has also just published an art book on Louis Cattiaux as he was not only a writer but also a painter. The book, entitled *Cattiaux, un Art magique* features a comprehensive biography and fine reproductions of 192 pictorial works showing a clearly hermetic and alchemical content. It also includes extracts from Cattiaux's essay on Painting. Readers wishing to know more about this author can find this essay in English under the title *Physics and Metaphysics of Painting*, as well as a collection of letters to his friends *The Collected Letters of Louis Cattiaux*.

Le Message Retrouvé has also been translated into several languages, with six editions in Spanish, five in Catalan, one in Italian, three in Portuguese, one in German, and a Dutch translation is coming.

Upcoming event from September 2024: The international traveling exhibition on the Berthe Weill retrospective and her gallery, which will travel from the *Grey Art Gallery* in New York (30th Sept. 2024-2nd March 2025) to the *Musée de l'Orangerie* in Paris (8th Oct.-25th Jan. 2025) via the *Montreal Museum of Fine Arts* (5th May-7th Sept. 2025), will feature the work of Louis Cattiaux, through the exhibition of the painting entitled « *La Vierge attentive ou la Vierge à l'étoile* », a knife-painted canvas that bears witness to Louis Cattiaux's first pictorial stage.

Now, seventy years have passed, and we have the honour of presenting this work to English-speaking readers, to their enormous benefit. We hope thus to have fulfilled the wishes of its author.

JEANNE D'HOOGHVORST
January 2024

PREFACE

The conspiracy of the imbeciles, the charlatans and the sages has succeeded to perfection.

The object of this conspiracy was to conceal the truth.

Each one has served this great cause, each according to his means: the imbeciles by means of ignorance, the charlatans by means of lying, the sages by means of secrecy.

The imbeciles do not want the truth to be discovered. They suspect, instinctively, that it would disturb them. If it were shown to them they would avert their eyes; if it were placed in their hands they would let it fall; if they were forced to confront it face-to-face they would howl in horror and run and hide below ground.

The charlatans do not want the truth to be discovered, for it would ruin their artifices, impede their profit and show up their shame.

The sages who possess the truth do not want it to be discovered. They have always kept it hidden for four reasons.

The first is that they know that knowledge is power and they want to keep it away from the unworthy. For knowledge in the unworthy one becomes malice, power becomes public danger and plague. That is why the reserves of knowledge accumulated over millennia in the temples of Egypt remained inaccessible to him who had not passed through all the stages of purifications and tests. Later, the unknown philosophers, the noble travellers, the alchemists handed down to one another the rest of the mysterious heritage in the same way, that is, by word of mouth, or rather, by their presence and by example, in symbols and enigmas, and always under the seal of secrecy. If they lived in the intimacy of the formidable powers of nature, they made sure the irresponsible knew nothing about them.

Where are you, oh, sages who know how to remain silent? You deserve that all living beings proclaim their gratitude to you, oh, sages.

Oh, sages who knew how to remain silent, now we have learned the value of your prudence, the grandeur of your humility, the depth of your charity.

Now that the profane ones have taken it upon themselves to acquire science and to propagate it as much as they can, now that they glory in their discoveries with the same zeal with which you hid your own, we have seen the result.

But their science is so small, exterior, superficial, precarious and limited, and we already see the result.

The result is that they have poisoned the springs, mined the earth, tarnished the sky, disrupted and perverted the peoples, corrupted peace, dishonoured war, furnished the common man with so many instruments of destruction and oppression that the entire family of living beings is threatened, while this canker continues to progress.

The second reason for the sages to keep the truth hidden is that *knowing* is an operation of life and a way of *being born*. And nothing can be born without a casing. A casing of flesh or of bark, of earth or of mystery. A seed, if you open it, will germinate no more; in a lizard, if you open it up to see what is inside, you will find only the remains of the corpse and not the inside of the lizard, which has gone, since the lizard is dead. Likewise, open, propagated, vulgarised science is dead science and the fruit of death. It is a desert of sand, and not a handful of seeds. It cannot be deepened, but only spread out, being exterior, and life escapes it. It cannot lead to the knowledge that is birth for oneself, nor to interior life. But the knowledge of the sages is an art of poetry that has the taste of joy and the breath of spirit. And like any living being, even a fly, it defends its form and refuses to spread itself.

The third reason for the sages to keep the truth hidden is their respect for the dignity of knowledge. They know it is the royal way that leads to the God of truth. It should lead to contemplation, to admiration of nature, to adoration of the creator.

It should bring light into souls, accuracy into thoughts, justice into acts. It should bring health and salvation. The sages have defended it as much as they could against vulgar men, for fear of it being diverted from its goal, denaturalised and debased, which is what vulgar men have not failed to do since they laid their hands on it. They have turned it upside down in using it. They put it to their use instead of serving it. It was here to deliver them from their desires and they have harnessed it to their tasks. They have forced it to increase their possessions. It was here to give them awareness and they have made machines out of it. They have taken the ciborium and made a piggy bank out of it; they have taken the crucifix to make a bludgeon. They have harnessed science to their motors, they have imprisoned it in their bombs.

But the oh-so-shrewd ones have been caught up in their own traps, they have let themselves be snatched in the gearing of the machine. Now, it clips them gently in times of peace, and devours them in great mouthfuls in times of war. The sages did all they could to avoid that.

The fourth reason for the sages to keep the truth hidden is that they love the truth, and that there is no love without modesty, that is, without a veil of beauty. This is why they do not want to uncover it but to reveal it, that is, to cover it with a luminous veil. Thus, they have taught it only by way of parables, so that those who have ears that are tuned in keep away, but equally so that those who deserve it learn the tones and the keys of the total music. For their allegories, their fables, their blazons do not explain the mechanical linking up of appearances, but rather the secret affinities and analogies of powers and virtues, the corresponding of numbers with sounds, of figures with laws, of water with plants, woman and the soul, of fire with lions and armed men, with the spirit, of the stars with the eyes, with flowers, with crystals of metals and gems, of the germination of gold in the mines with that of truth in the heart of man. In their obscure texts, where the recipes of Great Art are interspersed with pious warnings, the solemn sentences with cries of wonder and prayers, gleam the threads that weave the mantle of the king of kings.

The sages having scrupulously hidden their knowledge, the charlatans took advantage to hide their ignorance under the same mysterious signs. The imbeciles confused them for a long time, believing in one and another.

But now there has emerged, halfway between the charlatans and the imbeciles, a new species that ensures the definitive triumph of the conspiracy.

This new species is that of the academics and official scholars. On the day of their arrival, they declared the philosophical mystery invalid; chimera, the research of the ancient masters; child's play, their science; a hoax, their art. The imbeciles instructed by the new scholars have once again confused the sages and the charlatans, but this time they do not believe in either of them.

They believe in nothing but the science of the newly-arrived ones, who teach simply that the truth is in their science and that everything they cannot discover or demonstrate does not exist.

But they have neither taught nor discovered nor demonstrated anything about life and death, sin and judgement, about love, pain and redemption, about the behaviour of man and the destiny of the soul, about sense, essence and salvation. The more they discover new nebulas or new electrons, new vitamins or new explosives, the more they distance themselves and divert us from the essential. And now the truth is so well hidden that one no longer seeks it.

It would even be totally lost if some simple spirits for whom the truth exists did not survive. They cannot resign themselves into thinking that no-one possesses or has possessed it. They go around the world questioning people, interrogating the stars and the grasses, interrogating the great book of nature and leafing through forgotten texts, interrogating their heart and God in prayer. They know they do not have the truth, but they know that it is. They are so hungry and thirsty for it that they are able to follow its trail and recognize its scent. Before a defamed man, before an absurd event, before a piece of illegible scrawl, they stop dead and cry:

Here it is!

They shall savour this book. It is for them that it is written, even though their brotherhood be few in number.

And you, Cattiaux my friend, have you found the stone?

Sitting in the workshop where you paint and meditate among filters and flasks, have you found the carbuncle and the violet?

Sitting between your wife and your cat, Cattiaux my friend, have you found the living gold and the elixir?

Have you visited the interiors of the earth, and rectifying it, found the secret jewel and the true medicine?

I do not know and I cannot say if the substance of the ancient texts is hidden in these pages. But how is it that one finds the perfume in them?

In what egg and in what still Cattiaux my friend, have you distilled the subtle essence that is called the perfume?

Whence comes this poetry whose name is perfume of truth?

LANZA DEL VASTO
November 1945

PRESENTATION

Many wish to heare and do not know how to listen.
François de Foix

Wisdom is as rare in Tibet as it is in Paris, said Louis Cattiaux. It may flourish everywhere, however, without anyone suspecting it. A man similar to, but not the same as so many other city-dwellers, has written these pages that it falls to the reader to judge. They are not for everyone, even though they are destined to circulate among the men of today who, through neglect of the ancient revelation, have allowed themselves to sink into profound ignorance.

Those for whom this book has been written shall know it well on reading it, for it is given to them, as the author puts it, to believe the unbelievable. They shall know how to read and understand it, they belong to the same spiritual family. Before leaving this world on 16th July 1953, the author left it for them as a rallying sign and a reason for hope;[1] he dedicated it most especially to the black peoples, still divided and as though in their infancy, but destined to become powerful in the world through the play of a Providence indifferent to the intentions and works of men.

The Message Rediscovered is not easy to approach. It contains, according to the author, a tightly-linked initiation and mystique presented in a concentrated form that demands more than a straightforward reading, the words being transcended by the revelation, and the work presenting itself as liquid air that has acquired other extraordinary properties, but which are invisible at first sight...[2] The verses are arranged in two columns, for there

---

1. *The Message Rediscovered* XXXII, 37 and 38, and XXXIII, 35.

are two men in us, the carnal man and the spiritual man, the external man and the internal man, just as there is also darkness and light, justice and love, the pure and the impure; all things are arranged two by two.[3] Each of the verses includes several profound meanings, the left column generally giving the earthly meanings: moral, philosophical and ascetic; the right column giving the heavenly meanings: cosmogonic, mystical and initiatory. Sometimes these verses are completed with a third one placed in the middle of the page, bringing together the two others in the alchemic meaning that unites heaven and earth, relating to the mystery of God, of creation and of man; as for this most profound meaning, it corresponds only to God to reveal it to the pious man. One will also notice that each of the XXXX books carries a double title, for example, for book 1, on the left: VÉRITÉ NUE, on the right: THE GREEN SHOOT. The forty titles over the left hand columns are anagrams of one another. It is indeed rare to be able to make forty anagrams by means of nine letters that are always the same. The knowing reader will realize that not a single word of this book has been put there without intention.

The Message Rediscovered speaks to us of but a single thing, in continually different terms, so that the multitude of verses is not a dissipation. The ignorant ones in search of a *new revelation*, coming to add something to or subtract something from the old one, shall be disappointed. One shall find here only a testimony[4] in favour of the old one that speaks to us of the fall of man in this base world, of the physical and moral consequences of that fall, and of the means of his bodily and spiritual regeneration, via the mysterious way that leads to resurrection.[5]

We may perhaps scandalize more than one reader in affirming here that the Spirit of Elijah, still alive, manifests itself through the ages;[6] let those people abstain, for here is the rock of scandal. Yet blessed is he who shall know, in the pages that are to follow, how to loose this spirit from its coarse outer shell, recognize its authenticity and take nourishment from it for an eternal life.

2. Louis Cattiaux. Letters to G. Chaissac.
3. *The Message Rediscovered* III, 98.
4. *Ibidem* XXIX, 36.
5. *Ibidem* XXIX, 33 and 45.
6. *Ibidem* XXXVI, 95. We have expressed ourselves at greater length on this subject in a study on *The Message Rediscovered*, published in the review «Inconnues», vol. 9, Lausanne, 1954.

The general dedication of *The Message Rediscovered* tells us that it is intended «for the glory of God and at the service of men who shall read with the eyes of the spirit and of the heart the signs inscribed in the flesh of the world». The eyes of carnal reason or of the intellect shall, in fact, teach us nothing, there where language addresses itself to the eyes of the spirit and of the heart. The first ones reveal to us only the outer shell or the changing appearance of the world; the second ones guide us towards the Essence and the Substance, its indestructible support, and allow us to recognize the interior light that God lit up at the beginning in nature and in our heart.[7]

It is, then, a work of meditation that demands to be read, re-read and studied in simplicity of spirit and purity of heart. Is it not multiplicity and restlessness of the spirit that deprive us of the possession of the Kingdom of the Heavens, and the impurity of our hearts that distances us from the vision of God?[8]

The testimony of the Scriptures teaches us that knowledge of the divine light should proceed, not from the exterior, but from within; awoken and stimulated through its free origin, this buried light then germinates, and, becoming the «right measure» and the source of our judgements, it «appears then outside and shines fully in union».[9]

A deaf man will judge music from the description one can offer him, since he lacks the use of the organ that allows him to experience it for himself. It is the same for the other senses. The light shines in the darkness, but if man is deprived of the use of the appropriate organ to apprehend that interior light, it is darkness for him just as long as he does not recover the look of the spirit and of the heart.

If you have faith and patience, wrote the author with regard to *The Message Rediscovered*, it will become clear by itself a little at a time, and everything that seems obscure to you shall then appear evident.

It is therefore that we suggest the reader should develop his own personal opinion on this work and should judge for himself whether or not it is identical to traditional teaching.

EMMANUEL & CHARLES D'HOOGHVORST
January 1956

---

7. *The Message Rediscovered* VIII, 50'.
8. *Ibidem* XIII, 32'.
9. *Ibidem* IX, 54'; IV, 36' and XII, 12' and 13'.

Louis Cattiaux, 1945

BIOGRAPHICAL NOTE

1904 Louis-Ghislain Cattiaux was born on 17th August in Valenciennes (France).
1922 He studied at the *École des Arts et Métiers* in Paris.
1928 He lived for some months in Dahomey, working for a trading company.
1932 He married Henriette Péré. Together with her, he set up a gallery of avant-garde art called *Gravitations*.
1934 Cattiaux was one of several poets and painters to sign the manifesto *Transhylisme*.
1938 He began writing *Le Message Retrouvé*.
1946 Publication of the first edition of *Le Message Retrouvé* (the first twelve chapters, with a preface by Lanza del Vasto).
1949 He met the d'Hooghvorst family, with whom he maintained a fruitful correspondence. From 1980, fragments of the letters were published and have been collected under the title *The Collected Letters of Louis Cattiaux*.
1951 He wrote an essay on painting *Physics and metaphysics of painting*.
1953 He departed this world on 16th July.

★

1954 Publication of an anthology of his poetry, including *Poèmes alchimiques, tristes, zen, d'avant, de la résonance,* and *de la connaissance*, by the publisher Le Cercle du Livre (Paris).
1956 Publication of the first French complete edition of *Le Message Retrouvé* by the publisher Denoël (Paris).

THE MESSAGE REDISCOVERED

OR THE CLOCK OF GOD'S NIGHT AND DAY

To the glory of God* and at the service of men who shall read with the eyes of the spirit and of the heart the signs inscribed in the flesh of the world.

«*Enter and rest, leave and shine, but remain always in one.*»

This book is not for all, but only for those to whom it is given to believe the unbelievable.

---

* HIM (In French *LUI*): the secret fire that gives rise to universes, that maintains them and that consumes them.

▲
Golden
Father
who are
everywhere
and who rest in
the sun and in
the holy earth. Give
us the intelligence of
your forms and the love
of your Being. Erase our stain,
pull us out of the mud into
which we have fallen. Make us
like the holy Mother and engender
us in perfect love. Hidden and most
evident Father. Possessor of the
eternal light. Magic creator of worlds.
Cure our bodies, soothe our souls, free
our spirits. Make us heirs to the glory
where your beloved children shine. Do it, O Lord!

Radiant Mother who are in everything and who transform the stars and the sea. Grant us the secret of your light and the love of your purity. Baptize us in the divine water and fire and receive us in your living bosom. Ripen us to the perfection of love. Luminous Mother surrounded by darkness. Substance of life and source of happiness. God's beneficial seed. Nourish our bodies, quench the thirst of our souls, illuminate our spirits. Show us the path that leads to the beloved Sun. Wash us, holy Mother

▼

THE LIGHT

Like a promised land sodden with innocence, I give myself to him who unravels my night, and my heart settles in repose, and shines.

O Shulamite, my only friend! I am your Solomon alone in the world. Sun and Selene united in Salt. Salvation of the myths and Salaam of the mounts.

Ancient solitude of the primordial forests where the emerald emanated from the stars shines! He who found you possesses the divine secret that a true master passed on to us in bread and wine!

BOOK I

*The rain renders life on earth sterile,
image of resurrection.*

KORAN

*A day of darkness and of gloominess,
A day of clouds and of misty shadows.*

JOEL

VÉRITÉ NUE

1. He who is in the wrong tries to impose it on others.
He who possesses the truth does his best to apply it to himself.
This is the mark that does not deceive.

2. Pure men reach God without the aid of clerics or scholars since they are already saints in the Lord, who instructs them as he wants, when he wants and where he wants.

3. The man who is superior spares others from the evil he has defeated.
The man who is inferior inflicts on everyone the evil to which he himself has been subjected.

4. One can harm someone against his will. One would not be able to do good to anyone against his will.

THE GREEN SHOOT

1'. Truth that separates and unites. Ones. Two. One and nothing more.
«Whatever it is that we have decided to do, let us persevere until the absurd or the light of God delivers us and sets us free in action and at rest.»

2'. The end is like the beginning, but the middle enlightens us.
«The Prayer, the Star, the Stone.»

3'. Death separates what life has united, and water delivers the prisoner from his chains.

4'. The loosened[1] stone does not visibly return, yet it shines like the moon in all its brightness.

---

1. The French *déliée* («loosened») also means «dissolved».

5. Only he who can bring back to life has the right to kill.

5'. One waters that which must flower again.

6. God recognizes his children in the fulfilment of his work.

6'. He sorts out the seeds and makes the magic fruit appear.

7. There is no collective salvation; this is a belief of the mediocre and the lazy.

7'. He who keeps afloat is named the Living One.

8. He who has nothing to defend has no-one to fight.

8'. The nakedness of the Father.

9. The sage is alone with God just as God is alone with himself.

9'. All rests in the circle of luminous gold.

10. The dead gather together in order to pray.
The living isolate themselves in order to converse with God.

10'. The cry that is not heard and yet reaches us.
The response that springs from the bosom of the abyss.

11. The sage only teaches men of his own stamp.

11'. Fire allies with fire to harden the blood of the earth.

12. The simplest thing to teach is the most difficult to understand.

12'. The nurturing mud lies abandoned on the path.

13. He who is strict with himself is indulgent with others.

13'. The perfection of the sphere engenders a lesser friction.

14. He who is intelligent examines the creation in order to know the creator.

14'. By consuming everything, one obtains the smoke and the ashes and sometimes also the light of God.

15. «Mad in the world, wise in God». Such is the motto of the living.

15'. Eating, drinking, working and sleeping is not the life of the believer.

16. The confusion and contradiction of the spirit are the very image of death.
«Immobile spectator, attentive and passionless; such is he who is awake».

16'. Too much misfortune and too much happiness lead to the forgetting of oneself for a while.
The divine union engenders it forever.

17. Many have arrived and have never left. They deceive themselves and deceive others.

18. The madman questions others.
It is said that the wise man questions himself.
Both are close to God, but only one of them knows it.

19. The sage veils the truth by making it evident.

20. To argue with ignorant people is to stir up the mud so that it becomes clearer.

21. All the works of the world cannot be compared to the tiniest of God's creatures.

22. Evil and hatred are so closely associated with death that they become unconscious through the weakness and mediocrity of our hearts.
But goodness and love are so well attached to life that they only subsist in the awakened consciousness and in the activity of a loving heart.

23. The science of men is the violation of the natural and divine laws.
It kills everything and resurrects nothing.

24. Intuition associated with goodwill engenders the power of love which leads to the perfection of union in peace.

17'. Clay pots enclose a precious thing, but they do not last very long when the thing abandons them.

18'. Who can differentiate fire from fire? Who can manifest, embody the sun in the morning star issued from the darkened earth?

19'. That which touches the eye is not seen.

20'. The earth remains at the bottom. Life goes upwards.
Only God can separate them and unite them once more.

21'. The smallest flower represents the Universe. But only man contains it entirely.

22'. We must detach ourselves from created forms, but in order to possess creation in its primary substance and in its hidden essence. Thus, the more rest increases, the more attention must grow in order to survive the dissolution of water and the coagulation of fire.
«One chooses nothing once one is dead.»

23'. A lot of work to do badly, and a lot of work to undo.

24'. Water and fire multiply and make all the visible creation and all the hidden creation of the Lord perfect.

25. It is necessary to observe nature patiently before acting; otherwise, one becomes senseless before God, unbearable to others and eventually hateful to oneself.

26. Clearly, true wisdom, ultimate knowledge, isolates man from his kind more surely than any crime, any leprosy or any death could do.
The union with God is the true reward of the perfect one.

27. What kills the weak strengthens the strong.
What decimates the impious multiples the believer.

28. Dogs bark at what dominates them, or at what escapes them.

29. The essential condition of all cures is the will to heal; one could not save those who have chosen death and who keep themselves there voluntarily.

30. The smallest atom is like the greatest Universe, and the mass of men like a particle of God.

31. All is within All;
Light within Light.

32. All is within Nothing;
Light within the Shade.

33. Nothing is within Nothing;
Shade within the Shade.

25'. The gardener is the most learned of all men, but he does not know it, because he works with darkened seeds and with a soil mixed with death.

26'. The stone is hidden in the flesh, the almond lies under the wood and the germ rests in the nurturing water.
«Who will separate the light from the darkness, and who will manifest the hidden fire of the Lord?
Who will transform the virginal milk into the bodily consistency of the newborn Son?

27'. The ordeal strips the truth bare and makes it shine fully.

28'. The mountain laughs at the wind, but it receives the water and the fire that fertilize it.

29'. Water makes everything flower again, and fire matures the new world up to the holy land promised to the sages.
«O hidden light!»

30'. The sperm is hidden in the body of the earth and in that of the rain.

31'. The germ lies within the sperm.

32'. The composite universal.

33'. Death envelops heaven and earth.

34. He who despises the teaching of the ancient sages condemns himself to ignorance for ever.

35. Nature brings forth all light and leads everything to its perfection.

36. Sages say to the senseless: You destroy bodies but we save the spirit; we shall all return to the earth but we shall not possess it in the same way.

37. It is easier to bring forth fruit by watering stones than to speak of God to the mockers in order to teach them.

38. One cannot be a slave to the world and a friend of God.

39. God through himself produces the Mother, God through the Mother begets the Son, the Son through the Mother multiplies God.
Therefore, God has neither beginning nor end.

40. He who has been instructed despises neither a religion nor any teachings of the ancient sages.

41. Man must pass through mortification and the darkness of death before reaching God.

42. The clear-sighted one praises God for the perfection of his work.

43. To trust an impious person is like throwing a stone and believing it will not fall.

34'. Those that cultivate the land often lack the main heavenly food, which is God's blessing.

35'. The sage places the seed and God opens it by means of water and fire.

36'. The world has been made with water and earth.
It will become like a slime again before being made like an earth again.

37'. God knows the interior of everything. He is Judge through time in eternity.

38'. The flask is cleaned before the heavenly wine is poured in.

39'. Divine acts are instantaneous and subject to faith.
Natural acts are slow and subject to hope.
Human acts are blind and subject to charity.

40'. The earth covers the sublime diamond.

41'. Fire and water purify the earth, but it is God that gives life to it again.

42'. Worms live off fire, but they do not see it.

43'. The rotten plank only enriches the dung.

44. Water that washes and gives life is a truly loosened spirit that comes from heaven and fixes itself in the earth.

45. True wisdom consists in separating that which is good from that which is bad, and in uniting what is good with what is better.

46. He who is intelligent compares the words of the sages meticulously in order to discover the place where they all agree.

47. The venomous and reasoning rage of the ignorant sanctions all holy works.

48. Incapable of reaching that which is beyond them, they try to bring everything down to their level.

Unable to tolerate beauty, they strive to soil everything around them.

Powerless to grasp the truth, they attempt to distort everything they cannot see and hear well.

49. Men in revolt are like trapped rats.

In their delirious confusion they rip themselves apart and bite into their own flesh in their blind and desperate rage.

50. Those that envisage life as the search for the power to annihilate everything around them only reap death.

51. The ignorant one is characterized by the desire to convince others, at any cost, of systems that momentarily reassure him.

44'. Fire that gives life and matures is a very pure soul that comes from the sun and unites heaven and earth.

45'. Water and fire purge mixed creation up to the star of renewal and up to the sun of completion.

46'. One must enter again through where one emerged if one wishes to rest in the peace of the Perfect One.

47'. Nature gives lessons, it does not receive any.

48'. «Death in the mud, the hell of mixture».

The mediocre will not always be able to bury the truth of God. The believers will spread it once again to the ends of the earth and will make it germinate up to the heavens.

49'. They fight over the excrements and disregard the balm. They transform the stones into smoke, but who will transform the smoke into holy stone?

50'. Truth can only be grasped by the sage, and can only be cooked by him.

51'. «In limbo, all is confused and yet to be born.» God expects of us our intellectual death and the spiritual birth of our heart.

52. True philosophy is based on the knowledge of perfectly experienced divine reality, which frees men from all worldly servitude.

53. False science is that scaffolding of delirious thoughts built in the ignorance of the natural laws, which constantly collapses into despair, madness and death.

54. The former edifies in life by means of death,
the latter builds in death by means of life.

55. Those who give themselves titles of scholars and philosophers are subject to the effects of the evil that they carry within themselves and do not know how to reject.
They are ignorant of the cause of their fall and the means of their deliverance.

56. They fabricate and distribute death on the hypocritical pretext of seeking life, but their works demonstrate definitively their pride and their insanity.

57. It is because mankind has a feeble and obscure heart that it repels the strong emotions of divine love.

58. All is spirit, All is matter, depending on whether the Unique One expands or condenses.

59. Divine science uses natural laws as means.
It transforms all and kills nothing.

52'. Death is a light veiled with terror; the sage considers it with serenity and experiences it with intelligence and benefit.

53'. Clothes become rags, and rags become clothes again; he who wears them and throws them away does not change.

54'. That which seems impossible is sometimes easily accomplished, and that which seems easy is often unachievable.

55'. DEATH is useful to everyone, but only one makes proper use of it.
«Very few know that the primary and ultimate wealth is hidden in the heart of exiled men.»

56'. The entire mystery of the world is enclosed in a single grain.
Who will make it green again? And who will make it bear fruit?
«Life is for those who respect it, love it, help it and give birth to it.»

57'. The pearl is hidden in the abyss, and the sun lies in the pearl.

58'. God will inhabit the slime of the purified earth.

59'. God's creation is accomplished with ease, like everything that is purified and perfected by the to-ing

It consolidates the sperm and multiplies the germ.
It manifests life by using death.

60. The living frighten the dead so much that not until they disappear is it announced that they exist.

61. The words of the sages are excellent, but those that claim to explain them are often bad.

62. Too many complications and too many subtleties bring anarchy and death.

63. Vulgar men hate the sage, but he does not despise the instruments of his work.

64. That which passes for madness, that which resembles a dream, that which appears incredible: this is what the sage studies with love.

65. That which the world despises, that which is rejected by all, that which appears vile and valueless: this is what the sage examines with care.

66. He who can do without the approval of men is not tempted to do a useless piece of work.

67. There is no greater punishment than that of ignoring God in the world, and there is no greater joy than to know him in one's heart.

68. Through man one can reach God more easily than through the entire Universe.

and fro-ing of liberating grace and unifying love.

60'. Heavenly water wears down everything and yet is worn down by nothing; it delivers us from the tomb.

61'. Food that is overheated is dead and unfit to sustain the hidden life.

62'. Nature teaches him who looks it in the face and who explores it until the secret foundation.

63'. In the most corrupt of men there lies a sublime and living light.

64'. Life in the shadow of death.
The cubic stone and the triangular stone hidden in the sphere of chaos.

65'. The mud of the abyss, the humility of the earth, the veil of death.
«The fundamental stone and the water of resurrection.»

66'. Freedom is conquered over passions, desires and death.

67'. Between the sage and the brute there is an abyss that only God can fill.
«Let us forgive lack of understanding and let us pray for the conversion of our enemies and persecutors.»

68'. On scrutinizing the image, the model is easily recognized.

69. He who imagines himself to be strong amidst men is the weakest of beings in solitude.

70. No-one will seek God for us. This is a belief of the lazy and of the cowardly.

71. Religions fight each other when God is ill served and ill loved.

72. When we repel a sage, a saint, an artist or a poet, we increase his glory and we multiply our ills.

73. It is always the same people that teach the world and yet are the most despised during their life and the most betrayed after their death.
It is always the same people that deceive mankind and yet are the most honoured during their lifetime and the most respected after their death.

74. The worst people avenge the best without knowing it, and all contribute to the enlightenment of man by man that leads to divine nature.
«He who knows the hidden meaning of the holy Scriptures no longer uses the word of God to curse men astray in death.»

69'. He who is true to himself is unfair to no-one.

70'. Only the food one chooses within oneself can be benefited from.

71'. Disputes show up the true interest.

72'. The tree produces its fruit without worrying about who will eat it, but it needs the rain and the sun just like all living things.

73'. The world prefers manufactured poison to the natural water from the sun and the moon.
«O sleeping individuals of the dying crowds, your lamentable straying could not delight God's simple children; will you awake to the voice of the Lord who begs for your love?»

74'. Our brother is,
this wise man or this madman,
this saint or this criminal,
this chief or this beggar,
this child or this dead man.
«O buried splendour! Holy water that delivers our souls from the foreign earth.»

The impulse of the faith that touches hearts is arduous for mortals and despised by them.
EMPEDOCLES

When faith is not total, it is not faith.
LAO TSE

BOOK II

> *It is hard to leave the familiar and present ways to return to the ancient ones, for appearances are delicious and the invisible is unbelievable.*
> HERMES TRISMEGISTUS

> *Woe betide you hypocritical scribes and Pharisees, for you roam the sea and the earth to make a proselyte, and when he has become one you make of him twice as much a son of Gehenna as yourselves!*
> JESUS

ÈVE TRI UNE

1. New men always cause scandal.

2. To instruct vulgar men in the secrets of God is to arouse delirious desire and pride, to engender disorder and misfortune for ever.

3. There is work that binds in death; it is that of the world.
There is other work that unbinds from death; it is that of God.

4. The first is accomplished with difficulty and only produces sadness and death.
The second is easily performed and engenders joy and eternal life.

5. One must be intelligent and instructed by God to recognize the obviousness of creation.

PURE LIFE

1'. The rude awakening makes everything frightening.

2'. Divine jewels only adorn pure men and only clean women.
«Those that are the most resplendent in God often appear the most obscure in the world.»

3'. Men make death appear by means of fire.
Nature makes life appear by means of water.

4'. The upright and simple spirit penetrates easily to the centre of the earth where the living gold reposes.
«It is the poverty of total void that we must attain in order to be precisely filled with God.»

5'. Men's malice leads them astray in the multiplicity, and pride seals them in the mud.

6. The science of men is a dunghill covered in tinsel.
The science of God is gold covered in mud.

7. The characteristic of truth is that it is self-sufficient; he who possesses it tries to convince no-one.

8. Do not blame the tool it you are a bad workman, and do not call it a crime if you surrender your life to death.

9. A single man may be right against a thousand, and a saint may speak the truth against the entire world.

10. There is as much merit in being silent on finding as there is in searching on knowing nothing.

11. Simplicity and love that have become alien to men make the clearest word the most neglected.

12. Let us reduce by our example the mediocrity and hesitancy of those with lukewarm hearts.

13. Death's sting is there to force men into searching for the purpose of everything and of themselves.

14. Work that increases needs is worthless.
That which decreases them is sacred.
The world practises the former.
The sages help with the latter.

6'. The earth's crust leads the most subtle observers astray, but the interior sea enlightens the simple and believing man.

7'. He who is satiated does not fight with dogs over the rubbish on the path, whose beginning and end he knows.

8'. The great battle eliminates dead filth and makes the moving light of God appear.

9'. A heap of mud contains only one grain of pure gold.

10'. God opens the eyes of his children and closes the mouth of his friends.

11'. What is more despised than the clothing of God?
What is more unknown than the light of the sun?

12'. Do what one does not preach and only preach what one has done.

13'. Few men meditate on the changes of the world as far as the secret centre of enlightening and enlightened nature.

14'. God makes the fruits of the earth spring up by means of water and fire united in one.
«O miracle of resurrection!»

15. When they are offered pure water they reply: «Give us back the poison we are used to.»

16. How many people reflect on God's general work?
How many people are taught by the renewal of all things?
How many people accomplish the particular work of the Lord?

17. There is no-one above he who knows God, except God himself.

18. He who is not stunned and full of admiration before the mystery of man and before the miracles of nature will never discover God.

19. The ignorant speak a lot and observe nothing.
The sage is silent and examines everything to discover the Unique One.

20. The ignorant person claims to instruct those who do not ask for anything.
The scholar is silent and waits to be asked.

21. Honoured or despised, the sage remains true to himself.

22. All time not devoted to God is lost time.
All work that does not end in him is useless work.

15'. To forget one's wretchedness for an instant is to find it again increased for all eternity.

16'. The great work that causes fear, that which frees from the shadow of death, that which levels the mountains, that which makes the earth germinate, that which makes life shine and fixes it in the glorious Lord.

17'. He swims in the great water, the Living One of eternity, the Unique One.

18'. New and innocent eyes see God in his primary nakedness and clothed in ultimate splendour.

19'. Knowledge of God is the only reality that saves one from death.

20'. God is lavish with everything that is precious.
The world hoards everything that is worthless.

21'. The gold that lies dormant in the mud is just as pure as that which gleams in the sun.

22'. Those that have gone astray rebel here, for they prefer the agitation that keeps them in the slothfulness of death.

23. They desperately believe they create with their hands, not understanding that they do not even know how to make hands.

23'. The science of science consists in preparing things and leaving God to act.

24. The first duty of both the smallest and the greatest is to acquire intelligence by praying to God, in order to know of the obviousness of creation.

24'. The love of gold means that it is even searched for in the rubbish, but few men are capable of grasping it from heaven and fixing it on earth.

25. The greatest battle and the greatest victory is to acquire generosity of the heart towards all beings by discovering God in oneself.

25'. The visible and the invisible sun ripens everything to the golden perfection of the most perfect fruit.

26. All the scholars of the world judge the work of God stupidly, since they only consider the work and not the worker.

26'. Middle matter provides knowledge of extreme essences.

27. Have they seen how earth produces water?
Do they know by which way water engenders earth?

27'. Fog condenses the rain, and darkness nurtures the light.

28. Will they disclose the proportion in which water softens earth?
And later how earth consolidates water?

28'. The rainbow announces the marriage of heaven and earth.

29. And how everything returns at last to earth by means of fire?

29'. The red fruit capable of saving the world.

30. They remain ignorant, proud and stupid, God mocks them and they deceive the world.

30'. Sages proclaim their ignorance before God.

31. They flatter themselves to be the masters of the world, but not one dares to confess his wretchedness.

31'. The son of God overcomes death in three days.

32. Their worthless self-complacency does not prevent them from eventually falling heavily and returning yet again to the muddy chaos.

33. Their science was born of sinister interpretations of the teaching of the ancient sages.

34. It changes like the shadow and the wind.

35. The science of God is immutable like the sun and like gold.
«We shall pass through fire and water and the sun of God shall set us on fire for ever.»

36. One part cannot judge the totality of the Being, and he who is on the periphery does not have the same vision as he who is at the centre.

37. Now it falls to man to take the first step towards God, since he has also taken the first step towards the shadow.

38. Immediately, like a magnet, God shall make man travel double the distance.

39. There is no true strength and authentic weakness but that of the heart.
All the secrets of the world are contained in it.

40. The greatest recompense is to enlighten another man after having discovered the light in oneself.

32'. Limbo is the antechamber of God that must be crossed in order to reach the new-born Father.

33'. Complication engenders inextricable madness and death.

34'. Fire takes on all forms but remains fixed on the inside.

35'. All the sages profess the same teaching.
Water in the earth and God in man.

36'. Fire is only visible in the middle of the sky. It lies hidden in the centre of the earth and in middle water.

37'. The freedom granted to man permits him all forms of madness and complete wisdom.
The curiosity that made him lose himself may also save him.

38'. Light descends on the earth and returns to heaven to reunite in God the dust of humanity scattered in the abysses.

39'. The water in grain and the fire in water are like the water of stone and the stone of water.

40'. Few disciples know how to profit from the lesson of sages and discover God's natural gift.

41. Imagination is the tool that discovers God.
Patience is that which makes him evident.

41'. Water dissolves all manner of things, but fire coagulates only one.

42. It is in the midst of corruption that truth appears clearly.

42'. The holy Mother shines amid the darkness of the world.

43. The creation of the Universe is accomplished in accepted and self-sufficient solitude.

43'. Nothing is added to virgin water except the fire to mature it.

44. When the symbol is a reality it is impossible to discover it without the aid of God.

44'. The obviousness of the mystery blinds the most scholarly.

45. The blindness and pride of men have become such that they transform everything good into evil in the name of science and progress.

45'. That which is cooked to excess only contains death and only engenders death.

46. True success is accomplished for the profit of everyone and at the expense of no-one.

46'. God gratifies his children, without depriving anyone of anything.

47. When churches and states lean on the strength of the world they submit to death, because the power of God abandons them.

47'. Those that possess true spiritual power control temporal power effortlessly; however, coercion and violence remain alien to them.

48. We would rather you did not concern yourselves with accusing he who scolds you, but rather to be upset with yourself at preaching the truth and not observing it.

48'. On rousing saints rather than scholars, we will finally deserve a sage.

49. Those that repel the young girl and the child condemn themselves gratuitously to death.

49'. They are abandoned along the path and covered with filth.

50. God does not wait for their approval to bring to light what it has pleased him to create.

50'. Holy water flows up to heaven and sinks into the earth in order to move everything.

51. The sage takes in the mother and gives her shelter until the child is born.

52. God mocks the sciences, laws and morals of men.

53. All events, good or bad, are useful to him who uses them for his instruction.

54. Even the holy books, what are they compared to the mystery of life that subsists in the sun and in the earth? Nevertheless, they contain the key that opens and closes the source of the abyss and the seal that covers the germ of the Lord of the worlds.

55. The truth is self-sufficient.
Everything that is added to it obscures it.

56. God opens the eyes of whom it pleases him to do so, without the aid of any scholar.

57. The sciences professed by men require subtlety and great effort in order to be partially mastered.
The science God teaches demands simplicity and patience in order to be known in its entirety.

58. The injustice that crushes us is there to remind us that God awaits us with his justice.

51'. Only he who has acquired the knowledge of God in the three states of creation can be called: delivered for ever.

52'. Men pass on, but the doctrine of the Spirit remains eternally.

53'. The whole world aids the man who seeks God, but rare is he who understands and who accepts the mysterious lesson.

54'. He who understands praises the Lord in his heart.
He who thinks he hears and he who grasps nothing must pray and remain silent.

55'. It is in common places that the obviousness of the mystery appears.

56'. The Spirit works before everyone. Few see it. Only one grasps it and fixes it.

57'. Knowledge of the tree is not as important as that of the fruit, and this is less useful than the knowledge of the kernel of the stone. In the end, it is the almond we must know in its purity and it is the germ that we must manifest in its perfection.

58'. Death expels death and makes hidden life appear.

59. He who is truly devoted to God bears no special mark that signals him out to be revered by the multitude.
He is naked and poor in the world.

60. Ignorant men despise the earth and the heaven that gave birth to them and that nourish them.
Sages strive to unite the low with the high to form one single thing.

61. There is no new truth. There are only new forms and expressions of the eternal life that is well-hidden and yet obvious.

62. One must be very well instructed and extremely powerful to become once again simple and humble as a little child.

63. God allows for temptation so that we are judged fairly by ourselves.
Such is the justice that any objection increases our sentence.

64. The sign of lie is change, that of truth, immutability.

65. The greatest joy man can experience is the perfect manifestation of his strength in God.

66. God, who is the perfection of science and love, only offers and accepts perfect science and love.

67. Reflection must necessarily precede all experimentation in order to reach true knowledge.

59'. The pure earth separated from its death.
The white moon emerged from its shade.
The red sun washed of its stains.

60'. Water emerges from earth and returns to earth until the white flower blooms and until the purple fruit ripens.

61'. He who embodies me, says the heavenly man, knows the holy way of God's ancient sages.

62'. God: the madman we love, the sage who terrifies us.

63'. He who is in God commands the very stars, for he possesses the pure body and spirit united in the perfect soul.

64'. Fire shall judge the rotten world, but God's living shall emerge safe and sound from the terrifying trial. They alone!

65'. The fixed and perfect sun issued from the pure and living light that it engenders in the beginning.

66'. The treasure buried in the earth.
The great concentrate of the Universe.

67'. The end of doubt:
the experience of God through the knowledge of nature and of man.

68. Freedom is knowing all and remaining silent,
having all and possessing nothing,
being capable of all and reposing oneself.

69. The natural and the supernatural are so intimately mixed together that God alone can separate them and reunite them.

70. He who works more than is required by natural needs marries hell and death.

71. The search for the science of God is the only work that does without any human approval.
Such is the fulfilment of those who achieve it that they are in a state of giving all, while the world can no longer offer them anything else.

72. When the best men seem lost for the world they are won over for God, who possesses all.

73. The master can free repentant prisoners, but he does not deliver voluntary slaves from death.

74. God created the world that perpetuates itself in oneself.
This is where the unique teaching can be found.

75. Men prefer their own systems that collapse, their inventions that kill and their work that enslaves.

68'. The quintessence of heaven and of earth, which produces the sun and which receives it in marriage.

69'. By turning around the earthly REA we shall discover the heavenly AER that makes the divine ERA.

70'. Nature produces everything through water and through fire.
The sage perfects the world in the same manner.

71'. The universal mother existing through God who moulds her according to his will.
She who is the fertilizing one of heaven.
She who is fertilized by God.
She who is the fertile one of earth.
«Truth is a curse for those who approach it and yet do not receive it.»

72'. The reunion of the four elements forms the fifth essence, root of the moon and of the sun.

73'. Under the Beast, the secret God, and in the mud, the hidden pearl.

74'. The body-spirit easily accomplishes everything, for it is already in everything from the beginning.

75'. The mixed world, deceiver and deceived.
The wheel that does not rest.

76. God mocks the scholars of the world because they consider him alien to his own work.
Thus, the more marvels they see, the more senseless they become.

77. God is all-powerful.
He renews everything without effort.

78. All can be understood with his inspiration.
All can be examined with his help.
All can be purified with his science.
All can be perfected with his art.
He possesses all names and has none.

79. Nothing is ever lacking for he who leans on God.

80. He who has obtained the friendship of God is neither happy nor sad. He resides in the peace of the Perfect One and helps reconciled men in the loving Mother.

81. The greatest will is the greatest patience.
The greatest patience is the greatest acceptance.
The greatest acceptance is the greatest wisdom.
The greatest wisdom is the will and the way of God.

76'. The extreme humiliation of death is the compulsory entry to the splendour of heavenly life, for earthly separation is the beginning of heaven manifested.

77'. The beginning in the earth.
The middle in the water of heaven.
The end in the sun.

78'. Earth produces water and lives on water.
Water engenders air and takes its life from air.
Air becomes fire and subsists on fire.
Fire turns to earth and emerges from the earth.

79'. The camphor of gold in which all the virtue of earth and heaven resides.

80'. The mad and holy poet who hears God and translates him.
He blazes while lighting up the world and speaks of life to the rocks of the earth until he awakens them from their solitary death. His joy and his sorrow are incommunicable.

81'. A thousand names and a thousand faces on the unique purity contained in our heart.
«O universal light of worlds!»
«O most secret fire of the Unique One!»
«O most holy perfection of the union!»

82. By confronting the doctrines of all the holy books, the truth of the Unique One can be discovered.

83. Let us study the triple ancient mysteries.
Let us revere the sacred doctrines and fables.
Let us search for the good that subsists in the evil.
Let us meditate on the works of the prophets and those of the saintly philosophers.
Let us understand that there is but one God, one science, and one creation everywhere and always.

84. Happy is he who keeps silent until the time of knowledge, for his ignorance will not turn against him to overwhelm him on the day of separation.

85. He who is discouraged at the first or at the thousandth attempt is not worthy of possessing God's gift.

86. The only way that leads to the possession of God is the knowledge of nature and of man.

87. The gift demands the commandment; mediocrity resides in obedience.
When the rule is violated, societies sink into chaos.

88. To know the three hereditary foundations of man is to possess science.
The soul that comes from God,

82'. The Father in the centre.
The Son on the periphery.
The Holy Spirit between two.
All of them in One always.

83'. All moisture shall be expelled from the earth, and fire shall consume the foul grime until the virginal salt appears, to which will be given back the heavenly water in order to form God's new world.
«Who shall make us hear this word from the beginning and from the end of time? Who shall show us the denuded germ of the Lord's perfect creation?»

84'. When one looks for God, one has no time for the world, just as when one runs after the world, one cannot rest in the Unique One.

85'. The water of the earth and the earth of the water, that is the mystery of the Lord embodied in the flesh of the world.

86'. The metamorphoses of the world teach the clear-sighted one and bring him back to the universal source of life.

87'. Finally fire dominates water in the hidden creation and transforms all into holy earth.

88'. He who delivers the buried man receives all from the Father by means of the Mother and Son clearly manifested.

the spirit that comes from the stars, the body that comes from the earth.

89. Quarrels stem from the confusion of spirits, the fury of passions and the inaccuracy of language.

90. The strong man commands without speaking, and is obeyed.
The weak man shouts incessantly and no-one listens to him.

91. There is no greater curse than to be locked in the pride of the spirit and in the coarseness of sentiment.

«We preach neither the wind, nor smoke, nor ashes; we preach life saved in the resurrected soul, spirit and body.»

89'. The earth hatches over the bright eagle. Who shall seize it as it comes out of the egg? And who shall rear it until its return to the holy earth?

90'. In order to know God in the Universe, listen and look within oneself; that is the direct way.

91'. The apparent madness of God's secret excludes the proud, the greedy and the impious.

We are children of the holy and we expect the life that God will give to those who are always faithful to him.
TOBIT

Many appear to be outside the Church who are inside; many appear to be inside who are outside.
AUGUSTINE

BOOK III

I am in the Father, and the Father is in me.
                                JESUS

O Father! you are in my heart, and no-one can know you if not I, your son.
                                AKHENATON

UN ÊTRE VIE

1. Prayer is the most accomplished means of developing the will in God.

2. Mastering others is an easy illusion.
Mastering oneself is a harsh reality.

3. Who is great enough to remain hidden?
Who is well-known enough to remain anonymous?
Who is generous enough to possess everything?
Who is powerful enough to demand nothing?

4. Has all the science of men ever made one of their hairs grow back? Erased a wrinkle? Given back youth? Has it saved them from death, as does the love of the Unique One for his secret friends?

GLOBE WITHOUT BLEMISH

1'. The water that springs from the holy earth falls again as golden rain on the darkened world.

2'. The study of the middle world gives knowledge of the great Universe.

3'. Everyone sees the ancestor, some recognize him, only one awakens him and delivers the world from sin.
«Give us your secret NAME, O Lord! if you judge our hearts pure enough so as not to die if you do so.»

4'. Liquefy the earth and make the water concentrated, then marry the earth with the water and enjoy the peace of the Lord in the stone sanctified by the union.

5. Dispersion and agitation engender the sad madness of the world.

6. Let us remain silent and solitary, let us attentively scrutinize nature in motion, let us pray to God with love and overcoming, thus we will easily reach the light which gives birth to the Universe.

7. When a saint cures a sick man, he then teaches him to help others. In this way, he cures him twice over.

8. How shall we grasp the mystery of hidden things if we do not understand the obviousness of those that blind us?

9. A chicken comes out of a hatched egg, but no-one notices it.

10. By becoming accustomed to the death of the spirit, the miracles of God and nature are hidden from us.

11. It is superfluous to attack the science of men since it destroys itself.

12. We can only rid ourselves of a wicked man by trying to correct him.
Time and misfortune achieve this easily, and separate in him that which is good from that which is bad.

5'. Love shall take possession of the virtue of the sun and multiply it until the repose of the ultimate Lord.

6'. Heavenly weddings make the brightness of the stars burst forth.
Earthly weddings manifest the weight and the virtue of luminous gold.

7'. From Saturn to the moon and to the sun there is only one way, which is the patient purification of the rough body until the union of the clear spirit with the perfect soul.

8'. The external star combines with the internal sun to engender the unique brightness.
«O secret beauty!»

9'. The light of the stars shines in the sky and in the interior of the earth.

10'. It is that which frees the fountain of life where the germ of the sky and of the earth lies dormant.

11'. All that is accomplished outside of the natural laws is dead and engenders death.

12'. The true nature of man is the heavenly light covered by the shadow of death.
«The man who searches for ideals is a dangerous madman. The man who searches for transcendental reality is a beneficial sage.»

13. By sheer force of idiotic intransigence and rigour, upright men are kept apart from holy things.

14. The simplicity and the laziness of crowds make an idol of the living god and make fear of a religion.

15. Arguing with an ignorant man means becoming weaker than him.

16. The sage reposes in the plenitude of the unique light.
The madman is agitated in the void of multiple darkness.

17. Truth is hidden under the veil of fables and parables. A very upright and penetrating spirit is required to discover it, just as a very practised eye is needed to recognize the diamond under the casing that protects it.

18. Divine philosophers, saints, poets, artists and children often think and act in God.

19. However, when the first ones speak everyone must listen humbly and be silent.

20. Coarse men are never surprised before God's astonishing creation.
They see nothing, admire nothing, love nothing, understand nothing and find nothing.

13'. He who remains poor in God can possess the world without danger of dying.

14'. The life of the sun is visible in the sky and perceptible under the earth's crust.

15'. Corruption shows up all purity.

16'. We glimpse God in a fleeting breath, but he considers us for all eternity.

17'. The mysteries of God are contained in the centre of the Universe and in the heart of man.
Who shall hollow out the abyss? Who shall manifest the life of the earth? And who shall consolidate heaven's dew?

18'. Self-oblivion magnifies man to the limitless origin with which the Unknown One is endowed.

19'. Knowledge makes man repose in the immutable centre that supports the moving sea of the world.

20'. Senses deprived of the spirit crawl miserably over the earth's crust; but the spirit without senses penetrates as far as the inmost depths of heaven and earth. However, it is love that makes us repose in the unique brightness.

21. The power of true philosophy is to consider what is, and not what one believes to be so.

22. Few men are capable of acting in God in wakefulness, in a dream and in death.

23. The functions of a superior man are perfect and complete, and it is in this that he draws closer to God.

24. The tiniest part of the Universe is an image of the whole and is self-sufficient.

25. Birth and death, action and repose, light and darkness, union and separation, they all come from the movement of the four that make the changes in the world.

26. The repose of God establishes itself in purity when the elements are united in perfect equilibrium.

27. One does not kill the dead in order to instruct them nor to save them, they are baptised with fire and with water and they are entrusted to earth and heaven.

28. The world is plural but man is singular.

29. The truth never loses men; it is they who forsake it.

30. The sage asks for nothing from those who believe they have everything and who are afraid of losing everything.

21'. The light of wood presages the God within man, and the fruit of our earth makes us heirs to the magnificent Father.

22'. Those who are dead to holy water are doubly deprived of the heavenly fire.

23'. It is not enough to reach the light for a few moments; one must be able to maintain oneself there for all eternity.

24'. The heart of heaven and earth is like an egg hidden in the sea of the world.

25'. The imagination of the Lord lives under the earth and flies in the sky to give life to the worlds. Who will seize it in his hands? And who will fix it in his heart?

26'. The joy and astonishment of he who discovers himself in God are endless.

27'. The patience of grace delivers us from the most sombre prisons.
The sweetness of love makes our hidden life bloom.

28'. Great knowledge dwells deep down in us.

29'. In the darkness, the light is one with God from the beginning.

30'. He who knows the outcome of all things is a sage among sages, a god among gods and a madman in the midst of vulgar men.

31. Those who, when reduced to bread and water, are still joyful, put an end to the world more easily than the world puts an end to them.

31'. The madness of death in the world can only be vanquished by practising the wisdom of life in God.

32. Hatred is the extreme point of weakness in separation, just as love is the culminating point of power in the union.

32'. The hardness and dryness of the earth for death.
The suppleness and humidity of water for life.
The battle between the two makes the glory of the whole appear.

33. Men sigh for the stars without knowing that the sun rolls under their feet and sometimes reposes in their blind men's hands.
«The uncut stone will become prayer and the prayer will become precious stone.»

33'. Everyone sees the sky exposed. Some use the influence of the stars. A handful grasp the moonlight. But only one embodies the life of the truly perfect sun.

34. Nature teaches the sage, and the sage aids nature so that the fruit comes to life and becomes perfect.

34'. He who knows how to unite opposites of the same nature possesses the science.

35. A simple shepherd can be more instructed than a hundred thousand scholars assembled in the world, and a wretched idiot can show the sage the light of the Perfect One.

35'. He who possesses the salt of the earth seasons the world to his taste, sprinkling it on all evil until he makes it disappear as a testimonial to the glorious virtue of God.

36. God is present just as long as we are here.

36'. Perfection that is accomplished in secret causes no hindrance.

37. That which appears absurd and unbelievable is often a barrier that is meant to stop men full of pride and malignity.

37'. On raising earth to heaven and on lowering the fire to the tomb, we shall obtain the glory of God through the middle water and air.

38. He who knows everything is like he who knows nothing.
However, one rests and the other is restless, one knows himself, the other is known, one creates, the other is created.

38'. The two are in one, but only one knows himself both inside and outside, and subsists in the gratuitousness of the perpetual gift.

39. The angel and the demon are incomprehensible to us but human nature enlightens us wonderfully.

40. The way of wisdom, of holiness, and of genius is internal solitude where the star of our divine birth is nurtured.

41. Each piece of earth brings to light what God has enclosed in it from the beginning and nothing more.

42. It is just as worthless to want to do without everything as it is to try to possess everything in this world.

43. He who knows all disputes nothing.
He who has all refuses nothing.
He who can do all boasts of nothing.
He who has love despises nothing.

44. We are often at fault when we consider others guilty. Great lucidity and great loyalty are required to discover that.

45. It is a hundred thousand times better to be the last before God than the first among men.

46. The wisdom of God far surpasses our short sight and our weak intelligence.

39'. «The purified man engenders the perfect world.»
Let us flee from the wicked and their works, for everything in them is impious and leads to death.

40'. He who sows and harvests the light of the sun possesses the highest virtue and the greatest treasure in the total world.

41'. The truth first appears raw, then must be cooked so as to be offered to men.

42'. The man who has been instructed asks all of God, but imagines no means, so as not to hinder the gift of heaven.

43'. The all-powerful sun awakens life even in dead earth and makes it germinate as far as the heaven of resurrection, but it is the mother water that makes the seed of pure gold bear fruit.

44'. The sage sees the fault and the virtue of all things, but he is too occupied with rejecting one and glorifying the other, to talk about it.

45'. The intelligent man eliminates the envious by proclaiming his incompetence before everyone.

46'. It is the prayer that springs from the entire being that breaks the barriers of the body and makes us one with God.

47. The primary power, supreme principle, creator and pivot of the world, is like God resting in life in the midst of death.

48. The Universe is the framework of man, and man is the framework of God.

49. The easiest and yet the most difficult thing in the world is knowing who we are.

50. When the world repels us it is because God attracts us, but how many respond to love with love?

51. No word must be accepted without a rigorous and lengthy examination, in order to separate the true from the false.

52. In God's work, movement and time are the judges that make the truth appear.

53. He who does not increase the work necessary to his life is a wise and free man.

54. When we believe we have lost or acquired something here below, let us offer it up to God. Thus, we shall always be happy in everything.

55. God dreams the creations for his knowledge and for his joy.

56. The sage is alone with God, as God is alone with himself.

47'. The beginning of beginnings, the mystery of mysteries, the protecting veil of eternity.

48'. The centre of the centre is like the fire in the middle of the great water.

49'. She who delivers us from all darkness.
She who makes perfect all purity.

50'. He who is worthy of receiving instruction designates himself before God by the force of his desire and the power of his love.

51'. The outcome of science is the experimentation of God in the holy Mother.

52'. Concentrated, it becomes diluted;
diluted, it becomes concentrated.

53'. For one saint that reaches God, millions of dead people fall into the mass grave.

54'. He who longs for the Universe does not concern himself with the shadow of the world.

55'. The bird that comes out of the rock returns to the stone.

56'. The light dilates out to the imponderable ether, and concentrates itself into the fixed and heavy sun.

57. The mysteries of God must only be proposed to holy men. It is a crime to speak of them to those that remain voluntarily in filthy death.

58. The Universe and the atom form the unique body of God. Who shall cook them on the gentle fire of love?

59. To apply our will exclusively to finding God in ourselves is to shorten as much as possible our time in exile.
«Let us strive to do nothing, so that God may speak to us and his angels serve us unhindered.»

60. Night contains day. Death covers life. Hardness receives softness. Thus God manifests life and life manifests God.

61. The ignorant man always speaks about what he does not know.
- The man who has been instructed sometimes discusses what he knows.
- The sage listens and is silent.

62. The most perfect joy is to adore God.
The highest science is to imitate his work.
The greatest treasure is to discover him and conserve him in oneself.

63. Inexpressible love accepts nothing else but itself.

57'. The cloud that flies above the mountains nests in the caverns of the earth, where it nurtures the unique brightness.

58'. The sage shines on the inside and appears dark on the outside.
He resembles the origin of the world that reposes ignored by all.

59'. The cold and the dry appear outside.
The hot and the dry manifest themselves inside.
The moist binds heaven and earth.

60'. On placing the inside on the outside, we shall make the invisible appear in the visible, and the light of God shall illuminate men's earth.

61'. There is no difference between the two faces of God except that between stone and stone, but one is dark and the other shines magnificently.

62'. If you want to know the beginning, study the end, and if you want to reach the end, take the beginning.
«To disunite is not to scatter. To reunite is not to add.»

63'. The water that comes out of the earth returns to the living sea of the great world.

64. Repose contains movement. Movement engenders change. Change purges creation.

64'. Purified creation manifests God in singular trinity and in triple unity.
«To consume is not to kill; to cook is not to destroy.»

65. He who has found God forces no-one to believe.
The plenitude of love and of knowledge is enough for him.

65'. All that is true within is equally valid outside, for the two make nothing more than one in three.

66. He who knows and can is like he who is.

66'. The central fire matures the heavenly light.

67. Shame is the only punishment of he who recognizes his ignorance. God is truly great and generous.

67'. There is nothing in the Universe that is not also in man.
The great world can thus deliver the small one, and the small one can also assemble the great one.

68. When a people despises, mistreats or kills its sages, its saints, its children, its poets and its artists, the nation is close to its end.

68'. The hatred that the mediocre feel for knowledge, love, life, greatness and beauty knows no bounds.

69. On presenting oneself to others as ignorant and incapable, one easily obtains the peace necessary for the quest for God.

69'. The reality best experienced by the saint appears precisely absurd to the great majority.

70. He who does good does not worry about the bad that is done around him.

70'. Instinctive life mastered, channelled and sublimated at its source leads to holiness.

71. He who instructs the multitudes is rejected by everyone, then attracts everyone; such is God's justice.
«The sophists certainly amuse us for a while, but in the end they leave our hearts and hands empty.»

71'. God, who is life and fire, manifests the Holy Spirit through death and through the resurrection of his Son.
«Among all of these intelligent who describe to us the world in which we are prisoners, who is the one that leaves it and frees us from it?»

72. The saint is alone with God in the midst of vulgar men, just as mercury and gold are united amidst the wastes of the earth.

73. There are spirits made to meet and commune among themselves; their number varies little across the ages.

74. External signs of merit are the proof of the impotence and the fair compensation offered to the mediocre.

75. Mediocrity ensures against excessive pains and joys.

76. Saints are not loved by the world because they demand too much of vulgar people.

77. When a good teaching is given to mediocre men, they render it more harmful than ignorance itself.

78. All that is public becomes debased and is lost.
All that remains secret retains its virtue and its price.

79. Imbecility is a brake applied to evil-doing, for it prevents systematic choice of what is bad for others and for oneself.

72'. Acceptance and detachment cure all forms of madness, for they lead to self-oblivion, which is the wisdom of God.

73'. The combinations of perpetual becoming are infinite. God alone remains unchanged in his garment of life.

74'. He who seeks God in thought and in action must move aside the appearances of death, which are opposed to the return of heavenly gold.

75'. Useless precaution and intermediate death.

76'. A second of intuition reveals what a thousand years of work does not allow us to glimpse.

77'. Water is universal, seeds are particular.
One dissolves, the others consolidate, but only one thing contains God in secret.

78'. Sublime virgin clothed in terror.
Living food of the world.
Nurse of the sun.
Holy Mother of men.

79'. Nature unveils itself before simple and patient men, but no coercion whatsoever could force it to reveal itself naked before idiots and the proud.

80. The limitation of desires and the acceptance of change engender the necessary detachment, freedom and repose in the search for the Perfect One.

81. Without the will to heal no cure is possible; therefore, one must interrogate all those that are ill before beginning anything.

82. Woman disintegrates man until the water of the air.
Man consolidates woman until the fire of the earth.
From these two springs the infinity of the perfect creation that manifests the glory of the Unique One on the earth of the living.

83. One must make sure that each one is judged by his acts and by his thoughts; this is the true judgement of God, to which no-one can object without condemning himself further.

84. The innate gift, which comes from the past, determines the present state, which in turn prepares the gift to come.

85. It is easier to bring a great work down to one's own level than to raise oneself up to it, but it is indispensable to grow and mature after germination.

86. To know is to understand that the smallest thing created by God is worth more than all human works put together.

80'. He who wishes to enter God must become like God, that is to say, most pure and most perfect, like heavenly water and fire.

81'. The prudence of the sage consists in instructing those who ask him to do so, and in forcing no-one to believe or to know.

82'. The liquefaction and the vegetation of the earth are the first mystery.
The solidification and the animation of water form the second mystery.
The alliance of the first water and the second earth constitute the third mystery.

83'. If our luck seems too bad, let us entrust it to God, who shall make it become excellent, for the Sage knows how to liberate and mature our light buried in death.

84'. There is no injustice in the state one finds oneself in; consequently silence and acceptance suit everybody equally.

85'. On the boundaries where the water rises and falls, and there where the light of the stars and the central fire join, life takes form: under the earth, on the earth, in the water and in the air.

86'. When we are prepared to follow death without turning back, we shall be able to play with the world without fear of dying.

87. The only useful goal here below is to reach God; everything else is like a dream, like dust and like death.

87'. Live, love, desire, suffer, experience, know, choose, come to repose; this is the destiny of man.

88. The patient and resolute projection of the will towards a chosen goal is the secret of the fulfilment of desire.

88'. Inspired prayer constitutes the means, and God is the goal.
«Sharpened senses, relaxed muscles, folded legs, closed mouth, short breath, purified blood, emptied head, appeased heart.»

89. The sage does not condemn the madness of men, for he remembers having emerged from it only shortly before.

89'. In the best men something bad remains, and in the worst a spark of light subsists.

90. Happiness is to adore God in peace and make use of the world as in dreams.

90'. We shall see the world without illusion when we have found God.

91. To erase misfortune and to forgive offences is not to forget them, it is only to master them, so as not to fall into the rut of hate.

91'. Let us preserve the life around us, thus we shall increase that which subsists within us.

92. If the truth delights and enlightens the sage, it wounds and leads the ignorant man astray; that is why it remains concealed in the world.

92'. He who looks for the secret of God shall find life if he remains simple and upright; if not, madness and death shall scatter him in the abysses.

93. The man who is superior accomplishes everything in solitude.
The men who are inferior corrupt everything jointly.

93'. Fire and water separate that which is mixed in the world, and concentrate that which is united by God.

94. The ordeal confirms the holy and teaches the impious.
«He who accepts is soon delivered from the pressure of misfortune, for he immediately receives the divine remedy.»

94'. He who has vanquished the world, in the world and by the world, is declared vanquisher before God.
«The first charity is to think of others; the last, to think only of God.»

95. If the obedience of those that are inferior must be based on the desire to perfect oneself, the authority of those that are superior must be justified by the will to help and to instruct.

96. If the book aids a man to reach God or to approach him, it will not have been written in vain.

97. The light of the world emerges from universal darkness to engender the day of God.

98. There are two teachings and several meanings. God will make them evident or conceal them as he wishes.

99. We shall lose nothing more by blessing those who think they deprive and coerce us; on the contrary, we shall become richer from their deprivation and more assured of their ultimate defeat or of their unexpected conversion.

100. To give form to nature is peculiar to God.
 - To destroy appearance is the work of fools, and sometimes, that of sages.
 - To imitate natural proceedings is the work of the artist.
 - To make poor imitations of the world is the madness of the ignorant man.

95'. Only sages know the art of teaching the world through the absurd, but no-one hears them any longer.
«Do what you have to do among men well, but expect nothing from it, and above all, do not believe in it.»

96'. Each thing emerges from its chaos and perfects in oneself.

97'. It shall be found by few men that are worth many.

98'. The resplendent virgin and her golden son shall reappear on the earth of the living.

99'. All those who preach God speak the same language, but we understand them in different ways.

100'. The creation, The science, The art, The artifice. Let us not explain anything to anybody. Let us rather strive to find and manifest the truth of life that shall teach everything to everyone.

101. The greatest among men is he who is able to bring into accord the teaching of nature with that of the holy books to make one single thing.

102. Religions, arts, sciences and laws must not be subjected to mediocre men who degrade everything.

103. If we hear the teaching of the Lord directly, let us abandon ourselves to him and leave the books to those that follow, who grope around in search of him.

101'. Trusting the leadership of men to those who have the greatest love and the greatest knowledge of them is to honour God and serve him usefully.

102'. The earth shall once again become like the mud, like life and like gold under the breath of the Highest.

103'. All belongs to God, even death, which wisely conceals him.
«Those who say now: 'It is dark', shall exclaim on judgement day: 'It was blinding and we saw nothing'.»

103". The intelligent explain everything, but they enter the ditch and do not come out of it. So, what is the use of all their science?

> *So is the kingdom of God, as if a man should cast seed into the ground: and should sleep, and rise night and day, and the seed should spring and grow up, he knoweth not how. For the earth bringeth forth fruit of herself.*
> JESUS

> *Truth shall spring out of the earth and our land shall yield her increase.*
> DAVID

BOOK IV

> *The stone which the builders rejected has become the cornerstone of the pinnacle. This is the work of the Lord; it is marvellous before our eyes.*
> DAVID

> *Oh! that I be regenerated, that my spirit be purified and sublimated, that the Spirit from above breathes in me, that I see the divine fire.*
> EGYPTIAN PRAYER

VERTU NIÉE

1. The admiration and the study of the works of nature lead to the love and the knowledge of God.

2. The alternatives of faith and doubt constitute the whole drama of our divine quest.

3. Abandonment to the divine will, that is the difficult admission of our ignorance and impotence.

4. The sage who loses a friend is neither surprised nor sad because he has been alone with God for a long time.
«True friends always remain united in the golden Lord.»

5. We must examine carefully all our earthly desires in order to understand that they are worthless, and that the love and the knowledge of God are the only desirable end.

THE VEIL

1'. The black earth lying dormant. The living light of the world. The truly perfect red Saviour.

2'. Everything that distances itself from nature leads to death, and everything that penetrates man ends in God.

3'. Let us give and receive all with detachment, in order to know the unity of men in God.

4'. Love delivers us from solitude, making us one with men on earth, and it leads us to knowledge, making us one with God in heaven.

5'. The way of knowledge resides in the confidence of love, which is the perfect faith in the power of the Holy Spirit in action.

6. The knowledge of good and evil caused the fall of the first created god.

7. Imprisoned in death, he can only be delivered by the part of him that has remained pure and free in God.

8. Knowledge of the divine secret frees one from the middle world. The new state of purity shall be aware and more accomplished than the first.

9. Unrest is avoided by making gifted, lively men participate in public offices and for the benefit of the nation.

10. The righteous man who is buried alive breaks all that opposes his resurrection.

11. He who meditates on the termination of everything acquires true science. The appearance is unfortunate, but the fruit is golden and alive.

12. The sage speaks little, he observes everything and rarely acts. He knows the inanity of everything that does not end in God.

13. Every man must let his fellow men benefit from the gifts he has received from God, so that he can participate in the general and particular deliverance of the mixed Universe.

14. All joy, all love and all life are in the contemplation, in the knowledge and in the possession of God.
«Let us show our faith in God

6'. The study of nature and of man leads to knowledge of the divine Universe.

7'. The brightness of the stars is hidden in the water that was used to bathe the leper.

8'. She offers silver and gold, the diamond and the ruby, but everyone rejects her hand because it is black.

9'. The dead themselves teach the saint, whom men stupidly reject from their darkened lives.

10'. He who aids a man in distress aids his own life.

11'. The triple life and the double death engender the middle Universe. Who shall anticipate the sharing out of the end of time?

12'. Wisdom consists in not prejudging anything in the world, but considering that which transforms it, in order to discover what it is.

13'. He who reads into souls is truthful with everyone, but very few are at ease before him, for he denounces the secret burdens of our darkened lives.

14'. Those who have found the Unique One forget everything, just as they have forgotten themselves in everything.

through the truth of the Book that manifests the light in our hearts.»

15. All desolation, all hate and all death are to be found in the worries of the world, in the frequenting of vulgar men and in exterior possession.

16. It is easy to impose one's law by force; it is difficult to propagate it by example.

17. Let us not scorn any thought or any work of our father, for it is thanks to them that we are alive.
«God's seer contemplates with amazement the cubic sea where the universes of the divine dream appear and vanish.»

18. Truth lies in the forsaken word of the ancient sages.
Who shall bring it out into the light of day? And who shall bury it again?

19. God's sons are sent by love to lead the men gone astray in the immobile darkness of death back to their source.
To reject or kill one of these messengers is to send back God's forgiveness and condemn oneself to exile for ever.

20. Secret justice wants men filled with God to be envied and persecuted by those that are most needy of him.

«He who says a word to his Lord has earned his daily wage, but he who hears a word from his Lord has earned his life.»

15'. God is secretly longed for by those who have lost him, because everything else always fails them.

16'. The law holds man back, duty enhances him, servitude debases him, but love raises him up to God.

17'. All is in body and in spirit.
All is below and all is above.
This lives and is transformed perpetually.
All is triple and double, and yet unique.
This rises and this falls.
All is outwardly female and inwardly male.

18'. The ancestor of the days smiles at us through death, but remains nameless and faceless in eternity.

19'. The light of the sun, of the moon and of the stars perpetually fertilizes the water of heaven that carries the seed to the depths of the earth, from which springs the life of beings and things.

20'. Let us pray to the Lord that he enlighten both our enemies and our friends, for if we must love everything within God, we must dread everything outside of him.

21. The sage teaches the world in repose and silence.
   The madman disturbs everything with his agitation and his screams.

21'. Let us meditate on God until all reflection disappears and our light becomes one with him.

22. Lord, grant us the love and the knowledge so that we are able to endure without dying and forgive our lamentable blindness.

22'. Let us discreetly help those that suffer, in order to avoid the thanks or the insults of the ignorant, who think they acquire or lose something here below.

23. Being unfair and a liar to men, one acquires the goods of this world.
   Being simple and upright before God, one obtains the eternal life of his realm.

23'. When death dominates the world, the holy life will be on the verge of appearing.
   «That which is done in the light of day is not necessarily accomplished in the open air.»

24. The proud one is vomited by the whole Universe.
   He remains alone buried in the dead mud.

24'. outside
   Death. Pride. Ignorance[1].
      inside
   Mare. Occultum. Igneum.

25. The general mixture was produced by the minute interruption of the contemplation of God by man, who wanted to know the Nothing and the All, by eating the fruit mixed with death.

25'. Before the beginning, everything lay in the repose of the hard darkness of death.
   Fire, on awakening in the water, ordered the chaos and the four elements engendered the living spirit of the Universe.

26. Thus, due to the fall of a fragment of the luminous Being into the dark non-being, the middle Being was born.

26'. The hot and the dry enlivened within the young light of God, and the cold and the wet manifested it outside; seven times the interior fire divided the Unique One, and the stars appeared according to their rank.

---

1. In French the initial letters of Death (*Mort*), Pride (*Orgueil*) and Ignorance (*Ignorance*) form the word MOI, which means ME, are just the same as in *Mare, Occultum, Igneum* (MOI).

27. The separation and the reunion shall be accomplished by the assembling of the living parts and by the rejection of the dead portion.
Accomplishment and perfection shall be brought about by the concentration of the light and through the ultimate marriage of heaven and earth.

28. Love shall achieve total deliverance; those who are deprived of it shall remain in death.

29. God attracts that which resembles him and repels that which is alien to him.
He could only unite himself with a thing that is perfectly purified.

30. The variety of the mixture of one part of the Being with the non-being produces the hierarchy of creatures from heaven to hell.

31. The Being buries itself and resurrects itself for his own knowledge and for his own perfection.

32. Friend of God, instructed in his work.
Dedicated to God, searching for him in oneself.
Artist, making holy nature appear.
Healer, soothing his brothers.
Instructor, leading men towards their perfection.
Producer, patiently accomplishing the work necessary for life.
Peacemaker, at peace with his fellow men, maintaining order in his house.

27'. Finally, all rested in the perfect sun.
Thus, the divine light manifested its noble origin.
God contemplated himself in man and gave him his soul. He then advised them not to try to know their limit, in order to remain immortal.

28'. No-one could be able to reach God without passing through the universal holy Mother.

29'. He who truly loves has no narrow-mindedness; that is why he is hated by the mediocre.

30'. He who possesses the holy light is complete and alive like his heavenly Father and his earthly mother.

31'. The first sage to recognize God had no books.
Nature taught him and he helped nature.

32'. «Let us revere our divine teachers as the most beautiful images of God here below.»
Our life in this world is a perpetual game of disguises, sometimes attractive and other times repulsive, comical or tragic, which put each person's perspicacity to the test.
Happy will be he who discovers, under the outer layer of the shadow, the triumphant nakedness of the intangible Lord!

33. All sadness comes from the importance that one attributes to oneself and to others.
All joy comes from the trust one has in God.

34. Misfortune came from the abuse of the freedom that God granted to us. Happiness shall be found again through the observance of the laws he gave us.

35. Spiritual and bodily evil appears through the diminishing of the pure Being that subsists within us and by the enlargement of the impure non-being that hems us in all over.

36. Spontaneous prayer, solitary repose, profound meditation, simple food and measured movement sustain the soul, spirit and body of the sage.

37. The sages, friends of God, possess the perfection of the world in one single thing despised by everyone.

38. The higher the climb, the greater the risk of falling. Let us therefore always set our sights on the Lord and not look behind.

39. The Being and non-being are the poles of the whole, between which the mixtures of the mixed Universe appear.

40. Darkness conceals light.
Evil covers good, and death masks life.

33'. Men can well forget themselves in God, because he himself had no fear in forgetting himself in mankind.

34'. It is by passing through hideous death that we shall attain once more the sublime life of the Perfect One.
«Certainly, the water of heaven and the light of God shall make us germinate.»

35'. The blaze of the world shall precede the benediction and the coming of the Lord, but how many will be prepared to confront the storm of fire? Those who have eaten that which is incombustible!

36'. The centre of the Universe lies in the heart of man, but in order to free it, it is first of all necessary for the free spirit to come to the help of the spirit imprisoned by darkness.

37'. It is the blessing of God that sends the water of life, and it is his love that embodies the holy fire.

38'. Let us accept the failures that bring us closer to God and let us mistrust the successes that maintain us in death.

39'. The woman, who has brought death to the world, is destined to erase it in man, with the aid of God.

40'. There is nothing in the world that is not stained with mud, except for the glorious clothes of the Lord in heaven.

41. The most distant point from God is a complete absence of God, and the closest point to God is a total presence of God.
The points in between form the graduated Universe.

42. When the first separation is made, nothing shall subsist but the Being and the non-being, which shall be rejected.
When the second separation is accomplished, the united Being which shall be exalted, shall remain there.

43. When we die, we shall wake up in God and remember our life as an absurd dream.

44. It is more effective to vanquish the world by confronting it than to not be vanquished by avoiding it. But both victories have their own recompense.

45. All habits lead to death.
The purring and the sighing of the cloisters are as much to be feared as the temptations of the world.

46. The natural sages have established societies, religions and arts. Let us bow before them, just as they kneel before God.

47. White in black and red in white; the whole creation is present here.

48. God is like a fixed, dry fire, hidden in a moving, humid one.

41'. All that is within must join with that which is outside, and all that is outside must join with all that is within, to engender the sun of the glorious resurrection.

42'. Let us think of God at the moment of death and we shall be with him at the time of life, for the ultimate perfection and for the utmost multiplication.

43'. Let us tear open the worlds and bring together their light in the sun made of stone.
«The Lord's very heavy ruby.»

44'. One can expect anything of a rebel, of a murderer, even of a madman. One can expect nothing of a man who is mediocre.

45'. He who looks at heaven for too long lets his food burn, and he who only sees the earth forgets its purity.

46'. The sons of the Lord are the brethren of the eternal sun; they already shine with the glitter of the heavenly jewels and possess the density of purified gold.

47'. He who knows the Mother, delivers man and penetrates up to God.

48'. The sage speaks and is silent in the same instant.

He who discovers it possesses the mastery of life.

49. God is incomprehensible to all others but himself.
Science operates externally.
Knowledge accomplishes all within.

50. The study of transmutations is the beginning and the end of wisdom.
«Who shall give solidity to the middle spirit of heaven and earth?»

51. We must humbly recognize the law of the world and shape our life according to the wisdom of God, who has established everything for our ultimate perfection.

52. It is by studying the work that one succeeds in knowing the master that has created it.

53. It is the duty of each one of us to imitate God and to separate the true from the false.

54. The greatest evil is like the greatest forgetting of God, and the greatest good is comparable to his greatest presence.

55. Misfortune is a corrective that has no purpose for him who goes towards God via the shortest path.
He experiences voluntarily, through his thoughts, all the joys and sufferings of men.

He discovers all, but vilifies nothing.

49'. When I think of him my heart melts into the water and my spirit flies in his immensity, but the weight of love fixes me in the peace of the secret centre.

50'. The sperm is the most concentrated and pure part of the body. The germ is the most perfect and fixed portion of the sperm.

51'. Water is unique in the whole Universe, but it is different in each creation, of which man is the most accomplished.

52'. The truth rests in the interior of each piece of earth.

53'. The spirit manifestly enlightens the purified man, since the unique Splendour has lived in us since the beginning.

54'. It is better not to be taught by God than to persist in not hearing him.
«Rest and you shall be roused, empty yourself and you shall be filled.»

55'. He who possesses love and knowledge acts without sinning, for he cooperates with the power of the Lord, who is total purity and strength in the life that is eternal and free.
«Perfect humility cannot go with-

He has immense goodwill towards God, and puts his trust totally in him.

56. Work dedicated to the search for God alone brings deliverance from the bonds of the world.

57. No creature can be preferred to God, even if that creature bears God within itself.

58. It is wiser to obey the divine will that knows us, than to try to escape from the law we do not understand.

59. The impatient man displays his ignorance;
he who can wait sees his desire fulfilled.

60. The thousands and thousands of universes that submerge us are like the millionth part of a drop of divine blood.
The most minute atom contains inconceivable worlds. Thus, the Universe is in God, and God is in the Universe.

61. God, through nature, effortlessly remakes everything that men think to destroy with great difficulty.
Thus, God, through nature, subtly teaches the clear-sighted observer.

62. The glory of the world makes man sad and worthless; it is a smoke that blinds the most clear-sighted. He who collects it changes his life for the wind.

out total poverty, and holy love cannot appear without both of them.»

56'. The word of life comes from knowledge through the channel of love.

57'. From the total and hidden God emanates the visible and perfect Being.

58'. The failures of the world wisely lead us back into the way of God.
«What has never been lost completely could not be totally forgotten.»

59'. The scythe of time separates all truth, but it is the secret fire that makes it evident and matures it.

60'. It is better to look into oneself and remain silent.
O germinative light!
O so-heavy fruit of the sun!
O secret marriage of identical opposites!
O fruitful splendour of the unique beauty!

61'. From «one total», of which there are five, via «one secret», of which there are four, is made «a living one», of which there are three. Male and female in two that engender the «one victor», which is the dot in the circle.

62'. The glory of God is a cloud that enlightens and gives life to he who attains it.
O benediction!

63. Spirits rise and fall to wash the earth of its blemishes, so that God can come and live on it once more.

64. He who puts his trust in God acquires peace of mind and heart, which renders the tribulations of the world indifferent.

65. He who stands above praise and reproach has vanquished the present world, for he already communes with God.

66. It is God alone that supplies protection and consolation, and everything fails at the moment of death if he is absent from us.

67. Those who despise the teachings of the ancient sages heap madness upon ignorance and provoke the death of everyone.

68. The work of the world is illusory and of little benefit, but time dedicated to the search for God is never lost for anyone.

69. Detachment from created things is the condition of God's love.

70. That which appears impossible at the start seems easy at the end.
That which is hard and dead shall become supple and living once more.

71. The lack of knowledge of natural laws sinks man into the disorder and pain of a useless revolt.
The observance of this universal teaching frees his life from the bonds of death.

63'. He has emerged from death and fixed himself in the glorious sun.
O redemption!

64'. Those who know how to go naked draw from the treasure of God.
O purity!

65'. The gentleness of the fire makes the source of the stars spring up.
O germination!

66'. The purity of water carries the breath of life beyond death.
O transfiguration!

67'. The path of deliverance is visible everywhere in this world.
O fertilizing rain!

68'. Faith draws close the marvel of the world.
Patience brings it to light.
Love multiplies its virtue.

69'. He who is in God easily recognizes the unity of the Universe.

70'. Let us pray to God to allow us to hear, see and savour that which is in him.

71'. Who shall become once more a pupil of nature and a child of God, so that the water of heaven and of earth deliver our life and make us similar to the holy Mother, and then like the most holy and most perfect Son?

72. There is a hidden sense and a clear word. God shall open up understanding to he who is simple, loving and faithful.

73. To scold an ignorant scholar is to make an enemy of him and sink him in his error for ever, for he reasons about everything, he explains mysteries and unveils the Scriptures, but in truth possesses nothing, not even the outer layer of things.

74. It is better to act by example without wanting to convince anyone: thus everyone can become converted without appearing to give in to anyone.

75. How can we believe what the saints see in us, when we do not hear what happens within ourselves?

76. Let us distance ourselves from madmen, abandon them to their contradictory agitation. Misfortune shall instruct them for free and calm them for a long time.

77. Let us search for him who moves little, who speaks little and who meditates a lot.
God enlightens him and delivers him for ever.

78. Let us not respond to mockery, to vulgarity nor to insult.
Let us pity in our heart he who shows himself inferior to love.

72'. Who shall seize the brightness that ascends to the heaven? And who shall fix the light that descends over the earth?

73'. He who clings to the outer layer of things perceives nothing but death.
He who discovers the essence of the Universe attains eternal life.
«The repose of wisdom means coming out of death and never having to enter it again.»

74'. To love creation, to penetrate it and to remain silent: such is the wisdom of the sage, and such is the prudence of the saint.

75'. The central fire currently lives in the heavenly water, under the veil of the foreign land.

76'. It is at the moment of conflict with oneself or with others that it is necessary, above all, to resort to God, for he is the unalterable love and peace.

77'. Those who flaunt holiness do not always possess it within themselves, because in this world what is outside is rarely identical to what is inside.

78'. Let us place our enemies in the hands of God, so that he may instruct them like he does us, through wretchedness, mourning, sickness, old age, abandonment and death.

79. The wisest reply can provoke the greatest fury, and the best teaching can engender the worst madness.

80. God lives and waits in each one of us.
It is enough to die to the world and to oneself to hear him and to see him at once.

81. Death separates that which is bad and brings together all that is good, but it requires the aid of heavenly life.

82. Some unknown sages possess the holy and mysterious land of God.

83. He who sees and loves God through all the appearances of the world is the only one who is not astonished and does not suffer when everything vanishes.

84. The man who aids nature gives rise to life.
When he tortures it, he engenders death.

85. He who admits his ignorance, his impotence and his faults has no competitor to fear, and God can speak to him without hindrance.

86. Each persecution that the world inflicts on the sage brings him closer to God, and distances him from death.

87. It is humility that leads to awareness of our ignorance and of our impotence as men who have gone astray.

79'. Let us devote our thoughts and our actions to God, so that they do not cause harm to anyone.

80'. Fire and water shall deliver the Universe from the darkness of death and shall glorify it until the living jewel of the primary and ultimate unity.

81'. When the body is vanquished, the spirit appears pure and free, and the holy soul unites them in God for ever.

82'. No-one listens to them, and now they barely speak any more.

83'. The moon and the sun shall reemerge from the sea at the end of the long night, and I shall praise the secret of my Lord in the eternity of his magnificent gift.

84'. The end shall see the pure fire transform the water of the world into its own nature.

85'. He who starts out from what it is, arrives quickly at what it shall be.
And he who accepts all with love, soon recognizes the miraculous help of the Lord's hidden Providence.

86'. Each wickedness enlarges the clothing of death of he who thinks it or commits it.

87'. The weakness of water moves in heaven.
The strength of fire remains in the earth.

It is pride that leads to belief in our science and in our power of fallen gods.

88. It is risky to look for the science for oneself, but it is even more dangerous to instruct men in that which they do not wish to hear.

89. Nothing can be said clearly without provoking incredulity, greed, hate, or death.

90. Creation is like the imaginative power of God made present, who, through an extension of himself, manifests life up to the limits of death.

91. Nature teaches the secret of beings and things; few men are able to understand what they see.

92. There is only one God, one truth, one teaching; but the confusion of words and the subtlety of thoughts mask the obviousness of the eternal and moving life.

93. The spirit of truth is a gift from God; the study of natural laws and the meditation of holy books develop it until the incomprehensible becomes understandable.

94. The sage who has given himself to God feels no hardship in lending himself to men.

From these two reunited emanates the perfect Being.

88'. Let us not tire of the apparent obscurity of the holy books.
Let us rather try to penetrate it up to the cloud of love and up to the sun of knowledge.

89'. The expert conserves obviously and secretly the key to heaven and earth.

90'. The body-spirit has neither a beginning nor an end. When it divides into two, universes are born in love; it is the time of movement. When it comes together, worlds disappear in knowledge; it is the time of repose.

91'. Time shall make the stones explode up to heaven, and it shall return them to the holy earth.

92'. Water rises from the abyss of death and falls from the heaven of life by the power of love that unites all purity in God.

93'. To instruct those that seek nothing is to disturb the order of the world, and to read this without meditating on it is to sow and not to water.

94'. If we do not find the God who lives hidden within us, we shall never know he who remains free in the centre of the Universe.

95. He cultivates the fertile land and abandons the shrewd ones to their proud ignorance.

96. Let us keep in our hearts the memory of those who have taught us to love God.
Let us evoke them with the Father.
Let us bless them with the Living One.
Let us pray to God that he fill them with his love in the eternity of the great alternating breath.

97. The saint lives on earth as if in prison.
The hour of death marks the end of his exile.

98. Each one of us forges a false image of the world and struggles in vain to make it coincide with the true one.
«Education is appropriate for everyone, but instruction is only profitable for some and revelation is useful for only one.»

95'. He who tries to convince no-one fears no dispute.

96'. Our life is eternally made pregnant by God.
Who shall make him appear before the term of death and resurrection of the great world?
«Nature shall deliver nature, and the mysterious child shall be born of the unique Mother.»

97'. He who smiles at the desolation of misfortune soon sees the light of God appear.

98'. God has manifested nature and created man.
Man gives birth to nature.
Nature gives birth to man.
Thus, nature and man reproduce God.

The truth comes from God. Man is free to believe or to persist in incredulity.

KORAN

It is God who reveals profound and hidden things, who knows what is in the darkness, and the light remains with him.

DANIEL

BOOK V

The fire did not melt that heavenly food that resembles frost and is just as fusible.
                                                            WISDOM

Because that which resisted the destructive action of the fire melted easily, heated by the slightest ray of sun.
                                                            WISDOM

TRÊVE UNIE

1. He who has placed his confidence and his love in God can lose or acquire all here below; he no longer worries about it.

2. The superior man enlightens and gives life to all that approaches him.
The inferior one obscures and kills all that touches him.

3. Let us lead the warriors before the bones of the dead and ask them: «Place your friends on the right and your enemies on the left; teach us justice».

4. Only God can reunite what death has dispersed. He shall place all dead earth outside and reunite the suns in his heart.
To him the judgement, the light and the glory.

THE HEAVENLY MOTHER

1'. The Lord recognizes his children by the madness of their love, which makes the wisdom of their wish.

2'. Water purifies the blemish of the world.
Fire makes the virtue of water perfect.

3'. Behind the changes of the world the eternal essence of life remains.
Who can recognize it now?

4'. The creating fire rested in the living water, and all was hidden beneath the mantle of dark death.

5. God's envoy experiences no prudence when the fire of the Lord possesses him.

6. God's friend is completely reserved when the light of heaven is his.

7. Those who tempt God lock themselves away in death.

8. Victory is obtained over the Beast that lives within us and does not want to yield.

9. Let us pray so that death finds us praising God with true poetry and adoring him with pure love.

10. Perfection would be to think and act as though the world belonged to us and that we had referred it back to God.

11. Krist, invited to the wedding, went to it without ceremony, and participated in the feast without flagging.
«The perfection in love, the simplicity in accomplishment.»

12. Meditation kills the dead and enlightens the living.
Useless discussions lead everyone astray.

13. One can only converse with God with inner peace, as one can only converse with men with outer calm.

5'. The saint spares the existence of others by sacrificing his own.

6'. The sage helps all men by leading his life towards perfection.

7'. The hero kills everyone and kills himself.

8'. What forces God destroys man, and what humiliates man erases God.

9'. He who has obtained the water of the earth must look for the earth of the water in order to bring the work of the Lord to perfection.

10'. The traveller of heaven and earth weighs heavy in the depths of hell and flies in the highest firmament.

11'. Between water and wine there is a place for the blood of the earth, and between mud and wheat there is a place for the body of the sun.

12'. He who possesses gold argues with no-one to affirm his wealth.

13'. The light of heaven springs from the great silence of death through the effect of grace and love acting on it.

14. The thought of death is no longer a curb on the madness of men, for the world which has become ignorant and weak repels this vision with horror or abandons itself to it passionately and blindly.

15. Wretchedness, slavery, illness, old age and death constantly bring us back toward the one reality that is God.

16. The greatest revolt against the world must end in the most absolute submission to God.

17. God only delivers those who implore him with a furious desire and an insane love.

18. Saints are hated by vulgar men, as they are the living examples of what they themselves are not.

19. God communicates his science and infuses his love in those he recognizes as his children.

20. The fingers of the hand are sufficient to count the chosen ones of one moment of the earth.
«O living jewels, hidden among the extinguished multitude of blind men!»

21. Original knowledge involves an immense temptation for the mortal man.
It is only revealed to those with pure, humble and faithful hearts.

22. Those who possess the science remain carefully hidden, except one, who teaches the way to pure men.

14'. The ignorant one is recognizable by the boredom, contempt or anger he feels before the natural teaching of God.

15'. He who does not look away from the wretched end of everything soon sees the glory of the Lord shine.

16'. The absurdity of misfortune clearly demonstrates to us the vanity of our judgements and our actions.

17'. He who gives up earth and heaven receives God without hindrance.

18'. Gold separates itself from mud through its own weight, and sometimes through its great lightness.

19'. The children of love are engendered by the heavenly fire; that is why they are alive in eternity.

20'. There is no encouragement here below for sages and saints.
The persecutions that they endure in the world add to their worth before God.

21'. God is like a treasure buried in the earth that we trample on, and like a secret hidden in the rain that falls on our heads.

22'. He who possesses love and wisdom judges nothing and no-one.

23. Let us pray to God to allow us to meet a true instructor before the day of judgement, and let us pray to him so that we recognize his envoy when he appears before us.

24. Let us give back to God the praises that are addressed to us, since the gifts that motivate them all come from him.

25. It is in misfortune and at the moment of death that man reveals what is inside him.

26. The prayer experienced for one minute is worth more than the dead lesson pondered on throughout a whole lifetime.

27. To preach renunciation and cling to riches is to condemn oneself to double death.

28. It is better to use the things of the world discreetly and praise God for the opportunities he offers us.

29. He who minds only his own business avoids gratuitous enemies and blind dispersion.

30. He who collaborates in God's work acquires substantial life and peace forever.

31. He who complains about men or about God shows his ignorance or his presumption.

23'. All that is patiently desired for is easily obtained. It is enough to choose well at the beginning, so as not to recriminate at the end.

24'. Heavenly water engenders the Universe, which in turn manifests it in holy and perfect stone.

25'. The water alive for eternity is the singular plural of the visible and invisible worlds.

26'. The saint that prays to God in his heart is more efficient than all the armies of the world put together.

27'. He who possesses the secret fire can acquire and give up all without harm.

28'. The holiness of nations appears in the detachment and simplicity of the masters.

29'. By remaining unknown in the world, one escapes the malevolence of the mediocre, the envious and the treacherous.

30'. The sage joins his action to that of heaven and earth, for he knows the beginning, the middle and the end of everything here below.

31'. He who pities men and praises God demonstrates his love and his knowledge.

32. There is neither peace nor security for anyone in this world. Misfortune keeps us awake constantly; it is the instructor of men gone astray par excellence.

33. Supreme remedies are often the most bitter to the taste.

34. The vulgar man is like a cork on the raging sea of the world.
He who has the love of God remains firm in all places and on all occasions; it is the subject of astonishment for those around him.

35. The ordeal tempers the strong and teaches the weak.
It is the law of the world.

36. He who reaches the divine truth laughs, cries, admires, praises and blesses eternally.

37. The idolatry of oneself leads to madness in death.
The love of God leads to final wisdom in the impassive life.

38. By avoiding worldly competitions, one easily acquires the freedom to pray and to search for God.

39. The ignorant one tortures nature in all ways and means and in every sphere.
He who has been instructed discovers it by only one way and in only one place.

32'. All that has come from mud shall return to mud, until the sun takes possession of all the purity in the world and fixes it in God's new land.

33'. The penetration of the thought of the sages leads the most ordinary men to God.

34'. The saint helps the multitude of men, but these can do nothing for or against his advance, for it is the Lord that wakes us or sends us to sleep as he wishes.

35'. Everything that we send returns increased to us, and we become what we have chosen to be.

36'. The morning star guides us to the moon of gentleness and to the sun of strength.

37'. The man who links light to darkness participates in the total world.

38'. Let us enforce nothing by violence, not even the truth, if it would provoke disputes and hate.

39'. Grace and love deliver us from filth and unite us with God in the secret of the primary substance and essence.

40. He who discovers God's truth smiles even at misfortune and death.

40'. When we possess the united truth, not one contradiction or agreement shall make our judgement waver.

41. He who obeys God displeases vulgar men.

41'. God magnetizes his children until he delivers them from exile before the appointed time.

42. Our joys and our pains are of no interest to the world; let us offer them to he who receives his children lovingly, for he is the sum of all the ancestors.

42'. Holy love is like a to-ing and fro-ing that links them together and at their source, men gone astray in death.

43. If we must speak, let us praise the perfection of God's works. If we must remain silent, let us pray to him in our heart in order to know him better.

43'. Knowledge is like the reunion of man with his eternal, living and free origin.

44. The entrance to science is to observe the world without prejudice and to study how it perpetuates itself in life and in death.

44'. Wisdom has not begun and shall not end, just like the Unique One that it nurtures in its bosom.

45. The more one belongs to the Being, the more unreal the world becomes; the more one gives oneself to the world, the more non-existent God seems.

45'. Love began with the first separation; it shall come to rest with the final reintegration in the identification of the total union.

46. The limitation of desires ensures the freedom and the repose of the intelligent man.

46'. Let us pray before God, so that he may re-engender us in the holiness of the perfect love.

47. The union with God engenders joy and peace without mixture.

47'. There is no common ground between God's work and the science of rebellious men.

48. The strength and security of the saint is to be ignored by the corrupt world.

48'. The virtue of each being is hidden in his seed.

49. The glory of wisdom is to converse with God and never entrust oneself to impious men.

50. Our plain reason conceals from us the obviousness of the divine science.

51. God possesses the gift of perfect humour. He laughs at the proud, the shrewd and the greedy.

52. Only he who has acquired mastery over himself can command other men.

53. Let us think first of God, and he shall supply our ordinary and extraordinary needs.

54. The health, riches, glory and the science of men are smoke soon dissipated by misfortune.

55. True power and greatness are always accompanied by great tolerance.

56. He who has been instructed considers the world as the veil that covers the living reality of God.

57. If the world ignores or repels us, let us turn back toward God, who has always known and loved us.

58. To be considered mad, incompetent, lazy or an idiot, and not be distressed by the fact, resembles wisdom.

49'. The four elements form the alphabet with which God teaches clear-sighted men.

50'. God mocks the scholars of the world in an unheard-of fashion.

51'. How many turn away from the futile agitation of the world?
How many pore over the agonies and resurrections of the earth?

52'. The man who possesses the knowledge of love perpetuates himself eternally.

53'. Silence, repose and detachment maintain the energy of the sage.

54'. The secret of true success consists in always following the greatest slope of love.

55'. The holy stone crushes only the impious and the profaners.

56'. Behind the changes of the world moves the holy Mother of men, and in her reposes the mysterious Father.

57'. What difference remains between the river and the dewdrop once they have rejoined the primordial ocean?

58'. The sage smiles even at death. He knows that no portion of God can be destroyed.

59. The greatest deficiency of vulgar men is not to admire, not to love and not to know God.

60. One cannot save someone against their will, but one can lose them without their consent.

61. Intelligence means using the world as a loan granted by God and giving him thanks for it in any circumstances.

62. Prudence means accepting no word without having gone over it a thousand times, and speaking only of what one knows well.

63. Great perspicacity and total rectitude of spirit are required in order to see the world as it is, and not as we imagine it.

64. There is more benefit and more joy in conversing for one minute with God than in arguing a whole lifetime with men.

65. The raison d'être of all things is God, who is without raison d'être.

66. God has raised us to be witnesses to his splendour, and to share his glory at the beginning and at the end of creation.

67. It is better to endure a thousand injustices than to commit one only.

59'. He is like the central dot of the purified luminous sphere.

60'. Man's fall was caused by the cold of death.
The assumption of the Mother is free in the heat of love.

61'. Let us accomplish perfectly what we have decided to do, but let us consider nothing in this world as definitive.

62'. He who fixes the fire inside the purified earth becomes master of himself and of the total world.

63'. Death makes the renewal of all things appear through the life that comes out and re-enters without us knowing how to seize and fix it.

64'. He who attains God makes perfect the whole humanity, for he thus attracts like a magnet his own substance buried in the tomb.

65'. The Being always remains the master of divided creation.

66'. The Holy Spirit makes the pure soul appear and exalts the clear body.
«O holy trinity, admirable sun of grace, of love and of knowledge!»

67'. To imagine is more unsettling than to do or to endure.

68. God at the centre of life.
Life in the middle of death.
Therefore, all is exposed to the view of each of us.

69. The intelligence of the water and the possession of the earth make man modest and silent.

70. He who believes in God saves nothing.
He who knows him possesses nothing.

71. It is love that unites the part with the whole, and it is knowledge that maintains all in one.

72. One is like moving water.
The other is like impassible gold.

73. The divine will is not violent, and its perfection is never hurried.

74. The most dangerous madness is to force those who do not wish to live to do so, and to teach those who do not ask to be taught.

75. The law of making perfect is accomplished in the ordeal; the most excellent of which is the life incarnate.

76. He who is most spat on without wiping himself is declared the vanquisher on earth and in heaven.

68'. The mystery of God is a treasure that one must keep carefully within oneself until the time of the universal judgement, on pain of being killed by the world or of killing the world.

69'. That which is obscure at the beginning appears luminous at the end.

70'. By withdrawing from that which is useless, one swiftly arrives at the solitude and the freedom necessary for the quest for God.

71'. The rejection of the passions of the world is the condition of the divine union.

72'. The glorious Universe shall be born from the union of man and woman.

73'. The former opens the earth until the centre of hell.
The latter builds the light up to heaven.

74'. Everything that constrains man is repugnant to God.

75'. From movement to rest and from rest to movement, there is nothing but the time of God's judgement.

76'. He who has mastered the passions sees the light of the Perfect One gleam through the night of the world.

77. Few men are capable of bearing the ordeal of humiliation victoriously.

78. He who puts himself to the test and humiliates himself voluntarily wards off misfortune and shame.

79. Success isolates man from his earthly companions.
Failure returns him to the common mass, but he who reaches God is never alone again.

80. The victorious one carries the light of the world.
The vanquished one remains shamefully in the shadow.
Who shall receive the glorious, living crown from the hands of the Lord of justice?»

81. The function of heaven and earth is to lower that which is high and raise that which is low to accomplish God's work.

82. One can destroy everything in the world, except the origin of the world.

83. All that which is extraordinary and beautiful is accomplished in the solitude of divine creation.

84. To come out of God is to fall into the multiplicity of death. To re-enter God is to be born again in the unity of life.

77'. The masters use the subtlety of grace to make the faithfulness of love appear.

78'. The secret victory over the world is made perfect in the solitude of God.

79'. The destiny of men is written in the stars and is reabsorbed by them; but he who fixes his life in God escapes the alternatives of destiny.

80'. He who explains has not understood.
He who has understood searches for the water of earth and heaven.
He who has the water of earth and heaven sows the sun on it.

81'. The perfection of heavenly gold manifests the glory and the power of God in his purified creation.

82'. He hides in the dark, stiff mud.

83'. Forced labour engenders only sadness and death.

84'. He who seeks to please or displease men shall never penetrate as far as God.

85. The man who has been instructed searches for the content of everything and aids the changes of the world.
The ignorant man perceives only the outer layer of things and thwarts the transformations of nature.

86. He who truly admires and loves God has but one desire: to return to him.

87. He who has rejoined the Mother and the Father is no longer disturbed by the appearances of the world.
He uses the things of the earth with detachment and submits with indifference to the needs of a life incarnate.

88. The imprisoned soul cannot escape the desolation of death without the help of its source that has remained living and free.

89. God can deliver our life from the mud that hems it in on all sides and that stifles it to death.
Only he can fertilize it and lead it to the perfection of an infinite generation.

90. Meditation unbinds the spirit, frees the soul and purifies the body of the saints, but it terrifies and kills vulgar men.

91. Let us not reject the most minute lesson of misfortune, for fear of immediately receiving a greater one.

85'. God's friends are not loved by the world, just as the friends of the world are not loved by God; nevertheless, all of them subsist in the hand of the divine expert.

86'. Those who argue about God are not in him.

87'. By considering the beings and the things without desire, one sees what they really are, and he who humiliates no-one shall know the freedom and the repose of God.

88'. The moving multitude of stars fulfils its destiny in the fixedness of the ultimate sun.

89'. To extract the perfume and reject the poison.
To reduce earth to water and turn water into earth again.
To cook heaven and earth until the birth of the most perfect sun.

90'. He who floats in the world like wood drifting on the river soon bathes in the divine ocean.

91'. To work on knowing oneself is to help the whole of humanity to be re-born.

92. Misfortune does not pursue for long he who faces up to it and smiles on it without coercion, for the constancy of love erases our blemishes and relieves us from the burdens of death.

93. The search for God engenders such passion and provides such contentment that all the troubles of the world seem erased.

94. God's science wears a terrifying mask in order to ward off fainthearted men.

95. The obviousness of the creation and the mystery of the sages' teaching cannot be understood without the aid of God.

92'. By abstaining from the works of death and participating in those of life, we reduce the sum of misfortune necessary for our instruction.

93'. Let us flee from the mediocre that speak to us of God, for the dead are not qualified to present the Living One.

94'. The perfume of the rose hides beneath the stench of death.

95'. The water that emerges from the earth engenders the sun of resurrection through the power of the fertilizing love of the Highest.

Who, then, could give back life to a dead thing by returning movement to it?

LAO TSE

They die before having known Wisdom.

JOB

BOOK VI

For if woman was drawn from man, man is also born of woman, and all comes from God.
PAUL

I reveal myself to you who are married, rather than to a bachelor.
ZARATHUSTRA

UNITÉ RÊVE

1. If we are intelligent, let us pray to God that we become intelligent.

2. He who knows the body, soul and mind, the way in which they separate and how they rejoin, is the only judge among men. However he does not intervene in their quarrels.

3. To die to oneself is to be born to God; few know of this and only a few dare do it.

4. Let us imagine all the joys and all the misfortunes in order to shorten the time of our experience and to reach the desired repose more quickly.

5. The cross unites the fire and the earth which are in the centre, and the circle unites the air and the water that surround them.

THE ETERNAL CIRCLE

1'. The ignorance of the sage is like the science of God.

2'. Misfortune and death separate all men efficiently, but few complete the work of the great purification.

3'. It is holy water and pure earth that formed the primary amalgam.

4'. Let us first seek abandonment in grace, and all the rest shall flower and ripen at its own pace.

5'. All that goes to heaven leaves from the foot of the cross, and all that goes to earth comes from the highest heaven.

6. The highest and most useful function of man is to examine the work which contains him in order to recognize God in it, to make him evident and to glorify him in his Being.

7. This is the true work of enfranchisement. All the rest is an immense illusion of necessity.

8. Exterior practices cannot raise man up to God on their own, but they prevent him from falling down to the Beast.

9. The most sublime religions leave men between life and death, because no-one seeks to penetrate them and to experience them.

10. War, epidemics and famine awaken men from their torpor. How few are those that understand the vanity of this world imprisoned by death!

11. It is better to risk madness and death while seeking God in the multiplicity than to rot in this sterile agitation that is the spiritual idleness of the world.

12. When everything breaks up and collapses in us God shall act in our hearts and the desolation of death shall change into the light of life.

6'. The way back leads to our lord the sun and to the sun of Our Lord, who is in the centre of the centre.

7'. The more intelligent we become in God, the more stupid we shall appear in the world.

8'. There is a great teaching hidden in the sacraments of the Church of Krist. Who shall discover it? Who shall accomplish it? Who shall apply it anew?

9'. It is the heavenly gold that we need, for the illness of death does not exhaust our desires.

10'. He who possesses in himself the seed of God shall see it germinate in the purity of his liberated soul; but he who does not have this fire shall dry out even when in contact with the water of grace.

11'. Our reason is the wall that makes us doubt heaven.
The absurd is what makes us abandon exile on earth.

12'. That which descends to the lowest point is the same as that which rises to the highest point, in order to bring together the scattered Universe.

13. The love and the knowledge of God makes us forget everything that is not him, within and outside of ourselves.

14. Misfortune keeps man awake even in the midst of death.

15. We see nothing, we understand nothing of what is inside us and outside us.
Grant us, Father of the waters, the intelligence of your laws, the love of yourself and the knowledge of your work.

16. One cannot be at the same time arrogant with men and simple before God.

17. By accusing ourselves of the evil that happens and by thanking God for the good that presents itself we are assured of never being wrong.

18. True philosophy is the search for the origin and end of all things.

19. Nature and the ancient sages teach the divine secrets quite openly, but it is God alone who makes them understood.

20. We have fallen onto foreign land by disobeying our interior life.
We shall return to our source by relinquishing death from outside.
«God has not put a cutlass in one hand and a torch in the other to kill all and burn all here below.»

13'. When the desolation and abomination of death have reached their peak, the purity of the holy life shall shine on a reconciled world.

14'. We shall smile at our agonies when we have rejoined him who fertilizes life and who concentrates it as far as him.

15'. It is good that youth repels the rottenness of the world.
It is excellent that ripe age considers the two faces of the Universe.
It is holy that the end reaches hidden purity.

16'. To submit ourselves and return to God is to exchange our dead carrion for the heavenly stone.

17'. It is impossible to rejoin God and his grace without passing once more through the darkness crossed on the first separation.

18'. The holy quest for God is accomplished in the darkness of nature and in the humility of man.

19'. Knowledge shall proceed inwards on three occasions: water shall appear first, then fire, and finally water and fire shall unite in God.

20'. It is our divine freedom that permits us to sink into death or come back towards the light, with no limits other than the reason of the absurd that makes us repent and the madness of love that makes us experts and possessors.

21. The sage imposes nothing on anyone.

He constantly perfects his science in the contemplation of God, and prudently communicates his teaching to those who are capable of receiving it.

22. The inspired holy books are the guides of humanity and form the most precious heritage of the ancestors.

23. Poets sing of the despair of the fallen God, but none of them provides the remedy for the evil that knocks us down. Artists are prodigal in admirable works, but none of them transports us to the living fire.

24. The unique sun cannot be approached without us feeling admiration, love and recognition for him who gives himself so completely to us.

25. He who is simple with God and with men will be filled to the brim in this world and in the other.

26. The highest point of love is to discover God in man and discover fire in water.

The highest point of science is to unite opposites of the same nature up to the concentrated perfection of the solar ruby.

27. A great deal of time and effort is needed to learn that we know nothing, are capable of nothing, and are nothing for ourselves, but that we

21'. They offered the wise expert piles of gold coins, sacks of precious stones, then fields, cities and armies, and finally the continents and the oceans of the earth, but he only asked for a little mud to prepare his harvest.

22'. They who know the movement and repose of the Being, the darkness and the death of non-being, are the only ones that can teach without ageing and without failing.

23'. The purified woman shall deliver man, and he shall lead her to God's repose in the so-heavy sun of the end of time.

«O pyramidal beauty of the cornerstone!»

24'. The path that leads to God is sown with terror, desolation and death, which are the outer clothing of unique clarity.

25'. The Art of God is free from all effort and all boredom, for the patience of the Lord is infinite and his love is sweet and perfect.

26'. He who helps to save a single man does more than he who tries to console everyone.

«If only we could arrive before our Lord staggering beneath the weight of the harvest and the wine harvest!»

27'. He who reaches the Lord no longer knows how to behave himself; it is God that leads him towards the truth hidden in the primary humility,

know all, are capable of all and are all in God.

28. He who has found God knows that the present world is like stinking mud, and that the world to come will be like perfectly purified earth.

29. By using possessions wisely and tolerating the evils of this world we are allowed to collect the water of heaven and to amass the salt of the earth.

30. He who does not desperately long for the secret kingdom will sooner or later be crushed by the world without being of benefit to anyone.

31. When we discover the astonishing work we shall be overwhelmed by surprise and by admiration, most ashamed of our blemish; and when we obtain grace, love and knowledge we shall be annihilated and transformed in God.

32. The more heaven confers gifts upon us, the greater the opportunity to raise ourselves or to fall becomes.

33. The ignorant one who is silent does just as well as the instructed man who speaks.

34. He who has found God and his love can no longer be forgotten, for God is life, love and union.

despised by the ignorant and by the scholars of the world.

28'. The sage is neither courteous nor rude, he is truthful; that is why few people can bear to hear him.

29'. The master teaches the disciples, but it is God that gives the intelligence of precious words.

30'. All that we ask of God in the sweetness and the violence of love shall be granted us, for it is the key that opens and closes the mysterious treasure of life.

31'. When we have sensed him in our heart, nothing will ever be able to make us forget him. But when we have tasted him in our body, nothing will ever be able to separate us from him, for we shall be in him in spirit, and he shall be in us in act.

32'. Let us pray to God in order to know what we must request, before being confused with the dead.

33'. He who masters the stimuli of the body, of the heart and of the spirit becomes master of that which is inside and outside.

34'. Nobody could be born in the light without radically transforming his present condition.

35. He who persists in the stupid alliance of death remains separated from the Lord for ever.

36. Who is God? Who are we?
That is the quest, that is the wisdom and that is the repose.

37. God is all, man is medium, the shadow is nothing.
«Of course death stinks, and of course life exudes this unforgettable perfume.»

38. All that the light does, the shadow undoes, and all that the latter undoes, the former does again.
Thus, man is like a dead person that lives, and God is like a living one that dies.

39. Separation is the beginning of the secret work that leads to God. Unification is its end.

40. The son of God can see and understand that which no other could even hear or suspect, for he who has been instructed by the Unique One hears with the ears and sees with the eyes of the Holy Spirit.

41. All hope, all life, all love and all science are in God alone, and he is always attentive and always alive in us.

42. Woman has set man at odds with the whole world; however, she will reconcile him with God.

35'. The narrow door is like a slit at ground level; some find it well, but few men are naked enough to pass through it without hindrance.

36'. Psychological analysis makes God appear in the conscience, physical analysis shows him in action in the world.

37'. Let us not reject that which is good because of that which is bad, but let us separate each thing patiently and praise the best.

38'. Let us apply ourselves to the mysteries of God from the first moment, for purification is painful, becoming perfect takes long and divine union, most secret.

39'. He who separates himself from filthy things shall find God concentrated in his life.

40'. Let us leave the stupid to their stupidity and the intelligent to their intelligence, for we shall not pay for them on the day of reckoning; but let us embrace the ancient Mother, in order to be made one with the newborn Father.

41'. He who has separated heaven and earth shall reunite them again and shall multiply them in the perfection of living gold.

42'. When we have found the refuge of the Mother, we will have to seek the impassible repose of the Father.

43. He who stands in the last rank does not have to fight against those who long to be in the first few, and the way out will be much easier for him in the end.

44. He who reaches the Being is the only one to savour peace in the midst of the world gone mad.

45. Each one will answer for himself on the day of judgement. Why bother ourselves with the faults of our neighbours and why neglect our own?

46. It is at the moment when we believe ourselves to be strong that we discover our weakness; it is when we think we have arrived that we realize we have never left.

47. He who repels men must not be surprised if he is not helped by them, and he who withdraws from God must not complain if he is abandoned by all.

48. Wisdom enables one to acquire and lose all without being disturbed. It possesses a great hidden power.

49. We can get on with all men without speaking.
We can quarrel with our best friend through a single word.

50. The enlightened man loves God to the point of forgetting himself in him.
The blinded man admires himself to the point of no longer recognizing himself in anything.

43'. We must descend the ladder of creation before being able to go back up to God and fix ourselves in him.

44'. True repose is in the centre of the light where the most perfect Lord dwells.

45'. The Book shall separate many men in the world, for some shall be confirmed in life, and others shall be sunk into death.

46'. He who does not descend voluntarily into the great water will be thrown into it some day and will drown miserably.

47'. Misfortune and corruption shall separate purity from mud, and each thing shall come together in its own sphere, either to be exalted or to be rejected.

48'. True rebellion against this world is only made known by God, who renders it mute and patient in the extreme.

49'. If the first man to come allows his light to appear, he would teach like a god and shine like a star.

50'. Having received his God, he was clothed in the primary splendour and participated in his glorious body in the eternal feast of the Father and the Mother.

51. By judging men wrongly we most probably deprive ourselves of everything good that they have preserved.

52. Man, sown in the world, cannot germinate without the aid of grace and love that have remained free.

53. The intelligent and instructed man makes a prudent use of the fire and water that is necessary for life.

54. The sage knows that God accomplishes all his works without effort, and that we carry out our own with great difficulty.

55. The saint accepts living and dying without recriminating, in order to better understand the secret teaching of the Lord.

56. The prodigious man is he who loves God, he who discovers him within himself and he who becomes one with the Perfect One.
Thus, the saint acts in this world as though nothing were separated by the death of sin.

57. Prayer is the perfect art of communication with God. It leads to love that consoles, to knowledge that enlightens and to the union that saves.

58. It is dangerous to abandon the world without having experienced it, because temptation still endures.

51'. It is God's grace that delivers us from death and that washes us of all our blemishes.

52'. Who shall set free the springs of water? Who shall make the holy earth germinate? Who shall harvest the Lord's Providence?

53'. He assembles opposites with weight and measure, for a lot of heaven is needed to mix with a little earth.

54'. The sage venerates equally the beginning, the middle and the end of the fertilizing work of heaven and earth.

55'. We know that everything changes, except the immutable that moves the Universe.

56'. To speak of God, to love God, to know God and to possess God are distinct things. The first builds, the second excites, the third instructs, the last frees and leads to repose for ever.

57'. The queen of the Universe is weak and soft like life; however she destroys all that is strong and hard like death.

58'. In order to have it all, it is first necessary to know how to do without everything, and then to abandon it all when one has obtained all things.

59. It is risky to experience the world before abandoning it, for the risk of losing oneself in it is great.

60. It is prudent to possess all and abandon all in spirit, so as not to be surprised by the event.

61. It is holy to consider the good and the evil carefully before undertaking anything, and it is wise not to force the fire when one has chosen well.

62. Too many people claim to teach us the hidden meaning of the Scriptures when it is clear they do not enjoy the blessings provided by such knowledge, for the works of life must confirm the wise and holy words, just as creation manifests the virtue of divine verb.

«If we are ignorant, let us study the holy books and if we think we have been instructed, let us become simple in God.»

59'. When we know ourselves fully, we shall understand that we no longer possess anything, not even ourselves.

60'. To search outside oneself is to divide oneself up indefinitely in death; to search within oneself is to increase infinitely until the unity of essential life.

61'. The sage is in accordance with the unique content of all things; he wears the visible world like a temporary garment.

62'. Many scholars think they reveal to us the secret of beings and things, but none are capable of communicating to us the light of heaven, the only thing that matters, being the truth and the life of God.

«They argue and fight stupidly over the shell, but the wise possessor keeps himself apart from the confusion of empty words and savours the almond in secret.»

In order to re-establish piety, I am born in different ages.
KRISHNA

To neglect the root and look after the branches is impossible.
KHONG T'ZE

BOOK VII

It is the blessing of God that provides riches, and all our efforts add nothing.

SOLOMON

Your word, Lord, is a dew of light.

ISAIAH

VU ET RENIÉ

1. The work of God is accomplished over time, and the light is the reward for the patient imitator.

2. The admirable sage is he who strips the earth, places the seed and awaits the harvest.

3. Our thoughts and our steps are worthless if God does not approve of them.
It is he who directs them mysteriously through the joy or through the sadness of the spirit, through the plenitude or through the desolation of the heart, through the euphoria or through the suffering of the rough body.

4. The love of God, which brings about man's enlightenment, leads to unique knowledge. All the rest is therefore like useless mud that conceals nothing but death.

THE SAVIOUR

1'. We shall seek God, first with great weariness, and finally in great rest.

2'. It is the soul of the great world that shall deliver and receive the soul of man, with his particular seed.

3'. When death invites the sage to take a step with her, he shall take two, and death shall soon find itself overtaken and alone.
«O mysterious and divine game of the forgetfulness and knowledge of oneself!»

4'. We shall have to return everything to earth and heaven. Let us only pray that this does not occur before we have voluntarily accomplished this sacrifice in ourselves.

5. Poor or rich, scorned or glorious, the intelligent and instructed man adores God without considering further that which surrounds him.

6. Genius manifests the unconscious call towards God through the pains and the darkness of exile.
Holiness is the voluntary offering of oneself in the joy of the return to the origin of life.
Wisdom is the detached possession of the Universe and of oneself.

7. The whole secret lies in wanting what one desires, and in desiring God until one no longer knows what one desires.

8. The vanity of the world can only be understood by experiencing its mirages and by pondering its reverses.

9. A great deal of study, much time, much pain, much love and much learning are needed to become simple and natural again, but it is then a simplicity that is known and retained.

10. The truth is naked and simple; men see it more or less clearly according to the purity, according to the love and according to the knowledge of each one.

11. Those who come from God use the same language and transmit to one another the true teaching through the ages.

5'. Let us pray to arrive at the death of the world, already dead to the world.

6'. He who abandons the exterior world, on his own impulse or through the blows of fate, finally conquers the interior world of grace, love and union.
«The repose that loves, that knows, that possesses and that is able.»

7'. The movement that engenders creation adds nothing to and removes nothing from the Being.

8'. Evil is like the exterior face of the total God, and good is like the interior Being in his flesh.

9'. Outside we shall find a thousand things to distract us, but we shall not discover a single one capable of making us truly content like inner peace.

10'. It is grace that saves the good that is in us.
It is love that makes it perfect, but it is knowledge that accomplishes the mysterious and ultimate union.

11'. The blessing of heaven shall multiply the generous one and enlighten the believer.

12. He who knows God easily tolerates being considered as ignorant. He remains in his joy and shows indulgence toward all beings.

13. Meditation first of all causes great vertigo, then immense disillusionment and solitude as poignant as death. Subsequently it leads to intense admiration for the Mother and to the dazzled love of the Father. Finally, it gives peace in the union that engenders the truly perfect Son.

14. He who trusts in men is ignorant of all related to them and does not know God.
«Mediocrity is to expect everything from others and nothing from God or from oneself.»

15. At present God neither judges nor condemns anyone, but we all remain indebted through our thoughts, our words and our actions.

16. He who wishes to please men ousts God, for one cannot satisfy both the multitude and the Unique One.

17. He who can know and correct himself easily becomes master of himself and of the world.

18. Knowledge of oneself allows one to endure all judgements and all abandonment in silence.

19. If it seems useless to vanquish ourselves, let us at least consider whether it is possible to command ourselves.

12'. The sun can only live on a pure earth separated from all faeces.

13'. Let us get rid of all passion for the world and all attachment to it. Let us go deeper into death, as far as her dark abysses.
Let us purify our life until the primary light.
Let us magnetize God until he engenders in us the sun of perfection.

14'. It is in earthly abjection that we shall know holiness better, but it is only in heavenly glory that we shall fully reproduce God.

15'. No-one knows before the term of accomplishment that which he has decided for each one.

16'. The grace of God is like immaculate water that frees the universes and returns them to the ultimate and primary Lord.

17'. There is only a small number of men capable of appreciating the dark origin of heaven and earth.

18'. He who shall rise up at the end of time shall govern heaven and earth, and everyone shall obey him like the heart that submits to love.

19'. All that we repel and all that we retain crushes us, but all that we accept and all that we give frees us.

20. It is easier to drag all men into the conquest of the world than to lead a single one of them to the possession of himself.
«The saint cries over the ones gone astray and runs away from the hypocrites. The sage is patient with the ignorant and even smiles at the wicked.»

20'. Nature teaches the world, but men prefer to rave subtly which ends in nothing, rather than follow her step by step to discover what they are.

21. He who prepares himself for death with application shall not be surprised on the day of separation and of reunion.

21'. The sage is like the stone of a fruit that one puts aside indifferently, and like a bone that one flings away scornfully.

22. It is difficult to bow to the will of the Being because it is hard to recognize our present ignorance and impotence.

22'. The child of God shall negotiate easily the twists and turns of the Book and shall follow faithfully the way that leads to the more than Perfect One.

23. Death painfully surprises those who ignore the perennial nature of the divine soul and the discontinuity of the terrestrial support.

23'. The sewer of the world exudes rottenness for everybody, but the sage is the only one to detect the ancient perfume entombed in death.

24. The grace of God is like the heavenly water that makes everything green again.

24'. Let us bless the holy Mother, for if we have emerged through her, we shall also re-enter through her ministry.

25. The Mother only shows herself naked to pure and simple souls; thus, he who falls asleep in God will wake up in his presence.

25'. When we have conquered individual immortality we shall have to abandon it in order to penetrate God's repose.

26. Since we must abandon everything one day, it is wise to get used to doing without anything from now on.

26'. Let us strive to become like gold, which is extremely incorruptible and malleable in its precious purity.

27. Desires that are not oriented towards God accentuate our mourning and make us sink into death.

28. Fervent desire led by a patient will becomes a force that can separate and unite, kill in the world and revive in God.

29. Death is a phenomenon that needs to be studied for a long time before being able to truly dominate it through the power of the living God embodied within us.

30. Oh that our final breath and our final thought be in God, so that we might enjoy the long awaited deliverance!

31. Man was created free, but he no longer knows it; otherwise he would return immediately to his source, which is God.

32. He who has been instructed banishes the illusion and makes the divine reality appear. He knows that everything emerges from the Unique One and that everything goes back into him. He knows himself completely and becomes alive and free like his eternal Father and Mother.

33. Thus, everything that has entered universal man must necessarily emerge from him, for he himself is the cause and the effect, and this

27'. To always see God behind the appearances that present themselves to us allows us to make use of the world without becoming its slave.

28'. Evil is not what goes against us, it is what prevents us from being simple and pure. Likewise, good is not what flatters us, but rather what brings us closer to God and unites us with him.

29'. He who opens himself to God shall germinate like the stone of a fruit that one waters, but he who closes himself to life shall become like a stone that is removed from the path.

30'. To receive communion is to allow God to enter us and us to enter him; it is to absorb life and to be absorbed by it.

31'. Let us follow those who teach us generosity, and we shall have abundance in everything.

32'. Precious water seems contemptible in its simplicity, and that is why the world neglects it, but the dead earth that appears adorned with so many promises costs the lives of men submitted to appearance.

33'. One needs to have the patience to break the bone in order to taste the marrow, and to take time to examine the earth before exploring

means that all that has emerged from him must go back into him and lead him to the perfection of a new and perfectly accomplished generation.

34. All that man sows he harvests, and all that he receives he restores.
Thus, the hidden life has neither beginning nor end.

35. Man's intermediate nature does not permit him to unravel the true from the false without the aid of God.

36. The multitude of disappointing experiences that are accomplished in the world rarely leads man to look for God in himself.

37. There are men as huge as the Universe, and others who are as small as an atom. Love makes the generous bigger through union with God. Hate makes the mediocre smaller through division in death.

heaven, in order not to forget life by sheer force of running after its shadow.

34'. Let us turn back towards the holy stone that engendered us in the beginning, and we shall know the grace, the love and the glory of God.

35'. Too many subtleties lead to madness, and too many desires lead to slavery.

36'. The art of the gardener, the art of the potter and that of the doctor are united in the art of the sage, in order to manifest the light of God in the world.

37'. Be like he who IS, without place, without space and without time in the eternity of movement, and become like he who IS BORN with body, with measure and with weight in the eternity of repose.
«Only he who has become reunited with the heart of the Unique One is no longer subject to change.»

37". One death engenders the other, and one life foretells the next; that is God's justice.

38. The angel fell for having turned his face away from his god, and man died for having wanted to know the limits of his Being.

38'. Wisdom is to prefer the hidden quality of each thing to the dark clothing of the world.

39. The patience of love consists in putting everything back into the hands of God and in staying awake in the night of this world.

40. To command men is to identify with them through love and to behave as one desires.

41. Man's first prayer demands great generosity of heart and great courage of spirit. It can be helped by joy or by pain, but preferably it should be the fruit of clear meditation.

42. The Saviour becomes incarnate in the snow of the north and manifests himself in the sand of the south.

43. The light of the sun is like the secret life of seeds fashioned by the fire of the Lord.

44. He who discards the stone of the fruit obeys the law without knowing it, and something can be picked by the world, but he who plants collaborates with God, and the fruit belongs only to him.

45. To share the joys and the pains of others means increasing our experience beyond all limits; it is to converse with madness; it is to learn to love repose.

46. The part is the image of the whole and man is like the Universe; however one is half veiled, while the other is fully veiled.

39'. The sage employs fire to mature; the others use it to kill.

40'. The Living One is obeyed by the whole Universe, and the great water itself is his servant.

41'. God makes his light shine in the darkest abysses, and then love fortifies the secret Being, according to the faith of the spirit and according to the generosity of the heart.

42'. A saint is worth more than the nation that rejects him, and a sage is worth more than the world that ignores him.

43'. The great water nourishes the Universe and remains whole. The great fire saves the world and reposes in its own unity.

44'. He who knows where life emerges from and where it enters again leaves the world and meditates adoring the Unique One.

45'. Let us seize the truth of the Book before the hour of death, for then it would be too late to apply it usefully.

46'. The sage is like a gold nugget hidden in a pocket of salt that is enclosed in a mountain of stone that rises in the middle of the desert.

47. All that man desires can be obtained by the ministry of the Father and of the Mother who stay awake in him as in the Universe.

48. Happiness is to gather together our desires in the great light in order to stay free in God.

49. Each thing is impregnated by he who has possessed it. Therefore, in each man the perfume of God persists.

50. Who shall bring into view the Living One, the most pure, the more than Perfect One?

51. Man was created free to remain with God; right now he experiences that, outside the creating fire, there is nothing but palpable darkness and death.

52. The unmentionable is like the union of the three purities hidden in the darkness of the beginning.

53. Clumsy bodies and souls fall easily into orgy.
Exhausted bodies and souls slip rapidly into delirium.
Purified bodies and souls are easily sustained in truth.

54. The sage prefers God made present to all the pasts, all the presents and all the futures of the world.

47'. The inspired man shall lead nature to its term, which is God.
«We have not completed our request yet, and here we are fulfilled even beyond our desire.»

48'. Let us consider the water of our rock and we shall see the stars, the moon and the sun shine in ourselves.

49'. It is the great water that shall lead the ferment of man unto God.

50'. Grace can only open generous hearts already provided with heavenly water.

51'. The life of this world is like a hidden game, destined to test the perspicacity of God's children.

52'. Nature comes out of earth and is perfected in oneself up to the peace of God.

53'. «Helping nature never means depriving it or forcing it.»
It is by experiencing the work of God and his holy promise that we shall be saved here below, and not by believing in it without preparing anything, purifying anything and maturing anything.

54'. «Ignorance that knows itself is a wisdom that is silent.»
The will of God is the absence of all preconceived judgement in man.

55. The exterior is multiple, apparent and illusory. The interior is unique, hidden and real. The whole is nameless.

56. The knowledge of the Unique One is like the wisdom and the madness of the sages.
The search for the multiple is like the madness and the wisdom of the world.

57. The three emanations of the Being seemed as though emulsified in the non-being and formed the hierarchy of the worlds.

58. Therefore, all that exists involves a divine part, however diminished it is.

59. It is therefore necessary to examine everything carefully before rejecting or accepting anything in the proposed work.

60. The further a creature is from its source, the more imperfect, impure and close to death it is.

61. The Book is dedicated to the glory of God, for the deliverance of men and for the plenitude of saints and sages.
«A great doctrine presented by mediocre people may seem nonsense.»

62. The intelligence of the holy books shall be granted to God's children according to the capacity of their love for him.

55'. The origin of the holy light is a secret that God reveals to the chosen ones of his heart.

56'. No Being could disappear completely in death, but all of them may rot and sink there indefinitely, or on the contrary, emerge from it to be reborn in the totality of free and pure life.

57'. Hidden nature shall be freed, purified and magnified up to her divine origin, to become the wife of the magnificent Lord.

58'. Evil has fragmented man infinitely, but it could not kill him completely.

59'. God cannot be called nothingness, according to certain confused and badly taught spirits, who therefore unsettle those that search for the truth.

60'. To entrust the Book to a mocker is to sink him in his straying and add to his secret burden.

61'. The ultimate knowledge shall be exercised from inside and outside, for it shall reach a unique place like the divine fire, which moves in the infinite time of the great water.

62'. He who remains in secret adoration is carried by the water of the Lord.

63. Some men shall receive here a magnificent revelation and shall cry with joy.

Others shall see only a nameless absurdity and shall snigger with contempt.

64. Impurity, pride and avarice are so blinding to perverse men that, always ignoring their own straying, they sink further and further into the most opaque and most foul death.

63'. God instructs us with love and patience, but misfortune sanctions his infallible word.

Let us therefore never separate ourselves from the holy books that spin the link that unites us with the Lord of all wisdom.

64'. To instruct a brute or show interest in him before he requests it is to expose oneself unnecessarily to abuse and blows.

«Only divine grace makes our hidden life bloom, and only the love of the Lord fixes it in eternity.»

O Earth! I place this man in your bosom. May you return him restored to me at the time of the triumphant regeneration of the world!... May we form part of those who will aid the regeneration of the world!

ZARATHUSTRA

To me who would adore thee, O wise Lord with good thoughts! grant me, according to justice, the successes of one world and of the other, the corporal and that of thought, in order to sustain myself through them and place myself in happiness.

ZARATHUSTRA

BOOK VIII

> *The Lord makes the earth produce its medicines, and the sensed man does not scorn them.*
> ECCLESIASTICUS

> *And God sent him out of the garden of Eden so that he could cultivate the earth from which he had been taken.*
> MOSES

| TRIÉ EN VUE | LOVE |

1. The spiritualization of the body makes appear the water and the air that give us life and sustain us.
The embodiment of the spirit engenders the earth and the fire that sustain and multiply us.
Who shall weigh up the portion of each thing?

1'. Man without woman is like a stone on the dry river bed, and woman without man is like a cloud adrift on the sea.
«Who shall make the union of opposites by means of what is similar?»

2. Knowledge of the interior man provides enlightenment and the possession of God.
«Who shall be able to walk like a blind man trusting in the sole voice of the Highest?»

2'. «All comes out of God and all goes back into him.»
He who knows this no longer pays attention to the world or to himself.

3. The Father of the world who inhabits the universal Mother is inaccessible to the blemish of the outside darkness.

3'. Therefore, those that always look outwards remain in death.

4. The holy Mother remains hidden in the centre of the earth or shines in heaven, according to the will of the Father.

4'. Creation may change its form, but it cannot change its Being.

5. The mortification of the body has to prepare the purification of the spirit and the regeneration of the soul.

5'. He who turns away from the mystery of death shall never know the power and the glory of God.

6. When the feet are sound, the eyes shall see clearly.

6'. Man descends into the earth and ascends to heaven, in order to know the mysterious totality of his Being.

7. When the mockers are submerged in the filth of death we shall ask them: «Where have all your witty remarks gone?», and there will be nothing but the howling of beasts in response.

7'. If we cannot be like he who instructs, let us at least strive not to resemble those that lead people astray.
«Lord, free us from the rebellious spirit that eats our heart.»

8. We are all more or less veiled figurations of the Lord. Therefore, no-one shall be able to present himself as being his perfect image, nor as being his absolute shadow.

8'. He who knows the inanity of the visible world smiles at the mirages of water that enlivens it and searches for the stone that supports it.

9. Only they who have seen the Lord uncovered can teach men and restore their laws, but they do violence to no creature, following the example of God, their father.

9'. The great sages and the great prophets are the shepherds of the immense flocks of men that belong to God.

10. God is like a sun hidden in the centre of each earth, and like a sun visible in the middle of each heaven.

10'. True wisdom resembles the madness of God, which is the safeguard of life in death.

11. Luminous nature is the primary and most beautiful manifestation of the Lord. The pure man is the

11'. Forty is the number of hope, of stripping away, of transformation and of maturing.

ultimate and most perfect creation of God and of nature.
Here is the summary of the Universe.

12. What is the use of denouncing and repressing the errors of others if we are incapable of discovering and correcting our own faults?

13. No-one can examine himself externally without coming across the obscurity of lie. How could someone know himself internally without finding the true light?

14. Let us ask God what can be useful to reach him, be it grace, love, knowledge or repose; and let us not occupy ourselves with the means he employs to save us.
The Lord refuses nothing to the believers.

15. He who appears abandoned shall produce an inestimable treasure, and the apparently disinherited Being shall reveal himself to be beautiful like a god.
The sweetness of grace and the power of love accomplish all miracles.

16. He who has the knowledge of God is filled with love for all beings, since he perceives the light that gives life to them from the beginning.

«It is impossible to separate God from present humanity, just as what we ask of heaven is often offered to us by men.»

12'. He who is intelligent and instructed keeps his knowledge to himself and deeply regrets his ignorance, but he who knows and possesses pure life is already established in the peace of the Perfect One.

13'. He who pacifies the sea of the world shall rest in the living core of pure gold.
«O splendour! O miracle of water and fire united in One!»

14'. The primary power was in virgin water.
The ultimate power shall be in holy earth.
«The skilful man brings into evidence the light of each thing and of each being.»

15'. Let us not confuse the repose of the Being with the nothingness of the non-being, as the ignorant who make mistakes with words, do because they do not know the secret nature of things. Therefore, many famous intelligent people construct on this error and end up in the desperation of the appearances of the absurd.

16'. Each son of God who teaches in the world comes back to the Father, magnified immeasurably by the multitude of beings conquered in love.

17. Corporal man dies with sadness.
Astral man passes with courage.
Spiritual man rejoins God with joy.

18. True possession is the science of God experienced in the secret of the heart.
Illusory possession is the science of men practised in the world.

19. The Universe can be known without moving, by identifying oneself with he who contains and gives life to it.

20. Knowledge without power is like a seed without water, like a spirit without a body and like the Lord without his creation.

21. He who seeks God outside himself only finds the confusion of infinite darkness and death.

22. He who takes refuge in God escapes from the hallucinations of the transitory world.

23. All mysteries are reduced to a terrifying and admirable reality: «God in us, we in God».

24. He who examines himself in death and in life learns to know God.

25. He who knows the Mother penetrates all worldly things and easily delivers him that he loves.

17'. Before being able to leap into the divine void one needs to climb for a long time the paths of asceticism, on pain of sinking into the mud of chaos.

18'. The ignorant one speaks of getting rid of evil, the sage is content with separating it and rejecting it, in order to glorify good without hindrance.

19'. Intelligent men according to the world only end up with doubt, desperation and death; it is the mark of the ignorance in which humanity remains a prisoner.

20'. You have been told: «Do not speak against the spirit», and we shall add: «Do not blaspheme against the earth», for you know neither one nor the other in their integral union.

21'. The great night protects the core of light where the fire revels eternally.

22'. The Lord remains in himself, through himself, for himself.

23'. Life in repose leads to repose in life.

24'. The peace of the centre governs the eternal movement of the heavenly wheel.

25'. She will appear naked in the heaven to receive the glory of the beloved sun.

26. Men indeed wish for light and peace, but on the condition that this neither dissipates their darkness nor hinders their agitation.

27. God hides in the darkness of death and manifests himself in the light of life.

28. He who sees him everywhere, who loves him in everything and who manifests him in himself, is truly enlightened.

29. Perfect knowledge and mastery of oneself cause the end of change.

30. Faith is like the certainty of God in ourselves, and knowledge is like the proof of his intimate presence.

31. He who does not thirst for living water and he who does not take the necessary time to draw it shall never be wise.

32. To make visible the divine unity hidden beneath the diversity of the world is the work of nature. To incorporate the highest spirit into the basest body and bring them to absolute perfection is the work of art.

33. Nature provides us with all that is required for life; it is enough to come to its aid without forcing or destroying anything.

34. The sage is the only one able to consider his two faces without recoiling in fright.

26'. Abstention from the tempered poison is characteristic of the holy, but its separation is the work of the sage.

27'. With one look the lover penetrated the loved one, and she reproduced the lover.

28'. The sun shall nest in our unveiled souls and we shall be made one in the Unique One.

29'. The terrestrial emerald foretells the lunar diamond and the solar ruby.

30'. The secret darkness nurtures the immortal light of the Perfect One.

31'. The fountain that springs from God's earth gives life to the entire Universe.

32'. Love obeys God and God concedes everything to love, but it is by means of grace that he unties and binds us.

33'. Those who are content with the shadow of the world are quite undemanding towards God.

34'. Entry into the night is the beginning of enlightenment.

35. Madmen talk about that which is not or with that which does not concern them; they love no-one and are in disagreement with all men and with themselves.

35'. Speculative learning with regard to possessing knowledge is what a wooden leg is to a healthy limb.

36. The senseless person gives asylum to the anarchic multitude of hell.
The saint lives in the pacifying unity of God.
The sage loves all, knows all, possesses all and returns all.

36'. All lies in our heart, in our spirit and in our hands. Few believe it, some sense it and only one experiences it.

37. He who knows all and he who knows nothing know how to be silent, but he who is half-taught cannot stop himself from speaking.
«Do great works and consider them as nothingness; that is intelligence before God.»

37'. «God's truth never coincides with the passions of the world.»
One needs an unheard-of boldness in order to listen to the inner voice that always contradicts us, but one needs the courage of an idiot to obey its holy injunctions blindly.

38. The holy Mother is light as air and changing as water.
The sacred Father is heavy as the earth and immutable as fire.
The union of the four engenders the triple Son, who manifests the prodigious creation of the Unique One.

38'. Those who scorn nature while praising God are like asses laden down with stones that trample the gold along the path. They tire themselves out uselessly and achieve nothing durable.

39. I have asked the impossible of the Unnamed One, and he has given himself immediately. Yet I have neither merit nor do I possess intelligence, but I love him beyond all reason and all science.

39'. «The astonishment of astonishment.»
The most beautiful title a sage can desire after «son of God» is that of «midwife of souls».

40. The means to know and to be known is to pray in oneself; it is to bring into evidence the particular seed using the universal water.

40'. Nothingness envelopes the all that remains in oneself.
«The stone, the almond, the germ.»

41. What use can multiple exterior knowledge be to us if we ignore the centre that summarizes it all?

42. The sage converses with God and argues with no-one.
«Yet how beautiful they are and how they shine, those who rise to preach the truth of God before the lightning flash of the end!»

43. Grace, perseverance and love lead to the knowledge of all things.

44. One begins by loving what one possesses and ends by being possessed by what one loves.

45. He who makes himself obeyed without speaking is worthy of power, for he communicates through the heart and commands through the spirit.

46. All that is not deeply felt, arduously desired and animated by faith is null and without effect.

47. The world is a balance between life and death; it is the expression of the greatest visible mystery.

48. Therefore, good and evil form the totality which only silence can name.
«It is useless to try and fight against Satan; it is better to pray for his conversion and for our own.»

41'. The fire that gives life to the Universe remains hidden in the earth and shines in heaven.

42'. He who receives God in his heart, in his spirit and in his body is chosen from among the chosen, and walks on the sea of the worlds.

43'. It is difficult to see and hear that which exists in oneself.

44'. The accumulation of exterior work is a prey offered to misfortune. The accumulation of interior love is a treasure that saves one from death.

45'. Blessed be the masters who lead us to the secret root of fire. Their memory shall be perpetuated in grateful hearts.

46'. O flowing fire that dissolves and coagulates our Lord that fertilizes!

47'. Nature is buried deep in the earth and placed high in heaven, but there is a particular place where it is more hidden and more evident than anywhere else.

48'. Here there is a great ruin for the shrewd ones, but also a great recompense for simple and detached hearts.

49. Death resembles the immobility of darkness in the cold.
Life is like the movement of light in the warmth.
The world is a mixture that subsists through desire and through change in eternity.

50. The love of God leads to terrestrial repulsion and to heavenly attraction. Thus, God and man unite in a certain medium, which constitutes the mystery of heaven and earth.

51. To be God is to be one with oneself in the totality of Being, inside and outside.

52. Divine will is accomplished from inside out, and is made perfect from the outside in.

53. Thus, God frees without destroying and makes perfect without forcing.
He commands and everything obeys him.
He appears and everything smiles at him.
He reposes and everything re-enters him.

54. All deliverance and all perfection are therefore accomplished in the heart of man through the ministry of God's grace and love, and not brutally on bodies through the coercion of individuals.

55. In order for man to be filled with God he needs to empty himself

49'. He who has stripped the world of its clothing of illusion smiles at the supreme good that appears in the centre of the moving immensity of life.
«And no-one has been the victim of violence, not even oneself!»

50'. He who wishes to reach God must abandon all the prejudices of the world and all the certainties of human reason, in order to follow nothing but the enlightening nature hidden in the darkness of primordial creation.

51'. The culmination of all, which is the possession of all, ends in the renunciation of all, which is the depth of all.

52'. Water comes out of the earth and returns to the earth in order to separate the clean from the unclean.

53'. The grace and the love of God are manifested mysteriously by the failures we suffer in the world, and his fearsome judgement practises surprisingly through the successes he permits us here below.

54'. God's fire edifies life. Man's fire consumes it. Nevertheless, the gentleness of the latter can manifest the virtue of the former.

55'. The sage in God is like an ignorant man among the multitude

of all terrestrial foulness that obscures him. It is then that the union is accomplished immediately.

56. Vulgar men pretend to be proud of the work that is imposed on them and of that which they give themselves, in order to mask the spiritual poverty that overwhelms them. They are deceived and deceive the ignorant.
«Only the precious blood of the heavenly and earthly Son can deliver us from the ancient poison brought into the present world by the woman gone astray.»

57. Misery, disease, old age, doubt and death should cast us into the arms of he who proposes wealth, health, youth, knowledge and life to us.

58. God manifests himself to man when he is desired, loved and recognized by the latter, in the silence of union: «It is there where the void of the spirit engenders the plenitude of the soul».

59. Everything is possible for the believer; nothing is successful for he who doubts.

60. The fact of being God and man is beyond all science, because it is the most complete experimentation of the all in the all.

61. Divine action is proportional to the purity of the creature, which is acquired through mortification; that is to say, through the water of grace and through the fire of love.

of scholars, yet he is the only one who knows the beginning and the end of all things.

56'. The sage glories only in being in God; that is to say, he rests and is silent as often as possible, for the union of men in God can only be accomplished on the holy mountain in the unity of restful silence.

57'. Few men truly detest the evil that is in death, and very few seek the good that is with life.

58'. Let us reject all that is complicated and all that is uncomfortable so as not to multiply the temptations that take us away from the Unique One.

59'. They stand before creation like beasts before a bolted door that no hand is able to manoeuvre.

60'. He who wishes to be great in life must become imperceptible in the world and stop existing in death.

61'. Holy Mother who appears amid the distress of the world, grant us deliverance and oblivion from our ills.

62. The letter is very little when one considers the spirit that enlightens it and the soul that gives life to it.

63. Eternal life is the coming out of oneself and going back into God.
«The luminous Mother is the substance of all that lives. The shining Father is the essence of all that moves.»

62'. Ignorance crawls over the earth's crust, knowledge penetrates to the centre of the sea of the great world.

63'. The saint may seem an idiot and the sage may appear strayed, but neither one nor the other are ever mediocre in the world and in God.

Only he who is not exclusively occupied with the struggle for existence can wisely appreciate life.
LAO TSE

Those who understand me are rare, that is without doubt the measure of my value.
LAO TSE

BOOK IX

The whole of our work has been made by thee, Lord.
ISAIAH

He shall lift up the stone of the summit amid the acclamations.
ZACHARIAH

VUE TRI NÉE

1. God is like an infinite ocean of living, luminous essence, in which all penetrates and knows itself through love.

2. If it pleased God to make himself man, it now rests with man to remake himself God.

3. The present world is like an intimate mixture of light and darkness.

4. Created things are unreal in relation to God, but they are real among themselves during the time of their appearance.

5. The current world is neither real nor unreal, neither good nor bad.
It is formed by a portion of divine light divided up infinitely in the darkness of non-being.

THE ACCOMPLISHMENT

1'. Grace and love presage the path to knowledge and repose.

2'. I have searched for the truth even in the corruption of the world and I have separated life from death.

3'. He who frees his life shall be freed by it.

4'. The eyes of the spirit perceive easily the obviousness of eternity and the hands of knowledge manifest it effortlessly.

5'. God subsists eternally inside and outside, without a why or a how.
Such is the mystery of eternity.

6. Here is the fall of Lucifer and the exile of Adam.

7. The return to God is like the separation with the darkness and like the reunion with the primordial light.

8. Here is the redemption of Adam.

9. The saints remain in the mud in order to help their brothers, who are a part of themselves, just as they are a portion of God.

10. All knowledge not experienced is null and void, since it has no effect.

11. The fearsome man is he who wants to force people to be happy; then comes he who wants to make them unhappy.

12. The polished skull of a dead man reflects the truth to us better than any magic mirror.

13. All comes from inside. All returns to the interior. All remains in the centre.

14. To live is to communicate with God without hindrance; to die is to be separated from him by filth.

15. Mental confusion, ineptitude for discerning and choosing, the lack of power of synthesis and clarity are

6'. Who shall save his soul from the mud? Who shall free it from the prison of death?

7'. Grace frees effortlessly that which the greatest violence could not reduce over a long time.

8'. Who shall present the holy virgin to the fertilizing sun?

9'. He who exposes himself for others receives a thousand spittles for a flower. That is the law of atonement.
«Who would not expose himself for the Lord of love?»

10'. The sons of God deliver from misery, from illness, from old age, from doubt and from death. That is the mark that does not deceive.

11'. Arguments are ignorances that confront one another in death, and those that argue, phantoms that fight one another in the void.

12'. Saints can help the entire world, but no-one questions them, and when they speak, no-one listens to them.

13'. The examination of the circular world brings the clear-sighted man back to God.

14'. The beauty of genius, the purity of grace and the holiness of love enrage the mediocre to death.

15'. The holy Mother of God aids pure and generous men, yet the ignorant say: «God doesn't give us

the signs of the mediocrity of vulgar beings.

16. The light of the sun contains all the other lights; it is like the essence of life.

17. To reduce one's own nature, to purify and to perfect it is to know oneself and become like God. «We must sow if one day we wish to reap.»

18. Happiness is to have all and possess nothing; it is to be attached to nothing, not even to oneself; it is to do everything and endure everything for the love of the Unique One.

19. We only abandon effectively that which we really possess or that which we can certainly obtain.

20. Thoughts and visions that are either sublime or atrocious must be accepted equally and reduced to the same divine principle by perfect meditation.

21. God teaches those who desire to learn, but only as far as they dare to know, so that no-one perishes.

22. Peace of heart and of spirit is obtained by offering God all that fills us and all that empties us.

23. The assembly of the stars is like the luminous sea where God moves

food» for they do not receive what they have been sent, or they receive it with ingratitude.

16'. Even if we were to be as dry as stones, the grace of the Lord would make us germinate up to heaven.

17'. He who reaches the Mother remains in joy, and he who penetrates up to the Father fixes himself in peace.

18'. He who rejoins God can no longer become lost, for the Lord is like a guard for himself and for his own.

19'. When we are broken, purified, emptied and naked we shall see God clearly, and he shall penetrate into us without hindrance.

20'. He who is advanced no longer prays to God, he praises him; in the end he is silent in him forever.

21'. The believer returns to his source like the buried grain moves towards the light, and this is a great example of heavenly love and earthly faith.

22'. We shall gain neither earth nor heaven by crushing other men, but we shall most probably reap the curse of God.

23'. Sages are neither upset by nor rejoice over the ups and downs of the

between the beginnings and the ends, and where he reposes between the ends and the beginnings.

24. By giving back everything to God we shall also rid ourselves of ourselves.

25. There is nothing men dislike more than the truth about themselves, because both the nakedness of the spirit, like that of the body, is only endured to the advantage of those who are perfect.

26. The creation of universes is like the experimentation of a part of God by himself.

27. There is neither possible instruction nor certain peace for he who occupies himself with the affairs of the world.

28. Krist had to drive away the merchants from the temple before being able to make himself heard. Shall we not also make ourselves empty to hear the voice of the Lord?

29. Helping those around us to live is an intelligent and prudent way of enriching ourselves.

30. All that is destroyed quickly belongs to the world.
All that is immutable belongs to God.

world, for they know that the Father and the Son remain immutably united in the bosom of the moving Mother.

24'. The Living One who penetrates the great water floats and sails effortlessly.

25'. It is not enough that God is hidden in us, he also has to shine immeasurably there like the star of our new birth.
«God does not go towards the mediocre, and the mediocre do not go towards God.»

26'. We pray to be broken and for our lights to be reunited in the love of the Unique One.

27'. The wisest of men could not avoid weeping at the suffering of all beings.

28'. If our hearts knew how to commune with God and with men, our lips would remain closed.

29'. He who clings to three things, when two are enough and only one is truly necessary, prepares disorder and ruin for all.

30'. In order to reach essential life, we shall first have to become absent like the dead.

31. The light comes to us from the stars and returns to the stars, which restore it to God.

32. The mixture of lights makes the infinite diversity of creation and manifests the unity of the creator.

33. Repose alternates with movement in God's work. He who unites these two in one no longer has any passion for the transitory world.

34. Holy water delivers, purifies, elevates and blesses.
God's earth nourishes, unites, fixes and consecrates.
Both work under the direction of the primary and ultimate fire.

35. God overwhelms obedient love beyond all limit.
- It is baptism in the water of the genesis that gives us the glorious body of pardon.
- It is the mysterious communion of the true blood and true body of the Unique One that communicates to us the divine soul of redemption.
- It is unction with the holy oil of the stone that confirms us in the peace of reconciliation.
- It is the secret blessing of the ultimate marriage that binds us and that multiplies us in the glory of the union.

36. Man is the main ferment of the regeneration of the world; his action on the earth is comparable to the work of yeast on the whole mass of dough.

31'. The pure and perfect man is the most accomplished point of equilibrium in the Universe.

32'. Outside ourselves is still ourselves, for we are a portion of he who contains visible and invisible creation.

33'. Grace frees all without forcing or destroying anything; that is what we need at the beginning.

34'. The teachings of the sages are in the image of the middle world, where the light subsists beneath a dark crust.
«Let us not argue, let us rather practise until we reach the perfect knowledge of our Art.»

35'. We no longer have honour, pride, courage or virtue; we are without learning and intelligence; our talents are like smoke, and our strength resembles spilt water. Our piety remains like an empty tin, and our days have become insensitive beneath the ardour of the divine regard. But grace multiplies the secret love that lives in our heart, and we can already taste the gentleness of the transcendental fire.

36'. Here there is more than a moral and more than an asceticism, more than a philosophy and more than a mysticism. Here is the key to the restitution of man and the world in God.

37. He who loves men despite their weaknesses shall be loved by God despite his blemishes.

38. Who shall be audacious enough to ask the impossible of God? Who shall be holy enough to obtain it without harm?

39. Lie, cowardice, betrayal and hate are the specific hallmarks of the weakness of vulgar men.

40. The best thing in man and in the world is the simplest thing we find in them.

41. Nothing provides as much joy as loving all men in God, after having recognized the Lord in each one of them.
«The only crime is to be separated from God.»

42. One cannot love God and detest men, but during the whole time of our exile we must fear the former and the latter.

43. True knowledge is accompanied by modesty and silence.

44. When that which is superior abandons that which is inferior, the body decomposes entirely.
However, when that which is superior unites with that which is inferior, the body becomes completely whole again.

37'. If we obey hate once, it will command a hundred times and remember a thousand.

38'. The grace of God shall soak us once more, and we shall become like mud before being remade as gold.

39'. True love and ultimate knowledge endure all, pardon all and grant all.

40'. By rejecting everything that hinders us and everything that complicates our life we shall rapidly reach the desert where God makes himself heard.

41'. We can rapidly reach God by dying to the world and to ourselves, and thus avoiding absurd experiences that go from disguised happiness to quite certain misfortune.

42'. Would that the words of the Book were never a condemnation for believers, but that they increased further, if possible, the glory of God, by making them become children of the great water!

43'. Let us accept to appear like idiots, poor and useless in order to remain free in God.

44'. Water shall sustain us when we have abandoned all earth, and fire shall consolidate us up to the holy island of love and knowledge.

45. There is no-one as free as a sage, and no-one as occupied as a madman.

46. One needs to beg and deceive men in order to conserve the right to agonize in this world, while it is enough to pray and to love God in order to obtain eternal life.

47. Everything that seems indispensable and urgent at present to us shall appear useless and empty at the time of death.

48. From now on let us practise abandoning all and turning towards God, before all deserts us and turns against us.

49. He who knows his solitude before God experiences no apprehension at the time of death.
The dewdrop is like the sea that produces it and collects it.

50. Men's madness consists in seeking the infinite in death.
The wisdom of God resides in the examination of the unity of life. Thus, the learned man is he who questions his Lord, who hears his reply and who shapes his life accordingly.

51. Wretchedness and wealth are equally opposed to the search for God and to the peace of the soul.

45'. It is beyond prayers, in the repose of the spirit, that God shall manifest his glory in us.

46'. A single word, a single deed can set even the most deeply buried man on the way to reconciliation and deliverance.
«Let us never want to be in the right with respect to anyone; let us communicate the truth only to those who love it.»

47'. The reason and the madness of the world are rapidly erased before the wisdom of God that penetrates everything.

48'. There is only one separation, only one solitude and only one death that are fearsome, which are the absence of God and the oblivion of his love.

49'. The will of God consists in leading man back to the perfection of his own person. «He propels himself through the word, he reposes through silence.»

50'. The Unnamed One could not eliminate evil, that night that surrounds him and hides him, just as he could not create good, that light that clothes him and guards him; but he can mix or separate the exterior light and darkness, for the knowledge of the powers and of the limits of his Being and his non-being.

51'. There are several ways that lead to holiness; but there is only one that leads to wisdom.

52. Prayer is like a secret conversation between the created God and the non-created God, that is to say, like the bond of love that unites the finite with the infinite, and that allows the totality to know itself in One.

53. Art consists in making the supernatural hidden in the natural appear.

54. The more the sky is seen from below, the more beautiful and profound it appears.
Thus, in humiliation and in misfortune one can often perceive God better than amid the pleasures and the glory of the world.

55. Nature provides the nourishment, and it is the internal fire that digests and transmutes it. He who claims to do it better is nothing but a presumptuous ignorant.

56. The sage's teaching displeases vulgar men, because it shows up the end of each being and the shadow of each thing.

57. The best vengeance is to pray to God to teach our enemies just as he teaches us.

58. The disgust for the world and the repentance for our straying form the ordinary path for the return to God.

59. Grace and love subsequently accompany the seeker on the royal route of the chosen ones.

52'. We know that we are approaching God when we are magnificently supported in misfortune and when we manage to smile at life, through the smoke of death.

53'. In all he undertakes, the sage counts only on God and on himself.

54'. God ponders over his way in the great night of man; that is why faith must accompany until the end he who accomplishes his work, since purification is done first inside, then it appears outside and shines fully in the union.

55'. Man becomes his own instructor, his own judge and his own saviour when he penetrates to the secret centre of his heart.

56'. If we are resolved to grow in God, nothing bad shall hold us back in this world.

57'. There is but one universal life, which is like a game of shadows and lights on the moving surface of the waters of the abyss.

58'. The proud spirit shall sink even further and remain sealed in the dead earth and in the dead water.

59'. There is only one knowledge, one union and one repose that are true, which are in the accomplished fixity of heavenly fire.

60. No-one asks us to free grace. No-one implores us to perfect love. No-one requires us to unveil the union. No-one summons us to manifest the Unique One.
If we do any of these things, let it be done freely and at our own risk and peril, for the love of the believers.

61. Many shall benefit from the light of the Lord on the great day of the reunion, and the saints shall live in his sun on the day of the accomplishment. Yet there shall only be a few sages who shall know the secret origin of the all and of the nothing.

60'. The origin of life and death must be kept secret, so that the divine majesty cannot be profaned by the first one that comes along, as already happened once in Adam.
«O beneficial pain of exile!»
«O multiplying virtue of the sun!»
«O sublime accomplishment of the innocence that knows!»

61'. The spirit is hidden in the body, and the soul manifests itself through the separation and through the union of both in the eternity of the Unique One.

God has chosen the vile things of the world and the most scorned, those that are not, in order to reduce to nothingness those that are, so that no-one glorifies himself before God.
PAUL

He who sanctifies and those who are sanctified all originate from the same Father.
PAUL

BOOK X

Arise my friend, my beauty, and come, my dove perched on the crack of the rock.
SOLOMON

If they should sprinkle with such wine the ground of a tomb, the dead man would find his soul once more and his body would be revivified.
OMAR IBN AL FARIDH

IVRE ET NUE	WISDOM

1. The beginning of the revolt is the rejection of all that harms; the end, is the acceptance of all that kills.

1'. The abandonment of oneself, the acceptance of remedies and the practice of divine love deliver man from the constraints of the world.

2. The ignorant one humiliates life and constructs in death.
The sage separates death and makes life perfect.

2'. It is better to try and leave our prison than to attempt to improve it and to settle in it.

3. That which appears too simple often masks a sublime truth, and that which is complicated almost always hides lies and death.

3'. What is lighter than sunlight? Nevertheless, it is what gives weight to all things in the world.

4. No religion holds the monopoly on God, since he is unique and they are diverse.

4'. He who has the will to learn finds everything useful, both death and life.

5. He who searches for God has only himself to strip off and know.

5'. Blind faith obtains from God that which reason dares not conceive.

6. Only he who has found happiness can indicate the path to it, but few listen to him and no-one believes him.

7. All science, all religion and all jurisdiction that distances itself from the natural and divine laws is false and leads to death.

8. He who knows and possesses the light of the holy earth is no longer restless, nor does he study and speak any longer; he communicates with heaven and teaches the world by his example.

9. The scholars of the world mask their ignorance with senseless words and mad subtleties.
They don't reach anything that is neither true nor durable.

10. No-one is as attached to the riches and apparent glory of this world as are the bad shepherds that lead him to death, through hate, through lie, and through greed.

11. He who has rejected death and reinforced his life in God shall read the Book while trembling with surprise and weeping with joy.

12. Devious intelligence, delirious subtleties, cunning, malice and abduction are of no use here.

13. Modesty and love are the finery and the safeguard of the wise man.

6'. Detachment from the world and abandonment in God engender rapid deliverance.

7'. Through nature one penetrates up to man, and through man, one reaches God.

8'. Peace is like the fixing of life in the purity of God's earth.
«O renovating perfection of the worlds, you ascend and descend effortlessly!»

9'. All that is tiresome and complicated is not God's. But goodwill uses all that appears for the best, without discussion and without judging rashly the life that is still veiled.

10'. Let us honour in the tabernacle of our heart the memory of those who lead us towards God, and let us bless them in the Perfect One.

11'. That which is inaccessible moves before our eyes and rests in our hands. Who shall make it visible? And who shall give it the weight of divine incarnation?

12'. No hand of man could force the entrance to God's garden.

13'. Who shall admire the most beautiful part of oneself?
Who shall humiliate himself before God?

14. We are born master or slave according to God's gifts, but men distort divine justice through their proud and greedy blindness.
«Teach us, Lord, our own desire, so that we are not tempted to ask for that which is not suitable for us.»

15. True knowledge is current and alive, silent and hidden.

16. He who promises is celebrated.
He who gives is despised.
He who takes is admired.
He who receives is humiliated.
He who gives back is delivered.
He who blesses is fulfilled.
He who finds is loved.

17. He who truly loves is attached to nothing because he loves in God and not for himself.

18. Mediocrity, hate, pride, avarice and malice are insurmountable obstacles to grace, love, knowledge, possession and repose in God.

19. Let us accept the good and the bad equally, and let us leave to the meditation of time the care of separating them within us, for the sages have said: «Patience is the ladder of the philosophers, and humility is the gate of their secret garden.»

20. It is absolutely necessary to abandon all, find all again and return all to God, in order to be like the Perfect One who, after having divided himself up in the multiplicity, finds himself again in unity.

14'. We can laugh at beliefs, corrupt churches, complicate laws, overturn powers, violate nature and disrupt nations; in this way we shall change nothing of the darkness of our hearts, where the light of the world waits patiently.

15'. The sage sees nature stripped of its veils and contemplates man in his heavenly glory.

16'. The sages have come straight to the point, but men have stopped up their ears.
The saints have operated before all, but the multitude has looked the other way.
God shall consume the stone in which humanity has buried its heart.

17'. Hate often takes on the face of duty and appeals to the love of humanity to seduce men better.

18'. Let us become pure and transparent as crystal, and the divine rays shall enlighten us and shall fertilize us wholly.

19'. Let us not be dragged along by the judgements and blind passions of the vulgar world.
Let us rather dedicate our time and force to seeking him who persists through pain and death, in the joy of life that is redeemed.

20'. Those who are still passionate about the world, after having known the Book, are blinded or are extremely weak, yet God shall never abandon them completely.

21. The trickery of the ignorant one is to explain the inexplicable with senseless words until the confusion has become such that no-one dares contradict for fear of appearing backward and stupid.

22. It is ridiculous to speak of that which one does not know, above all with unknown or borrowed words.

23. To accept that which comes and release that which goes is wisdom beyond desire and renunciation.

24. The only efficient defences available to us against the temptations of the world are those that we build in ourselves, and not those that we borrow from others.

25. The height of madness is to speculate on the future, regret the past and ignore the present that lies within us.

26. A gentle and clean woman is a fragrant blessing from the Lord.
A bad-tempered and soiled woman is a stinking curse from hell.

27. He who knows how to maintain his life in grace, love and wisdom pities those who speak so much and yet say nothing, those who busy themselves so much yet do nothing, those who study so much yet know nothing and those who work so much yet possess nothing.

21'. The wicked and the mad can become saints and sages by turning towards the God who sleeps in their heart from the beginning of their straying.
«He who eats life shall inherit life. He who eats death shall inherit death.»

22'. Let us give up being understood, encouraged or admired by the world, for it is only success in God that truly counts.

23'. Flee from misfortune and it will pursue us.
Confront it and it will fade away.

24'. He who acts with detachment is not soiled by any action.
He who meditates without desire is not tarnished by any thought.

25'. The intelligent man repels all work and agitation that are useless. He concentrates his thoughts on God and seeks him in himself.

26'. Life and death laugh at our stupid blindness, which knows neither how to separate nor unite the marvellous light of the Lord.

27'. Everyone can study the Book, but those who understand nothing or understand little must love and believe simply in their heart, so that the fidelity of love counterbalances in them the effects of ignorance.

28. The saint remains unknown among frantic and greedy men, just as God stays hidden to the eyes of the proud and the brutes who use force on everything.

29. That which cannot be accomplished naturally and supernaturally is useless, because it is without foundation and Being.

30. False prophets deceive the ignorant, but they are denounced by their works, which lead only to confusion and death.

31. The sages teach gifted and perspicacious men; their work is recognized by the Lord's enlightened ones.

32. The love of God and of men must never go as far as dementia, which is a destruction of oneself and others.

33. Our search consists in discovering life, our goal is to fuse ourselves into it and to fix it within us. Everything else is a dream without importance.

34. The pure and perfect man shall receive no more than nine clean women and no fewer than three.

35. From the moment of conception until the moment of childbirth, the virgin shall remain in the care of the sage.

28'. The coarse and obstinate nature of certain individuals can only be improved by the repeated blows of misfortune.
Let us beg God that we be neither judges nor executioners.

29'. It is through the grace of the Mother that the Son multiplies the love of the Father.

30'. He who has been instructed remains in solitude, in destitution and in the peace of the perfect Being.

31'. Holy adoration scorns clothes, postures, rites and conventional languages.

32'. Illumination is often expansive.
Wisdom is never fanatical.

33'. God's grace and love deliver from all blame.
The Lord's knowledge and possession free from all servitude.

34'. A holy envoy of God justifies, balances and fertilizes an entire nation of believers united through grace and through love.

35'. The changes of the world purge creation; interior perfection leads to repose in eternal peace.

36. Divine gold is the most accomplished body of the world. Who shall know how to wash it? And who shall know how to cook it?

36'. Help given to humanity is a balm spread over oneself.

37. He who knows the two faces of creation and who invokes God in his heart commands the mirages of the world, in wakefulness, in dreams and in death.

37'. Those who understand nothing exclaim: «No-one knows anything worth knowing», and there they are, reassured in their night.

38. The madman ignores the sage, but the latter knows of his straying, and can deliver him if he is begged to do so in a holy way.
«Let us never lie to flatter the world, for in any case the world will eventually abandon us.»

38'. The apparent defect of beings and things deceives many intelligent men, and the secret beauty of the world is manifested only to sages and saints.

39. The word of God engenders joy and its possession provides happiness.

39'. Holy union makes us escape from the enchantments and desolations of the world.

40. When a believer scolds us, let us first examine whether there is not a small piece of truth in what he says to us, and we will end up discovering that the image presented falls way short of the reality.

40'. He who adores God in thought and in action is unable to sin, for it is the Lord who speaks and acts in him.
«Let us be entirely ourselves in the freedom of the Unique One, without worrying about the eventualities of our earthly prison.»

41. It is better to reach God in pieces rather than to remain whole in death.

41'. The destiny of man is God, and God is like the unity of the Being in the immensity of life.

42. Making everything perfect is accomplished through death, through resurrection and through the multiplication of the Being.

42'. The sage experiences everything with patience and detachment, until he has discovered the unique clarity and multiplied the divine seed.

43. Let us accept all patiently, let us use all modestly, let us abandon all wisely. Therefore, we shall have all and we shall be possessed by nothing, we shall savour the world and we shall not be poisoned, we shall handle the fire and we shall not be consumed.

Let us not plunge anyone into death through belated reproaches, through useless exclusions or through hazardous condemnations. Let us offer love that understands all, that excuses all, that comforts, that enlightens and that leads back without constraint to the way of the truth of the Unique One.

«Let us never adopt the tone of a master with anyone, so as not to offend God's freedom that lies dormant in each one of us.»

43'. Humanity that has gone astray no longer knows how to nourish itself, how to rest, how to reproduce. It has forgotten prayer, meditation and play. Its men no longer know the earth, their skin has forgotten the sun, the wind and the rain, and their eyes no longer see the stars. Their mouths no longer taste healthy herbs, their noses are filled with smoke and their ears reverberate with nothing but the noise of death. They have lost the simplicity and the intelligence of their primary nature. They have blunted the astonishment that led them up to God, and the vision of the world around them no longer instructs them. They have become senseless and miserable through their proud madness. They tear each other apart and break up the world with the obstinacy of blind madness.

44. The ignorant one destroys creatures furiously; he scatters and gathers thousand of things at random.

44'. The way in which everything disappears shows us clearly how the world renews itself.

45. The wise man gently unbinds the world, separates and joins up a single thing according to nature.

45'. The man who has been instructed knows the general essence of the Universe and the particular germ of each being.

46. God is the clearest and the most hidden we possess in ourselves.

46'. Knowing and possessing water and fire in the holy earth, the sage fears nothing and desires nothing.

47. The multitude of dispersed lights in the heaven and earth is like a more or less concentrated portion of the substance of life.

47'. When the suns unite, the worlds shall be splashed with a light that shall draw them like a magnet unto God.

48. He who recoils before the terror and the stench of death remains in the darkness of ignorance.

49. One needs to break the stone of the fruit in order to release the seed, and one needs to consume the man to free his light.

50. The greatest gift given or received is like the greatest test of faithfulness to God.

51. God has given us life and freedom, and we have offered ourselves imprisonment and death.

52. If a man weakens after having approached God, he falls back into an even more opaque death.

53. The holy and wise man judges no-one, he instructs by example, just as the Lord's nature does.

54. We retain the world's faeces and we let our life escape over time, that is the stupidity that makes us the heirs to death. Let us abandon the filter full of filth and patiently sublimate our life in God until the perfection of eternal peace.

55. He who works to unite men lends his hand with the restitution of the unity of the Being.

48'. You shall rise into my light and you shall plunge into my darkness until you have found me again, says the Lord God.

49'. There, where water and fire do not act, men work in vain.

50'. The suns increase their perfection by condensing the dispersed light to the fixedness of their glorious Being.

51'. We shall once again become like the light from which we were born and like the moon and the sun that make us grow and multiply.

52'. There, where there is no mixture of opposite things death is powerless.

53'. The mystery of God is so evident in the world that the sages are dumbfounded and stupefied.

54'. We divide through the fire of the earth.
We purify through middle water.
We unite through heavenly fire.
We multiply through holy water and earth.

55'. It is in our hearts that the hidden wisdom of the Lord reposes.

56. The doubts, sarcasm, temptations and persecutions of the world are difficult obstacles to overcome. But faith, prayer, grace and love break through all the dark outer layers.

57. We can, without danger, be rich in gifts in the world if we remain poor in spirit before God.

58. Self-denial towards others is the best charity for oneself.

59. We shall pray efficiently in desire, imagination and love; and not with lips, gestures and fear.

60. Not being able to please everyone, let us strive at least not to oppose the Father and the Mother who engendered us in the beginning and who subsist mysteriously within us.
«The wise man meditates on the light of the world until he finds it. Then he meditates on its content until he has manifested it.»

61. He who is filled with the visible goods of this world is known and loved by God for his unique faithfulness; or he is abandoned as incurable and as if already dead.

62. God fulfils those who are wise enough to obey the laws of creation for the love of him, but he does not disdain sometimes to satisfy those who are mad enough to dare to command the world in his NAME.

56'. The sage does not turn away from the corruption of the world, he separates that which is good and he makes it perfect in himself. Thus, the saint also separates himself from the world in order to reach God more easily.

57'. There is he who seeks, he who loves, he who knows, but only he who possesses is like he who is.

58'. Grace is like the water that delivers, and love is like the fire that unites.

59'. God is like the water that brings together the universes, and like the fire that matures them.

60'. We adore you, Water, mother of the waters, for the living fire is at your centre, and you are excellent over and above all other lights. The sun is your magnificent production. Holy Mother of fire, come to our aid right now and at the time of the difficult passage. Let it be done this way!

61'. God chastises no-one, it is our alliance with evil and its extirpation that make us endure so many evils here below.

62'. We must take the balm with the poison, then separate one from the other to obtain the pure truth.

63. The sons of God gather together life from the midst of death itself and glorify it here below.

63'. He who shapes the light with his voice and gives life to it with his breath
is like
God.

64. Everyone wastes his time and his life before God: believers and the impious, honest men and criminals, workers and idlers, intelligent men and idiots, ascetics and libertines, scholars and ignorant men, geniuses and mediocre men, the glorious and the unknown, the skilled and the clumsy, the young and the old, the rich and the poor, the civilised and the savage, everyone, except he who searches madly for his Lord here below without distraction and without repose, except he who puts his hand on the primary slime and does the work of God.

64'. The scholars and the intelligent shall be ridiculed before God and driven far away from his light; only the simple and the believers shall find grace before him. As for the sages and the saints, their heart has always been with the Lord of wisdom and love.

«The Book in which God has written his secret is heaven and earth. Therefore, the holy and wise man studies the science of the Lord in the peace of the garden of Eden.»

65. We shall not change the nature of beings and of things through our little deeds and, if we restrain it for a moment, it shall then rise up stronger than ever.

But God is all-mighty, for he changes even the darkness into the light of life.

65'. Oh! who shall give us absurd faith and mad perseverance?

Oh! who shall teach us derisory simplicity and totally naked humility?

Oh! who shall make shine the holy light of God before us so that we become like the gold of the Perfect One?

To him who triumphs, I shall give to eat the fruit of the tree of life that is in my God's paradise.
JOHN

I am the origin, the dissolution, the place, the deposit, the seed, the unalterable. I am the cradle and the grave of everyone... It is the science of sciences, the secret of kings, the supreme lustre.
KRISHNA

BOOK XI

You are an earth that has not been purified, that has not been washed by the rain.

EZEKIEL

This book has been composed by Isis for his brother Osiris, in order to revive his soul, give life to his body and return vigour and youth to all his divine limbs, so that, finally, he shall be reunited with the Sun, his father.

SAHU

RIVE TÉNUE

1. The maddest man can become wise if God enlightens him, but the sage could not become senseless because it is the Lord who sustains him.

2. Work that suits the ignorant and that keeps them in obedience and in order could not be applied to men who have been instructed and who are masters of themselves.

3. Intellectual subtleties are paltry things if we consider the knowledge of the total world.

4. The sage and the madman do not have doubts; however one possesses and the other is possessed.

5. Life in God is first sweetness, gladness and liberation, then it becomes lost in the contemplation of the Being without possible analysis.

LIVING EARTH

1'. It is better to resemble an idiot praising God than to seem intelligent while denying the obviousness of life.

2'. If we do not find God during our wakefulness, we shall not possess him while we are asleep.

3'. Let us throw our science into the fire, and at last it shall produce for us something good, like the simplicity of the ashes.

4'. Let us abandon all useless malice, and God shall appear naked before our dazzled eyes.

5'. He who reaches God in spirit and in body is like the quintessence of heaven and earth.

6. The great revolt is to seek God ceaselessly.
True success is to reach him without returning.

6'. In the hidden place, the luminous jewel currently lives.
«By doing good, evil disappears by itself. By combating evil, one runs the great risk of sinking into it even more.»

7. He who imagines that he does evil or does good according to men, sins because of ignorance.
He who has been instructed arranges things and leaves to God to concern himself with the accomplishment of his work.

7'. There is no law for him who inhabits the law, for he is already the law and love with the Unique One.
«Let the ignorant ones explain nothing, and life shall not be divided any more».

8. The joy of God is in the union of sages and in the prayer of saints, as it is in the inspiration of artists, in the games of children and in the songs of the whole nature.

8'. He who is truthful is rapidly delivered from the world of the mediocre, for the light separates itself from the darkness that surrounds it.

9. The Book is dust and ash compared to the living reality of God. However, it gives the means to recognize the source of heaven and earth.

9'. Knowledge frees the sage and faith saves the saint, but it is love that unites them in God.

10. Morals of sages does not violate natural laws.

10'. It is our hands that prepare the earth, but it is the blessing of the Lord that makes it produce its fruit.

11. That which flatters the brute may torture the saint, and that which pleases the sage may disgust the vulgar man.

11'. I shall forget those who have not remembered me, says the Unique One.

12. A life of work, pleasure, repose, suffering, resignation or revolt is not worth a minute devoted to seeking God in oneself.

12'. He who crosses the barrier of liquid fire shall attain the true knowledge of love.

13. Resignation is like the renunciation of God, for it maintains us in the filth that separates us from him.

14. Happiness is where there is neither separation, nor change, nor death.

15. He who knows where death leads has filled his life well.

16. The good doctor aids nature, and the sage is patient with all men.

17. No belief should be made obligatory.
God hates the persecutors and the mediocre.

18. The sage and the madman ignore fear; however, one dominates death and the other is its food.

19. When they want to make heroes of you, you are not far from being dead.

20. Misfortune saves those who were being dragged towards death by routine.

21. Sleep, prayer, love, work and drugs make one forget misfortune for a time; but only the knowledge of God delivers us from it forever.

22. To scold a senseless man is to sink him into his madness and gratuitously make an enemy of him.

13'. Let us return everything to God, and we shall possess the world without damage.

14'. How could there be repose for the sage while a portion of the Being remains exiled in death?

15'. God offers light and receives only light.

16'. It is necessary to make use of the end of everything to know the beginning of everything.

17'. If you find God, do not proclaim it from the housetops, and above all do not try to convince anyone.

18'. It is the absurd that delivers us from the prisons of the spirit.

19'. Let loose, before they wrench off.

20'. It is the excess of love and never self-satisfied mediocrity that brings us back to God.

21'. All that man has dragged with him in his fall shall be rehabilitated with him, and creation shall live again appeased in the bosom of the unique Splendour.

22'. We shall not strike except out of compassion, and only to instruct when the Lord formally demands it.

23. To argue with an inferior man is to stoop to his level and lose all chance of being heard.

24. He who is truly right never tries to prove it, for he knows that even misfortune itself is not understood.

25. The bramble and the wicked one are moved aside with a stick; he who puts his hand on it becomes entangled and rips himself up unnecessarily.

26. It is the primary and ultimate knowledge that constitutes the teaching of all the holy books.
«O invaluable treasure trampled on by ignorant men!»

27. Few men perfect themselves in peace, for many become bored and softened by it; and few are taught by misfortune, because almost all of them tense up or become desperate through it.

28. Who shall free his soul from the foreign land? And who shall make the Lord descend into the holy land?

29. It is through the madness of love that we draw closer to God, and it is through the world's reason that we move away from him.

23'. The Living One goes to the dead to save them, but they stupidly try to kill him, for they do not recognize the light that inhabits the Universe.

24'. Holiness is confidence in God, generosity towards all, abundance in everything, joy for oneself.

25'. Ultimate wisdom is like primary innocence, with the only difference that the one knows itself and the other ignores itself.

26'. Let the believers that love the Book pray in their hearts and say: «Let he who has told us of your grace, your love and your science be inebriated with you for ever, O Lord!»

27'. We play with everything we believe to be, but we shall conserve only that which truly is.
«The incombustible purity.»

28'. When the form disappears, the substance of water emerges from the chaos and manifests the essence of the divine fire.

29'. Let us observe the spectacle of the world till we are on the point of laughing or crying, but let us never participate in it seriously, on pain of losing ourselves in its night.

30. God lives and moves beyond all human reason.

31. If we wish to reach the Father and receive the promised inheritance, we must first cease to be orphans in the darkness of death, and secondly, fix ourselves in the holy Mother, where love shall mature us.

32. Evil has no intrinsic existence, it appears as the slowing down of whichever portion of life that distances itself from the source of the eternal good, which is God the Being.

33. Suns die and are born again in the nurturing water and earth.

34. Let us not commit ourselves on anyone's behalf. Only God can take on such a burden, for he can deliver us from the nets of death.

35. Too much freedom leads the ignorant one to the slavery of death.

36. Only he who has come out of death knows the value of repose in rediscovered life.

37. Let us not violate the limits that God has set us, in order to avoid sinking into a more opaque death.

38. The end of our rebellion shall be the end of our agitation. We shall one day become tired of misfortune, and we shall remember God, and return to him.

30'. The smallest experience of God is worth more than all the theologies in the world.

31'. Love is characterized by confidence and the limitless gift of oneself in the freedom of the Being. But when the slightest constraint appears, love and freedom disappear immediately.

32'. A corrective for others and an injustice for oneself: that is how misfortune appears to the ignorant.

33'. That which has been separated by fire can only be reunited by it.

34'. Malice has lost us, simplicity shall save us and we shall live once more in the garden of delights.

35'. If something annoys us, let us examine whether it is useful to others or to ourselves.

36'. O splendour! O life! O nucleus! It is you that we adore, O Eternal One of the eternities!

37'. Let us stand before God like a corpse in the hands of the embalmer who prepares the resurrection.

38'. The sages of this world shall humiliate themselves before the simple one who possesses God and his light.

39. God smiles at men's rebellion, for he knows that they shall return wiser and more loving after their migration into the darkness of death.

40. We can lose ourselves eternally if the absurd does not stop us on the path that leads us astray and if love does not bring us back to our holy origin.

41. God punishes no-one; misfortune is merely the effect of us distancing ourselves from the original source.

42. He who hands over all his gifts to God reaches divine simplicity, which is like perfect humility.

43. Misfortune is illusory in relation to the Being; however, it is what leads man back to his source.

44. The scholar knows many things, but possesses none of them.
The sage possesses just one and knows all the others.

45. Let us not take sides for anything or for anyone; let us seek God, who is more urgent than everyone put together.

46. Man becomes aware in separation, in absence and in return.

47. It is God who commands and it is the deity that executes.

39'. He who knows and possesses the truth does not tire himself out trying to be right against anyone.

40'. For some, God is a sublime reality.
For others, he seems like an incredible madness.
«The intelligent have rejected the Book, and the scholars of the world have completely failed to understand it.»

41'. The truth shines eternally, but its earthly clothing is dark.

42'. When we give and receive without a care, we shall be close to God.

43'. The laws of God and those of nature oppress those that violate them, and deliver those that observe them.

44'. It is by ascending and descending that we shall discover God's movement and repose.

45'. The sage acts freely because he knows everything is in God.

46'. We remain united in God, but we are several in the world, according to places and according to times.

47'. Just as water was used to form all things, all things shall once more

It is man who sows and it is woman who gives birth.

become like water.

48. We shall never find God by destroying beings and things; in fact we shall divide ourselves and sink further into death.

48'. The children of the Unique One imitate the work of the Father, and already live in peace in the present world.

49. Skilful dialectics do not lead the experts astray, for the holy light orientates all their thoughts towards the Unique One.

49'. It is the work that provokes arguments, and not the latter that engender the former.

50. Our faith is like the fragrance and the memory of the invisible sea of the world, where the Perfect One reposes.

50'. The sage and the saint do not tire themselves out admiring and praising God's creation.

51. The love of God is like the intense memory of our freedom and of our primary unity in the purity of heaven.

51'. The fulfilment of the wish depends on the accuracy of the image conceived, on the power of the projection of desire and on the patient regularity of prayer.

52. The light of our hearts screams at God through the darkness of the body that imprisons it, and the Father delivers she who has gone astray, and the Son appears in the splendour of the union.

52'. There is a great beauty and a great virtue in the Lord's work; that is why he keeps working on it and does not reject it.

53. The ignorant one does not know the ancient teachings and muddles up the present truth.

53'. There is intelligence in recognizing the origin of the misfortune that knocks us to the ground.

54. When the sterile tree cannot be restored, fire renders it to nurturing ashes and to fertilizing water.

54'. The only perfection is ascent, descent and repose.

55. No-one shall convince he who says no, except for the absurdity of this no, become evident in death.

55'. Holiness is like a curse for those who have seen it, heard it and not recognized it.

56. I have admired the luminous patience of life and I have praised him who matures it until God's repose.

57. Let us apply ourselves to becoming immense, in order to receive God in his totality.

58. True knowledge implies possession, absorption and transmutation.

59. He who has allowed everything to come and go can usefully turn towards God, for he is already in him.

60. The friends of God are powerful, yet they appear like worms. They possess all things and they are treated as if they are wretched. They live with wisdom, and the world believes they are mad. They overflow with love and they appear hard.

61. The best thought, the most beautiful action are those that bring us closest to divine gratuitousness.

62. The love of God is the beginning of knowledge, and his possession is the end of science.

63. Shyness is almost always a pride that does not name itself.
Who shall beg the Highest for his life?

64. He who restrains himself is a sage, but he who bullies himself is a madman.

56'. The intelligence of water and the memory of earth form the body-spirit of the Universe, but it is the love of fire that confers on it the living soul.

57'. There is nothing to understand there where everything must be felt.

58'. It is divine nature that consoles us, heals us, instructs us and saves us.

59'. The blessing of God shall flow over him who is naked, and the grace that is inside and outside shall form one single water.

60'. The most complete expression of love is generosity and patience towards all the beings of creation.
In the example of the Lord whom we eat and who eats us, the sage shows the light of life to the beings gone astray in death.

61'. Acceptance, detachment and self-oblivion are the perfection of love in God.

62'. The first duty is to make God appear in oneself; the second is to contribute to manifesting him in others.

63'. He who has delivered himself from the will to do good and the fear of doing evil is close to the freedom of God.

64'. The saint that wishes to go to God must free himself from the bonds of sin and from those of virtue.

65. All masters have been called proud by those who could not follow them, but they smile without replying, for they know that they have forgotten themselves in God for ever.

66. It is grace that delivers, it is love that unites, it is knowledge that perfects and it is union that provides repose.

67. When the mouth moves, let us listen to the words of the heart, and we shall know the truth about those who speak to us.

68. The world's obligations seem of very little urgency to him who seeks God.

69. Few men have been favoured with possessive knowledge here below, since few saints among the best are capable of acquiring divine power without adversely affecting themselves and others.

70. When we reach God, let us not omit to hand over everything to him; if not, we shall lose him immediately.

71. Language may change, the spirit of the Book shall not age, for it teaches the beginning and the end of apparent and hidden creation.

72. To vanquish the world by fighting it or by fleeing it, is the apparent alternative offered to all, if we wish to avoid being crushed, torn apart and bogged down.

65'. Let us observe the dead of this world to understand to which senseless dream their ignorance of God resembles.

66'. Wisdom has not begun and shall never end. In it love is manifested in unity.

67'. The weak one who says yes and who never acts accumulates the scorn of men and separates himself from God, since the rotten plank is of no use to either water or fire.

68'. He who is instructed asks God.
He who is not asks men.

69'. To be possessed by God is to be holy.
To possess God is to be wise.
But to penetrate God is to be senseless and become like God, who is the primary and ultimate sense.

70'. Our love and our knowledge shall fuse in the divine union, and living repose shall be our eternal reward.

71'. The Book is for the most subtle and the most slow-witted, for it partakes of heaven and earth. Each one shall draw from it according to his capacity.

72'. The perfection of the manifested One emanates from the union of the golden jewel and the luminous lotus, which emerged through the power of the divine breath from the

However, the sage knows a third solution that delivers us from all evil, servitude and ignorance, for it is that which patiently separates life from death within us.

dark and hidden chaos.

«The last-born is the cherished child of the Father and of the Mother, and the beloved brother of great souls.»

> *Senseless one, that which you sow does not come back to life if it does not first die... The body is sowed corruptible, it resurrects incorruptible, it is sowed contemptible, it resurrects glorious; it is sowed infirm, it resurrects full of strength. It is sowed as animal body, it resurrects as spiritual body.*
>
> PAUL

> *That which is below is like that which is above, and that which is above is like that which is below, in order to create the miracle of a single thing.*
>
> HERMES TRISMEGISTUS

BOOK XII

It is a closed source, a sealed fountain.

SOLOMON

I am everything that has been, everything that is and everything that will be, and no human has ever raised my veil. The fruit I engendered was the sun.

INSCRIPTION ON THE PEDIMENT OF THE TEMPLE OF ATHENA, IN SAÏS

NUIT RÊVÉE

1. It is perfect knowledge that demonstrates to us our absolute ignorance.
«He who prejudges God's choice cuts himself off from the love of his Lord.»

2. Our glory is to let God operate in us without hindrance.
«The intellect is the blazing and whirling sword that prohibits our entrance into the garden of Eden.»

3. The tree of life is planted in the centre of the garden of paradise, but the tree of the knowledge of good and evil grows straddling the boundary wall.

4. Man is the middle term of the graduated Universe and the expression of its greatest mystery.

THE SOURCE

1'. It is through the pure gratuitousness of our thoughts and our acts that we shall acquire and conserve peace of heart.

2'. Holy love is like a to-ing and fro-ing that links together, and with their divine source, the creatures gone astray in death.

3'. The sage meditates on the nothing where everything has come from.
He is the guardian of the wisdom issued from heaven and earth.

4'. It is in heavenly light that the life of the world resides, but it sometimes acts also in the earthly shadow.

5. Man was made from the best part of heaven and earth, and if he were cleaned of his filth, he would be seen shining like the stars, the moon and the sun.

6. Coercion is something totally alien to God and to the sage, for they inhabit the freedom where there is neither darkness nor death.

7. Let us control once our agitation and we shall enjoy life in the very middle of the death of the world.

8. The sage is like the precious stone hidden beneath its gangue.

9. Those in whom there is neither baseness nor mediocrity are repelled and set apart by the world, which thus returns them to God without knowing it.

10. Adaptation to the world is like forgetting God.

11. We shall suffer in the worlds for lengthy times, we shall play in the mother for eternities, but only in God shall we rest forever.

12. There is a state that is higher than all prayer, which is absence, presence and union. This grade belongs to masters.

5'. The Book teaches us how to come out of death and repose in life, but how many of the believers are passionate about this mystery?

6'. The mediocre shall rot in death until they open up in the abandon of grace and in the generosity of love.

7'. Let us conserve the detachment and joy of holiness, and all shall become easy and simple for us.

8'. Let our secret virtue be the union with God.

9'. Let us be rich to the point of no longer possessing anything.
Let us be lovers to the point of being able to give everything.
Let us be faithful to the point of tiring the darkness.

10'. Separation and union make the impassive appear.

11'. Love began with the primary separation. It shall repose with the ultimate reintegration, in the possessive and uniting knowledge of the Lord of the worlds.

12'. Man's heart is like a stone that seals the entrance to God's treasure.

13. When we feel great fatigue due to the agony of this world, we shall be ready to live in God.

14. He who has forgotten himself in God remains indifferent to the promises and threats of this world.

15. The wisdom of the sage is like an ignorance that knows itself and remains silent.

16. When we have obtained everything in the spirit, the heart and the hands, we shall understand that the only desirable thing is repose in the centre of the centre.

17. Let us consider the instability of the present world and let us turn towards God, before change has broken our particular will and attachments.

18. Without the lessons of misfortune and without the failures of this world, how many men would be sunk in death forever?

19. We shall honour God by making the Book known to those who seek a way out of their troubles.

20. The Book is powerful as fire and conciliatory as water, subtle as air and faithful as earth.

13'. Dissolved in the water of grace and the fire of love, it manifests the holy light where all of them move and some of them repose.

14'. The great purification is to love, contemplate, know, possess and repose.

15'. Silence allows us to hear all and say all, without exciting the incredulity or the anger of the mediocre.

16'. He who does not roar in his heart and who does not shed the tears of desperation in the midst of the death of this world cannot be instructed by God.

17'. Three-times mad, those of you who believe you can organize yourselves definitively in the unsteady mud of this world; the great tide shall erase your works and shall return you to naked humility.

18'. We must live more and more in the spirit, otherwise we shall remain slaves on foreign land for eternity.

19'. Nothing is more urgent than the search for God, and nothing is more useless than human dispute.

20'. God speaks only to God and is heard only by God.

21. The mediocre think they are afraid of death, but in reality it is life that they fear above all else.

22. The art of healing is noble, for it prefigures the art of regeneration, which is holy.

23. No joy and no pain in this world could make us forget the agony of the earth.

24. No-one can change nature, but some know how to purify it and mature it fully.

25. Let us consider interior peace and let us remain as absent as possible from this world.

26. God makes the worlds move by attracting that which is luminous and repelling that which is obscure.

27. A little dust tarnishes a mass of gold, and a small defect sometimes masks a great holiness.

28. There is only one true misfortune here below, which is to be unaware of God and his repose.
  «O mysterious and hidden Father!»
  «O luminous and living Mother!»
  «O radiant and perfect Son!»

29. He who believes he can reach God without knowing man and nature is more ignorant than an earthworm.

30. Mediocrity is not to give or receive freely; not to love or increase;

21'. Let us offer a praise to the Unique One every day, so that his joy remains with us.

22'. It is more advantageous to be saved by someone simple full of experience than to be killed by a scholar stuffed with science.

23'. Clear-sightedness towards oneself is the most accomplished form of courage.

24'. God is everywhere, but he is found only by those who search for him in the limbos of the world.

25'. Wisdom is like the union with the living, eternal and free centre.

26'. The sun fertilizes the life that rises and falls. It is like the centre of each world, be it infinitely large or infinitely small.

27'. Few men taste the beautiful things of the world, and even fewer admire those things that are wise.

28'. Let us take advantage of the slightest respite the world grants us to converse with him who is always attentive inside ourselves.

29'. All that falls from the heaven accumulates in our souls until the light delivers us from death.

30'. Unmask yourself, strip yourself down, and the Mother shall ap-

to have neither generosity nor gift; to hate greatness, beauty, genius, holiness and purity; to be separated from grace and deprived of love; to think and act basely; to be weak and cowardly in all circumstances of hidden life; to oppress that which is inside and to be crushed by that which is outside.

31. One can be mediocre; one could not boast about it.

32. No repose without knowledge.
No knowledge without love.
No love without grace.
No grace without abandonment.

33. The primary light was drawn from the chaos by God and made quintessence in Adam, who did no more than mix this sublime light once more with the exterior darkness of non-being; through curiosity, presumption, vanity and disobedience.

34. The new Adam, the true son of God that came, is coming and shall come, separates once more the light from the darkness, through humility, love and obedience to the law of the Unique One.

pear to you without a veil; but take care that no-one adds nor takes away, on pain of clouding the truth that enlightens you and that gives life to you.

«If we could see the world laid open, we would be petrified by the surprise and crushed by the shame of our voluntary exile, for God is the conscience of life, and life is the body of God.»

31'. All that we accomplish with love is exempt from boredom.

32'. He that fertilizes resides in the sun.
She that nourishes remains in the earth.
She that delivers moves in heaven.
He that unifies reposes in the heart.

33'. The union of water and earth makes the purity of the Lord's luminous garment appear, and fire manifests the secret virtue of God's treasure.

34'. It is the interior woman and man that we have to bring out of the chaos, through the divine succour of grace that opens and of love that fertilizes.

35. The first revolt exiled man in the foreign land. The second makes him organize himself comfortably in it. The third makes him give up this world and leads him back to God.

35'. The mortification that prepares for the new life is accomplished in the darkness of faith and in the vacuity of the Being.

36. The particular will of man only accentuates more and more the failure of his revolt against God.

36'. God does not ask us to please, he asks us to be simple and true.

37. He who has experienced the humiliation and the sadness of exterior death duly appreciates the joy of life rediscovered and the glory of God recognized.

37'. It is abandon, grace and love that deliver us from the prisons of death and that give us access to the abodes of heaven; but it is possessive knowledge that fixes us in the secret centre.

38. It is the responsibility of each one of us to arouse God in oneself with one's particular faith, be it patient, sweet, bold, wilful, or even violent; but always animated by the fire of love.

38'. The saint that prays to know his Lord refrains from imagining the place, the moment and the arrangement of the meeting, so as not to hinder the mysterious union of the Unique One.

39. God may remain deaf to all kinds of prayer, but he could not resist for long the generosity of love.

39'. Deep intention determines the means of accomplishment, be it for good or for evil.

40. The science of men has brought blood and fire upon the world. What would happen if the science of God were to fall into the hands of the wicked?

40'. Intelligence without love is like a gear without oil which, despite its perfection, ends up grating unbearably.

41. Even the sage, who knows the perennial nature of the world's support, sometimes cries like a baby at the pain of separations.

41'. The truth possesses a thousand garments, yet it has only one body, one spirit and one soul in the One.

42. Let us not wait to be stunned by misfortune before turning towards God.

42'. When a temptation becomes too violent, let us offer it to God, who makes everything bearable.

43. The vanities of the world are of no use here, for it is not a case of being overloaded with memory or puffed up with importance, but rather of being simple and naked as on the last day of creation and on the first day of our birth.

44. The mediocre in power bring down a people with much more certainty than a coalition of all its enemies would be capable of doing.
«The Lord becomes dark in the shell, but remains luminous in the secret centre of his creation.»

45. There where temptation does not exist, there is no combat, nor defeat, nor victory, but rather repose for the chosen ones, stagnation for the mediocre and death for the rebels.

46. We need God and his kingdom right now, in order to escape from the vertigo of the abyss opened up in this world.

47. Let us strip down those who recommend misery to us and thrash those who preach resignation, to see if they speak the truth.

48. Let us support those who search for the Unique One so that, on having reached life, they help us to climb the ladder of creation.

49. My Name is like a golden dot in the tabernacle of the ancestors. Who shall make it shine on the earth?, says the Lord. And who shall make it shine in the heaven?, asks the Unique One.

43'. We shall rejoin God's treasure and we shall remain in his splendour and in his peace forever.
«Only holy water can wash us of the dark filth and make us live again in the light of the Lord.»

44'. He who is at the peak of love and of knowledge is like a vessel full of the nectar of the gods, where all beings quench their thirst; but he who stops halfway on the path to knowledge is like a jug full of ashes that is of no use to anyone.

45'. Let us use the goods of this world modestly, so as not to deprive ourselves of what is necessary, on the one hand; and so as not to be excluded from the superabundance of God, on the other.

46'. God is closer to man than to any other earthly body, except for the salt of the earth.

47'. It is identification with God that gives perfect omnipotence and gratuitousness.

48'. He who possesses light in its primary purity is a coadjutor of God.

49'. He who does not have the patience of water, the constancy of earth, the subtlety of air and the purity of fire, which separate and unite, shall not enter the glory of the Lord.

50. There is one thing that God would not be able to do: destroy himself.

50'. Matter. Matrix. Matrass. Mater. Patria. Part. Pastor. Pater.

51. He who cannot reach God in ecstasy tries to approach him through vulgar drunkenness, for each one tries in his own way to find the repose of the Unique One.

51'. It is in the apparent madness of God that subsists the deep reason of the Universe, just as the spark of fire remains hidden in the uncut stone.

52. It is characteristic of a saint to lend himself to men and give himself to God.

52'. The study of creation could not do without the love of the creator.

53. Do to others as you would have done to you, and the dew of the sun shall make all men's earth flower once again.

53'. It is only the purity of childhood, of holiness and of love that can approach God.

54. The sages shall give up their wisdom in order to become united with God, and the saints shall forget their holiness in order to rejoin the unique clearness.

54'. This world is like a house of madmen, and we shall only get out of it by becoming madder than the maddest, that is to say, wise in God.

55. The past is like the time of madness.
The present is like the time of ignorance.
The future is like the time of illusion.
Only life in God is like eternal wisdom.

55'. Let us attach ourselves to God from now on, so that when misfortune comes it passes over us like water slides over a duck's back.
«O brilliant truth that erases all blemish of death!»

56. We must recognize ourselves in all those who suffer and lack assistance, and offer them the water they need for purification and the fire that is essential to union.

56'. The madman kills and disperses that which lives.
The sage vivifies and concentrates that which seems dead.
«One single substance, one single essence.
One single food, one single drink.»

57. All that bores us is precisely that which is useless to us at that moment; that is why each one goes towards that which attracts him most, in order to experience the world to the best advantage.

58. Work is a chain and ball imposed upon the pride and rebellion of the fallen man.
Pain is a bit and a bridle placed on the lies and disobedience of the unfaithful woman.

59. It is better to become unconscious in the truth than to remain conscious in lies.

60. The proud one must not complain, nor cry, nor curse, for he has chosen to live alone in the midst of the darkness of death.

61. It is the faculty of expansiveness, of giving and of love that makes us one with God.

62. Pride considers that which is outside.
Humility looks into oneself.
Wisdom fixes God.

63. Let us pray that we become simple and flexible in the extreme, in order to possess the joy that never ends.

57'. It is better to stammer the Name of God in our heart than to name him in a learned way through the lips of others.

58'. One must be mad to be proud of a wound, and demented to keep it in the hope of obtaining relief, for it is only the medicine of heaven and earth that delivers us from all evil and from all death.

59'. The tortuous way is tiring, and the straight way so easy.
«Wisdom does not do violence to anything, yet it discovers everything.»

60'. Pure air and bitter herbs make the blood clean.
Detachment and self-oblivion make the soul clear.

61'. The anarchy of love prepares the Lord's way.

62'. Without the ordeal, no-one truly knows himself or possesses himself.

63'. Our safeguard lies in generosity towards all beings and towards ourselves.

64. It is better to squander in charity than to save for destruction.

65. All that comes from man is human, even that which appears inhuman.

66. All creation is precious before God, since its change makes the salt of life appear.

67. Let us first pray with humility and perseverance in the darkness of faith. Then, we shall praise with abandon and gratefulness in the light of love. Finally, we shall adore, with overcoming, and with integration into the unity of knowledge.

68. The power of man resides in the generosity of justice.
That of woman is in the grace of virtue.

69. He who has closed the circle of creation knows that nothing exists outside of the primary and ultimate essence, where the germ of the marvellous creations of eternity reposes.

70. Violence may lay the world low for a time, but it could not convince anyone.

71. Creation is like a delirium whose generator barely manages to keep control.

64'. Let us begin by giving, so as to receive without sinning.

65'. Let us not make ourselves rigid before anything, and we shall not be broken by anything.

66'. Man subsists only by his exchanges with God through creation.

67'. He who rebels before the weakness and mislaying of men must strive for holiness, so as to erase in himself that which displeases him so much in others.
«When our dream is like our wakefulness and our wakefulness is like the absence of the world and the presence of God, unity shall be accomplished in us.»

68'. He who observes the commandments of his heart can ignore those of ordinary men, for he already surpasses all of them in the love of God.

69'. The equilibrium of opposites is established in the accomplishment of perfect love and in the repose of final knowledge.
«We shall eat the glorious sun and we shall be alive for ever.»

70'. When we are afraid for our lives as we are afraid for that of an ant, we shall be close to being instructed.

71'. By joining heaven and earth we shall obtain the glory of God.

72. To be absent does not mean becoming drunk in a vulgar fashion: it means remaining empty of desires so that God can visit us freely.

73. To accept does not mean lying down and waiting: it means doing well what one must and not considering the result.

74. To be detached does not mean becoming insensitive to creation: it means letting everything come and letting everything go without coercion.

75. To forget oneself does not mean cutting oneself off from the world and humanity: it means merging into them until one is able to love everything and judge nothing.

76. To repose does not mean remaining in death: it means living in God, and not interfering in the running of the world or the affairs of men.

77. After having lost oneself in God, the greatest joy consists in finding oneself once again in him.
«Who shall present himself pure and complete before the Lord in order to be made one with the Unique One?»

72'. GRACE that opens.

73'. LOVE that causes germination.

74'. PURITY that enlightens.

75'. KNOWLEDGE that unites.

76'. PEACE that balances.

77'. GRATUITOUSNESS that perpetuates.

There are three possible solutions for men here below:

To rely only on oneself, as the ignorant ones who have gone astray in the night of the world do.

To rely on oneself and on God, as believers that have heard about the light of the beginning do.

To rely only on God, as do sages and saints that know or approach the origin and end of all things.

Trust in God with all your heart and do not lean on your own intelligence.
SOLOMON

In order to receive the kingdom, the only means is to do nothing for it. While one acts to achieve it, one cannot attain the kingdom.
LAO TSE

BOOK XIII

Accursed be the man who trusts in men! Blessed be the man who trusts in God!

JEREMIAH

Do not extinguish the Spirit, do not despise the prophecies, try all things and retain that which is good.

PAUL

VUE... ET RIEN

1. He who speaks outside continues to be ignorant. He who is silent inside lives with wisdom.

2. Identification with God engenders perfect power and freedom.

3. The conqueror of the three worlds shall repose forever in the translucent sea of the beginning of the beginnings.

4. It is the pacification of the whole Being that leads to interior vision and divine union.

5. It is the contemplation of the primary and ultimate unity that engenders true union and peace.

THE MIDDLE

1'. Do not abandon your God and he shall not leave you, and you shall be in one forever.

2'. Enlightenment transfigures he who becomes empty after having searched for a long time.

3'. I have made an absence of my prayer and a stupor of my praise. Ah! When shall I be able to make a death of my love, so as to become reestablished in your imperishable life?

4'. Let us cry for being so full of the world and so empty of the Unique One.

5'. We are all in God, but few know it and hardly any experience it in this world.

6. Let us wait for his presence night and day without ever tiring, for when we are ripe we shall fall from ourselves into his arms.

7. If we truly love God, let us reject all that is not him so that he may manifest himself in us without hindrance.

Let us forget sects and sectarians, sciences and scholars, laws and lawyers, homelands and politicians, slaves and masters, and let us serve only our inner peace, taking counsel only from our deep conscience.

8. Let us allow life to come and go, for it is movement and change; he who inhabits it does not vary.

9. Let us not be too scrupulous with that which comes to us, so that we are not too scrupulous with that which leaves us.

10. Not one ignorant person could blaspheme the Name of God, for no-one knows it except he who is already living eternity.

11. Let us meditate on God and his light when we come out of the night, and let us think of them when going into it so that we do not break the bond between us and him.

12. He plays at frightening us in the world, but when we awake in him, he laughs at our delusions with us.

6'. All our thoughts and all our acts are inept or lies. The sage knows it, the saint believes it, the poet sometimes suspects it.

7'. The Mother is found in faith and in patience, and she acts immediately. She is the one that delivers and cures. The water from heaven makes the earth germinate, but all remain deaf and blind before the miracle of God, for they think they are more intelligent and wiser than the creator of innumerable worlds.

8'. He who becomes hardened in battle, how will he then manage to be penetrated by love?

9'. A thief who gives is closer to God than a righteous man who preserves what he has received.

10'. There is nothing tragic in the world, except the idea that we have of the things of the world.

11'. Let us love with no other hope than love, knowledge and repose in the peace of the Perfect One.

12'. It is the infinite division into two of the Unique One that makes creation, and it is the re-uniting of the parts that makes repose.

13. Let us abandon our rights and our possessions and we shall be delivered from our duties and our burdens.

13'. He who says: «God does not exist» asserts the reality of creation.

14. Let us allow God to speak and act in our place, and let us not worry about the result.

14'. Let us interrogate the Lord in all circumstances and we shall know the truth about everything.

15. Let us not trust anything and anyone, except God, and we shall not be torn apart by anything and by anyone, for the Lord is the only one that does not disappoint those that give themselves to him.

15'. Let us not ask ourselves questions, let us rather interrogate him. Thus, that which we desire shall not hinder us, but we shall accomplish that which is useful to us.

16. Teach us the vigorous prayers like the ruts of love.
– Give us the impulses that shall carry our souls beyond the abyss.
– Sing us the NAME that forces open the gates of death.
– Nourish us with the essence dragged along by the living gold.
– Offer us the redemptive sun of our lives gone astray.

16'. When our reason, will and intelligence are annihilated by the length and by the violence of our quest, then innocence, grace and love shall hand over the long-desired secret of the unique Splendour.
«O poor idiot!», it is enough to remain silent and stop being restless for the Perfect One to give life to you once more in your primary perfection.

17. The worst idleness is to despair of God and of oneself.

17'. Let us explore our heart and we shall be enlightened by our own light.

18. In vain we try to believe, see and even touch; if we do not possess the eternal Mother and the divine Father we shall never attain the holy Son.

18'. The virtue of the tamed lion prevails over the natural gentleness of the lamb, and the two re-united engender the perfection of the ultimate Lord.

19. The magnetization of love is communicated to those who are sufficiently pure to let it in. Thus magnetized, they in turn become magnets, and the chain of reintegration that forms in the world merges into God.

19'. Our curiosity for the Lord is a grace that is ignored, but our love for him is a confirmed blessing.
The door and the key.
«O holy light that shines in the mysterious grotto of Adam!»

20. The extraordinary adventure is not to carry out dangerous actions in foreign countries. It is rather to search for the divine Mother and Father hidden behind the apparent banality of the things of this world.

20'. There are few believers in the world that are truly disgusted by the leprosy that covers them and that poisons them more each day. All that is thought and said about them shall neither add nor take away anything from what they really are.

21. When the world judges our patience as stupidity, our faith as idiocy and our love as madness, we shall be close to perfection.

21'. Our rebellion against the world corresponds to the condemnation of our own straying, but few know that.

22. We shall know that we are prepared for the divine quest when we are tired of running away from ourselves, tired of getting passionate, tired of lying to ourselves, tired of becoming lost, tired of rebelling, tired of becoming distracted, of becoming agitated and of scattering ourselves in the world.

Then we shall no longer consider the place we occupy here below, but rather the emptiness or plenitude of our hearts, which is the only thing that matters. Then faith shall be in us like the superabundance of the powers of the divine life that overflows our narrow bounds under the irresistible drive of love.

22'. Build your house, cultivate your garden, weave your clothes, sew your shoes, cut your wood, make your bread, bury the dead, water the earth, help the woman to give birth, raise the child. Turn your hand to these things once and meditate on the beginning and the end of the middle world, in order to know the beginning of the lower world that unites with the perfection of the higher world. Thus, you shall remember where you came from, you shall understand where you are and you shall know where you are going, and the deliverance of peace shall live in you forever.

23. Few men become worthy of God's gift, which is the freedom of the Being in eternal life, that is why so many creatures struggle or languish in the shackles of death. Let us therefore make of our life a perpetual act of thanksgiving, and let us be aware that all we imagine and name with faith and love is accomplished in heaven and shall soon be manifested on earth.

24. Each of us must bear until the end, and without recriminations, the burden he has chosen by sinking into the exterior darkness. For it is solitary germination that separates the good seed and prepares the fruitful harvest.

25. By hating and condemning those that have gone astray, we sink them into error. By loving them without judging them, we help them to emerge from the chaos of death.

26. Even those who know that one floats on the sea without moving do not dare to launch themselves naked into God.

27. Let us act gratuitously as often as possible so as not to fall into the traps of the appearance of numbers and accounts.

23'. It is absolutely necessary for the shrewd, the proud and the violent to experience the absurdity of their systems. Unfortunately, this is first done at the expense of the innocent before turning against them. Let us then stop being so intelligent in the world in order to become ever simpler in God.

«The worst deceit is to have clean hands and a dirty heart.»

24'. When we feel tempted beyond our strength, our intelligence or our love, let us pray in ourselves so that the rebel is subdued and returns to God like a prodigal son taken in and introduced by maternal love.

25'. Let us put into practice the virtues contrary to the vices that we find so repugnant in others. Thus, the visible evil shall help to lead us to the hidden good.

26'. First break the barriers inside so as to become one in oneself, and secondly, break those outside so as to become one in the totality of the Being.

27'. Let us try to acquire detachment from temporal forms in order to attain the knowledge of inside, which will allow us to fully enjoy the hidden life.

28. The extrinsic filth and the intrinsic substance of the Universe are uncreated, infinite and contain he who can only be named by silence. But the forms emanating from the secret centre are created, finite and temporal in the mixed world.

29. Let us not be moved by anything, but let us be attentive to all that happens to the world and ourselves, so as to learn to distinguish divine reality from the appearances of mixed creation.

30. If we do not meet the master, let us become the master by releasing our God inside and outside of ourselves.

31. Holy love laughs at systems, methods, logics, complications, and even death; for it takes in a single stride madness and reason, darkness and light, to fix itself in the peace of the Unique One.

32. Let us not accuse anyone of the difficulties that occur, simply so as not to increase them uselessly.

Let us remain as much as possible in the repose and in the silence of God until we become nothing more but one with the One; thus, we shall easily command the beings and the things of the total world without doing violence to anything.

The sage and the saint are the only ones truly disgusted by the filth of uncleanliness; the former separates it and rejects it here below, the latter waits patiently with it until the time of the general judgement.

28'. All the waves of creation pass and disappear, but the sea of the great world and he who gives life to it subsists eternally.

«The climax of repose ends in the creative act, the climax of movement leads to regenerative repose.»

29'. Let us pray to God in ourselves so we recognize the means that permits us to discover the hidden substance beneath the crust of the foreign earth.

30'. Let us converse only with our soul, it shall teach us all we wish to know.

31'. The loved one submits herself to the lover's desire, and the lover fulfils the desire of she who is loved.

In this way they manifest the unity of perfect love.

32'. Our light separates by itself from the darkness that imprisons it. It is enough for us not to hinder it through our restlessness in the world and our particular will, which are opposed to the secret decanting of the chaos of the abyss; for wisdom is like our intimate union with the primary essence and substance, which form the indestructible basis of the changing creation.

«There is flesh around the stone, but there is much more precious flesh inside the stone, and in this precious flesh there is also a highly secret and very holy stone.»

33. When we know how to remain absent from ourselves to the point at which God can fill us entirely, all will be possible to us without effort and without difficulty.

34. Let us consider in ourselves and in all beings the buried image of the Lord, so as to love everything according to the reality of life, instead of hating according to the appearances of death.

35. A thousand little simplifications of a thousand little problems make a life full of light.

36. True perspicacity is to discover God beneath his clothing of light after having discovered life under its shroud of darkness.

37. We shall obtain from the Lord everything we ask of him. Let us therefore be very careful about what we choose, so as not to remain ridiculously inferior to the gift of God.

38. Ignorance is like strength outside and weakness inside. Holiness is like weakness outside and strength inside. Wisdom is like strength inside and outside, and sometimes also like weakness outside and inside; that is to say, like God in the holy ignorance of love, which is kept or lost according to his will.

33'. When we have pacified and clarified the inside, the outside shall obey us in the same way and shall seem equally lucid to us.

34'. With their intimate praise, the saints produce a harmony that delights all creation, but with their secret operation the sages collaborate in the reintegration of the Universe in God.

35'. Love towards all beings engenders clear-sightedness and peace for oneself.

36'. When we believe we have seen him, we shall only have caught a glimpse of the shadow of his robes, and when we think we have touched him, we shall only have brushed against the dust of his footsteps.

37'. He who penetrates knowledge risks death, madness or blindness, but if he emerges again unscathed, protected by love, God establishes him in his eternity and in his royalty.

38'. He who reads until the end the Book of opposites and knows how to unite them in the unique, double, quadruple and octuple NAME, shall seem wise to the wise men, holy to the holy and foolish to the fools.

Thus, many have lectured magnificently on God, on his attributes and

«O mystery of the Unique One's choice and gift!» his creation, but how many have glimpsed the hem of his robe, and how many have kissed his footprints? But how many, then, have contemplated the splendour of his body, and how many — what astonishment! — have savoured the delights of his heart?

39. When we see our enemy depressed and asking for help, let us rush to his help, for it is a unique occasion that is offered to us to make a friend of him. In the meantime, let us pray in ourselves for his conversion, and therefore he will soon leave us in peace.

39'. The curse of God is like ignoring or returning his blessing. Thus, it is never he who condemns, but rather us, who remain stupidly and proudly buried in the solitude of death.

40. When we have separated, classified, labelled and stuffed everything, we shall have to reunite and unify everything in life, on pain of remaining sealed in the letter and the multiplicity of death.

40'. He who can unite with the penetration of the spirit the impulse of the heart and the purity of life, shall know neither doubt, despair nor death; for God shall allow him to drink at the source of the living.

41. In this world, there is nothing but clothing that isolates us and possessions that shackle us. For this reason we need to become naked and poor, so as to penetrate unhindered the bosom of the eternal Mother, where the living secret of the Unique One reposes.

41'. We all have the same light, but it is more or less veiled and slowed down according to the thickness of the dark outer layers that separate us from the primary magnet. But incarnate life decants and enlightens the attentive and reposed man.

42. The most direct and naked love gives peace. The simplest and best prepared food gives health. The humblest and most unified knowledge gives wealth.

42'. Let us abstain from dreaming of the world in the world and through the world if we wish to touch the truth of the Unique One.

«There is no universal void. There is nothing but a total fullness, but it is a translucent fullness that makes us believe in the void.»

43. If each one of us simplified ourselves without waiting for our neighbour to begin, all humanity would soon shine with beauty and holiness.

44. He who opens himself up entirely to love is no longer subject to the teaching of the absurd.

45. All created things serve as vehicles for returning up to the source or for distancing oneself from it. Let us abandon them with good grace at each stage of the divine journey.

46. The intelligence of bodily food and that of spiritual food is not simply to choose well that which suits us, but also to reject that which does not suit us, so as to conserve in ourselves only that balsam that maintains and makes the body and the spirit perfect, until the glorification of the soul in the marvellous Lord.

43'. To meditate is to cook the body and the spirit gently to the glorification of the soul.

44'. Those who know how to separate but have never learned how to unite shall never repose in the unity of the hidden essence.

45'. It is only in solitude, in the middle of misfortune and at the time of death that we shall measure the certainty of our faith and the purity of our love in God.

46'. It is gentle and long meditation that turns all things fixed and perfect, for it separates at the beginning to unite better at the end. In this way, we shall see One in everything and Everything in One when we become simple and naked.

The goodwill in God uses as well as possible all that presents itself, but desires nothing. It is like highly sustained attention amid the most perfect quietness.

46". «The chosen ones shall ascend to live in the sun of life. The reprobates shall descend to live in the dead stone.» This is not a fable.

47. The peace of the sage is like the unification of the three worlds; it is a particular reintegration of the creation; it is the repose of the forms in the centre of the pacified essence, and not their destruction.

47'. If we are disturbed by the world it is because we are no longer in God. In fact, nothing could bully him who bathes in the light of the beginning and the end of time.

48. Those who through love and through knowledge teach the way back to the Unique One are sages among saints, but those who penetrate the Lord's secret through the silence of adoration are saints among sages.
In this way, the goods of the earth through earthly affairs, the goods of heaven through heavenly commerce, but God through God alone.

49. There is the Being, there is the act, and there is repose, and there are all those who try to explain one or the other because they are not in that unity that is self-sufficient.

50. In creation, all is loans and restitutions. Thus, after having returned our bodies to earth and our spirits to heaven, in the end we shall also have to give back our souls to God, who shall reunite everything for purity or for filth, on the judgement day.

51. All mysteries are contained in the sweat of the earth and the dew of heaven.

52. Only the sage does not wear a disguise, neither outside nor inside, for he knows that the mantle of shadow protects the light of the Lord naturally.

53. It is the divine fire that manifests the holy light and propels the forms in life, and when something goes astray in death, it is still he that delivers from it.

48'. The words of the Book are nothing; it is the palpable light of the Unique One that is all. When we possess it in our head, in our heart and in our hands, we shall no longer need the teaching, the consolation, the work, nor the care of anyone, for it is the Lord in person that shall be in us and that shall make us live in him.

49'. It is the verb that diversifies the primary substance, and it is silence that unifies it again. Thus, art that gives form to matter is a noble function of man because it brings him closer to his creator.

50'. It is God that creates and gives life to the forms, and it is nature that maintains and multiplies them until it is time for them to return to their initial source.

51'. The divine bird makes its nest in the dust of men's earth.

52'. The birth of the world is like the expansion of the Unique One. The end of creation shall be like the repose of the ONE.

53'. Men's works have become a tremendous temptation for those who do not realize that they only conceal death.

54. Every priest, every chief, every judge, every legislator must experience the human condition of the most humble in order to know the needs of each one, so as to keep alive love, justice and peace among the children of men.

55. The madness of wisdom and holiness is to no longer take seriously the mirages of the world; it is to accept being spat on and say thank you because you have been washed, and to receive blows with gratitude because they open; it is to respect the mud and nail your sandals with gold; it is to smile at the absurd and teach others to cry over it. It is to sense, beyond all reason, perfect freedom and absolute repose in the luminous bosom of the Unique One.

56. It is our God that we must release inside, and not pray to that of others outside.
«The centre of the centre.»

57. Let us thank and praise God in all circumstances, and he shall thus deliver us from the evils of the filth and shower us with heavenly and earthly goods. This is certain.

58. We must never lose sight of the permanence of the essence of crea-

54'. In the beginning, our indiscreet curiosity cost us the freedom of heaven; at present, our exterior science could well deprive us of the life that is left to us in this world.
«The Lord reserves his greatest gifts for those of his children who laughingly tolerate the failures of the world.»

55'. Although we accept personal injustices, insults and annoyances it does not prevent us from replying to those that are directed to the weak and the holy.
«The tempter and the tempted shall meet one day in that which tempts, as the lover and the loved one shall finally subsist in the Amen.»
«We only hear the echo of your voice, we only perceive the reflection of your brightness, and here we are totally bewildered, totally blinded and without strength before your greatness.»

56'. Let us learn to do good with our heart, then with our spirit and finally with our hands; and let us remain silent and in repose until the time of union.

57'. When something annoys us here below, let us check if our desire is still in God. Thus, we shall return to the right path instead of struggling uselessly in the swamps of death.

58'. He who pacifies and decants the interior sea shall repose forever in

tion, so as not to be led astray by the ascending and descending forms of the transitory world.

59. It is life mixed with the non-being from outside that constitutes suffering, for the pure substance of the beginnings is still eternal pleasure in oneself.

60. The smallest abandonment of our particular will is like the first pledge of our heavenly coronation.

the peace of the Lord's light.

«By correcting the sourness of humours, we also correct the sourness of the spirit.»

59'. That which is not, is that which cannot be transformed in oneself, through oneself, for oneself. Nothingness, darkness and exterior death.

60'. Let us not become restless over nothing, for then even death would no longer be able to calm us.

He who falls on this stone shall be broken, and whom it falls on shall be crushed.
JESUS

All follow their own path, each according to his profit, from the first to the last.
ISAIAH

BOOK XIV

Born with a composite body, you are subject to the law of dissolution.
LIE T'ZE

Dissolution is inherent to all formations; work tirelessly for your deliverance.
BUDDHA

ENIVRE TUE

1. When we have been instructed by the Lord, our filth shall horrify us and that of others shall terrify us. Then, we shall pray that our blemish be erased and that everyone's burden be lightened.

2. We shall observe God's commandments and we shall bring joy, through our secret gifts, to the heart of the poor and the unfortunate.

3. «Never despair of God and of oneself», such is the law of salvation. We must therefore persevere, trust in the Lord and act according to his law for it is the act of faith of the sower and the act of love of heaven and of earth that save us from death. But how many shall penetrate this mystery and how many shall accomplish it before the hour of judgement?

THE PRESENCE

1'. When we realize that we are blind, deaf and stupid, the fear of God shall no longer be an enigma to us. And when we see his light, the love of the Lord shall enlighten us and shall give life to us forever.

2'. «The grain which is sown dies and is born again to life, but no-one is astonished and no-one admires the miracle of God.»

3'. The Book is God's and shall return to God, and we, who are of the earth, shall also return to the earth, and no-one shall be able to rejoin the Lord without having been washed by his blessing and without having been revived by his Holy Spirit, for that is the judgement so longed for by some and so feared by others.

4. It is through reading and through meditation of the holy books that we maintain and develop in ourselves the sacred fire of the Lord.

4'. He who reads the Book to his nearest awakens life in their hearts and makes them germinate before God. In this way nothing shall be lost, for the believers shall be confirmed and the mockers put to the test.

5. Who shall take responsibility for the Book and who shall present it to the believers? The blessing of God flows over them.
«We shall search outside, then we shall search inside.»

5'. To go to God is not a duty; it is the greatest of pleasures.
«We shall manifest outwardly, but we shall keep inwardly.»

6. Perseverance in the practice of divine and natural laws provides immunity and leads to the freedom of pure and holy life.

6'. The Lord shall send his showers onto the seed he has hidden in the earth. He shall certainly make it germinate.

7. Queuing up for the spectacles of madness, stagnating at the famine counters, jostling at the doorways of death, exhausting oneself in the service of machines, vegetating in holes without light and air, listening to, reading, breathing, drinking and eating death; this is what men currently call «living freely».

7'. The further man distances himself from God, the more he must work and fear, accumulate and go without, suffer and doubt, become restless and destroy himself. He that claims to live without the Lord's aid is senseless, he loses his water like a bone that dries up, and no hand of man shall deliver him from the desert and the shadow of death where he agonizes.

8. The Lord has sown and we have produced the Book for all men on the earth, for all those who are and for all those who are coming, of all races and of all nations. For all those who have intelligence and who have put their faith in the omnipotence of God.

8'. The wisdom of God is veiled by a darkness and by a nameless chaos, but it shines sometimes like a very pure light. The wisdom of man is like a twilight and like a dawn that gravitates between these two poles.

9. And we have not claimed a salary from anyone here below, for the

9'. Let us remember that the worship of the holy ancestors completes

gift of the Living One of eternity shall be our prodigious and real share.

10. God is truly magnanimous, for he delivers us from death. He is truly patient, for he waits for us to return to him.

11. Let us thus leave aside self-esteem, intelligence, reason, and individual will to go towards the Lord, as the child returns to his mother when he is tired of playing with the muddy water of the stream.

12. Are we able to read the Book and not praise God in our heart when he inundates us with light? Are we able to receive the unheard-of word and not bless the Lord who offers us the truth that sets free? Are we able to catch a glimpse of the deliverance of death and not cry with joy?

13. Would we say to the sons of the same Father and the same Mother that one is legitimate and that the other a bastard? Or that one is white and the other is black? Or that he who keeps the patrimony is more worthy than he who recovers old credits?

14. Let us fear the moment of confusion when the Father, the Mother and the Son shall not ratify

the worship of God, who is the Living One of eternity.
«Let us adore the sun of life and not despise the ashes of the ancestors.»

10'. When we can bear the abandonments, the treasons, the reproaches, the mocking, the insults, the blows and death without a murmur, we shall be close to God and his salvation.

11'. Let us limit our cares in the maintenance of incarnate life and we shall have the sufficient time for the quest for the Perfect One.

12'. We shall magnetize in ourselves the light of the Perfect One for the safeguard and renewal of all creation.
Who can verify this thing right now?
Who can put to the test the truth of the Book here below?
Who can hold in his hand the weight of height?

13'. Do we not see that it is the light that illuminates men and the world, and that the stars are nothing but the instruments of its manifestation?
– When the torch goes out, there remains nothing but a half-burned log of dead wood.

14'. Will we still keep confusing the tool with the workman for a long time? And will we render a profane

our blind judgements, the stupefying moment when we shall see only one God there where we would have thought to discern plurality, the cruel time when he who we shall have ignored and rejected shall not recognize us and shall reject us in turn.

15. There has been the Book of sacrifices and of rites, the Book of the dead and of the wait, the Book of the way and of water, the Book of fire and of purification.

16. There has been the Book of revelation and of the beginning, the Books of law and of justice, the Books of grace and of love, the Book of judgement and of the end, the Book of sowing and of renewal.

17. There has been the Book of faith and of resurrection, the Book of the secret and of knowledge, the Book of obedience and of imitation.

18. God sends us now the Book of science and of union and the following one, which is the Book of accomplishment and multiplication.

19. But in each one of them, the others are already contained in their entirety, and what one says in secret the other proclaims before all.

20. If we remain so deaf and blind to goodness, let us try our best to also be mute and inert to evil.

worship to the propagators of the Unique One?

– Only he has the right to our homage and our gift.

– His sons, who have returned everything to him, know it well. They proclaim it loudly from the beginning, and not one of them has tried to pass himself off as God.

15'. Have we ears to hear the word?

Have we hands to purify the earth?

Have we eyes to see the light?

16'. Have we nostrils to smell the perfume?

Have we a palate to taste the nectar?

Have we a mouth to kiss the holy stone?

17'. Have we a tongue to praise God?

Have we a body to purify?

Have we a spirit to simplify?

Have we a soul to embody?

18'. Have we a whole to glorify?

Have we intelligence to manifest the flower and the fruit?

19'. Have we a love to multiply them?

Have we a wisdom to collect them and make them serve the glory of the All-Powerful One?

20'. He who swears by a holy book and rejects the other writings of the prophets denies the members of the Unique One.

21. And if we are so stupid before the creation of God, let us not explain to others the word that we do not understand.

22. Let us examine the good and the evil that happen to others and to ourselves, and let us praise the Lord for the masterly way in which he teaches the blind and the clear-sighted.

23. The waves of the sea do not have their own permanent existence, yet the sea exists both in its parts and as a whole.

24. Let us work to maintain our lifestyle, let us never work to amass riches.

25. Let us be intelligent about everything that concerns love and good, but let us become idiots about everything that relates to hate and evil.

26. Let us flee the illusion of the past and that of the future by establishing ourselves in the divine presence, which is like eternity made present.

27. What most infuriates the ill-bred pedants is not being able to integrate the sages and the saints into their flat reason of incurable mediocrity.
«The obscurity of plenitude is not the obscurity of the void, for the light inhabits the first and the darkness populates the second.»

21'. It is preferable to reach God whole than to arrive in pieces. Yet it is better to arrive in pieces than not at all.

22'. Let us strive to be like God, who unites in himself, with fruit, opposites of similar nature.
«God's sages and saints bless the Book that confirms and honours their inspired word.»

23'. The Absolute is unknowable in its totality, but it is possible to approach it in its parts, which are like images of the whole.

24'. Let us be satisfied with what we possess, and let us realize that it is still highly superfluous.

25'. People who boast of their purity are a thousand times more rotten than the sinners they habitually denigrate.

26'. If you are seeking the world, run after it; but if you desire God, wait for him to come to you.

27'. The sons of God fraternize in the centre of the «unique Marvel», for their teachings are One for those that penetrate the divine word in a holy way, instead of examining it with curiosity from outside.

28. God is not served by constraining men, by torturing beasts and by forcing nature; but rather by loving the uncreated Being through all the created beings and by accomplishing his hidden work.

28'. The sages do not invent anything; they simply put men back on the way of light and love that leads to God.
«Who shall purify his body?»
«Who shall simplify his spirit?»
«Who shall embody his soul?»

29. The powerful and the rich are generally against sages and saints because the latter demand freedom for all men and generosity towards all beings.
«It is up to us only to plough, for it is the Lord who makes the holy seed germinate and ripen.»

29'. There is but one crime before God: to be mediocre and to love nothing freely, not even oneself. Likewise, there is only one sin: the lack of pure, fragrant and luminous life within us. And there is only one sanction: dark and stinking death that hems us in on all sides.

30. Let us practice our own rule and let us not worry about our neighbour's, unless it is to borrow what seems useful for obtaining and conserving the peace in God.

30'. It is restlessness in the world that makes the temporal hell, and it is repose in God that makes heaven of eternity.
«Who shall give us the bread of heaven and earth? Who shall give us the wine of water and fire? Who shall give us the blood of the Living One of eternity?»

31. The true sage is he who sees the two faces of God and contemplates what is hidden inside. For it is in the union of opposites that the truth of the Unique One appears.

31'. The secret of the sages is God and his light placed within reach of the heart and the hand of the man sanctified by love.

32. Men subjected to a life of exile, hunger, cold, pain, illness, decrepitude, doubt, appearance, solitude, desperation and death must help one another to live and hope, but without forgetting, however, to search for the way of divine purity that leads to the place where nobody lacks anything.

32'. Those who do not make use of the secret counsel of God and who do not draw directly from his hidden Providence are forced to rely on men's opinion and science to govern themselves, maintain themselves and cure themselves here below. But this is not the truth of the Lord.

33. Let us accomplish what is necessary to maintain our earthly lives, but when we have to die, let us offer ourselves joyously and in a saintly way to God, who welcomes, pardons, consoles and renews beyond all limit.

34. Those who, on receiving the Book, do not read it, and those who, on having read it, do not respond in their heart, proclaim themselves satisfied in the stinking death of filth. They judge themselves, and their subsequent complaints shall not be received.

35. The sages, who know the interior of beings and of things, are moved by the disappearance of those dear to them. How, then, shall ordinary men, who only know the exterior face of the world, not be cruelly ripped apart?

36. Glory to the Father who engenders him mysteriously. Praise to the Mother who manifests him clearly. Love to the Son who offers himself to all.

Acknowledgement of the sages who pick him up, raise him and lower him for the salvation of the world, in the land of the living.

37. First of all, we shall ask to live in order to learn to praise God. Then we shall ask to die in order to better remain silent in him.

33'. We are only really brothers in God, for it is the only place where there is neither separation, darkness, nor death. Likewise, the revelation of the sons of God can only be heard clearly in hearts purified by love.

34'. Love, which is the food of the soul, does not need to be digested like grace and like food, which are the nourishment of the spirit and the body, for it is already like the divine fire: accomplished and perfect.

35'. Evil has taken shape through man's straying, and part of creation has become lost with him.

Evil shall cease with man's return to his source, and this shall once again magnetize the world to the purity of the Living One of eternity.

36'. The sun of God shall gather together the lights gone astray in death, and concentrated life shall manifest the glory of the Unique One for the mysterious communion of sages and saints, in the united body, blood and spirit of the Most-Perfect One.

37'. Even though they offer us heaven and earth and all creation in between, we would always ask for HIM, HIM, HIM, because he is the seed without which nothing would be.

38. The divine gift of freedom only wants the man who is lost in death to be able to reach the pure, living source through that other divine gift that constitutes the reciprocal magnetization of love.

39. When we weigh the works of our whole life with the minutes that precede death, we shall be terrified by the lightness of the former compared to the weight of the latter.

40. By considering ourselves responsible for all the difficulties and all the evils that humiliate us in this world, we shall be delivered from the worry of attributing them to others, and by patiently bearing them we shall soon be delivered from them if we do not abandon the Lord of souls.

41. He who has handed everything over to God, including himself, no longer has the temptation to do violence to anything in order to reinforce an isolation that he has definitively given up. «Through his denuded vision and inhuman detachment, the saint is an object of scandal for those who remain subject to appearances and given themselves over to the bonds of this world.»

42. When we are weary of pursuing him with our reason, we shall eventually be obliged to attract him through the folly of our love, on pain of extinguishing ourselves forever in the dead ash and dead water.

38'. The sons of God possess the Unique One and are possessed by him from this world. In this way, secret love accomplishes for some chosen ones the total gift of the ONE to the One in the One, before the universal separation and judgement.

39'. It is only in privation that we shall measure our love for God, for in abundance we would only be able to praise his love for us.

40'. Silence and fasting effectively absorb the stimuli of impatience and anger, as the love of God and the self-oblivion suffocate the seeds of greed and pride.
«Eternal life is like the fixedness of the fire of conscience among the moving creations of the mother water.»

41'. It is through assiduous study of the sacred books that the grace and the love of the Lord are awakened in us, and it is through the practice of holy works that they are manifested in the world; therefore, we can only be legitimately proud here below of our goodwill towards everything and everyone.

42'. Where are the well-loved sons always rejected by men and always attracted by love? There where the absurdity of reason shall engender the reason of absurdity. There where the old stump shall flourish again and give its golden fruit.

43. The great pain of the saint here below is to stumble many times over the stupid blindness of the impious as well as against the conceited sectarianism of believers.

43'. The love of God could not justify violence towards oneself or towards other creatures.

«It is not a question of repressing passions, which provokes fatal accidents; it is rather a question of removing the opportunity for them to arise.»

44. The mediocre bury God in the depths of their death; that is why they hate the freedom of life that manifests the spirit of the Lord so much, and that they label the letter of all the holy Scriptures, thinking they pin down the prophets just as they pin insects in their dusty collections.

44'. They try without success to reassure them in their night, but the rottenness of confusion and the dryness of death are their certain heritage.

«Only the saint possesses precise awareness of his past and present straying and responsibility. That is why he cries and searches every day of his life for the light lost by the elderly one.»

45. Let him who sees nothing and hears nothing in the Book look and listen in the world; and if he sees nothing and hears nothing in the world, let him look and listen in himself; and if he sees nothing and hears nothing in himself, let him lie down in death; but above all, let him be silent, so as not to drag anyone into his blind and deaf solitude.

45'. Sadness comes from the unconscious yearning for free life in God.

Love is born when approaching the beloved source.

Knowledge appears through union with the Impassible.

«We all receive the same love, but we do not all recognize it in the same way nor at the same time.»

46. Those who praise God in the secret of their hearts are the only ones admitted into interior creation; all the others are parasites that he tolerates on his skin due to the effect of his infinite mercy.

46'. He who is enlightened is called «idle, idiotic and useless», for it is his only justification before «the Peaceful One, the Holy One and the Gratuitous One».

47. We are great neither for the gifts received nor for the privations endured, but only through their overcoming in God.

47'. O my secret Lord!, all my progress in you is due to you who accomplishes it in me, and my nakedness remains as my only ornament before your splendour.

48. The ignorant man judges everything rashly because he only perceives the outer layer of the things that maintain him in the apparent chaos of the absurd. The alert man condemns nothing and no-one, but searches for the good that is in each creature and exalts it to the Lord's repose.

48'. We were like blind and enraged beasts locked in a narrow and sordid cage, and here we are free and in repose, bathing in the light of the Unique Father and Mother.
«O wonder of the Perfect One! O blessing of the Generous One!» «O love of the Gratuitous One!»

49. Everyone is useful for something or for someone here below, but we seem useless to others and to ourselves. It is therefore to console us that God sometimes agrees to say a little word to us.

49'. If we do not empty the body through fasting, the spirit through prayer and the soul through contemplation, how shall the Lord be able to fill us with his presence, which is triple and unique?

50. The most advanced amongst those who pass through this world is he who tolerates the ups and downs of incarnate life without grumbling, and who no longer ever asks this question: how? and why? for the faith that reposes in God's Providence does not question.

50'. He who knows the underside of creation is not scandalized by any injustice, does not come up against any appearance and is not moved by any upheaval in the world, for he knows that everything in us and around us conforms to the interior vision.

51. Poets and artists are lovers who do not consent to converse with God without signs and without witnesses, while sages and saints do.
«O extreme bashfulness of holy loves! O sweet light of divine union!»

51'. The return of the soul to its source is like the prefiguration of the end of time, for all is accomplished according to a geometric progression; that is to say, with the acceleration of pure bodies rejoining their primordial centre.

52. The reward and the joy of saints and sages is to offer God the thanks, the praise and the love of those who they have removed from death through their teaching, their example and their sacrifice.

52'. Madmen work against creation and do it a disservice, but they do not know it. Sages deliver creation and help it to be born, but they know the purpose of their efforts.

53. Let our hidden virtue be the daily frequenting of the Unique One in our self-oblivion.

54. Here below we are constantly in danger of definitive blindness and death, as up there we shall be under the perpetual threat of a solitary eternal life, if we do not fix ourselves in the heart of the Unique One.

55. The final poetry of love and of knowledge appears in the silence of God.
«Today I go to everyone, but who welcomes me and who listens to me? Tomorrow everyone shall come to me, but who shall I receive? And who shall I hear?», says the Lord of grace and love.

56. When we have understood with our head, we shall be like dead in life. When we have felt with our heart, we shall be like the living in death. But when we have touched with our hands and tasted with our mouths, we shall be like gods in the Unique One.

57. He who adores God in his heart, loves humanity in the world and respects all living beings, justifies all present creation, because he is already the only one justified before God.

58. He sings himself in every one of his poets.
He announces himself in every one of his prophets.
He plays with himself in every one of his children.
He praises himself in every one of

53'. The saint who serves his Lord faithfully shall not be surprised to be served by his Lord.

54'. He who delights in the prison of this world, how shall he discover the freedom of the other world? And he who settles in that plenitude, how shall he enter in the repose of the most secret union?

55'. He delivers us from death and then withdraws us from life so that we remain with him in the secret of his secret forever.
«O holiest repose in the centre of the centre!»

56'. To be possessed by the multitude of the Universal is to be mad. To be possessed by the Uniqueness of the One is to be holy. To possess the Unity of the Unique One is to be wise.
But to penetrate the plenitude of vacuum is to be God with God.

57'. If we were to free that which is hidden in man, we would become like the Lord of light, and we would bless all humanity and creation in the very midst of the darkness of death.

58'. Let us penetrate the apparent folly of the teaching of the saints and sages and let us consider their deep intention, which is the gathering of all beings in God. In this way, we will be able to laugh at all that happens as we laugh at a farce that is as continu-

his believers.
He loves himself in every one of his saints.
He knows himself in every one of his sages.
He shines in every one of his sons.

59. We shall only obtain greater slavery by running away from ourselves more and more, whereas we shall reach the freedom of the Unique One by patiently forgetting ourselves.

60. Intellectual knowledge that does not lead to unifying love and to the transforming possession of the Lord, is as illusory as the reflection of the moon in a glass of stirred water.

61. The power of God can only be granted to him who has abandoned all competition, all demonstration, all approval, all possession and all vengeance; that is to say, he who has given up himself.

62. Those who read the Book and do not choose in their heart the love of and the quest for the Perfect One are more excluded than those who bustle about blindly in the world without an inkling of the truth of the Unique One.

63. True sages and saints magnetize all men of goodwill to God, and that is why they are the only sons and faithful servants of their Lord.

64. He who is no longer moved by the grimaces of death, sees the smile

ous as it is illusory, until all ceases to reassure us and frighten us here below and elsewhere.

59'. He passes into us, we pass into him, and here we are fertilized and renewed through the sole merit of our death in him and his birth in us.

60'. What is the use of all our marvellous work if we neither discover nor incorporate the Unique Splendour of sanctified life? What is the use of the magnificent speeches on the light of God if we do not see it and if we do not eat it in a holy way?

61'. When we contemplate him in wonder, what can we ask of him but him, nothing but him, always him? For, who is the expert who would not wish to contemplate the splendour and live in it?

62'. Only God offers us love without disappointment, because it is always greater than our own gift.

«The Living One shall bear witness to the truth of the Book before everyone, but few men possess the eyes of the spirit that permit them to approach the obviousness of life bared open.»

63'. He who does not know how to extract his life from heaven and earth knows nothing of God, possesses nothing of God, is nothing in God.

64'. Let us prepare the earth, let us be simple, let us be confident, let us

of the unique brightness shining everywhere.

be patient, let us remain in peace, and God shall make us see his salvation.

65.	NO	NO		The beginning	65'.	YES.	YES.	YES.
	YES.	NO.		The middle		YES.	NO.	YES.
	YES.	YES.				NO.	YES.	NO.
	YES.	YES.	YES.	The end			NO.	NO.

66. If you love me and you seek me with all your spirit, with all your soul and with all your body, I shall put a spirit of discord between you and the world so that no strange consolation diverts you from my righteous way; your dear ones shall hate and reject you, you shall be odious to them and they shall be unbearable to you and opposed to everything, says the hidden Lord; even your wife shall rise up against you, and your children shall make fun of you because of me.

Cruel words for the ignorant world; perfect and holy love for him who knows, for when we have found him, all shall be given back to us according to our desire and much more besides.

66'. Let those who teach the mysteries of God that they only know through hearsay be humble and timid, and let those who have experienced them in their hearts and who have held them in their living hands remain hidden.

O – YOU – ME – US – ONE WHO IS – THROUGH ONESELF – IN ONESELF – FOR ONESELF – ALWAYS – LOVER – LOVED ONE – LOVE – AMEN.

All books not based on the holy Scriptures have come from the hand of man and shall perish.

LAWS OF MANOU

Every true word, whoever its author, is spoken by the Holy Spirit.

ST. AMBROSE

BOOK XV

The bolts of the earth were closed on me for ever, and you have made my life rise again from the grave, IEVE my God.
JONAH

When men resuscitate, the earth shall become white, united and pure.
KORAN

NUÉE REVIT

1. A worker, a good-for-nothing, a peasant, a tramp, a shopkeeper, a wanderer, a thinker, a simple person, a believer, an impious man are the first to have read and loved the Book. O derision on the scholars, on the academics and on the religious officials who have not received it!

2. This one is called founder of religion and he does not even understand that of his fathers. That one calls himself a sage and can neither sow nor reap. The other one adopts the title of scholar and he does not know how he subsists and why he dies.

3. Some are said to be religious and holy because they wear a habit; just as another proclaims himself to be intelligent and courageous because he shows off a diploma or a medal.

THE WAY OUT

1'. How original and simple is the way of God! How secret and exposed to the eyes of all! Yet how noble and common it is! Who shall seize now the primary and ultimate sense of the inspired word?

2'. It is because we are too occupied with ourselves and not enough with God that the Lord is no longer heard and is no longer manifested in us.

3'. The kingdom of the Lord shall come when the seed of God covers all the earth, and no-one shall reach God without passing through the creature of God, which is the excellent creation of the Lord.

4. When we comment on a holy Scripture, a rite or a symbol let us add for the listeners and for ourselves: «Here is one of the numerous interpretations of the One truth. God alone is master of clothing and of nakedness.»

5. Amen is God's verb manifested, the right side of the All-Powerful One, the executor of the judgements of the Righteous One. He does not argue; he takes action. Bad luck for those who would not have recognized nor received him at the time indicated, for on the day of general judgement they shall be swept away just like the dust is carried along by the equinoctial storm.

6. God is the distinguished creator and excellent organizer. He sketches out his work with a luminous touch and completes it with a non-perishable architecture. He is surely unique.

7. Also, the prophets and the sages who glorify themselves in God consider themselves personally incapable and unintelligent before the Lord, for they truly believe, hear, see, feel and taste the unique light. They alone!

4'. He who hears, sees, smells, tastes and feels the truth without veils can do nothing but remain silent and adore in the unique Splendour. He may well appear senseless before all, since he is the only one to be instructed before God.

5'. Religions may become confused with dead morals, and holy initiations may seem like masquerades; the science of God shall always be reborn from their cold ashes, and the guardians of necropolises shall once again give way to the builders of life. It is the law of renewal of all things.

6'. He began his work as though making child's play of it, and he finishes it by showing his excellence and his perfection over all the works of the world. On the day of judgement, the splendour shall be on his saints, but the mockers shall be steeped in consternation and cast into the anarchy of death.

7'. O cruel moment in which a portion of ourselves shall rot in nothingness! But the Lord is merciful; he puts off his judgement and pardons our souls gone astray, when our hearts of stone open up to his active grace and to his transforming love.

7". The sages and saints that possess God in themselves shall once again come out unscathed from the burning cloud, for the Lord God, who is the essence of fire, is incombustible. The evil ones shall be reduced to ashes and shall serve as fertilizer for the new plantation of God.

8. Let us not take the law into our own hands, for we would lose the benefit of our ordeals and we would erase the iniquity of the evil one. Let us refer ourselves to the judgement of the Lord, who knows how to discern deep intentions and distant goals.

8'. It is the goodwill in God that saves us from death, and it is goodwill in ourselves that hurls us into it. In fact, though both are blind, the first is guided however, and becomes receptive and organising, while the second is errant and becomes anarchic and destructive.

9. Let us bless he who has gone astray and the rebel so that we may benefit from his ever possible conversion.
«If we kill the evil ones, how shall we then convert them? And if the evil ones kill us, how shall they be saved?»

9'. One thinks one can make do with evil, but it is always evil that sorts us out. One thinks one can make a pact with death, but it is always death that surprises us.

10. Let us train ourselves to let go of the little things so that when the big things let go of us we remain serene, because we shall be rich in God.

10'. God preferentially grants the enormity of his sons' demand, because it is more in keeping with his magnanimity and his omnipotence.

11. She was a courageous and self-sacrificing wife, then she became rebellious and blind, for she judged the Book as being a useless thing without ever having opened it. Finally she accepted the God's way out of love for us.
«Are we not all stupid before God's truth that blinds us?»

11'. Let us not boast about our health, our intelligence, our learning, our beauty, our fortune, our work or our family, for they are loans granted by God that misfortune and death transform rapidly into smoke and are soon converted into ashes.

12. Indeed, we know neither the angels he arouses to guard our ways, nor the demons he authorizes to test our hearts. God delivers those who follow his way without rebelling and forgives those who repent sincerely. Judgement and glory belong to him.

12'. Let us rather boast about our faith in God and in his omnipotence, that shall return to us eternal and pure life if we are found as we must be, that is to say, faithful, pure, simple and loving.

13. An ignorant young man by nature tends to despise all that appears weak, old, abandoned and dead in the world; and his blindness is excusable.

13'. When we become aware of the difficult passage awaiting us, we shall reform our thoughts, our judgements and our acts, and we shall no longer play at imitating the histrion among the senseless ones.

14. But an instructed old man who does not recognize God's Providence and science in action in the Universe and in his heart is as stupid as a petrified stump.

14'. Let, oh Lord! our eyes and ears open before the beginning of the end, or, at least, before the end of the end.

15. God does not force us to reject our parents, wives, children, friends and goods to please him. He asks that we do not attach ourselves blindly to the transient things of this world so as not to be deceived and cruelly ripped apart on the day of separation; for true poverty is in spirit, and true wealth is in God alone.

15'. God does not demand that we do violence to our nature nor that of other beings in order to please him. On the contrary, he asks us to purify it, to allow it to settle and to gently mature it so that he may be fully manifested in us.
It is neither violent repression nor forced labour that count for salvation, but rather awakened attention and the persevering quest.

16. Yet no-one can be judged guilty of abandoning the world to go to his Lord, for that is what we shall all have to do in the end.

16'. Just like the people of the world, the saints forget what they possess and deplore what they do not have, but the things concerned are not the same.

17. The sage and the saint concentrate all their attention on the quest for God and seem absent from the ordinary occupations of men.

17'. What appears to you empty appears to us full, and what appears to you full appears to us empty. For the world seems turned inside out for those who see the inside of beings and things.

18. If we could read the Book openly we would be terror-stricken and we would remain rooted to the spot in stupor, then we would run to hide it in the tomb for fear of the impious abusing the divine mystery and profaning the light of God forever. But the Lord has precisely foreseen this, for he is sage amongst sages.

18'. Many brilliant books contain the wisdom of men, but how many enclose the wisdom of God? Many men stutter the holy Scriptures or make blind commentaries about them, but how many hear the word of God directly? How many transcribe it clearly? And how many experience it in their heart here below?

19. Thus, the scholars and the intelligent, the cunning and the greedy remain stupid before the lock and key without being able to open anything. Let us notice how they then affect to denigrate or ridicule that which they were unable to steal or do violence to.

19'. «God seeks madmen to make sages of them. He mocks reasonable people. This is what fails to please all.»
– It is not learned speakers that we need, but prophets full of the Holy Spirit.

20. Morality is a barrier and asceticism a parapet. Law is a dyke and rites are a guide. Sacraments are a memento, symbols are eloquent images and the holy books show the way, but the science of God invalidates everything because it surpasses everything.

20'. Each time we have read the Book we have learned to behave in God, and we have remembered the way of the Lord. Then, we have blessed his sacred Name and adored his holy Person, hidden in the light of the beginning and the end.

21. Yet who would be so ignorant as to scorn the steps that allow us access to the tabernacle of the Lord of life?

21'. How much more will be learnt those who read the Book and have not written it?

22. If God were to abandon his children, it would be all the worse for God and for us, but the Lord is neither forgetful to himself nor ungrateful to his own.

22'. Ah! how close to God are the poets, the poor and the simple, and how ignorant they are of their proximity!

23. That is why we must place our hope in him despite all appearances in this mixed world, until the day of reckoning and the elimination of death.

23'. The feet of humanity are still healthy, but the head is rotten and blind. It is therefore necessary to sow that which is below so that which is above is cured and renewed, just as in the past that which was below was saved and whitened by that which shone above in purity.

24. Everything that Christ said about the Pharisees is still true for the majority of present believers. O derision! O cruelty! O penitence!
«O derision!» We have rejected the secret of God's science and here we are at present adoring the science of Satan for fear of appearing backward. We have reserved for ourselves the sacrament of knowledge and since that time we have become blind and deaf to the will of God. We are conciliatory with death and transigent with evil for money, and we hate those who denounce it and who do not adapt themselves to it.

24'. «O penitence!» Now, we shall once again enter the dust and we shall end as we began, hiding ourselves below ground, in tombs, in cellars and in abandoned quarries; and we shall once again become a small number before God, for the mediocre and the cowards will have abandoned us, like the dead branches ripped off by the storm. When the chief has crossed the water, we shall know that the time of penitence is about to begin for us. Four figures will be enough to enumerate the survivors of the end, but we shall be like a holy seed that will produce a magnificent fruit before the Lord.

25. «O cruelty!» We have distanced ourselves from the simple ones and paupers, and the latter have even forgotten the Name of God. We have rejected the sages and the saints, and our science and our faith have vanished in reasonable discourse. We have hoisted the flags of

25'. It is the Book of the height and the depth that shall unite us in a single body before the Perfect One, for a remainder of each faith and each belief shall be recognized in God and shall fuse in love on coming together with the unique root, and the man of water and fire shall be our guide and

nations on the house of God while peoples cut one another's throats, and we proudly wear the decorations of murder. Let us consider from where the warning comes: from an unknown but loved man, from a poor but fulfilled man, from a layman, but linked to God.

26. Let us recognize the love and humour of the Lord who thus calls us back to the holy order that he established for his friends and for his disciples. For gold shall not save us, nor diplomacy, nor allies, nor moans, but rather our faith, our hope and our charity in action, and above all, knowledge of the omnipotence of God which withdraws from death.
Shall we finally understand?

27. The rebel's revolt is his failure that has hardened him instead of instructing him.

28. The wicked one's cruelty is his suffering that has closed him instead of opening him.

29. Everyone's hell is the refusal to accomplish the pact that we have signed with death benevolently.

30. If we would consider first the apparent or hidden evil that gnaws away at each being here below we would become more attentive to his complaints, more patient with his cries, more compassionate with his weaknesses and more helpful with his pains.

our saviour, for the way of God, which is his, shall also be ours on that day.
The old stump shall then secretly flourish once more and shall manifest its holy fruit in a reconciled world.

26'. The wicked ones shall see the beatitude of the saints and that shall constitute their greatest torment, for then, hopelessly, love shall be behind them, instead of being in front, as it still is now with hope.
«Rediscovered innocence can contemplate everything, for it is only surprised at nothing, judges nothing and profanes nothing.»

27'. The safeguard of the sage is to run away from the assemblies of men and take delight in the solitude of God.

28'. The sanctification of the saint is to give in extreme poverty and bless in suffering.

29'. Faith for the believer is to erase the desolation of death by the sheer force of hoping for the resurrection and the joy of the new life.

30'. If we first thought of the light of the Lord buried at the bottom of each being, we would bear more easily the contradictions and blindness of his exterior darkness, and we would be confused by our own interior darkening.

31. We are without merit, like small children who can only count on the love of their parents to maintain them. Do we send children to work or to war? Are they hauled before courts or thrown into prison? Are they condemned to torture or to death? Or instead do we keep them carefully in the family bosom for games, for joy, for love and for future life?

32. Let us imagine our contradictors and our enemies as they soon shall be, that is to say like the dead: then, we shall no longer feel resentment or hate towards them, for one can only pray for the dead while awaiting the time of their resurrection and of their enlightenment.

33. Our gifts are more in keeping with the quest for God than with the conquest of the world, for that which comes from the Unique One must go to the Unique One, as that which comes from the world must return to the world.

34. Failures in the world are the safeguard of those blessed by God, so that they are not distracted from the quest for the Perfect One and that they are not indebted to anyone for anything here below, but on the contrary, that men are their debtors for the revelation of love and of the knowledge of God.

31'. To what summit and to what depth can the rebel who submits himself to God not hope to reach?

– To what recompense and what gift can the poverty-stricken one who gives himself to the Lord not aspire?

– What consolation and what sweetness is not promised to the violent one who seeks the peace of the Unique One?

– To what blessing and what union is the abandoned one who has hope in the love of the Perfect One not destined?

32'. They are as ignorant as those who ask for money in order to explain the word they do not understand. At least the latter transmit, unknowingly, science to the children of God, who well know how to recognize it, always identical to itself among all the holy Scriptures.

33'. Let us not kill ourselves either in work or in pleasure, let us rather kill ourselves while searching for God and his salvation, which are in eternal, evident and hidden life.

34'. The saints that are currently ignored or rejected shall later be known and sought out, for if the world treats them as nonentities and nothing, they shall be set up as masters by God over those who have ignored them and over their descendants. «That is the Lord's justice that no-one can falsify.»

35. Everyone becomes exhausted, and no-one reposes.
Everyone hurries, and no-one arrives.
Everyone amasses, and no-one profits.
Everyone makes an effort, and no-one obtains.
Everyone worries, and no-one sees.
Everyone explains, and no-one understands.
Everyone preaches, and no-one practises.
Everyone struggles for life, and no-one saves his own.

35'. If we feel weak: let us help.
If we feel rejected: let us welcome.
If we consider ourselves poor: let us give.
If we suffer: let us relieve.
If we are disconsolate: let us comfort.
If we are hated: let us bless.
If we are tempted: let us pray.
If we are alone: let us praise God.

36. Where is the intelligent one who expects all from God and nothing from the world? Where is the ploughman? Where is the reaper? Where is God's fulfilled one?
– There where the light of the Perfect One germinates!

36'. Where is the Lover? Where is the Loved One? Where is the Amen?
– In our heart of stone, from which we must extract it and manifest it clearly!

37. Let us not wait to be struck down by misfortune, suffering or death to remember the God of our childhood and to speak to him without witnesses and without reserve.

37'. Each one accomplishes here below work that is useful for and pleasant to men and to oneself, but who is the one that secretly puts his hand to the work of God?

38. Our most useful and most admirable works shall be worthless on the day of judgement. Only the love of God, the observance of his law and the practise of his way shall open the gates of life to us without mixture.

38'. Human intelligence and reason are humble servants that must never usurp the place of inspiration and love, which are the masters of God's house.

39. If we could contemplate ourselves after having meditated on the Book, we would be surprised at our

39'. The appearances of this world are strangely deceptive and baffle the most experienced, as well as mislead-

own spectacle. How much, in this case, should others not be troubled by these same appearances? Therefore, it is only the spirit of God that unravels, in us and in the world, truth from lies, and it is for this reason that we must ask insistently for the light that illuminated us in the beginning and that shall enlighten us in the end.

40. «Who could believe, without having seen it, that a contemptible, dark worm transforms itself into a butterfly glowing with light?»

41. The light that conceals the Lord is like the clothing and the luminous shadow of the Perfect One, with which we must be covered if we are found to be simple, faithful, loving and pure, as on the final day of creation and as in the first time of our new life.

ing the best prepared. That is why it is preferable to reserve our judgement until such time as all things and all beings are manifested to us without veils or disguises.

«Many criticize everything and propagate discouragement and hate. Very few console and offer their aid and their love.»

40'. Let us flee from the wicked ones that beget evil, that nourish it in themselves and that spread it in others; and let us seek the advice of those with no interests in the world nor passions in the heart.

41'. Once, ten times, a hundred times, the Book will tell us nothing, but let us believe that the thousandth time it will speak to us a little and that, in the end, it will appear to us too clear and too evident, that is, excessively imprudent.

41". Thus, if the Book were weighed for us by the weight of our gold, if it were counted by the number of our days and if it were measured by the measure of our blood, it would still be a small thing compared to the Lord's gift.

42. He who weighs up his weakness in this world and his strength in God no longer considers himself worth much here below.

42'. What can the world offer to him who God has already provided with his love? to him who follows his way? to him who accomplishes his work?

43. God does not rejoice in our agony nor in our death in this world. That is why he proposes to us life delivered from suffering and from death forever.

43'. If the holy books are so beautiful and deep, it is because they directly reflect the splendour of the divine light and they speak to us of the unfathomable mystery of God's work.

44. It is the secret revelation of God that makes us enter the dust and that illuminates us at the same time.
Thus, he who recognizes his Lord becomes humble among the humble, yet shines like the moon that reflects the light of the sun.

44'. He who is fully aware of his fault before God is precisely he who tries the hardest to erase it.
– What shall be, then, the remorse of him who has forgotten himself in the world when the solemn and unforeseen hour strikes for him?

45. A long and solitary task, the indifference and mistrust of everyone, rejections, hostility, poverty, silence and solitude for companions.
– Such is the holy work offered to the dead, such is the salary of the dead who do not receive it.

45'. It is not the host that shall be deprived, but in fact the guests that voluntarily abstain.
– As regards he who is charged with announcing the feast of the holy union, he shall benefit with his friends from the absentees' part.

46. But of what importance is this for him who has the vision of the astonishing promise of the Perfect One? For his progeny shall be like the stars in the sky, and his children shall populate the holy earth.

46'. Their lot shall be formidable and as though absurd, for outside there will then be hunger, suffering, desperation and death, and no-one shall be able to close the gate of hell, and no-one shall be able to open the gate of heaven.

47. It is apparently logical, for those who perceive no further than their exterior senses, to deny the salvation of God and to plead for the salvation of man through the work of man.
«Poor work, poor salvation, a foretaste of hell!»

47'. How can we condemn those who do not hear the Lord's truth, when it has taken us so much effort to penetrate the temple of God and so much time to discover his living heart?

48. Now let us not say: «If we had known the Book, we would have honoured it and made it known to those around us», for many have read and almost all have abstained.

49. Let us instead thank God for not being tempted by a common appearance, for he who writes is nothing, but he who dictates is all.

50. Not one word of a holy Scripture actually contradicts the word of another holy Scripture. Thus, God appears multiple in people, yet he is unique in action and in repose, as he is the Being par excellence, that is to say the Primary and the Ultimate in everything.

51. It is right now that we must cease to make new enemies, and now that we must reconcile ourselves with our old enemies. It is right now that we must look after and help all the beings of creation. It is now that we must make good the enormous deficit of our acts of love toward the creator and toward his creatures.

«Let us take note that what happens to us is precisely what we wish for others or what we make them undergo.»

52. Have the poor, the simple, poets, artists and true saints ever cursed and exterminated their kind in the name of the holy Scriptures, or of charity, love, beauty, or in the name of God and of his justice?

48'. Let us sow the Book as we sow our hearts, so that the seed of God is multiplied in the world and the kingdom of the Perfect One is thus brought forward for all.

49'. It is enough for the ploughman to plough, for it is God that sows, waters, makes germinate, flower and bear fruit, and multiplies the seed.

50'. Therefore we need to know all the holy Scriptures and study them until we have discovered the primary and ultimate identity of the inspired word.

«To think of God and meditate on his creation is to pray and praise God.»

51'. The impious have taken over the doctrine of fraternity that the believers have rejected, and now everyone is fighting instead of converting themselves, be it to patience and sweetness for some, or humility and generosity for others; that is to say, to the love of God for everyone. When many are wounded, stripped and reduced to nothing, will the survivors perhaps recognize the wisdom of God's law and the safeguard of his holy way? Perhaps they will not be greedy nor hateful, having lost everything?

52'. Those who secretly help their fellow-being in thought and action receive without delay God's inspiration and the help of humans, but they often do not perceive them.

53. «Sectarians, torturers and criminals are surely not of God.»

54. When celebrating the mysteries of God in a dead language, is it not surprising that we are not heard by believers and no longer listened to by the simple ones? Perhaps this now leaves shepherds and flocks indifferent?

55. Why do those who profess to teach the law of God, to transmit his word, and even to speak in his name or to represent him here below, why do they ignore the collaborators who are not from their side? Why do they reject poor or independent believers? Why do they treat their colleagues who preach the unique God as competitors, and their faithful as undesirables? God himself, however, judges our hearts and not our situations or our belongings.

«Let the holy priests who preach the salvation of God of the end of time be blessed; but let the wise priests who teach God's deliverance from this time of exile be fulfilled!»

56. Who, then, among these advises the Lord on the choice of his envoys, his inspired ones, his chosen ones, his saints and his sages?

«We must convert ourselves, that is to say, turn around, and, instead of looking at the outside where the past disperses, contemplate the inside where the eternal Present of life reposes.»

53'. How can one quarrel with the world and hear the voice of the Lord in oneself or realize the opportunity that is offered?

54'. A whole team is necessary to write a book on Satan, and the curious ones rush to admire. A single believer is needed to write a Book on God, and no-one moves nor says a word.

«O how stupid the intelligent have become by the sheer force of intelligence!»

55'. Who among us can judge the work of God, and how many know his hidden way? Who among us can prejudge the Lord's choice and decision? We have become like blind men who fight over a false coin, and like deaf men who insult one another for rags. Alas! Those whom we have stupidly abandoned and forgotten shall make us agree. The nonbelievers shall lead us back to the humility of our condition as exiles, for we shall be lying in death, without distinction and without forgiveness, piled up like dead game, dispersed like husk from grain, thrown into the ditch like rotten meat.

56'. Then there shall be no more subtle discussions, derisory priorities or men's salaries, no more scholars and no more sermonizers. Only piles of humble and anonymous bones and the eloquent silence of the open jaws of death.

Then shall we understand?

57. O Lord, how many hear your voice?
How many receive your life-giving shower?
How many half open their heart of stone?
How many bear fruit before you?
How many reach your promised land?
How many multiply in you?
How many reap your harvest?
How many reclothe your life, O Lord?
«Do not reply right now, so that the stupor and desperation do not knock us to the ground irremediably.»

58. All of that is difficult and almost beyond our strength, but let us at least do something for the holy communion of love; and however wretched and pitiful may that thing be, let it nevertheless remain secret and free.

59. Let us choose a free man's profession and let us abandon our disguises. Let us officiate and preach in the language of the country where we happen to find. Let us act so that nothing distinguishes nor separates us from believers, if it is not the virtue and example of holiness.

60. Let us stretch out our hand only for ourselves and not for others. It is enough to signal in secret the distress of a faithful one for all to come to his help, if we are as we must be, that is, sanctified by love.
– It is better to obey God alone

57'. Let us go to those who cry and not to those who rejoice.
Let us go to the humble and not to the powerful.
Let us go to those who suffer and not to those who dominate.
Let us go to those who are lost and not to those who are saved.
Let us go to those who are deprived and not to those who have plenty.
Let us go to the seed and not to the dried fruit.
Let us go to the holy earth and not to the false gold.
Let us go to death in order to save our life.

58'. He who seeks God may appear tormented and difficult to mix with, but he who has found God is serene and is patient with all men and with himself, for he no longer leaves the company of the Unique One.

59'. Let us officiate and preach in the house common to God and men, and let us preach and officiate in the house of the believers that receive us. Let us accept from the poor man and distrust the rich man for our sakes, for it is the poor that we should enrich and not the rich that should corrupt us.

60'. It is enough for them that they help directly those that we designate for them in secret or that they themselves discover.
Thus, let us not distance ourselves from the simple and the poor and let us not neglect the root of the peoples

rather than men and the world, as many do now.

where the glory of God is hidden.
That will be for us the joy of the heart that appears in the fraternity of the humble, the true children of God.

61. Let us, then, be imprudent and gratuitous like true poets.
– Let us be free and unworried about our lives like true artists.
– Let us be simple and trusting like children of God.
– Let us be good and helpful like the ancient Samaritan.
– Let us be detached and clear-sighted like the ancient sages.
– Let us be attentive and humble like ignorant men who know themselves.
– Let us be assured and consoling like God's saved ones.
– Let us be inspired and convincing like the prophets filled with the Holy Spirit.

61'. Let us sow, then, and we shall live in the abundance of the Lord.
«There are among us more sleepers than dead, more prudent ones than cowards, more timid ones than hypocrites.»
Let us wake up, then, before death put us completely to sleep.
Let us read again the sacred books and let us practise the holy way like imprudent ones and like God's madmen, for we are here to warn, to help, to excuse, to console, to pardon, and certainly not to insult, to denounce, to judge, to condemn nor, above all, to execute our fellow-being.

62. Let us not worry too much about how we shall live, for God shall provide through inspiration and help if we ask it of him with trust, for he watches over, he inspires and he supports his children on all occasions.

62'. Our God is a God that can be eaten, can be drunk, that communicates life, that sustains it, that frees it and that restores it in its admirable primacy. He is a God that gives himself to save in us that which subsists of life gone astray in death.

63. He also allows them to be tempted very often so that they become firmer on his way. Thus, it is best to remain in the trust of the Perfect One without asking ourselves useless questions about the world.

63'. Thus, possessing in ourselves God's deposit, we must open ourselves to his blessing and to his love so as to be delivered from the exile of death and so as to be made one with the Unique One.

64. It is therefore recommended to pray, to praise and to remain silent

64'. We must expect everything from natural sowing, germination

while waiting for the revelation to become clear and perceptible to us, for it is in our heart that God's mystery resides, and it is he himself who accomplishes our deliverance within us.

and ripening; and we must fear everything to do with the constraint, the impatience and the violence of well-intentioned ignorant ones.

65. Let us wake up with the Book so as to begin our day with a salutary thought.
– Let us move around with the noble tool so as to work usefully in between our futile occupations.
– Let us fall asleep with the message so as to have it before our eyes on the day of judgement.

65'. All shall see God's judgement.
– Many shall live off the truth of the Unique One.
– A small number shall live in the heart of the Lord.
– Some shall contemplate the secret work of the Perfect One.
– But how many shall know the mystery of the origins and of the ends that make the eternity of eternities?

66. Thus, we shall be able to verify point by point the prodigious work of the Highest, the truth of his law and the excellence of his way.

66'. O mortal terror of the unveiled secret! Who shall resist the vertigo of knowledge and love united in One?

67. We are overcome by the beauty of the Lord's work, we remain stupid before its depth and we are dumb before his greatness.
– Some sneer to keep their composure, the majority pretend to ignore it so as not to discover their blindness. The hole that shall receive them is already half-open, but even that does not instruct them.

67'. How admirable is his prudence, and how mad is his audacity!
– How impenetrable is his science, and how his love shines!
– How subtle is his grace, and how faithful is his heart!
– How dark is his way, and how luminous is his salvation!
– How merciful are his blows, and how perfect is his peace!

68. Re-make the mud.

68'. And cook it.

69. We shall search for the work of the Highest like a curious thing and like a game without importance. Then we shall study the work of the Unique One with a scholarly assur-

69'. We shall no longer cry from desperation and suffering, we shall cry for joy and for recognition, and yet this will be the same water and the same salt; but the heart will have

ance and with a sharpened awareness. Finally, we shall be caught in the trap of the Perfect One without knowing how it has happened, and we shall be just as likely to be calling for help in the mysterious darkness as savouring the repose of his divine love.

70. But the Lord is merciful with his dreadful children; in the end he shall let them see his salvation and his glory so that they live before him forever.

opened under the shower of the Lord, and the spirit will have been lit up by the miracle of God.

70'. O how mysterious, how assured, how powerful, how transforming and how salvatory is the way of the great Healer!

70". It is through a wise judgement of God that the brute and the impious trample underfoot the pearls of his crown, and that the shrewd and the greedy cannot see them in the mud where they are hidden here below.

All things are resolved in fire and fire is condensed in all things, just as goods are converted into gold and gold into goods.

HERACLITUS

All shall be judged and devoured by the fire that shall strike.

HERACLITUS

BOOK XVI

And the water was given to them from a rock, and from a stone their thirst was quenched.
SOLOMON

Who is a stone if not our God?
SOLOMON

RÉUNIT ÈVE

THE ROCK

1. Let us examine carefully what is said or asked of by each one of us and let us see if the thing conforms to the law of God and not the laws of men, and God will reply to us in our heart. But few of us listen to the voice of the Lord, for it upsets our routines, contradicts our passions and destroys our false tranquillity of blind and deaf dying people.
«Who will stop up his ears to hear better and who will close his eyes to see better?»

1'. He who does not possess the Spirit of God shall judge the Book as a boring, obscure and useless thing, for too many of the mediocre have discredited the inspired word, emasculating the word of God, propagating imbecilic writings, fabricating dead images and making erroneous comments. In a word, using the holy Scriptures for the petty affairs of men, instead of serving the greatness of divine revelations.

2. Do we no longer know how to recognize the tone of God's truth nor the language of holy poetry? Would it not be because our wretched reason, our little intelligence and our assured mediocrity have stifled in us the voices of humility, inspiration and love, which do not deceive the true children of God?

2'. By mutilating our receptor antennae, we cut ourselves off from inspiration and become deaf. By removing our emitter antennae, we deprive ourselves of our virility and become blind. It is then that our wives rebel, and scorn us when they have to take on our weakening roles.

3. Make us humble, patient, loving, innocent and pure so that we are fully fertilized by your love and led to your everlasting glory, magnanimous and perfect Lord.

4. When we meet a believer we shall say to him: «Speak to us of God». In this way, our conversations will always be interesting, beautiful and useful. Yet, silence in God is far superior to noise in the world.

5. «We do not have to be patient and courteous with the wicked ones, the hypocrites or the mediocre, who ask for our approval of their evil doings and their platitudes. Let them keep away from us as we keep away from them!»

6. Those who have been instructed by God recognize the religions and initiations of men, for it is they who establish them when they are lacking and who straighten them when they deviate.

7. Agriculture is surely the most useful knowledge for humanity, yet many ignore it, and almost everyone despises it. «Strange blindness!»

8. Sowing, mortification, germination, ablution, flowering, fructification, multiplication: such are the successive states of our becoming perfect in God.

9. Communion is accomplished in us by the marriage of bread and wine which unite, by means of the water

3'. Finally, it is our children who treat us as nonentities in our own homes, then anarchy takes over nations, and lastly, slavery establishes itself in the world.

4'. He who unveils the mystery of God to anyone, and he who incorrectly receives it, would be cut off without forgiveness for eternity.

5'. In fact, only God lays bare his truth before the one he has chosen, for he is the one judge of our hearts and the one owner of his secret. The sages, prophets and saints of God can only reveal it in images to believers with fear and trembling.

6'. If we do not attract in us the Spirit of God, we shall remain here below like wretched animals, limited to their exterior and stupid senses before the living creation of the Unique One.

7'. We shall be called «the planter of men and the gardener of God». They are prestigious and glorious titles for those who understand.

8'. God's truth reposes inside our darkened hearts. Only the grace and love of the Lord can manifest it clearly inside and outside ourselves in the dark world.

9'. He who has received life directly from God can also give it to whoever he pleases. Yet he prefers to

that is contained in all. Thus, they maintain and develop the life that has lived in us since the beginning, and they mysteriously deliver it from the claws of death.

10. While we ignore God's way and are deprived of his holy light, we might imagine that we are the only ones in possession of the truth and that practise the true religion. But when we penetrate the mystery of the unity of the saints in God, we shall be amazed to recognize at the same time the unity of God's teachings in the world.

11. Rationalists resemble ants who see nothing but their anthill, ignoring the sky that shelters them, the earth that contains them and man who observes them. For they conceitedly believe themselves the masters of their works and of their destiny, without foreseeing the flood, the fire or the kick of the distracted walker that will scatter them.

12. An attentive god also watches them, and they do not know it.
«Having fallen into the filth, they organize themselves in it instead of getting out of it. Unfortunate intelligence, useless courage in truth.»

13. There is the essence that fertilizes, the substance that is fertilized, the medium that is born, the matter that is created.
There is inversely the matter that is

leave this fearsome choice in the hands of the Lord, for God alone is the perfect expert. He knows what our hearts conceal. He knows what time produces. He possesses what makes eternity.

10'. Thus, we must confront the words and thoughts of the holy books of humanity, so as to reach the transcendent unity that causes all God's enlightened sages to agree from the beginning to the end. Let us remember, however, that the mean reason of exiled men is definitely opposed to the inspiration and revelation of the Lord of light.

11'. The temples have become public places that the profane trample on and cross like deserted squares, and the faithful go there like those who go to a station, a market or to do a burden; and the officiants have installed themselves there behind the sales counters and begging posts.

12'. There are no longer any candidates for the science of God because there are no longer any believers in the omnipotence of God.
Thus, God's initiated have become imperceptible in the world, and his adepts have completely disappeared.

13'. We must first be patient in the land of faith.
– Secondly, we must be purified by the water of grace.
– Thirdly, we must be fertilized by

solid, the medium that is aqueous, the substance that is gaseous, the essence that is fluid. For that which descends is like that which rises in the bosom of the Unique One.

14. Right now we cry about our agony in the world, but one day we shall cry when we see the fate of those who deny us and who overwhelm us here below.

15. Alas! neither the pity nor even the love of the saved ones will be able to do anything for those who have chosen the excrements of death.

16. Aid comes to us from God through the inspiration of the angels and through the ministry of men.

Who shall be so stupid as to reject the advice of saints and refuse the help of men after having asked for the aid of the Highest? Who shall be so ignorant as to praise the instrument while neglecting the artist?

Who shall be intelligent enough to go back as far as the worker, via the tool and the work?

17. The wicked ones shall be obliged to swallow their life mixed with filth for as long as their wickedness lasts. For the eternity of hell is made up of the obstinacy of revolt in ignorance, pride and wickedness.

the air of the Holy Spirit.

– Fourthly, we must be matured by the fire of love.

– Fifthly, we must be multiplied by death and by resurrection in the Unique One, for everything ends as everything began.

14'. Let us be careful that death does not strike us like a thunderbolt, and that it does not find us naked and empty like chalices drunk dry.

15'. He who wishes to make his peace with God must first make his peace with men and with himself.

16'. He who is invited to the Lord's banquet receives the promise of life.

– He who eats at the Lord's table benefits from the gift of life.

– He who drinks from the Lord's glass obtains the knowledge of life.

But he who kisses the Lord on the lips reposes in the bosom of life and commands with the Perfect One.

«Who can give without feeling important? And who can receive without feeling diminished? Only he who lives in God!»

17'. O believers in God!, rejoice in your tears and laugh at the sufferings of exile, for you shall live in the light of God one day and you shall become transparent and pure.

18. It is the absurdity of forced and useless labour, it is the sin of life mixed with death, it is the infection and the horror of the ever-agonising and ever-renascent rottenness.

18'. All shall be given to you without vile mixture and without mercenary work, you shall drink from the sacred source and you shall suck the holy stone, you shall live in splendour, you shall praise and bless the magnificent Lord for the eternity of the union.

19. Let us strive every day to strengthen our faith in the amazing promise of the All-Powerful One. Let us strive to increase our love for the generous who nourishes us. Let us strive to bear without weakening the ordeals of our darkened lives. Let us not tire of asking for the help of the Providence of the Highest. Let us never lose heart in our quest for the holy treasure.

19'. Now, my God, if we have spoken according to your holy truth and if we have acted according to your righteous way, let your blessing flow and make your love rain on your beloved children. Grant your repose on your obedient servants. Provide your peace to your devoted heroes. Communicate your wisdom to your faithful friends. Multiply your love in your loving sons. Make your pure life bloom in your darkened images. Send your salvation to your sleeping bones.

20. The only work that truly counts is work that we do on ourselves. The rest is a provisional stopgap allowed for the necessities of our imprisoned lives.

20'. Now, Lord, that we have ploughed and we have prepared your harvest, grant us the first fruits of your abundance and give us the pledge of your glory without equal.

21. Are there no longer among us anything but hunters of clouds and collectors of smoke? Are there no longer anything but conquerors of dust and conservers of death?

21'. Let us honour the saints and let us remember the faithful believers that have illustrated the word of faith and love, and who have shown us the way of acceptance and of patience in all things.

22. Are there no longer anything but empty shells that the wind shakes as it passes?
Are there no longer anything but

22'. Let us praise and bless in our hearts the sons of God, the sages and the prophets who have transmitted the Lord of life's ancient promise to

sterile conceited and stupefied beasts? Are there no longer anything but delirious ones gone astray in the darkness of the outside, and pigs that wallow in their excrement?

23. When the wind blows the desert seems alive, but when it stops everything falls back into dust. When passions rise the world appears to be in movement, but when they calm down, we see only the platitude of doubt, and we only hear the rumblings of the beasts' agony.

24. The devil appears smooth-tongued and flattering, kind and prudent, full of promises and easy-going, seductive and sugary, disguised and skilful, evasive and vague, obliging and charming, eager and servile. The world seeks him and is easily ensnared; his salary is deception, desolation, torment and death.

25. O temptation, O trap! the impious seize all the apparent goods of the world and relinquish the treasure of life.

26. Let us not take on airs of saved ones nor affect holiness, for the mud that covers us from head to toe would make us even more grotesque and more laughable in the eyes of everyone.

Let us neither stop in our falls, nor sleep on our small victories. Let us walk towards the centre, for it is that alone that counts, and not the sneer

us, and who have revealed the holy way that saves from death to us.

23'. Let us adore in our hearts the all-powerful God who showers us with his grace, who warms us with his love and who makes us germinate to the heaven of resurrection.

«The repeated failures of seekers of arts, systems, sciences and laws should open our eyes and bring us back to the way of the intimate quest for the Perfect One.»

24'. The saint seems hard and coarse, disappointing and severe, rough and brutal, clumsy and offensive, demanding and uncompromising, scandalous and outraged, repulsive and bitter. Everyone flees from him like the plague. His gift is truth, consolation, peace and life in God.

25'. O temptation! O safeguard! the seekers of God have to beg to survive, when in fact they possess the gold that never runs out.

26'. Do we not hear the word that rings true?
– Do we not recognize the tone that vibrates in tune?
– Are we not amazed by the inspired word of God?
– Are we not moved by the interior voice of him who speaks to us?
– Are we not awakened by the clamour of God's envoys?

or the acclamations of the ignorant crowds.
«Let us first of all make our submission to God in the secret of our hearts, then it will not be hard for us to publish it before all.»

27. Let us laugh at the mockers while thinking of our recompense, and let us cry for them while thinking of their salary. O sadness, O pain of the rejection of the dead and the dying!

28. He who looks humbly at his Lord leaves to time the care of decanting the mud of sin in which he languishes wretchedly, while those who wish to analyze it proudly only render it even more opaque and malodorous.

29. God's saints bear a closer resemblance to wandering beggars on earth than to powerful men established in their palaces, but God's sages can be found everywhere, for the temptations of the world can no longer make them forget their magnificent Lord.

30. Following the example of the germs that develop for a long time in the darkness and suddenly shoot up to the light to mature and fructify into the gift of themselves,

31. Thus, our love in God hatches for a long time in the darkness of faith, to appear on the day of hope and become fully accomplished in the multiplicative virtue of love. «Such is death, and such is life in God.»

– Are we not upset by the groans of the crucified innocents?
– Are we not frightened by the calls of the Highest asking us for love?

27'. It is better to help a believer than to be enriched by an impious one. How preferable it is, then, to help a single believer than to enrich a thousand impious ones!

28'. Knowledge of the holy work is the obtention of grace, it is the possession of love, it is the entry into glory and into the kingdom of God.

29'. By putting our hand in the seed, we shall have dough, by putting our hand in the dough, we shall have yeast, on putting a little yeast in a lot of dough, we shall have the abundance of bread that cures and nourishes the children of God.

30'. we shall reappear from the earth, we shall walk on the water, we shall travel through the air and we shall repose in the fire, to the astonishment of all and of ourselves.

31'. For the Lord is a marvellous companion who saves us from distress, from abandonment, from falling and from dispersion in death. «Free your God, nourish your love and you shall never be sad or abandoned.»

32. Everything can fail us and abandon us, for we ourselves can deny all and relinquish all, but the Saviour could not mislay a portion of his flesh nor forget a drop of his blood in the world. Such is the promise and such is the love of God.

«To benefit from the sacrament of life does not necessarily mean one has it available, and to have it available does not necessarily mean one knows it.»

32'. O safeguard of crucified love!
O memory of dispersed blood!
O power of the exploded centre!
O vertigo of the magnetized hub!
O miracle of rediscovered life!
O splendour of purified gold!
O stupor of the maintained unity!
O fervour of the ecstatic heart!
O terror of the exalted union!
O death in the life of the Be-loved One!
O peace in the bosom of he who IS!

33. What is the use of praying hypocritically to God in his temples, if we violate his law in our houses, if we veer off from his way in our lives, if we hamper his work in our hearts?

33'. Why not tell the truth? Only hypocrites and wicked people fear it, because it disrupts their machinations, lays bare their lies and shows up their dishonesty.

34. A sincere believer who prays, who praises and who adores God in his heart is worth more before the Lord than all the right-thinking ones who exhibit themselves complacently in the temple squares.

34'. The illusion of lies will sooner or later be cruelly dissipated by misfortune and death, which will be the share of the deceivers and the deceived.

35. Shall we continue to reject or pretend to ignore the Book for much longer when in fact we call ourselves believers in God?

Who among us can fault it and who can refute it before God and before men?

O ingratitude, O hypocrisy! we remain silent and we try once more to bury God's talent.

O unfortunate ignorance! we still do not know that God's truth breaks all the locks of death and finally shines in broad daylight before all the men of

35'. We are all endowed for material pleasures because they flatter the Beast and require no effort. A large number of men are endowed for work because it allows them to avoid thinking and forget themselves in the world. An equal number of individuals are endowed for business because it goes hand in hand with lies and encourages greed. Many are endowed for sciences because they arouse curiosity and dispersion.

A small number are endowed for laws, because they require subtlety and

creation, so that they can freely choose and thus God's judgement becomes irrevocable and final.

36. How unfortunate is the fate of the timorous, but what lamentable fate awaits those who oppose the light of the Lord!
«Our crime is unforgivable, for we are right compared to the impious and the hypocrites, the scholars and the ignorant, to the intelligent and the mediocre.»

37. The artist is a perpetual newborn who is astonished by apparent creation.
The scholar is a perpetual curious one who looks for the motive of present creation.
The saint is a perpetual agonizer who hopes for repose in hidden creation.
The sage is a perpetual living one who is active and who reposes with the Perfect One in the bosom of purified creation.
«In man's semen lies hidden a germ that consolidates the substance of woman. Thus, God's conscience is like a dot that coagulates the Universe and gives it form.»

38. It is the assiduous reading of the holy books that engenders and maintains our faith and our courage in God. It is daily frequenting of the sacred Scriptures that gives birth to and keeps our fervour and our hope

reflection. A minority are endowed for the arts, because they demand intuition and renunciation.

36'. A few are endowed for the quest for holiness, because it needs love of one's fellow-being and self-oblivion. Almost no-one is endowed for the mystery of God, because it is necessary to meditate upon it for a long time and acquire the whole knowledge of nature and of man. However, the love of God is enough for everyone, and everyone can acquire it easily.

37'. There are those who are promised through the revelation of the Lord of charity. There are those who are committed through faith in the Living One of eternity. There are those who are bound by the grace of the All-Powerful One. There are those who are chained by the love of the Beloved One. There are those who are nailed through the union with the Most-Perfect One. There are those who are agonizing through the integration in the unique Splendour. There are those who are dead through the knowledge of the Most-Hidden One. The latter no longer speak or act personally, for they remain in repose and in act with the Unknowable One who IS.

38'. If we abandon or even simply neglect the holy books, we shall rapidly fall back into the chaos of hell and death. If we study them patiently and if we practise them in our hearts, God shall give us access to his mag-

in the Unique One. It is the repeated study of the revealed words that enlightens and increases our science and love of God and of men.

39. It is patient and attentive practise of the sacred teachings that delivers and that makes our life in God perfect.

40. Well-meaning commentators are often sinister, but direct relationship with the Lord is never boring.

41. The saints and the angels of God are those who shall deliver the true believers when the latter are reborn in the glorious world of the Perfect One, and the wicked ones and the demons are those who shall deliver the impious and the hypocrites into the world of brutal beasts.

42. All the wise and holy books are of the word, they come into the word, they remain in the word and they come out of the word again for the instruction and the safeguard of some and the condemnation of others. God imposes the test and in this way prepares the judgement of the end of time and the hierarchy of his new creation.

43. Thus, among the believers who currently serve many will be served, and many among those who

nificent life and shall lead us to his peace without mixture.

39'. Let us pray to the Lord that he allows us to reach the bottom of things and of ourselves so as to be able to accede to his divine grandeur and to his holiest repose.

40'. The light lives in us and surrounds us. But we remain in the darkness of doubt, of desperation or of faith, as long as the Lord does not lift the dark veil that hems us in tightly on all sides.

41'. No, the Lord's fantastic promise is not an old wives' tale nor a story for entertaining children. It is a reality that everyone shall see with their own eyes, that only a few shall touch with their hands and that only a few shall know in the secret of their heart.

42'. There is a certain number of faithful among the nations. There is only a small number of believers among the faithful. There is only a small number of saints among the believers. There is only a small number of sages among the saints. There is only a small number of God's sons among the sages. And there is but a single word of God among the divine sons.

43'. It is he who does everything, for everything comes from him and everything returns to him. It is he

command will have to obey.
«Let us notice that God's envoys have always proclaimed themselves servants of God and of men.»

44. Let us not despise anything or anyone, for all that we despise no longer brings us any good, and even ends up turning against us. Then, hate and misfortune succeed scorn and privation. Indeed, he who cuts himself off from life and from love is finally cut off by men and by God. Thus, we must be careful never to despise the beings and things that make us live; on the contrary, we must hold them in esteem and love them ever more, so that they too become more and more beneficent and loving.

45. How much, then, must we love he who has given us life, maintains it, delivers it and restores it in its primitive splendour when we beg him to do so in a holy way!

46. The great sages, the great saints and the great artists are marvellous examples that must not discourage us from playing our small personal part, for they are there as examples and as guides to the perfection we can all reach through the simplicity and through the purity of the actions of our hearts.

47. Let us go and visit the dead, the sick, the imprisoned, the unfortunate, the abandoned, and after hav-

who inspires the holy Scriptures, it is he who brings them to life, it is he who spreads them, it is he who keeps them and it is he who renews them according to his desire.

44'. Let us not argue over any religion or any doctrine. Let us study all the holy Scriptures assiduously.
– Let us follow the law of the Unique One, which is the love of God and of his whole creation.
– Let us practise his way, which is the return to the pure and holy life of ancient times.
– Let us accomplish his work, which is the fixing of our lives in the most perfect centre. Thus, all things shall be accomplished in the ultimate and primary splendour.

45'. God's chosen ones perceive him in essence, contemplate him in substance, feel him with their hands in birth and taste him in resurrected body. O holy and perfect mystery of the totality of the Being!

46'. Let us never despair of God in this life and let us never abandon ourselves in the world. Let us ask, rather, for the Lord's help and let us put ourselves in his skilful hands, for he delivers our life from the filth, he purifies it marvellously and he leads it to the perfection of his admirable Being.

47'. The Book may appear easy or difficult, but it is never obscure nor far away for him who chooses to help

ing helped them, let us consider in ourselves the respite that we are still enjoying, and let us immediately set about the quest for God before it is too late.

48. We wish to collaborate in the rehabilitation and reintegration in God of all creatures that have gone astray in death. This is our wish, for the noblest work before God is to separate with him the light from the darkness and cook his truth until the fixed and perfect splendour.

49. There are many more well-intentioned faithful than enlightened believers.
– There are many more people of good will than instructed men. And there are many more people who have gone astray than wicked ones in the world.

50. Each one condemns his neighbour in the name of the morality of men, instead of seeking the love of the Unique One for oneself and for one's own.
«It is nature that makes us get to know man, and it is man that makes us get to know God.»

51. How is it that those who come most recommended from God condemn one another and rip one another apart, instead of loving and helping one another like brothers born of the same Father and the same Mother?

and love without judging.
«During temptation, let us pray for our conversion and for that of the enemy.»

48'. We need great boldness to bless our enemies, but it is the only sure means of delivering ourselves from them, freeing them from the evil that darkens their hearts and that keeps them in blind death.
«Does not God also make all things flourish again through his holy blessing?

49'. If we understand nothing after having studied and meditated upon the Book, it is because we are still darkened due to the filth of sin, which prevents us from seeing the miracle of God in action in the world and in ourselves.

50'. There is but one response to wickedness: to pray in our hearts that the evil one becomes converted and ceases to torment us and himself.
«God crushes the rebels and forgives the repentant.»

51'. Because of their conceited and hypocritical attitude, some turn the worship of God into something suspicious or even odious to many. Others, through the effect of blind zeal, leave it noisily and split it up infinitely.

52. It is because they have more confidence in themselves than in God and in his holy law of love.
«They fight one another like dogs and they bark stupidly at wise and holy men. But the divine whip shall soon calm them down.»

53. They are ignorant of the hidden meaning of the inspired word, their moral explanations are the saddening proof of that. If they understood, they would ascend once more to the source instead of losing themselves in pointless justifications and idiotic disputes.
«God shall erase fatherlands, ideologies, confessions and sects, for believers are all brothers in the unity of the Unique One.»

54. Let us not be afraid of seeming relentless supplicants and troublesome beggars before the Lord, for he grants his treasures only to those who pray to him with humility, with perseverance and with love.

55. On every occasion when we are tempted, let us pray with love for the conversion of the devil, that is to say, for his submission and for his return to God. Thus, he shall either become converted or he shall distance himself from us and in any case we will be delivered.

56. Intimate frequenting of the Lord removes all timidity from us and makes our faith effective and our love miraculous; it is that which gives us the necessary and that showers us with the superfluous, so that we are

52'. All of those people only live off the outer layer of the Scriptures, and do not suspect the precious almond they conceal.
«He who studies the holy books and speaks to the Lord in his heart practises true religion.»

53'. God proposes the unheard-of adventure to us and offers us the incredible share. He presents us with the keys to death and life and indicates to us the way that can save us from the chaos of the absurd. But we stupidly persist in pursuing the dying rottenness and we cry out against injustice. Will we always be so stupid and incurable?

54'. We are plagued by debts before the Highest, but we always ask him for more so as to test his boundless generosity and to go deeper into his bottomless love.

55'. It is not by cursing the accursed that we shall bring him back to the fold, and it is not by fighting him that we shall save ourselves from him; it is by asking God's forgiveness for him and for ourselves.

56'. When we are tormented, let us pray for him who torments us. When we are fulfilled, let us praise the Generous One, but when we are abandoned, let us humbly draw up the inventory of our nakedness and

the living witnesses of the blessing of the All-Powerful One.

57. Many men and things shall pass, and the Book shall be always new and sealed as on the day of its birth, in poverty, in anonymity and in abandonment.

58. God is not particularly interested in our situation in this world. He considers instead the state of our hearts, for it is from it that our rescue or our perdition comes from, and the colour of our skin neither adds nor takes anything away from that.

59. Stupid and incurable, those scholars confuse God with an ideal, and living reality with dead ash.

60. Let us leave the world to its affairs, which appear to it so serious and so important, and let us occupy ourselves with the affairs of God, which seem so unreal and so distant from the world, and let us remember the proverb that says: «He who laughs last laughs longest», for the echo of this laugh will invade the world and will cover the screams of the reprobates.

61. Why always beg from men, who only give grudgingly, and never ask anything of God, who satisfies us so generously?

our uselessness, and let us strive to re-establish contact by meditation on the holy books.

57'. No, we have not written the Book in vain, since multitudes of believers will be confirmed in their faith, fortified in their love and enlightened in their quest. And our reward already shines in the hands and lives in the heart of the magnificent Lord.

58'. Everyone makes a living from working, trading, playing or stealing. Only he who searches for God is forced to beg for his bread like a useless person. O marvellous humour of the Highest for him who knows!»

59'. Let us imitate faithfully the procedures of nature, but let us not copy stupidly its deceptive appearances.

60'. The mocking of the intelligent, the vulgarity of brutes, the malice of the wicked ones, the avarice of the greedy, the pride of the powerful, the vanity of scholars, the blindness of sectarians, the hypocrisy of the skilful, the indifference of the ignorant, the satisfaction of the mediocre, keep away the divine treasure that contains life without mixture.

61'. Some have found while reposing that which multitudes have not come close to by working hard.
«O unfathomable mystery of the divine gift!»

62. The violence of desire eventually prevents its accomplishment. Thus, after having prayed a lot, it is wise to entrust God with the task of granting us our desires, while simply remaining highly attentive to what happens in ourselves and around us.

63. Who could extinguish the movement of life? Death itself masks it, but does not eliminate it.

64. Let us give all in the name of God, so that the thanks, the praise and the blessings go to him and then return to us through the effect of his overflowing grace.
«The saints love those who love God, before loving those who honour them.»

65. Let us patiently till the Book, and its harvest shall enrich us and nourish us in the peace of the Unique One.
«The characteristic feature of the scholars of the world is profanation. The characteristic feature of the sages of God is revelation.»

66. We do not have a poetic or literary genius to attract men to God, we know and we preach nothing but the holy truth.
«Weak bait: terrible hook!»

67. By demanding much of oneself and very little of others one achieves all the victories one desires.

62'. It is always necessary to wash in order to separate the almond from the filth that surrounds it, and it is a great secret that nature displays every day before all. However, without God's inspiration we are unable to understand the obviousness of divine science.

63'. All remains in the unity of the One; nothing lasts indefinitely in numbers.

64'. We are united with all believers, with all good men and women, like twin sisters and brothers that share the same body and the same spirit in the transcendent unity of the Unique One.

65'. The forger may counterfeit the appearance of the holy word, but he could not imitate its mysterious and living content. Oh, let be silent all those who describe to us the holy light that they have not seen nor touched!

66'. Our goal must coincide with God's goal, which is our conversion and our complete restitution, that is to say, the atonement of the Beast and of all creation in the re-conquered unity of the divine body, soul and spirit.

67'. By examining ourselves naturally as far as our heart and by reposing in the world, one rapidly reaches God.

68. Rationalist philosophers and delirious false prophets are they not like the thorns that crown the Lord and like those that surround the mystical rose?

69. HE SHALL CHOOSE HE WHO WANTS TO.
HE SHALL UNDERSTAND HE WHO IS ABLE TO.

68'. The truth does indeed shine inside the well, but the opening is covered in inextricably tangled brambles.

69'. HE SHALL TAKE HE WHO DARES.
HE SHALL VEIL AGAIN HE WHO SAYS.

Division is not death, it is the separation of the mixture. Bodies are divided, not to be abolished, but to be renewed.
HERMES TRISMEGISTUS

And God, who resurrected the Lord, shall resurrect us also through his power.
PAUL

BOOK XVII

But a vapour rose from the earth and watered the whole surface of the ground.
MOSES

For him the precious gift of heaven, the dew.
MOSES

ÈVE NUE RIT

JOY

1. How cruelly are the hypocrites mocked by the impious and how ferociously condemned are the impious by the hypocrites! For as neither are the children of God, their destiny is to mutually destroy one another.

2. Now the preachers exalt the scholars and their poisons in the holy place to flatter the ignorance of the world and so as not to appear behind the times; for the faith, the love and the science of God seem too puerile and too old-fashioned to them, and they are ashamed of the simplicity of our first fathers.

3. Who inspires these shepherds who speak highly to us of the century, the factory, the machine, poison, politics, patriotism, social issues, intelligence, work and men's vanity over and above the knowledge and the love

1'. True believers do not exhibit themselves, do not judge and do not upset themselves; for, having their spirit constantly fixed on God, they have no time to concern themselves much with the world or its matters.

2'. Satan has taken such a lead that the sanctuaries of God now serve him as benches and propaganda agencies without their knowing.
«O compassionate Lord! who shall save us from hell if you do not come rapidly to our help?»

3'. O priests, O monks, O laymen, who still believe in God in your hearts, throw away the leaven of Satan's proud science! Realize that it is useless to want to organize the rottenness of the sin of death here be-

of God? Who inspires these panegyrists of human pride and blindness?

4. The intelligent are annoyed, for they cannot turn the Book inside out as one does with the finger of a glove, and their intelligence is humiliated.

Will not Satan whisper to them a miserable explanation, and will he not veil their nothingness with some sordid rags?

5. And then the wicked ones and the hypocrites, will they not come to their help like natural allies?

low. Remember the word of the master who said: «The works of the world are bad», and like him do not fear the hate of the world by bearing witness to it before all.

4'. The wicked ones shall cover us in filth, as we have covered them with forgiveness, but the Lord shall deliver us forever from the stench of death and the company of evil ones.

5'. They shall live forever with her, that infamous and rotting companion, and her devouring fire shall consume them without respite.

5". When the virginal water bathes us once again, we shall sit up in our tombs, washed of the filth of death, and we shall praise the Lord God with one voice and with one heart.

6. Let us pray to God in a holy way, and he will reveal to us in one way or another the truth of the Book and the authenticity of its inspiration, if we still have any doubts.

7. Many thought they were doing the right thing in seeking the death of Jesus, but not one has followed him in resurrection, which is the only justification of the passion of the handsome Lord, and which confirms our deliverance to come.

8. The great sages and the great saints are their own mould, and they have no need of that of others, for

6'. He who deals with filth ends up smelling bad, and he who frequents the holy Scriptures ends up transpiring God's perfume.

7'. Let us not desire to become martyrs so that our successors are not tempted to be executioners.

«Wickedness is the absence of God; holiness is his assured presence.»

8'. Uncover yourself prudently, Lord, so that we are not crushed by your glory, but that we live more and

they hear God directly. But it is good and even excellent for the weaker ones to follow the ways traced by the strongest ones.

9. We have nothing to explain, nothing to demonstrate and above all, no-one to convince; for the love and the peace of the Unique One are enough for our contentment.

10. The proof of the divine origin of creation is its revolt in the face of death and its innate habituation to life that does not perish.

11. Let us pray madly to God so as to know the means to our immediate deliverance, or at least to benefit from this deliverance on the day of the great lordly judgement.

12. A rich man can become poor and humble and a criminal can become converted to love, but how could a shrewd one ever become simple? And how might a swine become pure?

13. The latter accumulate rare books and pursue hidden knowledge, but they deny God and the holy Scriptures, which are the only ones that could give them the intelligence of the veiled texts and the key to the buried treasures.

14. Too often we take for ourselves that which is not meant for us, and too frequently we also direct to others that which is not due to them, for we consider the outer part of the world too highly and we neglect the inner part of man.

more before your splendour, so that your saints dwell in your light and so that your sages reach your most secret core.

9'. All has been said, all is reiterated and all shall be repeated until the Lord's chosen ones have entered the luminous secret of the word of life.

10'. What destroys us and others is evil. What gives life to us and conserves others in God's freedom is goodness.

11'. He who is sufficiently detached from the world can see all and hear all without disturbance or harm, but he who is not perfectly bared may die, even of God's truth.

12'. Those that are too simple take gilt for gold, and those who are too intelligent reject gold because of the gilt, but all of them eat the filth of sin without knowing it.

13'. They proudly think they have stolen the secret of creation without asking the creator for it, and their subtle intelligence and their great learning have become like the greatest stupidity there could be, for all of their works are dead and engender death.

14'. Let us respond to the accusations, the insults and the persecutions of the world by moving closer and closer to the Lord of life, who purifies us in the blaze of holy solitude and love.

15. The religious and the impious ignore us, scholars and ignorant men despise us, the intelligent and the stupid mock us, workers and the debauched reject us.

If a friend recognizes us, it is still superfluous, for our consolation is only in God.

15'. We cannot convert a hypocrite, an impious one, a wicked one or one who has gone astray by pointing out his evil and reproaching him vehemently, but we can improve him by cultivating the good that has remained in him, encouraging him and loving him as he is, however disfigured he may be.

15". Do we not have to wash a great quantity of earth in order to discover a small emerald?

16. The pleasures of the world disappear for he who gets old, since the diminished body can no longer endure them; but the gentleness of the love of the Unique One increases for the believer, since the soul disengages itself from the ties of the rough body and communicates more and more with its Lord. Therefore, getting old is a sad decadence for some and a sweet enlightenment for others.

16'. Wisdom and holiness in God do not depend on worldly opinions, on general or particular obediences, on figurative rites, on social positions, on patriotism, on the number of wives or children or on the quantity of goods, but rather on knowledge of the primary cause and the ultimate effect.

17. He who draws close to God's truth no longer disputes anything with anyone, for he is too busy trying to remember the forsaken word.

17'. If we are not strong enough to convert the bad company, let us flee from it before it perverts and ruins us completely.

18. To become converted is to turn over in the great water and contemplate the light of heaven face to face.

18'. The report of a blind man will always appear more sensible to other blind men than the description of a clear-sighted one.

19. Would the prophets have deceived us by announcing the resurrection, and Christ himself, would he have cheated us by being the first one to resuscitate?

How, then, can believers be distressed at the death of their loved ones?

19'. Let us defend the jewel, but let us not defend the filth that covers it; let us instead resolutely throw it away, taking care however not to throw away the jewel at the same time.

20. Surely they should rejoice in the hope of new life and of their coming meeting with God, if their faith is not worthless and if their love is not dead.

21. Only the ignorant complain and protest here below, for the saints bless in poverty and the sages repose in the very middle of the chaos of the absurd.

22. A little charity is better than great learning.
A little love is better than great wealth.
A little peace is better than great power. But then, what are the grace, love and knowledge of the Perfect One worth?

23. When the bad word and the bad blow have been delivered, who can then hold onto them and who can erase them?

24. When we are disgusted with the vanities of the world, we shall come back to the Book, which will give us back the taste for the faith and the peace that are so necessary to the manifestation of divine love.

25. Sobriety, simplicity and charity are the three great doctors of the body, the mind and the soul, but divine love is the only remedy for the sickness of our exiled lives.

26. We shall act with an absurd faith in wakefulness until we act in the same way in dreams; then, unity shall be accomplished in us.

20'. We shall name our hope with faith against all contrary appearance and against all opposing reason, thus eliminating the doubt and fear that kill the soul.

21'. Let us practise daily acts of faith, naming the desired thing in a holy way until it is accomplished before our eyes.

22'. When we bless our enemies in a heartfelt way, we shall be close to the Lord, who is the source of the love that springs up. In the meantime, let us strive to bless and love our friends as befits believers in God.

23'. The holy Name of God is an all-powerful magic in the mouth of him who truly believes and loves.

24'. Each imagined thing seems absurd until it is accomplished in the world, then everyone is surprised; then everyone becomes used to the prodigy, and finally no-one pays attention to it any more.

25'. By eliminating the doubt of reason through the constant exercise of faith in action, we shall not only manage to disregard contrary appearances, but even to modify them miraculously.

26'. How could he who is false before men be true before God? And how could he who has abandoned himself to the passions of the world still hear his Lord?

27. How much do men harm their bodies! How much do they torture their spirits and bully their souls!
«Let us thank God for the good creature and praise him for the excellent fruit.»

28. They have cunningly and criminally substituted their profane words for the holy words, and now the mediocre blindly follow their countersigns, without even knowing the teaching of the divine master, whose name they give as a reference with impudence.

29. How to believe when injustice and death undermine us?
– How to bless when misery and despair crush us?
– How to be virtuous when we lack everything, and how to be detached when the world oppresses us?

30. It is better to deal with a thousand nonbelievers than with a single blind and ignorant sectarian.

31. Many claim to have the exclusive monopoly on God, and consequently, each one excommunicates his neighbour in the name of the grace, love and knowledge he clearly does not possess.

32. Let us not flaunt diplomas, decorations, titles or grades, nor any other disguise to delude the world

27'. By giving up the mirages of the world and devoting himself to the quest for divine unity, the sage avoids many complications, many excesses and many useless pains.

28'. Those in charge of souls have abandoned the harvest of life for the harvest of death.
Both the deceivers and the deceived shall be rejected, and there will be stupefaction, tears and a frightful desperation like the mire of the swamp where they shall be relegated with the wicked.

29'. Holiness is truly a test of endurance and strength that very few men can tolerate without succumbing.
«To seem this or to seem that, to be here or elsewhere, what does it matter to him who has forgotten himself in God?»

30'. To take oneself seriously and to believe in one's own intelligence here below, is that not the worst ignorance?

31'. Let us not allow ourselves to be marked, numbered, led or exploited like cattle. Let us respond to the oppressors with the sobriety, with the simplicity, with the charity of our lives, and let us propose to them the freedom of believers in the bosom of the Unique One.

32'. Let us prepare neither speeches nor sermons of men. Let us speak of God only when the Holy Spirit

and ourselves.
Let us rather remain in God's truth that is enough for everything.

33. The wicked who call themselves religious have simply swapped their natural impiety for social hypocrisy, and their wickedness has multiplied itself within them, poisoning them irremediably.

34. Those who obey the law externally are right in doing so. Those who live the love of the Perfect One in their heart do even more so.

35. Those who experience defeat or fear feel great resentment as a result, and exercise great vengeance, and those who surrender to the passions of the world are lost according to God.

36. How secure they think they are, the mediocre who live only for themselves!
– How skilful they think they are, those who frustrate their brothers!
– How intelligent they think they are, those who dominate the unfortunate!
– How strong they think they are, those who crush the weak!
– O believers, consider the end of those who say «ME» and never «GOD».

37. How will they manage in the quagmire of death?
– How will they falsify justice in eternal darkness?
– How will they seize the best por-

inspires us, or let us humbly remain silent so as not to be found boring or untruthful.

33'. The pretension of some false believers is only equalled by their lamentable blindness. How cruel their disillusionment will be when the truth of the Highest appears! How much will they regret their worthless judgements, and how much will they weep for their absent love!

34'. Who would dare to expose himself to risk like a dog before all? And who could converse in public about love with the Beloved One?

35'. He who threatens disappears suddenly before being able to strike, and he who promises slips away before giving anything.
«Only the promises of the Lord are accomplished with certainty.»

36'. O how successful have been the powerful and the shrewd!
– O how proud are the intelligent and the well-off!
– O how self-assured are the herds of the mediocre and the hypocrites!
The earth is half-open to receive them and they do not realize, for their self-contentment blinds them, and all of them go into the pit from which there is no return.

37'. O believers in God! change your way of living now that you still have time and seek relentlessly the keys that open the doors to the abode of life, of joy, of love and of peace.

tion for themselves in the pit of filth?
— How will they be able to be astute and mendacious among the unchained demons?
— How will they be able to be ferocious and pitiless amid wild beasts?
— How will they digest in peace in the slaughterhouses of hell?

38. We do not bend life to our laws; it is life that adjusts itself to our laws and that persists in spite of them.

39. O Lord, forgive the ignorant, the ones gone astray and all the repentant sinners, but strike the hypocrites who publicly fake piety and virtue and who are full of hate, deceit and pride.

40. Those who only count on their learning, their intelligence, their courage or on their skill here below condemn themselves unknowingly to forced labour forever, and all their effort remains useless and sterile before God.
«Our fathers who received the Holy Spirit, were not mad, and what they teach is the truth.»

41. Prove this to us, make us see that, say the nonbelievers with the conceited pretension of idlers who want to know everything without searching for anything.

Abandon your cumbersome baggage to the greedy ones, and ask the Lord of love and knowledge for the way and for the viaticum, like lost and repentant children, for we must ask of God, who is all-powerful to satisfy us with the unheard of, the incredible and the enormous.

38'. Happy is he who recognizes his incapacity and his uselessness here below, for he is not afraid of begging God for his life daily!

39'. It is not a question of being pleasing and kind to the wicked and the hypocrites. It is rather a question of fleeing from them when we meet them and of then avoiding them at all costs.

40'. Let us note carefully how the ignorant and impious ones systematically reject all that could help them, take care of them, console them and save them, for their ignorance and their rejection of God hinder the aid of the holy men and the aid of the Lord's Providence.

41'. How susceptible are the conceited, how vexed they are at not understanding the obviousness, how much they punish themselves for being pedantic and ignorant!

42. Not even a miracle would be able to satisfy them, while the spectacle of the grain germinating illuminates the spirit of the believer.

43. It is not the clothes that make the sage, nor the beard that makes the prophet, but only the inspiration of the Lord who visits his living ones in secret, as he wishes and when it pleases him.

44. Could a handful of nonbelieving scribes or hypocrites bury the talent of God forever? Will not the believers one day publish the testimony of their eyes, their ears and their hearts?

45. The money of the wicked burns like hell, for their wickedness is attached to it like a bad smell is attached to filth.

46. Everyone has a profession, a job or a pension that allows them to live and prosper. Only he who has devoted himself to the quest for and the praise of the Highest receives no salary here below. But is his reward not already visible in heaven, and is it not inscribed on the land of the saints?

47. Many rich men say: «We do not care about money», and their life is filled with contemptible base acts and plundering to acquire it.

48. Others boast of their good works and, under the cover of charity, make the wretched work for half of the salary that is their due. How seriously they greet one another at the

42'. How could we free those who voluntarily lock themselves in spiritual coarseness and in the worship of themselves?

43'. He who does not try to pass himself off as something that he is not, and who even accepts being taken as something other than he is, already has great peace.

44'. We shall recognize the hypocrites and the impious ones in that both shall remain silent when they are invited to speak spontaneously of the Lord of life. «Always saddening and always sinister like dead people.»

45'. But the field transforms the manure into harvest, and God's grace transfigures sin into light of life.

46'. He who has endured poverty and abandonment without weakening, for the glory of his Lord, shall one day be showered with the riches of the Universe and given the task of distributing the manna of life to the charitable and faithful believers.

47'. How could he who possesses divine freedom and love, still forget his Lord to run after the wind and death in the world?

48'. Those who are well-off, O how pleasant, how fair and how orderly do they find the world, how satisfied are they with their superstitions, their vanities and their hypoc-

entrances to God's temples, and how joyously they feast in infamous places!

49. O how humble when faced with money are those who make a livelihood begging the rich, how supple are their backs, and how ready are their hands to bless before the triumphant hydra!

50. How accommodating are they with the crimes of the winners, how resigned are they before the injustice that crushes the unfortunate, and how patient are they with the despair of the abandoned ones!

51. The sages no longer guide nations, because they seem too ignorant in this world.
And the saints no longer inspire the churches, because they do not appear «right-thinking» enough.

52. Some play at being sages and reply only by nodding their head gravely and subtly stealing away, but most often it is to hide their ignorance, their powerlessness and their platitude of incurable mediocre men.

53. Each one remakes his small experience of a blind man and each one proposes his little system of a dying one, without noticing the immensity of God's creation and without suspecting the presence of the uniting doctrine of the masters.

54. It is a security for everyone to refuse to introduce and to maintain death in oneself and in others, whatever is the motive put forward by the merchants of death.

risies, and how well-installed do they feel in their putrefying sewer!

49'. If the salary of the hypocrites and the wicked is hell, what will be the punishment of those who encourage them and bless them in the name of the Lord of love and justice?

50'. No believer can think of this without his hair standing on end in terror. «The pure man is the only one who does not bow and scrape before money, and that is the rare and precious sign among all.»

51'. If the gifted occupied the places that correspond to them here below, what would become of the multitude of the mediocre and failures who bustle about in their useless ventures?

52'. Others speak highly of the bestial life they enjoy at present, and mock the spiritual life they ignore.
Instead of saying humbly: «We see nothing», they state proudly: «There is nothing».

53'. Let us not break our head over the Book; instead, let us break our heart over it, so that our precious soul germinates and fructifies before God in the secret of the beginning and end of all things.

54'. No faith, no help, no medicament, no food, no assurance should be imposed by force on anyone on the fallacious pretext of saving him.

55. There is no chance for the believers, chance is for those who remain voluntarily astray in the quagmire of dark and stinking death.

56. The world gives its approval only to professional destroyers and poisoners, to criminals and brutes by trade, to licensed oppressors and thieves; and the names of the saints and the righteous are replaced everywhere by those of the wicked ones.

57. The quantity of believers is not of importance before God, it is only their quality that counts. Therefore, those who do not shine in the night shall not reach the light of the primary splendour.

58. Perfect freedom means to have no needs and no desires. «That which scandalizes hypocrites does not even surprise God's saint; as for the sage, it is enough for him to consider attentively what he possesses for him to feel fulfilled.»

59. The devil cannot be opposed to God as an equal, for he is still a part of the whole that works without knowing it in the hierarchical purification of dispersed creation.

60. The holy Scriptures are not stupid, and the Churches are not idiotic, for what they teach is preferable for man and what they prohibit is dangerous to him. Experience demonstrates it clearly, for intelligence is

55'. The wicked are the instruments of the destruction of the impious ones, just as the saints are the instruments of deliverance of the believers.

56'. Those who sow prepare the resurrection, and those who pray make God's blessing descend. Therefore, the most useful and the most estimable of all men appear the most useless and the most contemptible in the blind and deaf world.

57'. How joyful and vivifying are God's saints, and how sinister and mortal are the wicked! «He who has replaced his intelligence with the love of God and of men is a master.»

58'. First of all, the Holy Spirit shall join the body to revive it; then, the divine soul shall unite these two in splendour to glorify them in the bosom of the magnificent Lord.

59'. Abundance and peace descend on God's saints, while desolation and misfortune fall on the wicked.

Thus, all are taught in different ways here below, but appearances are deceptive.

60'. Those who travel by ship fully clothed, must not despise those who swim naked in the great water; and the latter must not mock those who are taken in small boats. For many of the former become shipwrecked and

not enough here to protect oneself from the effects of the primordial sin. Obey the laws of God, that is the intelligence that enlightens and saves!

61. Sobriety, simplicity and the careful study of the holy Scriptures are the safeguard of God's wise investigator.
«How much do warm climates and peaceful places facilitate the quest for the Lord of truth!»

62. It is our bad thoughts, our bad words and our bad actions that allow the demons of misfortune, of despair and of death, and above all, the imprudent curiosity of our first parents to enter us.

63. If Satan were to place the love of God above his own intelligence and his own esteem just once he would be saved and reintegrated in the living unity of the Unique One.

64. How skilled are the wicked ones at tearing apart and destroying, and how poor they are at encouraging and helping!

65. Those who have supported the destructive works of Satan, be it for the taste of lucre or because of a natural bent, should not have recriminations at the time of the settling of accounts, for no-one shall have made them to increase the disorder of death.

some of the latter are devoured by the beasts of the sea before being able to reach the goal.

61'. As regards those who remain in the foreign land, they destroy themselves mutually and are separated from essential life for as long as their voluntary exile lasts.
«The wicked are sometimes the tools of God without anyone suspecting it.»

62'. It is our good thoughts, our good words and our good actions that save us from the infamous mixture and from putrefying death. But above all it is God's love that enlightens us and purifies us of the ancient poison.

63'. For us, it is not a question of convincing the world, it is rather a question of helping men of goodwill, as our handsome Lord did by showing the way out of mitigated hell.

64'. Raw roots, coarse bread and clear water with the peace of the Lord, rather than all the riches of the earth with the poisonous rage of the wicked!

65'. Many bark after the Jews through incitation or through jealousy, unaware that it is they who transmitted to us the light of God inherited from the land of Egypt, and who were deprived of it because of their bad behaviour, as occurs with us at the moment.

66. The justice of the Lord shall be minute and implacable for the wicked ones and the hypocrites, let us be assured of it, and let us tremble at the thought of being counted among them to our great astonishment.

66'. Misfortune strikes the rebels and the impious hard, but the Lord's forgiveness and blessing descend in abundance on the generous and on the believers.

67. The sages have penetrated and revealed the mystery of the fall and of the restoration of man and of all creation in God. However, for the believers it is more a matter of saving oneself than of understanding and explaining the divine secret.

67'. True philosophy does not rest on the frenzied subtleties of the spirit, nor on rigid moral principles, nor on the meticulous observance of rites, but rather on knowledge of the content at the core of all things.

67". Here below, all is like the moving shadow of the unique divine reality.

There is diversity of gifts, but it is the same Spirit; diversity of ministries, but it is the same Lord; diversity of operations, but it is the same God who operates everything in everyone.

PAUL

Your judgement is the light that will rise up.

HOSEA

BOOK XVIII

> *Ah! the shepherds are stupid. They have not sought IEVE, also they have not prospered, and their whole flock has been scattered.*
>
> JEREMIAH

> *And I, in my turn, have made you contemptible and vile before all the people, for you have not kept my ways and you take notice of people when applying the law.*
>
> MALACHI

VIE NEUTRE

1. On that day there will be several of us in one single body and in one single spirit, and the mystery of communion in the bosom of the Unique One shall be revealed to the believers, without them knowing the why or the how of the holy union.

2. It is a great deliverance to be ready to leave this life at any moment, in the hope of the Lord's day.

3. Some work like madmen in sinister places to produce the death that shall cripple them, poison them or volatilize them, and they snigger when one speaks to them about hell, for their little intelligence and their derisory pride have blinded them totally.

THE WAIT

1'. Wisdom is to repose in peace and observe the renewal of the Lord's creation attentively. Holiness is to remain silent and listen in oneself to the voice of the Unique One.

2'. It is hard to believe without having seen, and yet who can see without having madly believed the unbelievable?

3'. Satan is, like ourselves, a hidden and spoilt light; however he tries by all means to attract the souls gone astray here below towards his miserable company, instead of submitting and returning to the purest bosom of divine splendour, as the sages, the saints and the believers in God hope.

4. While living by tricks in a fake world they collect the most horrible physical and mental illnesses and speak of their science that shall save humanity, for their old background of revolt has made them deaf to the voice of divine wisdom.

4'. Who could judge the rebel if not the righteous and clear-sighted Lord? As regards ourselves, it is enough for us to do good and to place our trust in God alone.

«Hell is full of fire, machines, stench and cries. Paradise is full of light, flowers, perfumes and songs.»

4". Nothing for the man rebelling against God.
Nothing for the woman rebelling against man.
Nothing for the child rebelling against woman.
Nothing for the world rebelling against the child.

5. The devil never says his name frankly, he prefers to hide behind a false identity or he says «ME».
«The outer layer.»

5'. I am the essence, I am the substance and I am the knot, says the Lord of the centre.
«The almond.»

6. The believers postulate the divine soul, the saints and the sages incubate it and manifest it here below; but the wicked and the brutes stagnate in the limbo of forgetfulness and dwindle away on the dark periphery.

6'. Due to their nature divine souls tend to separate from the crust of sin and rejoin their eternal, pure and living centre. «The prophets have come to collect the gold dust dispersed in the mud of this world.»

7. In order to be able to fully taste the beatitude of divine union, we must become indifferent to material goods and as if absent to spiritual gifts. «This is the poverty to the world, and this is the wealth in God.»

7'. The innumerable outer layers of creation attract men much more than the substantial almond enclosed in it. Therefore, many prefer the subtle and superficial explanations that lead them astray in the multiplicity, rather than the concise and deep thought that would centre them in the light of the Unique One.

8. If we wanted to develop the teaching of the holy Scriptures systematically we would finally realize that all creation is like the prodigious library of the incarnated word.

9. He who begins to see clearly in himself is not really proud of his life in this world; subsequently, he is not even ashamed of it, when he knows the weakness of his condition of incarnated creature in the dark, foul-smelling mud.

10. Who is the greatest among the prisoners of the dark, stinking gaol?
– Who is the most estimable among those who rot in the cul-de-sac of death?
– Which one is the most known, but which one is the best?
– Which one is the most honoured, but which one is the most useful?
– Which is the intelligent one, but which one is the saint and which one the sage?
– Which one is the saved, and which one is the saviour?
– Who serves, and who is truly served?

11. The poets and artists sing of lost beauty, but very few know that they are weeping for their repudiated Lord.
«Evil IS NOT, but it remains as the casing of that which IS.»

12. Everyone asks themselves what others will think of it, but no-one ever thinks about what God will say of it.

8'. Intelligence has been given to us so that we can ride it and it serves for our deliverance, and not so that it crushes us and enchains us in this mixed world.

9'. Sin is what engenders in us the stench of misery, of crime, of disease, of decrepitude and of death.
«Who can boast about living on the dung heap here below? And who can boast of having purified himself of its bad smell?»

10'. He who shares his bread, or he who makes it for everyone?
– He who cleans the gaol, or he who organises it?
– He who consoles, or he who looks after?
– He who prays for the deliverance of all, or he who suffers with the damned?
– He who rebels in slavery, or he who installs himself in it?
– He who preaches good behaviour, or he who shows the hidden exit?
– He who wants to force the locks of death, or he seeks the key that opens all of them?

11'. Even when God inspires the wise and holy man, the mystery of creation, that of the fall and that of the regeneration still remain at his size, and the result of his quest is not assured!

12'. The worst temptation is to want to reform and save the world instead of achieving one's own happiness and salvation.

13. There is only one response to attractive or repulsive temptations and to the absurd of the present world. It is the prayer of the saint, the repose of the sage, or the laugh of the absent one!

14. God's sages and saints are as intelligent as anyone, but they have more confidence in the knowledge and the love of their Lord than in their own particular capacities.

15. If we reject the work of a man, so much the worse for him, but if we reject the work of God, so much the worse for us. Therefore, it is better not to know the Lord's word than to refuse it when it is presented to us.

16. We can equally take action or rest when we laugh as much at our scholarly works as at our ridiculous disguises.

17. For the inspired, revelation.
For the intelligent, instruction.
For the skilled, work.
For everyone, education.
For hardened brutes and hoodlums, the whip.
For informers, death.

18. Who can bite into a juicy fruit without giving thanks to the divine gardener?
– Who can contemplate the perfect curve of a woman's breast without praising the magnificent artist?
– Who can repose naked on the hot sand without smiling at his Lord?

13'. O subtle trap! O phantasmagoria of the world of images! It is enough that we are right in God just once for the contradictions and approbations of the world to affect us no longer.

14'. He who believes in God is like he who no longer believes in anything in this world, but with the difference that the first is joyous, while the second is desperate.

15'. Look how the hypocrites rear up before the truth and before the simplicity of God's word when they cannot make use of it for their cowardly platitude and for their security of moribund blind men! Worms are definitely more intelligent!

16'. It is our absence that permits his presence, and it is our divestment that makes our royalty.

17'. Only the Lord knows the rank and quality of each one of his envoys, and makes them shine in different ways for the teaching of the ignorant, for the safeguard of the believers, for the illumination of the saints and for the resurrection of the sages.

18'. Alas! now the worm is in the fruit, the parasite is in the sand, malice is in woman and death dwells in us.
– Who shall deliver us from the putrescent foreigner and her infection?
– Who shall return to us the total pleasure of life without mixture?

19. Who can feel alive and healthy without singing a hymn of love to his creator?
And what else, if not, did our father ADAM use to do in the garden of Eden?

20. No wicked man shall enter the peace of the Lord, and no shrewd one shall discover the tree of life, for the wicked shall be crushed by their wicked deeds and the shrewd shall be entwined by their tricks. It is the justice of God that bullies no-one, but that gives to each one his own salary.

21. Creation is like God's imagination coagulated by the word. Repose is like the divine imagination liquefied by the Holy Spirit.

22. True wisdom does not consist in living, like a prudent blind man, a transitory life in this mixed world; instead, it consists in searching for, discovering and eating the life purged of death so as to become like it, immortal and pure.

23. The holy and wise books are quite necessary to know the Lord, but a spade and a watering can are not useless in approaching the holy Mother.

24. Those who sow love shall be delivered by love. Those who sow hate shall be crushed by hate. With a little patience the thing is easy to check in the world.

19'. O handsome Lord of compassion, come to us who beg you madly and desperately in our exiled hearts.
– Deliver your beloved little children before horror swallows them completely.

20'. He who is attacked by others can find a benevolent defender or even flee or take pity on his executioner, but he who does violence to himself, by who shall he be defended, and by who shall he be delivered?
«He who is awake and strong in God seems asleep and weak in the world.»

21'. Life eats life and life unites itself with life; what is irremediable, and what is sad about that?

22'. The wisdom of men is no more than a forced arrangement with the rottenness of death.
– Divine wisdom is the possession of eternal life and deliverance from death.

23'. There is a great difference between the intelligence of men and that of God, but few understand that.

24'. Reality is that which man embodies with sufficient clarity to make it perceptible in the world.
– The ideal is that which man does not embody with sufficient power to give it life and body here below.

25. He who takes care of his own happiness and his own salvation is not tempted to trouble the world under the fallacious pretext of saving men and of giving them happiness and peace, which in reality for others are called «violence, coercion, slavery, misery, despair and death.»

26. He who does not do violence to himself is a wise, happy and loved man, for neither is he tempted to force surrounding nature or other creatures.

27. O believers in God, recognize the authenticity of the voice that is calling you to earthly regeneration and to heavenly union. «Shall we always approach God and his saints to beg sordidly and never to praise freely?»

28. Man's greatest error is like the greatest doubt and the greatest timidity towards God, and, inversely, the greatest truth is like the greatest faith and like the greatest familiarity with him.

29. Creation is a secret of God that very few have known or shall know clearly, and this humiliates the intelligent of the world, who cannot manage to penetrate it with their limited intelligence.

30. The true sage is like a little child who follows divine nature and who makes the elements obey him, without being surprised by it at all.

25'. The only serious occupations here below are not work, pleasure, profit, power or glory, but certainly contemplation, prayer, love and the life that germinates in us and around us constantly.

26'. True luck is to be sufficiently at repose, sufficiently gratuitous and sufficiently empty to hear God's interior voice and receive his blessing without hindrance.

27'. The ignorant ones and the hypocrites present themselves as sad, severe and boring monitors, while God's saints are passionate, joyful and free. The former are as complicated and sinister as the latter are simple and upright.

28'. He who has worn out the Book begins to live with God.
– He who has understood it begins to live in God.
– He who has experienced it begins to live God.

29'. There are also many nonbelievers, but there are very few sons of God ready to manifest the incredible, for where, then, would be the merit of our quest? And how would the hierarchy of the future world be established?

30'. God has come to rest in man who is pure to enjoy his own creation that is so marvellous and so varied.

31. If we fall or if we think we are falling, let us keep our eyes fixed on our handsome Lord of eternity instead of analyzing the mud in which we have been lamentably struggling since the primary fall, for it is neither intelligence nor the intervention of man that separates the true from the false and that saves from death, but rather the grace and the love of the most learned and all-powerful Lord who forgives and who delivers his beloved children.

31'. Having given up the mud on the outside, my Lord gave me a pearl; having given up the pearl, he offered me a diamond; having given up the diamond, he presented me with a ruby; but as I did not stretch out my hand greedily, he gave himself, and I ate my Beloved One with prudence so as not to die of his great perfection.
«O unique savour of the Living One of eternity!»

32. Generosity towards others and towards oneself is the best investment that can be made in this world and in the other; let us then give a little of our property before everything is taken away from us, and let us not refuse our help to the humble seekers of God.

32'. Finally, each one will have to be faced with the good or bad images of his particular faith. Only he who has hoped for God without imagining anything else shall fully enjoy the repose and the freedom of the Unique One.

33. Nothing to hope for among the impious and the mediocre.
Nothing to hope for either among the intelligent and the scholars of the world.
Nothing to do, above all, while in the company of hypocrites and of the wicked.

33'. Our fellow-being is he who wakes up to the reality of God, and not he who falls asleep in the dream of the Beast. «Who can boast of conversing with his Lord while in bad company?»

34. Let us not constantly bother God's wise children with indiscreet and worthless questions; let us, instead, strive to silently perceive the thought of their heart, which shall lead us to the life and the repose of the splendour of the Unique One.

34'. Who shall lead us to the dwelling of God's sage, and who shall introduce us to him? Who shall show us the holy place, and who shall reveal to us the light that lives in it secretly? O hidden crib! O primary and ultimate secret!

35. Let us imprudently seek the Living One who can save us from the pit of filth, and let us run away from the dying and the dead who drag us into their imbecilic and satisfied darkness.

«How many worldly sages on whom it has been forgotten to stick the label «factitious»!»

36. It is not scholars and thinkers that we need, but rather a single wise expert and a single holy possessor of God's secret.

37. It is not up to us to unveil before all the secret beauty of God's creation, it is up to us only to affirm its existence in the heart of man and of the Universe.

38. How indifferent and light everything becomes to us when we taste the love and freedom of the Unique One, and how everything rips us apart and crushes us when we attach ourselves passionately to the beings and things of the transitory world!

39. Grant us the absence of ourselves, O Lord, so that we enjoy your holy presence and we find your hidden truth that saves from death.

40. It is not enough to study, we must also understand what we study,

35'. Many are asleep to the point of forgetting themselves in worthless or sinister occupations, and very few are sufficiently awake to seek themselves in the holy books and to find themselves under the veil of mixed creation.

36'. O holy light of life that shines in the darkness of the end! How many have seen your salvation? And how many shall see it before the definitive judgement?

37'. O fleeting life, the Lord of heaven shall fertilize you and shall fix you in the peace of the holy gold, and your glory shall illuminate the worlds and your virtue shall quench the thirst of the believers of the grandiose Universe!

38'. Let us not be afraid so much of sinning in detail, let us rather be afraid of not loving God and his creatures as we should, and let us dread behaving like satisfied hypocrites in this divided and darkened world.

39'. Make us hear nothing but your true voice, make us see nothing but your radiant face, make us receive nothing but your vivifying breath, O holy and veiled beauty!

40'. Prayer and praise are not ends in themselves, but rather the learning

and what good is understanding if we do not experience in ourselves the truth of God?

41. Many have become sinister by the sheer force of taking themselves seriously; let us therefore pray to the Lord that he teaches us to laugh at ourselves before the trap of the world closes on us forever.

42. The religions of tears and of repentance are for the beings who have gone astray in death. The religion of joy and of freedom is for God's children found again in life.

43. Who would have the intelligence to listen within himself to the voice of the Highest, and who would have the wisdom to conform to it? That one would see that the greatest submission to God engenders perfect freedom in this world and in the other.

44. The prudent ones who now reject the Scripture shall become the guardians of the precious words. O most subtle humour of the Perfect One, who has the children of heaven's light guarded by the blind!

45. It took ten years to write the Book; who, then, would refuse to read it for the same time before asking useless questions?
«The more we stir up the mud, the murkier it shall become, and the more we let it repose, the more it shall settle naturally.»

of silence in God, which alone instructs us fully.

41'. God is free and alive, that is why he also duly understands the absurd humour of death and the astonishing freedom of life. «Long live our Lord the fire that is embodied in our lady water!»

42'. We shall obtain nothing here below and elsewhere but that which we are able to hear, see and taste without danger of perishing, for the Lord does violence to no-one, not even through the inestimable gift of eternal life.

43'. Goodwill in God does violence to nothing, not even oneself. Goodwill in oneself does violence to everything, even to God.
«Who strips bare the almond and who makes the seed germinate? Is it not the spirit of the all-powerful Lord?»

44'. True freedom is like a holy madness that knows itself and keeps itself in God.
«Who could prevent the children of God from taking up possession of their holy heritage?»

45'. In wanting to go directly to the light of life, we run the risk of wearing ourselves out against the glass of human reason and not feeling the draught of divine inspiration that comes from the narrow door, hidden in the shade of our earthly prison.

46. Suffering is useful as it makes us disgusted with our exile in this world mixed with death.

46'. He who knows everything is like he who knows nothing, but with the difference that the former is free, while the latter is a slave.

46". Prohibitions, separations, limitations and blind judgements are in our heads and in our hearts before being in our houses and in the world.

47. When he who has lived in a holy way on this earth in union with God is asked: «What good have you done?», he shall reply: «Nothing», for only the wicked excuse themselves in the worthless hope of hiding their innumerable crimes.

47'. It is our silence that allows God to state in us his holy truth, and it is our repose that allows him to accomplish in us his ultimate perfection.

«Sobriety, Simplicity, Solitude, Salvation, Saintliness.»

«Solution, Salt, Sanity, Succour, Sagacity.»

48. Let us climb the ladder of love and of knowledge without worthless discussions over how to grab hold of the rungs, and without worthless regrets about what we are leaving below.

48'. Here we are submerged by the scholars and the intelligent of the world, who explain everything to us, but who give us nothing of imperishable life.

49. The great man is he who attracts God in his heart, who fixes him in his body and who manifests him in himself and in the world.

49'. It is not a question here of arguing over words; it is rather a question of finding the God who delivers us from death.

50. Let us be sinners who sometimes do good, rather than devout ones who often do bad.

50'. All that is noble, generous and great frightens the mediocre and arouses their hate. «Only love could still save them.»

51. No-one could hate those he prays for before God, for they are like the deposit of his victory over death that has dispersed us here below.

51'. Let us note well that the action of God tends to unite gently, while the action of the devil tends to separate brutally.

52. When we reach the permanence of hidden life, we shall bear

52'. We shall be enlightened by what we have not invented, and we

everything in silence and we shall witness the catastrophes of the absurd with a smile.

53. We must love God and his creatures for themselves and for what they really are, and not for ourselves and for what they seem to be. Such is true love.

54. The Book is not for the scholars of the world, nor for the satisfied, nor for the agitated, nor for those who have been sold out, nor for the impious, nor for sectarians. Above all it is not for hypocrites.

55. Sunk in the mud, we must wash ourselves daily. Going round in circles, we must persevere in our march towards God. Blind and deaf, we must seek the light of the Perfect One and listen to his holy word.

56. Many believe they can fool God, without seeing that it is God who tricks them.
«Lamentable blindness, derisory triumph!»

57. He who holds his tongue avoids the most frequent opportunity there is for sinning.

58. The primary freedom and power are similar to leaving of individual conscience and like immersion in the divine conscience, where God takes action and reposes eternally.

shall be saved by what we have not done. (Strange words for the intelligent and for the scholars of this world.)

53'. The truth scandalizes the ignorant, that is why it remains veiled in the world and is only shown to he who has given up all human passion and judgement.

54'. Is there no longer anything on earth but men satisfied with their little intelligence and reassured by their miserable reason? Is there no longer anything here below but ruminants of ignorance and those sated with vanity?

55'. Repose, silence, prayer, meditation, self-oblivion are the ways of reaching the divine presence and communion with God, who shall provide us with everything we ask of him.

56'. Let us always add this after having prayed to the generous Lord: «Satisfy my desire, all-powerful Father, if it does not harm me or your children.»

57'. The man of weight and the lofty woman engender the perfect world.

58'. All arguments over words are paltry things with respect to the tangible reality of the embodied Lord that our eyes see, that our hands touch, that our mouth tastes and that our heart secretly shelters.

59. True faith in God and in his salvation can only be born and grow in the absolute freedom of individual choice.

60. Let us become sufficiently poor and simple so that no-one can rob or humiliate us, or let us become sufficiently rich and instructed so that nobody is capable of impoverishing or of disappointing us.

61. We need mad generosity and senseless love to forgive and to bless our enemies, but we need holy humility to ask their forgiveness for being right against their hate and against their blindness.

62. Let each one honour God in the secret tabernacle of his heart and let each one listen to the interior prophet who shall lead him to the Most-Unique One, the Most-Perfect One, the Most-Living One, the Purest One.

63. Love, beauty and the gift are repugnant to the mediocre and the hypocrites, for they themselves are hateful, ugly and dull, and it is for that reason that they try to soil and suffocate everything that surpasses them.

64. It is God who marks us for the quest of life, and it is he who leads us to the goal when we are humble, lov-

59'. The Father is hidden in the Son, as the Son is hidden in the Mother and as the Mother is hidden in the darkness of our hearts.

60'. If God lives in us and submerges us, we shall also do the works of God like beloved sons overflowing with love. «How much good it does us to listen to our God, and how marvellously his word fertilizes us when we are found to be pure, simple and believing!»

61'. If God does not pass into us, and if we do not pass into our fellow-being, we shall not be able to receive and transmit the blessing that saves from death.

«The wicked punish themselves for their wickedness, rejecting the Lord's help and that of holy and wise men.»

62'. Everything is possible for us, Lord, when you appear in us, but when you withdraw, it is there where we are more impotent and more stupid than the stones of the road.

63'. It is the Lord who makes us holy and alive forever, but it is we who grant or deny the secret entry of our hearts.

64'. The sages and the saints transpire God in spite of themselves, and that is their only source of virtue.

ing and obedient to his law of love. «The union of heaven and earth makes the light of the Perfect One appear.»

65. Our hands are powerless to sort life from death, and the humble knowledge of this truth is the only thing that allows God and nature to accomplish our deliverance here below.

«Thus, that which we do is nothing; it is that which God does in us that is everything.»

65'. The holy Name of God is a living and palpable reality that is capable of everything. It is a mystery that very few have known or shall know.

65". Let us be pious and believing, let us be simple and patient, let us be sober and peaceable, and let us cultivate the earth of the garden of Eden with the aid of the all-powerful Lord.

66. Love penetrates, love gives life, love exalts, love multiplies, love unifies in splendour.

66'. It is through the purity of grace that we magnetize divine love and that we embody God in ourselves.

67. The scholars and the intelligent of the world shall be quite disappointed on reading the Book, and shall say: «I cannot make head nor tail of this», for, precisely, the Book is a circle that guards the soul and that speaks to it inside.

67'. The word of God first humbles our reason, then secretly communicates its light to the soul, before enlightening the spirit, if we are attentive and persevering in our holy quest.

68. Who shall present to the Highest a mirror of love and purity so that he lives again among us in the primary and ultimate splendour?

68'. Our virgin has conceived under the gaze of the Highest and she has given us a son who has vanquished death and who shall make all his Highest brethren perfect.

69. There is no longer chance and there is no longer doubt for him who fixes God in spirit and who houses him in his heart. There are no longer tribulations nor death for him who is one with the Perfect One in his holy light.

69'. He who has seen the Lord, who has touched him and who has tasted him no longer has faith, fear or hope, for the possession of life enlightens him and enlivens him fully in the experimental certainty of the Unique One.

70. If we wish to stay alive, we must magnetize heavenly life within us, so that, in its turn, it attracts us to it, where there is no longer a place for death.

71. Many have nostalgia and the secret desire for God and are deeply troubled by it and sorry about it, for they do not know to whom their love is addressed.

70'. Who has seen the light of God shine on the land of the dead?

– Who has seen the Lord's gold fertilize the land of men?

– Who has seen the most-perfect Saviour multiply himself in the land of the living?

71'. It is the sincere love of God and the ardent desire of his knowledge that provoke the conditions of our meeting and our union with the living glorious one.

What use would it be to a man to win the world if he lost his soul?

JESUS

In everything and above all, repose in God, O my soul, because he is the eternal repose of the Saints.

IMITATION OF J.C.

BOOK XIX

Yes, in those days, I shall scatter my Spirit over my sons and my daughters, and they shall prophesy.

JESUS

He who is of God hears the word of God; it is because you are not of God that you do not hear it.

JESUS

NUEVITRÉE

1. The prophets have spoken to us of the substance and the essence of God, but we dissect their texts to discover in them history, morals, poetry or divination.
O stupid blindness of the intelligent and the scholars!
O self-satisfied mediocrity of the believers!

2. Who shall know how to trap the life of the Highest? Who shall know how to mature it and who shall know how to eat it so as to become like it, pure, free and eternal?

3. If we frequent the brutes, the wicked, the shrewd or the impious, we shall become like them. Moreover, if we frequent God and his true friends, we shall also be made in their image and we shall taste the beverage of pure life.

THE MIRROR

1'. Let us not adapt the holy Scriptures to our little thoughts, for in the end everything will go badly for us. Let us rather bend our desires to the word of God so as to enjoy the protection and aid of the All-Powerful One.
«If we cling blindly to our opinions, how will God be able to instruct us in life?»

2'. They are beautiful thoughts, say superficial people on leafing through the Book, but those who have been instructed think: «These are the locks and the keys of the gate of life.»

3'. The Book speaks to intuition, to love and to deep memory, and not to men's intelligence, will and superficial reason. «What the Book says is great, but what it induces in each one of us is incommensurable.»

4. The authentic sages and saints attribute to God alone the merit and the praise for everything they do in his NAME.
«O perfect humility of true knowledge!»

5. Religion and initiation transmit a precious teaching; it is up to us to resurrect it through our faith, enliven it with our love and manifest it through our knowledge.
«False believers are a thousand times more repulsive than impious brutes.»

6. The Book may well conceal the truth, but if our hearts do not participate in it, it is like a useless treasure before which all die of hunger and thirst.

4'. The science of nature leads to substantial knowledge, and the science of God leads to essential knowledge. He who possesses these two treasures is heir to the eternal and living Lord.

5'. What will the hypocrites say of him who calls Jesus-Christ his elder brother?
«Silence, then calumny, then persecution if they are allowed; it is the devil who now inspires them since God has left them.»

6'. Let us not think: «We shall become rich, then we shall seek God». But let us rather say: «We shall seek God, then we shall be rich».

6". Let us not sit at the table before a multitude of complicated dishes and drinks; let us rather prepare a tray with a simple dish and drink such as the bread and wine that satisfied our wise fathers.

7. As we cannot bear the simple, naked and perfect truth the Lord has to decorate it with foliage and flowers to content us. But he has also put thorns there so as to keep away the superficial and the inconstant.
«The Lord's crown may well poke out an eye of the imprudent and the presumptuous who throw themselves thoughtlessly at his head instead of adoring his holy and perfect feet.»

7'. If we are faint-hearted in our quest and if we dread to examine the foundation of all created things, we shall never find nor taste God here below.
«How weak, sad and poor we are when the Lord is absent from us, and look how lively, joyful and fulfilled we are, when he dwells once more in our hearts!»

8. The Book confirms the holy Scriptures just as a self-sacrificing child answers for his beloved parents.

9. «The more we give, the more we shall receive.» Thus, enrichment comes from the free circulation of goods, and impoverishment comes from their immobilisation.

10. He who hopes to seat himself at the divine banquet should not be surprised at not receiving here below the crumbs that satisfy the passers-by unfamiliar with love.
«O faithfulness at the primary and ultimate hour!»

11. Whoever we are and whatever we do, let us keep our spirit and our heart fixed in God so as not to lose ourselves in the darkness of this world.

12. He who adores God in spirit and in deed is assured of not making a mistake here below and elsewhere.

13. There is no insurmountable obstacle for he who cultivates goodwill in God, for the terrors of the night vanish before the light of the Perfect One.

14. If the mediocre can still germinate, it can only be through the warmth of brotherly love. Who would not want to try and save the most disinherited of humans?

8'. God became man in the flesh of Adam so that we could become God in the gold of Christ.

9'. He who loves God and his creation shall also be loved by all beings, for by loving we shall save and we shall be saved.

10'. He who curses the rich and the powerful denies himself ever becoming like them, on pain of being cursed by himself; but he who despises the poor has already condemned himself to the solitude of death.
«O how the secret gift washes the blemish of sin!»

11'. Let us see to it that our final thought is always in God, so as to purify our visions during the contemplation of wakefulness, during that of sleep and during that of death.

12'. He who seeks God goes to the solitude of nature. He who has found God returns to the society of men.

13'. Our Lord, who dwells in life, shall not abandon us at the difficult time of separation and deprivation, as long as we shine at least like glowworms in the night of the world.

14'. Let the sages and saints that have set us on the way to God be blessed forever in the most pure and most living bosom of the unique Splendour!

15. He who recognizes his faults disarms his enemies and transforms them into allies.

16. God looks for us in spite of ourselves when we hide from him. Why would we not look for him in spite of himself when he shies away from us?

17. Legions of ignorant men explain profane wisdom to us. Hordes of scholars impose foreign science on us. Crowds of intelligent men unveil to us the secrets of creation. A multitude of courageous men promise us happiness for tomorrow. Millions of delirious men multiply the madness of all. Thousands of false prophets describe their darkness to us.

18. And we continue, quite flabbergasted by their shouts and their gesticulations, to perish in ignorance and in fear, in doubt and in hatred, in solitude and in despair, in slavery and in misery, in old age and in sickness, for like them we have lost the divine knowledge, and have repudiated God's conscience, believing stupidly that we order the chaos with our derisory intelligence, reason and will.

19. It is the stench of sin that has led us to the pit. But it is the blessing of God that shall save us from death, and it is the warming love of the Lord that shall confirm us in the splendour of life.

15'. All that we love serves us and frees us. All that we hate escapes us and oppresses us in the end.

16'. The baptism of water delivers us and purifies us, but the baptism of the Holy Spirit fertilizes us and enlivens us fully.

17'. And you, poor rebels who are restless, who howl and who curse in the exile of death, you are lent some genius and you do not even have the intelligence to seek in silence and with patience the way out of your dark and icy prison.

You collide with the surface of words and things, and uselessly you throw words and things at the surface of the world.

18'. You are as lacking in perspicacity like your counsellor the devil, who stupidly judged by his appearance the first man that God presented him with. You who glorify hate daily, God has already excluded you from the land of the living, and you shall hate yourselves more and more until the final scattering.

«How brutal and unexpected is the fall of the wicked! And how forgiving is God towards those who return to him freely!»

19'. Our fellow-being and ourselves form the same Being and contain the same light. It is a secret of God that very few get close to and that only some chosen ones possess in its entirety, for souls remain different even in the bosom of the Unique One.

20. It is up to each one of us to seek Christ, to find him and to accommodate him so as to be saved, transformed and made perfect in him.

21. The stupid and the ignorant always want to be right in everything because they rely on themselves or on others.
The sages and the saints easily accept being wrong, for they refer it to God, who knows the foundation of all things exactly.

22. Many are filled with good intentions towards the holy Scriptures, but they are equally full of ignorance as regards their essential meaning.

23. The stars, the moon and the sun shine on the world while the intelligent and the scholars argue and rave about the invisible God who sends life and who attracts it towards himself.

20'. It is heavenly gold that we must embody (after ridding ourselves of the rottenness of sin), in order to be strengthened in eternal life.

21'. Let us consult the Lord and obey him in everything if we want to conserve the life, the health, the peace, the honour and the possessions he has granted us here below.
«God's saints radiate love for all his creatures.»

22'. If we possessed a simplicity and a faith capable of experiencing the incredible, we would penetrate the secret of the divine words and we would find the immortality of the garden of God again.

23'. He who is pure, luminous and living does not worry about it, yet he illuminates in the thickness of the night.
«To be and to forget it.»

23". The Spirit of God, by turning back on itself, produces the light.

24. When we have seized the Lord by his golden hair, when he has transformed our miserable thatched cottage into a palace, when he has become our victorious and unfailing companion, then we shall bless, with full knowledge of the facts, the holy Scriptures of all nations and we shall praise God and his work without books and without instructors.

24'. It is easy to reprehend the sinners, to denounce the hypocrites and to overwhelm the impious, but it is difficult to convert them by example and save them through love when one does not visibly know the unity from which they have emerged, and to which they shall return.
«He who knows the mystery of God loves his fellow-being naturally without hesitation and without effort.»

25. The whole creation is offered to us by God; we only have to choose and to sow in order to reap in abundance, be it the works of life or the works of death.

25'. Everywhere there are the scholars who dissect the holy Scriptures, everywhere there are intelligent who desecrate the mysteries of God, and not a single saint who purifies the earthly body, and not a single sage who accomplishes the divine incarnation.

26. The earth is black and shall become even blacker, then it shall whiten little by little and the stars shall reappear, the innumerable stars, the pure, white moon and the living, golden sun, which shall be the signs of the triumphant incarnation over death.

26'. It is the hand of man that prepares the earth, but it is nature that operates and God that gives life.
«If we constantly love and bless God and his creation, he will in his turn always love and bless us through it.»

27. Let us become benevolent and courteous to our fellow-beings and let us send good thoughts even to our enemies, so that they are converted to God in their heart. For curses can only entrench them in their opinions and in their obscure hatred.
However let us keep away from them until their wickedness has become extinguished.

27'. The wicked come from our lack of goodness, the poor from our lack of charity, the nonbelievers from our lack of faith, the rebels from our lack of obedience, and so on for all the rest. There we have the reason why it is always our fault and never that of others, contrary to what we commonly think.

28. O derision! The Lord has given us the Book first, and strangers have received it before us, for thinking ourselves intelligent in the world, we have become stupid before God.

28'. The better we come to know our indignity, the more we shall be terrified by the immensity of the Lord's mercy and by the greatness of the gift he grants us.

28". Who shall wash himself in the fire and in the water so as to become once again pure and white like the salt of life?

29. If God is badly served, let us distance ourselves from the bad servants, but let us not reject the Lord,

29'. He who feels free and rich in God no longer laments his poverty or the slavery of this world, for he

like the ignorant ones who crudely judge the inside from outside appearances, do.

30. We must strive to imitate God, who constrains nothing and no-one in the name of his truth and of his justice, but who matures everything patiently through the sweetness of his grace and of his love.

31. Men's wisdom is not God's wisdom, for the former looks at the outside while the latter considers the inside.

32. Let us not condemn or repel those who have gone astray, for it was not so long ago that we were still among them. Let us instead pray so that they come with us through the delivering grace and through the unifying love of the Highest.

33. Grace, love and faith engender living works; when they disappear, duty, law and coercion make for dead works.

34. If we bless God and his creation, life shall open up to us and receive us in its bosom. If we curse everything, life shall close itself to us and we shall remain abandoned in death.

35. Who shall go up to the end of the Lord's word? Who shall penetrate the luminous truth of the holy writings? Who shall practise the divine science on earth? Who shall enter the kingdom of eternity alive?

already tastes the deposit of eternal life.
«Inebriating promise! Incredible donation!»

30'. Goodwill in God delivers us from the constraints of the world, for it allows us to hear the Lord's teaching and gives rise to the action of his hidden Providence.

31'. Water comes from the body, and the body likewise comes from water, and the two unite in the glory of the most perfect Saviour.

32'. When the Lord visits us, here we are like enlightened gods, but when he leaves us, here we are like stupid beasts. Who can foresee the moment of his coming, and who can predict the time of his departure?

33'. Our desires are ten thousand things scattered and dead; God's will is a single thing concentrated and alive.

34'. Our holy spiritual masters are the instruments of God's blessing. Let us honour them and let us pray to them in the Lord so that they lead us to the holy light of God, which we lack so much here below.

35'. Lord, we kiss your sanctified earth, we sow your hidden heart and we preciously reap your incomparable glory that makes us live eternally.

36. If we possess grace and love and if we practise them with everyone, we can ignore law and duty, but if we still do not live in God, law and duty must guide us like the hard, dry cane guides the steps of the blind man.

37. A single verse shall enlighten one, while the other shall see nothing in the whole Book. «There is no why nor how for that which IS.»

38. Let us be those who do not manage themselves, but who have faith in the God who brings order to the chaos.
– Let us be those who demand nothing, but who seek eternal life.
– Let us be those who do not take possession, but who pray to him who showers us with blessings.
– Let us be those who do not envy, but who enjoy the gifts of the God of love.
– Let us be those who do not bustle about, but who work with the God of resurrection.
– Let us be those who do not condemn, but who ask God's forgiveness for everyone.
– Let us be those who do not amass, but who imitate the God of charity.
– Let us be those who do not fight, but who are patient with the God who separates and unites.
– Let us be those who do not kill, but who manifest the life of God by uniting heaven and earth.

36'. Prayer and praise that ascend towards God fall back on us in multiplied blessings, just as the good thoughts that we send to the living and to the departed, return to us in the form of unexpected gifts.

37'. Look how the word of the Lord makes the believer germinate, and how it hardens the impious one! «O depth! O mystery! O secret judgement of the Perfect One!»

38'. The ungrateful and the impious are not close to God, but neither are the flatterers and the hypocrites.
– The debauched and the lazy are not close to God, but neither are the moralists and the workers.
– The ignorant and the stupid are not close to God, but neither are the scholars and the intelligent.
– The rebels and the blasphemers are not close to God, but neither are the resigned and the narrators.
– The sensualists and the spendthrifts are not close to God, but neither are the inhibited and the thrifty.
– The wicked and the furious are not close to God, but neither are the well-intentioned and the snivellers.
– The righteous and the experts are close to God, but so are the charitable and the simple and, above all, those who have goodwill in God.

39. Let us examine where others are right and where we are wrong. Thus, an agreement shall easily be made by the coming together of similar kinds and the moving apart of opposites.

39'. All that we think, name and do becomes embodied and rushes towards us. Let us, then, pay close attention to our thoughts, to our words and to our actions, so as not to create our own misfortune without knowing it.

40. Hypocrites, proud men and the wicked destroy themselves mutually and blaspheme the word of God, either by blessing crime or by cursing love, for those who are swollen shall be emptied by the storm, and those who are hardened shall be crushed under the millstone. False brothers against enemy brothers. False devotees against devotees of dead science.

40'. The Lord does not abandon his own, those who love him in their heart and are submissive to the hidden wisdom. The net of misfortune and of extermination shall not close in on them, for the humility of their love and of their knowledge shall pass even through the tight mesh of death.

«How wretched is our love for the Lord, and how nonexistent is our faith in his Providence!»

41. Many wish to make us believe that they know more than anyone about the mysteries of God, quoting at random the magnificent words of prophets and sages, and interpreting them according to their wretched thoughts of the moment.

41'. O derision! they fight with the light of the holy and wise words, and yet they stagnate in the darkness.

O cruelty! they fight one another with sentences of life, and every day they rot more and more in the dung, for now the deaf lecture us and the blind show us the holy way!

42. Thus, one moralizes and the other emasculates. The latter dissects and the former stuffs; and they all look like penguins explaining the holy Scripture to other penguins.

42'. It is the practise of God's word and science that shall save us from death, and not our good intentions, our fine words or our great works.

43. All that we ask with faith and perseverance shall one day be accomplished before our eyes here below.

43'. Let us therefore keep watch attentively over all that enters and all that leaves, so as not to fall into the trap of the deceptive appearances of this world.

44. Let us do everything to please God and let us endure the blind judgements of the world patiently, without challenge and without profane justification.

45. O how does the good thought, the good word and the good deed erase the world's sin!
O how does praise, prayer and charity in God deliver the soul of the believer!

46. What shall be the ridicule of all those who shall have explained to us the word of God without having understood it themselves? And what shall be their assurance before the manifested obviousness on the last day?

47. The nonbelievers have named us «happy man», for the Lord's love has made us shine even before the blind!

48. They will want to affiliate us to churches, sects or secret societies to explain the inexplicable, for even the believers no longer believe that God is still capable of speaking directly to his children.

49. The wisdom of God is the freedom and abundance of life offered freely to simple and upright men.
The wisdom of the world is the noise and vanity of the hollow words which the blind reassure themselves with in their night.

44'. The Book shall still be new and present when all the proud productions of the world have returned to nothingness.

45'. He who gave us Being can also take it all back from us and give it all to us again.
Who can believe this in his heart before having seen it with his own eyes?

46'. He who has sown good seed waits confidently for harvest time. (Let us not think we can easily penetrate the inspired word of God if it has not itself first penetrated us.)

47'. The Lord's temple is his grace within our heart, and the sacrifice is his love for us and our love for him.

48'. We are not looking for slaves, sectarians or sheep, we are looking for men and women capable of living in a free and holy way in God. For the time of flocks is over, and the time of freedom is coming.

49'. The atheist thinks he will survive through his work and his intelligence.
The religious one thinks he will save himself through his hope and resignation.
Hardly one or two sages per century work the miracle of God here below and enter eternity alive.
(Their number is exaggerated on purpose.)

50. It would be better never to have been born rather than to despise the life we have been given by God, and that we have stupidly darkened.

51. Not a cent and the reprobation of everyone in exchange for the naked truth.
Money and the aid of the whole world in exchange for the disguised lie.

52. The brutes at least provide the repose for the spirit, while the hypocrites destroy faith, and the delirious communicate the madness of the devil. Happy is he who finds a believer in God and who converses with him about the Unique One; and blessed is he who reaches one of God's saints and who listens to him speak of the Lord of love.
Blissfully happy, most of all, is he who discovers one of God's sages and remains in his divine silence.

53. Satan is there to lose the wicked, but he is equally there to send back to God those souls enlightened by love and knowledge.

54. Do we know by any chance who this little child dying before us right now of the plague is?
Is it not the tight-fisted old employer who made a quarter of the town perish from misery?
Who judges God's justice here with the piercing sight of a mole?
Who condemns the wisdom of the Highest with the unshakeable assurance of a log?

50'. God's reason is beyond the absurd, the reason of men always remains this side of it.

51'. To be fulfilled by God and to live ignored by the world, and not to be fulfilled by the world and to live ignored by God.

52'. Lord, teach us the humility of your holy quest, place a heavy weight on our back and earth in our mouth until we consider the stump from which we were taken, and until your blessing delivers us from the stench of sin and the darkness of death.
Lord, out of compassion, make us be silent and explain nothing profanely and vainly to anyone.

53'. There is nothing obscure nor hidden in God's love, but in his science all is depth and mystery.

54'. O misfortune! The blind have set themselves up as strict judges and the deaf have become merciless executioners. Therefore, faith and charity have grown distant, and misfortune and confusion have now reached their peak in a world disfigured by sin, hate and fear.
«Who can firmly believe in the protection of the Unique One? And who can desperately hope for his holy gift?»

55. O how subtle is the devil, what a reasoner he is, and how well informed he is about the world!
O how the deceiver disguises himself, how he worms his way in and how skilful he is at trapping God's creatures!

55'. Let us be magnets of life and not magnets of death, and let us know that all that we think takes shape in us and around us and is fed by our words and our acts.

56. Well-named tempter, how well you test us in the blaze of envy and of pride!
You say «ME», but we reply «GOD».
O enemy, who shall save us from the vertigo of your darkened face, if it is not the love of our brilliant Lord who is so pure?

56'. Therefore, let us pay close attention to what we think and what we say, for if it is good, good shall appear, and if it is evil, likewise evil shall come.
«It is only God's love that truly fulfils and satisfies us. All else quickly disappoints and bores us. But it is also his holy science that saves us from death here below.»

57. He who pursues the things of the world is quite disappointed at the end of his pursuit, but he who looks for nothing dries up in his sad mediocrity.

57'. He who tirelessly seeks God and his truth has an opportunity to find them here below and the holy assurance of approaching them in heaven.

58. Let us confide in the Lord, who shall erase our pain and who shall multiply our joy, and let us not confide in the world, which shall envy our joy and reject our grief.

58'. If we love God in humanity and in nature, God will also love us in men and through all his creation.

59. After everything has been consumed, grace, justice, simplicity, obedience, forgiveness and love shall germinate once again and our God shall repose visibly in his saints, and all those that are saved shall give one another the kiss of peace on an earth whitened and reconciled by resurrection.

59'. The Book could be spun out infinitely; it is enough that it has made us touch the sacred root of the beginning and had a glimpse of the holy light of the Perfect One, for the Lord in person shall be the living word of the end for his sages and his saints.

60. The essential and substantial world shall be separated from the excremental world, and the former shall be glorified with God's saints, while the latter shall be thrown out with the rebels and the wicked.

61. We shall find God neither through the speculations of our intelligence nor through the work of our hands. We shall find God only by imitating God, for the sowing of our death prepares the harvest of our life.

62. Our reason, our courage and our work are powerless to open the gates of life for us if divine blessing and inspiration do not accompany them.

63. Why work hard and why fight ferociously to obtain life's shadow when the Lord generously offers us divine reality that never runs out?

64. It is good to offer a present to the spiritual master, but which is the intelligent disciple that shall send him a good thought of love?

65. Let us be like orphans seeking their Lord feverishly day and night, and then let us become like empty wine-skins waiting to be filled with the heavenly nectar.

66. We have fallen into the pit of filth and we have swallowed the dark rubbish.
Who shall deliver us now from the

60'. In the crepuscular beginning of the end, the stars shall come together to form, with the sun, the moon and the saints, the earth of the living fertilized by God, and that shall be then the dark medium of the end.

61'. Then, the light shall return little by little and the queen and the king of heaven shall appear in the divine splendour, and there will be the brilliant end of the end, announced and blessed by the Lord God's prophets.

62'. The Lord opens up understanding for him who is docile to his voice, and everything turns out for him effortlessly, but he blinds the senseless one who listens only to his own counsel, and leads him to his perdition.

63'. Do not force the Desired One, my friend, for if she is to come to you, she will appear by herself.
The Lord knows what he is doing, and you still do not know it.

64'. He who blesses God and his saints in his heart makes part of the Unique One's vestments shine visibly.

65'. A living person is forgiven everything, except for being present among the dying ones of this world.
«O holiest sacrifice of the sons of the Unique One!»

66'. O miraculous Lord, open our hearts to your holy dew and come and live in us once more in the primary splendour; if not, we are lost

stench of the sin that submerges us on all sides?

Who shall cure us of the virulent poison that eats our hearts out and that extinguishes our spirit?

Who shall separate the sanies from the living God?

67. It is of course our idiotic presumption that prevents us from recognizing the grandiose work of the Lord of life and light, and it is of course our attentive and holy humility that permits us to discover it in the world.

68. The sin and the fall is to have eaten the poisoned fruit from the dual tree, to have absorbed the living substance with the dead filth and to continue to do so.

forever and no-one shall feel sorry for us in our disconsolate lament here below.

«Wash us, rain of the heavens, and sow us, glorious sun.»

67'. First, we shall admire the works of men while we are sleeping; then, we shall admire the works of nature when we begin to see clearly. Finally, we shall admire those of God when we are fully awake.

68'. Regeneration and redemption is to discover and to eat the pure fruit of the unique tree that shall expel from us the stench, the darkness and the fatal inertia of death.

There will be a reunion of saved ones, as IEVE has said.
JOEL

Search for God, you all so humble ones of the country who have practised his law. Make search for justice, for humility. Perhaps you will be protected on the day of God's wrath.
ZEPHANIAH

BOOK XX

Due to disgust towards you, you were thrown onto the surface of the fields on the day you were born.

EZEKIEL

If you separate that which is precious from that which is vile.

JEREMIAH

VÊTE RUINE

1. He who perceives only the exterior wrappings of beings and things is separated from God's essential and substantial unity until his blindness ceases with the birth of the Saviour's light.

2. The holy Scriptures have been complete since their beginning, and each new book revealed does nothing more than confirm them without adding anything or taking anything away from the mystery of the incarnate spirit, which constitutes their sacred foundation.

3. Who can say this without blaspheming and who can hear it without being scandalized? Our sacrifices and our crimes are equally illusory before God. Our blessings and our curses are likewise worthless before his greatness.

SALT

1'. It is the purity of the Mother's substance that will allow us to embody the splendour of the Father's essence, and thus become true sons of God throughout eternity.

2'. Teach us to hear you and obey you.
Teach us to love you and imitate you.
Teach us to receive you and mature you.
Teach us to conserve you and multiply you, O Lord of imperishable life!

3'. Why try to advance and why fear retreating? Why strive to ascend and why dread falling? For it is enough that the grace of the Unique One strips us of poisonous sin and that his love clothes us in golden splendour.

4. Our thoughts of love or hate are completely derisory before his splendour; only our repose and our goodwill in him are approved of by the Unique One.

5. For even our love for the Lord is only a reflection of his glory and it does not belong to us, while obedience and acceptance are the acceptable offerings of a heart buried in death and broken by exile.

6. We are all unworthy of receiving the word of God. Because of this, he does not stop reminding us mercifully of it so that we should never forget the humility of the creature and the glory of the creator.

7. On asking my Lord one day: «What must I do to please you?», he replied to me: «Nothing, above all nothing, so that I might water you in total peace and so that I might mature you in total safety».

8. There are two ways to get out of everything, either from above or from below. He who leaves the world the high way is holy and saved. He who leaves it by the low way is mad and damned.

9. Like the monkey who remains a prisoner in his gourd, his hand obstinately gripping the bait, it is also enough for us to let go of the fistful of mud that we stupidly clutch in this world in order to be returned to our primary freedom. However, every-

4'. Is the goodwill of our heart towards the Lord and his creation not enough to be forgiven for the imbecilic fault and to be saved from the foul death at the end of time?

5'. Teach us, O Purest One, to behave according to your holy will, and give us the intelligence of your sublime teaching, as well as the understanding of your sacred work.

6'. If the world rejects our works and our gifts, let us turn towards God and let us offer him our attentive silence and our relaxed uselessness, which will certainly be more welcomed and more appreciated by the unique expert.

7'. We shall stop our ablutions when we gleam with purity, and it is then that God's sun shall fully fertilize us, for it is a viriginal and light heart that we shall offer to the Lord and it is a sown and dense heart that he shall give to us in exchange.

8'. We shall await him in order to be awaited. We shall look for him in order to be looked for. We shall find him in order to be found. We shall repose in his peace in order to be unified in him.

9'. My Lord asked me once: «What shall you bring me on the day of judgement?» And I replied: «You in your secret in me». Then he said: «Very well. Go then, germinate, ripen and produce fruit for my harvest» and I cried bitterly at being still

one makes fun of monkeys, and no-one barely makes out his own greediness.

10. Who would still wish to argue with ignorant creatures when God converses with us so marvellously in our hearts?

11. O music of musics!
O perfume of perfumes!
O flavour of flavours!

12. How shall the spring that has not been tightened be released? And how shall he who has not madly looked for the Lord in the world discover him in himself?

13. We shall pray in order to learn to praise, and we shall praise in order to learn to be silent before him.

14. This one explains to us in detail the incarnation of God, without even knowing the virginal nature of the holy Mother; that other demonstrates to us the mystery of Christ, without even knowing the virtue of the sun that illuminates him.

15. Therefore, too many scholars overwhelm us with their science, while they hear nothing, see nothing and taste nothing of the unique truth, for their knowledge of God is intellectual and bookish, instead of being experimental and experienced.

16. One day, returning to the world after a conversation with my

covered by the mud of the foreign land.

10'. To put the mud of the world in order is a stopgap measure; to come out of it, there is intelligence!

11'. The science of men organizes the pit of death, but the science of God delivers us from it forever.

12'. God's judgement is not man's judgement, and what one exalts the other despises.

13'. «When you love one another as I love you, you shall be one with me», says the Lord of the unity of love.

14'. Finally, the ushers came and threw out all those who were waiting in the antechamber in the house of the Highest, but I continued to wait on the steps of the threshold, until sleep came to calm my despair and cover my solitude.

15'. And it is there that he found me and took me in his arms to console me, and when I awoke I was in his very bed. He smiled at me like an attentive and happy mother that has found her lost child again.

16'. When we have found the Lord in the inside of our heart, shall

Lord, I felt sudden nausea and frightful sadness. Thus I knew that my great pain was beginning here below, when in fact I thought it was over.

he perhaps make himself seen also outside in the world?

O distinguished rarity! O supreme confidence! O terrifying test of the total gift!

How many have been able to bear without dying your visible presence and your incarnate splendour?

17. We shall think we are making a sacrifice by giving up the world and turning towards God. Then, we shall understand that it is the Lord who sacrifices himself by turning towards us.

17'. «We do not choose God, it is he who chooses us.» By being in repose and remaining attentive, shall we perhaps hear him and see him one day here below?

18. How can we believe in God in this absurd world when the light of the Perfect One has not been seen to shine?

18'. O infinite mercy of blind faith! O amazing security of divine love!

19. There are no competitions, juries, examinations, prizes, medals or diplomas that count in the quest for the Highest.

19'. It is God's idlers and God's blessed ones who shall win the celestial stake, and not the workers and the intelligent of this world.

20. Only a broken heart, in which the Lord gently separates the truth from the lie, so as to come and dwell in it in all his rediscovered glory.

20'. He who keeps his eyes fixed on his Lord moves forward stepping equally over the gold and the mud of mixed creation.

21. The best way towards God is the greatest attention in the greatest abandonment, after the long and arduous quest in the darkness of faith.

21'. How difficult it is to find again the joy of one's Lord when one has pursued the world and when one has received in payment its flowers or its spittle!

22. We shall easily do without the exterior world on the day when we can no longer do without the interior Lord.

22'. Two things distress us: our estrangement from the Lord and our stupidity before his creation, but a third one terrifies us: the filth that masks for us the light of the Perfect One.

23. If the world reveals itself to us like a rotten plank, let us lean on the Lord who never shies away when a beloved one comes to rest in his bosom.

24. The best way to serve God is to be like a signpost that indicates the road of the unique Splendour for other men.

25. To contemplate one's Lord and organize the world is impossible. It is necessary to choose at the beginning so as not to hesitate at the end.

26. He who approaches his Lord here below shall say: «My life has been a perpetual feast» and the others shall add: «He was a saint» after having spat on him. As for the wise possessor of the unity of the Unique One, very few shall recognize him in his mortal wrapping.

27. Having rejected their Lord, they have plunged themselves into horror to forget their grief, but they have only increased it tenfold. Who shall now give them back the peace of the Perfect One?

28. The Lord has not given us any recipes for coping in the mud of the world, but he has made us see how we can emerge from it altogether.

29. The saint is neither distant, nor important, nor superior with anyone, but he is truthful with everyone,

23'. We shall be able to love men all the more insofar as we ask nothing of them, and we shall be able to love our Lord all the more insofar as we ask all of him.

24'. How marvellous is the presence of the Lord, and how terrible is his absence!
Most secret companion. Most holy company. Most beloved one that is accompanied.

25'. Neither the joys nor the pains of this world must make us forget the refuge of unique candour.

26'. God's idlers receive all from the hands of their Lord, while the workers of the world suffer severely to lack all here below.
«These idlers can work like the workers, but what worker could idle like these idlers?»

27'. How could the love of God and of the saints turn away from a being, however disfigured he may be because of the fall? Isn't Satan himself likely to rejoin his Lord some time if he desires it once?

28'. He who contemplates his Lord can laugh frankly at himself, after having cried about himself for a long time. He no longer has anything to fear of misery nor anything to expect of the riches of the world.

29'. Some have persevered with the love of their Lord in the midst of griefs and pains, but how many have

and that is why he exasperates the hypocrites and the mediocre.

30. How many, among the better ones, have been kept away from God by the mediocrity of those who teach his salvation! How confused shall be the ones gone astray who will have rejected the Lord because of the bad servants! But what shall be the fate of the mediocre servants who will have hindered men of goodwill!

31. Death cuts us down unexpectedly and rakes us up in the blink of an eye, and there go all our little worries and all our little thoughts, vanished in an instant.
Oh! Who shall have the intelligence to search assiduously for his Lord here below in order to obtain the victory of life?

32. O believers scattered over the earth, you shall one day resuscitate and embrace one another in the name of God, crying for joy, like brothers and sisters who meet again in the place of their birth, and you shall live in the purity where there is no death.

33. Let us enter the repose and distance ourselves from the issues of the world, for it is the only means of obtaining the leisure and the peace that are indispensable to the quest for God that shall make us beautiful, rich, glorious, powerful and immortal, when we have found the unique treasure.

remembered him amid the joys and possessions of this world?

30'. Any son of God, if he received the order, would reveal the secret of the Unique One, and all creation would revive in the primary splendour. Only the insufficiency of the mediocre and the malice of the wicked are opposed to it, but the Lord of the centre knows the hour of judgement.

31'. Let us not sleep on the Book, let us also put our hand to the resurrection and to the transfiguration of the darkened world; thus, we shall have the immortal and pure life of the beginning, which fulfils God's children.

32'. Have intelligence, and the light shall illuminate your way.
Have purity, and the Highest shall sow your field.
Have patience, and your land shall produce salvation.
Have simplicity, and heaven shall multiply your virtue.

33'. Have heart, and you shall possess the treasure of the children of God.
Have sobriety, and you shall swim in the wealth that never dries up.
Have faith, and the Lord himself shall work for you.

34. It does not matter what we look like in the eyes of the world, it is only what we are before the Lord of truth that counts.

«The insults and spittle of the wicked shall add nothing to the garment of mud that covers us, just as they shall take away nothing from the core of light that lives in us.»

34'. The intelligent of the world shall mock us and shall shower us with insults because of the word of the Lord of life, but it is enough for our joy that a simple and shrewd heart understands and practices here below God's way before the time of the great judgement, which shall consume all filth and shall separate all faeces from the glorious body.

34". MARANATHA.
He is surely coming.

35. Not a thought, not a look, not a word, not a gesture for evil; thus, it will not take shape and life in us nor around us, and if it appears due to the effect of the ancient fault, we shall think the good, we shall see the good, we shall name the good and we shall accomplish the good, so that the light of life invades us and subsists alone in us and around us.

35'. Let us tie the good words around our neck and live with them until they have entered us.

First, let us rely on the Lord's Providence, then let us work in a holy way so as to give body to his transforming blessing.

«Who shall eat the word issued from heaven and earth so as to possess the life that does not perish?»

36. The jobs that are necessary for the maintenance of our lives do not amount to much for those who think about God more than about the labour of their hands.

«Deliverance from the curse of death flies towards him who prays to his Lord with love and with overcoming.»

36'. Let us associate God with our works and with our suffering, but let us also associate him with our leisure and our pleasures, so that evil cannot enter us during the absence of the Perfect One.

37. Let the intelligent and the scholars of the world not get upset if they remain at the door of the Book with all their intelligence and with all their learning, and let them forgive us that which seems obscure to them, for we do not wish to convince nor to instruct them despite themselves.

37'. We must teach our brothers to pray to God so that they obtain his grace and his help, instead of carrying them on our back, which could not teach them to walk in faith, and which could not make us move forward on God's children's road to freedom.

38. If we are strong in our weakness, it is because then the strength of God lives fully in us and acts in our place.

39. Let us not enter any competition in this world, for our performances are ridiculous before God.

40. He who knows that God alone operates all in everything is not tempted to boast about his works here below. Let us therefore place our hope more in the Providence of the Lord than in the works of our hands. Hard words for the intelligent, for the courageous and for the reasonable of this world.

41. He who has learned to fall also knows how to pick himself up again without hurting himself, but he who has not learned this runs the risk of breaking one of his limbs or even his whole body due to his excessive rigidity.

42. Let us not do anything that we would not also dare to accomplish in the presence of God.

43. Those who will have been cleansed by the fire of *Gehenna* will have to be purified with middle water and revived by the celestial spirit so as to acquire the incorruptibility of the kingdom of God.

38'. Prayer and praise to God make the joy of saints and sages, but it is absence and silence that make the presence of God's word and the union of the perfect ones.

39'. If we cannot push ourselves unto God, let us boldly pull him towards us. It might work better that way.

40'. Our works are useless without the blessing of the radiant Lord, for they can do nothing without it, while it can do everything without them; however, by uniting them through a natural means, we shall obtain the repose and the glory of God.

41'. No-one knows the thickness of the mantle of filth that covers us, except the saint who consumes it, and no-one knows the weight of the light that dwells in us, except the sage who matures it in secret.

42'. He who associates God with all his thoughts and with all his deeds becomes one with the Perfect One.

43'. Oil joins with salt by means of water, and water becomes fixed in salt by means of oil, and everything remains in One.

> 43". O humble ashes of mortification!
> O living water of blessing!
> O pure salt of baptism!
> O holy oil of resurrection!

44. Who shall study the Book and who shall travel along the way of the Unique One?
«When in doubt, let us place ourselves in the hands of God, who speaks to us through the interior voice, and let us do his will, for he knows perfectly the right, the left and the middle of man».

45. Let us manifest the inside outwardly, as our handsome Lord, descended from heaven, has done.
«Blessing and curse proceed from the interior vision of the spirit and from faith in action through the word.»

46. The Providence of God is manifested preferentially through the mediation of believers of goodwill; but it can exceptionally act by means of spirits, or even directly by combining primordial elements.

47. God forms and dissolves images, but he saves some of them through the Son, who is similar to the Father.

48. All is potential in the hidden substance, and it is our thoughts that manifest the desirable or the undesirable.

49. It is our interior vision that we must exercise and animate until it appears alive and pure in the world.

50. Let us neither imagine nor name the undesirable so as not to give it body and life in us and around us.

44'. Let us free our virginal queen, and she shall give us a son who shall save the human race and restore it in its primary splendour.

I.N.R.I.

45'. Desire gives the substance. Imagination gives the form. The word gives the weight.
Faith gives life, but the purity of the heart is the only thing that allows for union with God the creator and renovator of all things.

46'. Let us not imagine the means of accomplishing our prayer, for the ways of the Lord's Providence are unpredictable, disconcerting and impenetrable for our petty reason.

47'. That which is clearly established inside is already on the way to being accomplished outside in the world.

48'. It is the world inside that shall change first, then the world outside shall also be made clear and beautiful.

49'. The living faith is mad and absurd, for it does not even take into account the reasonable appearances of death.

50'. It is safer to be with God than to be against anyone, for in this way we are certain of never being wrong, and of taking the shortest path.

51. Let us go there where the Providence of God smiles on us, and let us leave the ways where it impedes us.

52. All that resembles a work of man is not of God, and shall disappear in the new world.

53. Hell is death maintained in us perpetually; it is life forever dying and being reborn; it is the stench and the horror of the rotting filth mixed with the light of life.

54. If we feel abandoned and sad, if we are tempted and agitated, let us immerse ourselves in the reading and the meditation of the wise Scriptures, which shall suffuse us with the joyous light of the Purest One.

55. He who has found the light of the Lord can abandon the Book; God shall establish him in peace through his love, just as he has introduced him into grace through his blessing.

56. The proud obstinacy of man is such that the weaknesses of his flesh and the fragility of his condition do not succeed in returning him to the liberating and renewing humility where God's secret reposes.

51'. Let us go where the heavenly life is embodied in the pure and holy earth.

52'. He engenders his Mother, and his Mother engenders him in the world for the safeguard of the saints and the sages.

53'. Let us work all the days of our lives at separating and rejecting the filth of death that has invaded us since the primary fall, for it is a pleasant and holy job in the eyes of the Lord, who shall come to our aid by delivering us completely from her, this putrescent foreigner.

54'. Let the desire and the will of our creator and donor, holiest and wisest Father, be accomplished in us perfectly, and let the pure rediscovered unity of the three worlds place us into the eternal presence of the Living One who IS.

55'. The purity of the Lord shall invade the whole earth and shall consume the filth of death, erasing our sin through the unheard-of miracle of the separation and the holy union.

55". For the height of mortification manifests heavenly life, which in turn engenders the eternity of God's peace.

56'. He who cultivates his garden and digs his own earth carries out a job that is agreeable to God. Most certainly, the Lord's snow shall consume his sin and he shall shine before all nations, and his word shall have the density of fermented gold.

57. Some receive the word of resurrection and life directly and entirely, but others can only absorb it little by little and with great difficulty.
Those who reject it are already excluded without knowing it.

58. Also, if we are allowed to cry with joy about the former, we are recommended to be patient with the latter, and above all not to put them off with blind and deaf intransigence.
«Priests condemned Jesus to torture and soldiers nailed him to the cross.»

59. Let us praise the Blessed One for all that we have and thank him for all that comes to us. Thus, we shall always be fulfilled and rich in the Lord.

60. When the ignorant of this world treat us as if we were useless, idlers and cowards because of our quest for the divine treasure, we may consider ourselves quite fortunate, because we shall be assured of being on the way of the unique Splendour.

61. The souls of the believers and the blood of the impious shall not rise up against us on the day of reckoning, for the Book shall be our witness before the Highest, and everyone shall remain silent before the prodigious revelation of the Unique

57'. Let us not go astray in the dispersion of our hearts, nor in the agitation of our spirits nor in the works of our hands. Let us rather remain in the perseverance of the quest for the Unique One, which shall fulfil us well beyond our desires.

58'. Who shall rejoin the Lord of the centre from this world?
Who shall return to the pure and inexhaustible Father before the universal judgement?
Who shall go through the darkness of earthly exile once again?
Who shall overcome the test of the mortal fall?
Who shall follow the Lord of resurrection here below?

59'. A good encounter is worth more than a thousand good ideas, and the frequenting of the Lord is worth more than all the riches of the earth.

60'. The rebel and those who serve him bustle about in blind dispersion and in frenzied work. The Lord and his nearest delight in the unity of the heart and in the holy repose of the accomplishment of all things.

61'. O intelligent ones! where will your tricks be?
O scholars! where will your lights be?
O workers! where will your works be?
O mediocre! where will your judge-

One, but some shall rejoice while others shall weep bitterly.

62. Let us place our causes in the hands of the Lord of justice, and our sleep shall be peaceful and no blemish shall throw a shadow over the light of our hearts.

63. Let us be demanding with ourselves, but let us do violence to nothing, either within or without; let us instead ask for the help of the All-Mighty One, who constantly holds out a helping hand to us.

64. The ignorant of the world shall mock God's science like those who seek it and will say: «If the thing were true, everybody would know it.» Thus, they cut themselves off from the lordly secret for ever, and their light remains buried in the darkness of death.

65. If we do not know how to pray, let us simply say: «My Lord and my God» and the dark void of our hearts shall change into the plenitude of the holy light of the chosen ones, and we shall hear the voice of the Most-Secret One and we shall do his will without vainly arguing.

ments be?
O important ones! where will your assurances be?
O hypocrites! where will your disguises be?
O mockers! where will your witticisms be?

62'. O All-Blessed One! remove the sack and the dead ash that blind us so that we can see your light of wisdom and so that we can praise forever your holy NAME in your rediscovered glory.

63'. That which we have done with our hands totters and already collapses behind us, but that which we have to do with our heart can become imperishable like the heavenly stone. «The ignorant ones separate brutally that which the sage unties with patience.»

64'. When all has become evident and clear, but there where no hand will be able to stretch out to seize the resplendent life of God's children, who shall weep and shall truly rejoice?

65'. The outside does not amount to much for him whose light shines within, for he sees through the outer layer and penetrates beyond death.
«The more we consume our outer layers, the more resplendent shall be our light under the gaze of the Highest. That is what the wicked shall not understand.»

66. We shall call ourselves incapable, useless and stupid when we rest in the contemplation of the Unique One; or else we shall call ourselves charlatans, jugglers and clowns when we teach his holy law in the world.

67. Thus, nobody shall be able to insult us or stain us, and the door shall remain closed to the proud, the hypocrites and the mediocre.

68. A multitude of goods engenders a multitude of worries, and too many things distract us from the quest for the Unique One; but poverty is only possible there where heaven and earth are generous and gentle.

69. We think we are intelligent, honourable and important, and this prevents us from living pleasantly in the simplicity and in the joy of God's children.

70. There is no success in the world for he who seeks God, but only failures and repeated blows, most opaque darkness and solitude that makes him cry over himself, but what a reward at the end, when the light of the Unique One illuminates God's children's way!

71. The most evident state of the unique Splendour is free and pure life. Thus, let us not victimize anything or anyone, be it in thought, word, or deed, if we wish the Subtlest One to establish his dwelling in our purified hearts.

66'. It is not up to us to take ourselves seriously, nor to demand of others that they do so. That is up to God, who is the only one to see the inside of creatures clearly.

67'. As for us, it is enough that our hearts germinate in the darkness of the world, flower in the light of the Unique One and become fixed in his glorious sun.

68'. Let us liquidate the superfluous so as not to be dispersed among the multiplicity, and let us constantly verify, through the inspiration of the Unique One, the need for our action and the rectitude of our quest in the world.

69'. It is better to pass for a madman by talking of the things of God, than to pass for a sage by talking of the things of the world.

70'. One must be mad for God to believe beyond the sinister appearances that blind us, that crush us and that drive us to despair here below. So let him make us mad, so that we become wise and find the light of life that is never lacking for those who have once known it!

71'. O compassionate Lord, move away from our bones the horrible stench that kills; remove from our hearts the dark filth that blinds us and make your light of life shine over your reconciled children.
O wisest and holiest Renovator!
O all-powerful and hidden Saviour!

72. The companion who rebels against the holy quest of her companion would be rejected in the end, and her remorse would be most cruel, for she would have had the greatest of all chances in this world.

«The fate of each one rests in his heart, and the Lord of equity is the sole judge.»

73. He who remembers God loves God.
He who loves God hears God.
He who hears God obeys God.
He who obeys God imitates God.
He who imitates God knows God.
He who knows God embraces God.
He who embraces God becomes one with God.

72'. O women! your malice in the world is great, but your intelligence in God is small. Therefore, retain your thoughts and judgements with regard to your fellow-being and do not despise the seekers of God, so as not to burn one day in the devouring fire of tardy regrets.

73'. Eternal glory to the living and splendid Lord who inspires his sages and his saints and saves them from death.

M.O.I.O.M.

«Perfect faith is simple and absurd; that is why it is all-powerful.»

73". There is an important and urgent prayer that we must repeat every day of our exiled life:

«Deliver us, all-powerful Father, from the disgusting filth that submerges us on all sides, so that we become resplendent once more in your purity, and fertilize us with your holy love, so that we become fixed in you for eternity.»

AMEN.

The stone hidden in the darkness and the shadow of death.

JOB

There, there will be a way that shall be called the holy way. No impure one shall pass along it... Those who will follow it, even the simple ones, shall not go astray from it.

ISAIAH

BOOK XXI

> *Many shall be purified, whitened and tested; and the wicked ones shall do evil, and no wicked one shall understand it, but the intelligent shall understand it.*
>
> DANIEL

> *They have perished because they did not possess the true science. They have perished because of their madness.*
>
> BARUCH

VUE NITRÉE

1. A single verse shall spark off vocations, and a single word shall bring souls back to God. Therefore, what will the whole Book not do in the spirit and in the heart of believers?

2. God has engendered us from his pure substance and essence, and we have thrown ourselves stupidly into the quagmire of death.

3. Satan was deceived by the appearance of Adam, that is why the Lord allowed Adam to be deceived by Satan through the appearances of the world, and for the sons of Adam to suffer the same disturbing ordeal.

4. The nonbelievers say: «This Book is nothing», but we say: «It is a monument that the believers of heaven and earth shall visit with veneration, while the name of the deniers will have disappeared forever

FROST

1'. The poorest is like the richest in this world before God's secret. However, the poor man is not tempted to disperse himself in the onerous complications that lead the rich seeker astray.

2'. If we ask him with tenacity and love, the Lord can pull us out of the pit of perdition in which we lie dying here below.

3'. Those who have fallen in the darkness and will then get up again in the light shall be established forever in the glory of God.

4'. Let us confess to the Highest in this way: «I accuse myself of having fallen here below through my own fault, and of being in the lamentable state in which you see me, but would your will deliver me from the horri-

from the memory of God and of men».

Let us not join the impious, for they shall not become believers, but they shall make us impious.

5. A sweeper is more highly esteemed than a prophet in this blind world, for he seems less useless than he who announces the truth of God to men. The latter is despised by his own, and passes for an incurable idler in the eyes of everyone.

6. Christ wants to save us from the filthy ditch into which we have fallen, while the antichrist wants to install us there forever. Behold God's action and behold Satan's, here lies a fundamental difference that must separate once and for all the true believers, who trust in the action of divine nature, from the hardened impious ones, who only count on the labour of their hands to save themselves.

7. How shall the Lord maintain us if we do not take care of the beings that we are in charge of here below? How shall the hand of our angel discharge us of such heavy burdens if we charge others immeasurably?

8. Machines are stupid, and their stupidity shall always drag us too quickly and too far from the contemplation of the Unique One and from his holy quest.

ble mud of the sin of death and clothe me in your holy light of life, O Merciful One! whose heart is a blaze of forgiveness and love, you, eternal Lover of beloved souls».

5'. I have doubted my Lord's care and aid, and he has satisfied me generously instead of scolding me and punishing me for my wavering faith. O how you take care of my weakness! O how patient you are with my stupidity! O how you illuminate my mire, attentive and hidden Lord!

6'. O all-powerful and merciful Lord! take off the sack that makes us blind and deaf, break the shackles that squeeze our necks and our hands, and untie the bonds that fetter our feet so that we can walk in your light of life, making public your bounty and raising our hands as an offering to your so-holy face. Praise be to you who delivers us from the outside through the inside, O Living One! for you make a mockery of all death forever.

7'. He who maltreats or neglects a child, an animal or a plant excludes himself from the blessing of God and falls into the hazard of the stone and the pit. However, the child that strikes us shall be whipped, the animal that attacks us shall be struck down, and the plant that tears us shall be cut down and burned.

8'. Let us not continually rail against that which displeases us: let us rather abandon it and let us be content with the bread of the earth and the water of heaven with the repose and the joy of the Perfect One.

9. All my friends remember me and make me happy with their gifts and with their good thoughts, without me doing anything for them. Thus the Lord, who fulfils me with his joy and his love, kindly reminds me that I am equally unworthy of his graces and his laughter.

10. Let us keep ourselves from identifying with the defective things we do every day so as not to be drawn into defending the indefensible nor justifying the unjustifiable.

11. Let us never argue vainly in order to be right; let us rather question humbly and then let us experience the truth of the reply in our spirit and in our heart.

12. When the clerics drop the torch of God, it is up to the believers to pick it up and place it back on the altar so that once again it lights up the darkened world.

13. And the clerics who have remained alert and faithful to their Lord must help these believers to restore the true worship of God, which is accomplished in the heart of men, instead of forming a body with the invasive frigidity of dead stones.

14. With their self-satisfied mediocrity and with their repulsive hypocrisy, some «right-thinking ones» can even disgust the impious. How

9'. I was drying up on the dead sand for a long time, but when the Lord's dew blessed me, I flourished once again in the airy secret of snow and I ripened in the weight of purified gold.

«If the Spirit of God is with us, who can oppose our preaching in the world?»

10'. The Lord's prophets have been held in contempt by their close ones and persecuted by their people simply because they have always been adamant in relation to God's revealed truth.

11'. O Most-Precious One! give us the intelligence of the mysterious sentences pronounced by the sages of your house and make our hidden life flourish.

12'. It is more intelligent and more advantageous for those who are in power to test and adopt those who are inspired and who scold them, than to stifle their voice in the silence or make them disappear through violence.

13'. For God's truth always re-emerges triumphantly from the dark prison to which it is consigned by the faint-hearted ones, and it always germinates irresistibly from the ashes with which the wicked cover it.

14'. If we truly «love», no evil shall reach us, and the freedom, joy and peace of the Unique One shall dwell in us forever. «God's children shall

could they not also be repulsive to the seekers of the Unique One? And how could they be known by God?

15. Whatever our aberrations and our faults, let us continually return to the quest for the Unique One without becoming discouraged and without doubting the end.

16. Let us stop fighting in the world in order to amass riches, for the hour is coming, and it has already come, when we must abandon everything and appear before justice with only our good thoughts, our good deeds and our repose in the Unique One.

17. Examined from outside, the rose windows of cathedrals only allow their framework to show, but seen from inside, their brilliance illuminates the believer. Thus, the word of life heard from outside only allows the bone of truth to be glimpsed, while this very word perceived from the inside allows us to taste the nourishing marrow of the creator of all things.

18. The Book has germinated in a man deemed by many as: useless, lazy, revolted, proud and even impious, for the humour of the Perfect One enjoys accomplishing great things with derisory instruments.

flourish in the peace of the Lord, while the rebels shall perish and dry up in it without return.» Behold the mark and behold the judgement.

15'. O my Lord! you speak to my soul and all else is erased, for your plenitude is established in me and invades heaven and earth.

16'. In the quest for God, we shall only come across brothers who shall help us with kindness, while in the pursuit of the world, we shall have to deal solely with competitors who shall fight hard against us. Let us note this well and let us distance ourselves from worthless controversy.

17'. O important ones! O powerful ones! O wealthy ones! O scholars! O intelligent ones! what do you contribute to the Lord whom you question with such conceit? or rather, what do you offer to humanity in whose name you speak with such impudence?

Worthless words that meet with the silence of death, and empty works that rot on the surface of the earth.

18'. The Book shall shine on the world like a sun, and when it has returned to the Unique One, its light and its warmth shall be still perceptible for a long time in the heart of men.

«Let us pray that he who gave it to us repose in the adorable peace at the centre of the Unique One.»

19. We seek the two columns of the Temple and we have them before our eyes and within reach of our hands, but our hearts are darkened by the sin of the fall and the truth of God has withdrawn into the well of the abyss.

20. Gratitude towards the creator is most rarely found in fallen humanity; beasts are unanimous in saluting his image, but we do not blush with shame at being the only ones to scorn it here below.

21. The symbols of God's mysteries can be proposed to all believers, but God's mysteries must be reserved solely for wise and holy men. Women are opposed to them by nature.

22. The nonbelievers do not hear the Lord because they are not the first to speak to God. How shall we open their heart and mouth if the Lord does not aid us in person? For pride is an impenetrable armour-plate under which life is dying, and none other than God can break it from outside or melt it from the inside.

23. Let us pray that the angel of death finds us praising and blessing God at the hour of separation and reunion.

24. When we are floating effortlessly in the light of life, we shall rejoice in God, but we shall weep on remembering our unbelieving companions who shall wallow in the

19'. Separate that which is united, and the darkness shall make you see the beginning of the work. Join together that which is separated, and the light shall lead you to the end of the divine work, which is the glorious sun.

20'. If we do not go boldly towards the Lord with our eyes closed, the Lord shall not come to us, and he shall not take off the blindfold that covers our eyes and that impedes us from drawing near to the amazing light of the Unique One.

21'. The inconstancy of Eve has dragged Adam out of Eden. The constancy of Adam shall lead Eve back and convert her within the bosom of God.

22'. O incomprehensible temptation! O vertiginous mystery! we refuse to judge and we lie on the ground, crying for our lost brothers, until the Lord takes us away through the sole power of his love, for we can do nothing but wait whimpering for the conversion of the ones gone astray and the forgiveness of God.

23'. Let us praise God and let us confess in our hearts before the Lord so that he washes us of the invasive mud of the sin of death.

24'. O beloved brothers who read this, convert yourselves in your hearts while your time is still measured! Stop being restless in the wind of the night and consider attentively

agony of beasts. Only the fate of the hypocrites shall leave us indifferent.

25. Our hearts are impatient on seeing the success of the impious, but we have chosen the reward of the Lord's life, and our hope shall not be dashed.

«The senseless serve the world that delivers death to them, the believers serve God who lavishes life upon them.»

26. We have only proposed God's truth, but the mediocre and the faint-hearted have become frightened before the rawness of the thing, and they have entrenched themselves behind their blind judgement.

27. Those who are capable of scrutinizing God's truth, even through the horror of death, are the only ones who deserve to see the lamp of the Perfect One shine.

the end of all things, so as not to let yourself be seduced by the appearances of this world.

25'. The angel of the Lord was in me and put pressure on me from all sides to proclaim the truth of the Unique One, «for», he said, «many ears are now attentive inside the Church and outside of the Church».

26'. It is not up to us to dress up God's truth to seduce the incapable. It is up to us only to present it in its nakedness, so that they can judge themselves, being scandalized, and pushing it far away from them.

27'. Who shall bind the spirit?
Who shall embody the soul?
Who shall purify the body?

27". O divine sun of God, you sow us in death, you make us grow in life and you establish us forever in your unequalled glory!

28. Let us not be afraid of developing our roots in the darkness of nurturing faith for a long time, for when we germinate in God's light, no storm shall be able to knock us down and the weight of our growth in heaven shall not be able to topple us into the abyss.

28'. The fugitive and scorned servant that mysteriously nourishes the world has become the faithful and most precious master that secretly nourishes the chosen ones of God. Who shall see the word gleam? Who shall touch the light? Who shall savour the perfume? Who? Who? O who shall embody his Lord in a purified heart?

29. Let us run from people who are agitated and in a hurry, for their heart is closed to the voice of the Highest and their madness is incurable.

30. A piece of glowing coal is enough to set a mountain of fuel alight, just as a saint is enough to make a multitude of believers germinate, and just as a single son of God is enough to renew and to save exiled creation.

31. Pride means to be showered with gifts and riches and not praise God, or it means to die of misery and despair and ask nothing of God. The first pride can still receive the lesson of misfortune, but the second would not yield, even before the abundance of the Lord's gifts.

32. All the prudent editors have rejected the Book, for the word of God does not pay, so it seems. Alas! They are right, for the number of lovers of God has become imperceptible in the world. Alas! They are wrong, for the word of the Lord pays more than anything else, since it gives life to God's intelligent ones.

33. The Lord is cruel, for he even mocks his saints. He plunges them into the darkness, he ridicules them, he humiliates them until they are like corpses in his miraculous hands that give life to the dead.

29'. If our interior life does not grow to the same extent that our exterior life diminishes, we shall have no inheritance but the filth of death on the day of judgement.

30'. The little pebble of God is worth infinitely more than all the mountains on earth and all the clouds in the sky. Who shall discover it before the veil is ripped away on the hidden creation?

31'. The professed impious ones and the disguised religious ones refer to the Book as «foolish words» and «blasphemy», but what shall they say when they are crushed irremediably under the weight of the manifested stone?
Alas! the pulp of men does not speak.

32'. We shall emerge again from the earth like mushrooms under the heavenly shower, and the Lord shall pick some to establish them in his garden, and shall abandon others to the rottenness of the foreign land, just like a judicious gardener who knows how to distinguish what is good from what is bad.

33'. Let us be wary of the scorned, the weak and the simple, for the Lord often moves and germinates mysteriously in them.
«O holy humility! O holy mud of the abyss! O holy chaos of the beginning!»

34. What bad luck for those who despise the Book and who sordidly judge him who has written it using the Lord's breath. What should we think of those who tear the soul and of those who lose patience and hit?

35. The Lord shall settle their disagreement, and his judgement shall be an example for those who believe.

36. Satan does not forgive and he is always at our heels, and the rebellious woman continues to be the main instrument he uses to drive us to despair and damn us here below. Wretched executioner, wretched victim of torture, wretched instrument of torture!
O Lord! have pity on us and deliver us from the malice and the blows of the indomitable demon. Save us through the grace of the heavenly Mother submitted to your fertilizing love.

37. Let us never associate with creatures without generosity and without nobility of soul, for in the end we shall be despised and oppressed to death without being of profit to anyone, and forced to flee their blind and deaf wickedness on pain of falling into the slavery of the Beast.

38. No jackpot of fortune here below for the rescued of the Lord, but only scorn, insults, blows and poverty in exile.

34'. The free believers shall save the Church of God that the religious ones leave sinking miserably in the affairs and passions of the world. They shall restore it in its fraternal purity before God's judgement.

35'. If the Lord's wealth dwells in us, our poverty in the world shall be light and healthy for us.

36'. Satan unknowingly leads us back towards God through kicks in the backside, and that is why, even torn and rolled in the mud, we must turn with confidence to the Lord of forgiveness, who shall save us and who shall restore us in his kingdom of peace through the grace of his love, which is incommensurable and mad.

37'. O all-powerful Lord, keep away from us the miserable hearts that secrete hate and ooze the vileness of hell. Deliver us from the unspeakable meanness of the mediocre and the corrosive envy of the wicked.

38'. What is assured is few desires, few worries and few cares in the world, with the consoling presence of the Lord of truth and of life in oneself.

39. Suffering is a spur that drives the intelligent ones of God towards the peaceful dwelling of the Unique One, but where can we catch our breath on this steep route?

39'. O my Lord, our defeats are too persistent here below, and if you do not come to our help, we shall lie down in the dust and we shall die before your face.

39". Do you want to see the wicked gloating while breaking our bones? Do you want to see them triumphing while insulting your holy Name?

40. The Lord's saints are the only ones who see his justice shine in heaven; as for us, we must walk with faith's compass in the darkness of the world, and we are often tempted to wonder if the impious who mock us and who live the present life are not shrewder than us who hope for the impossible and believe in the incredible.

40'. Satan blinds us with all sorts of tricks and mirages and discourages us with all sorts of blows and falls. Let us remain, then, in the holy community of God's children and let us hold on to the chain of love, so that the killer of souls does not find us isolated and exposed like sheeps gone astray.

41. We shall accept everything that offers itself and that is given, and we shall leave all that denies itself and that resists. Therefore, we shall accomplish God's will, which never does violence to anything or anyone.
«He who seizes is a criminal; he who picks up is none other than a parasite of God.»

41'. Crushed by blows, mad with pain, inebriated with desperation, here am I like a stupid man who adores his Lord, crying in the dust. Scandalous stupidity, disarming stupidity, disturbing stupidity, blessed stupidity, triumphant stupidity that makes the light spring from the darkness.

42. We say this clearly to you: You have fallen into the mire and you have been clothed in the skin of a beast. If you behave like angels who have remained in the celestial homeland, God will bring you back to him and you shall enjoy his holy repose in his light of life; but if you behave like rebels, Satan shall plunge you forever into blind and deaf bestiality, and

42'. What joy at having written the Book, and what reassurance at hearing the approving voice of the Lord!
Oh, what an overwhelming reward ours will be when the multitude of blessed souls comes towards us, so that we can deliver them as a homage into the hands of the Perfect One. He shall choose and eat those

your screams of damned ones shall not pass through the layer of death that shall surround you on all sides.

that shall have eaten him, so that the unity of the unique heart is accomplished in One. As for the others, he shall establish them in his garden of delights like stars in heaven.

42". The Unique One divides and the Unique One comes back together, and each one offers his little judgement about the why and the how he does not know, instead of returning to the unity of the One and remaining in it until the day of the Unique One's choosing.

43. When the impious and the wicked of the world discourage us, let us re-read the Book of the Unique One, and the triumphal way shall shine in our hearts.

Then, the laugh of our joy shall surprise and scandalize the blind, filled with the assurance of their darkness, and the artifices of death itself shall seem worthless to us.

43'. When we have put a holy book in a generous heart, we shall have sown the grain of gold that shall germinate and set aglow heaven and earth, but if the heart is dry we must not be discouraged, for in those close to him the light of the Lord may repose, awaiting the free dew of the Unique One to flower and to appear in the world of love.

44. The sterile heart is jealous of all friendship, even of God's love, for it embraces like the octopus that sucks life until the last drop and rejects the emptied remains. Let us therefore flee from the wicked who only love for themselves and never for God, for they take everything and give nothing.

44'. Your father, your mother, your brothers, your sisters, your companion, your children, your friends may turn against God and weigh you down with their bad thoughts and their sarcasm. It is not up to you to judge them, but you can run away from them as quickly and as far as your two legs can carry you, for the Lord shall accompany you and he shall replace your family of vanity to your advantage.

44". After the corrosive tears of bitterness, behold the sweet tears of unbounded joy, for the abundance of our Lord's gift makes the water that is

the prisoner of our hearts flow, and
his love condenses it into a holy and
precious stone.

45. When I had stricken the rebellious woman on the way to the Highest, I thought I would be deprived of my Lord for a long time, but he immediately overflowed in my heart with magnificent revelations and with loving consolations; and my surprise was great that, on having hit, my heart was even more open inside.
«The Lord can even convert stones if it pleases him.»

46. When I had given up my small possessions in the world, my Lord inundated me with riches in my heart, and I knew that, on having lost everything on earth, I had gained everything in heaven.
«Is it not necessary to throw out the dead ballast so that the balloon flies into the freedom of the heavens and reaches the island of happiness?»

47. Let us pray that the wicked ones who surround us are converted in their heart, and if they persist in their wretched judgements, let us run from them and let us pray for those who seek the Lord gropingly in their pained and troubled hearts, so that the light of the Holiest One germinates in them and so that it illuminates their route until the end of their quest.

48. Who has found the holy chalice?
Who had opened the sealed vase?

45'. I hear the voice of my Lord and transcribe the word of my Lord.
What reward is more wonderful?
I see the light of my Lord and I eat the life of my Lord.
What gift is more adorable?
I swim in the love of my Lord and I repose on the heart of my Lord.
What more divine state is there?

46'. The names of the heroes of the world and the names of the believers shall be erased from the stones, from the monuments and from the memory of men, but the names of the holy prophets and of the wise friends of God shall remain engraved forever on the heavenly stone and shall live the eternity in the heart of the Unique One.

47'. If it happens that we suspend our work in the world to pray and to praise our magnificent Lord, that will bring us no evil, despite the threats of the impious and despite the blows of the wicked, for the smallest praise to the Highest is worth more than all the works of men here below put together. «The Book has indeed been judged as an idle thing by the blind and the deaf of this world!»

48'. Show us that one, merciful Lord, so that we can kiss his feet and his hands and follow him blindly to

Who has looked into the secret?
Who has drunk at the spring?
Who has fallen in heaven?
Who has died in life?
Who has resurrected in love?
Who is established in knowledge?
Who reposes in the peace of the Perfect One?
Who has become ONE with him who IS?

your secret garden, to your hidden house and to your virginal and so-holy heart, where the joy of life dances eternally around your immutable love.

49. O my Lord! you are my father and my mother, you are my brothers and my sisters, you are my wife and my children, you are the good and the unfailing friend who remembers his beloved ones in this world.

49'. Here we are in the eyes of the Lord like a cinder that he does not disdain to fertilize and lead to the eternity of his peace.

«Who shall understand the love of the All-Powerful One for his nascent creature?»

50. How many women would not have cried with joy on discovering a companion who was assiduously seeking his Lord, and would have helped and served him with love and gratitude?

50'. That which we have denied and fought against can never belong to us. Let us be quite careful of what we think and what we say about the resurrection and the judgement announced by the prophets.

51. That which God has given us has doubted our quest, and has revolted in her heart.

«The Lord is jealous with his beloved ones, and he does not allow their love to go astray in the world, but anyone can convert himself to him if he desires it in his heart.»

51'. For the accomplishment of the thing shall irremediably close the exit and the entrance gates. Let us think deeply about it before the crash of the bolts and bars mark the time of irrevocable choice!

52. We shall recognize the hardened impious in that they are hard with themselves and with others, in that they are filled with courage for the things of the world, and in that they rely only on themselves and on the work of their hands to settle and organize themselves here below.

52'. If only they could one day stretch out their hand humbly and meditate on their weakness, as well as on the power of God's Providence, which makes everything grow and ripen without the work of men!

But would they understand?

53. Let us be wary of the impious who, having denied God throughout their life, scorned his teachings and spat on his people, become afraid in their old age and attempt to underwrite an insurance by endowing religious works or by building and decorating chapels, for it is still their names that they attempt to impose proudly on God and on men, and not their hearts that they offer with repentance to the clear-sighted Lord.

53'. If we do not have the intelligence to do otherwise, let us accomplish our silly things in the world, but sometimes let us at least give thanks to God in our hearts for the life he grants us here below with his patience and generosity, and when we see something beautiful, great and noble in the world, let us abandon our wretched thoughts and let us praise the Lord for that small reflection of the admirable and secret work that is accomplished before our blinded eyes.

54. Their cunning and their hypocrisy shall not save them if they do not enter humbly and sincerely the path of penitence that is offered them by the Merciful One.

54'. What does it matter that our hands are empty of the works of the world, as long as our hearts are replete with the love of God!

55. Some pursue in secret the quest for God beyond symbols and figures, for they are thirsty for the reality that can be seen, touched and eaten. Who could scold them, and who would dare to exclude them from the universal Church of the most-learned Lord?

55'. If we do not embody the Highest in the purity of our hearts, we shall not feel with our hands the body of the Lord here below and we shall not enter alive his magnificent eternity and peace.

56. «They are disciples of Jesus, but in secret, for fear of the priests» says Emmanuel. But did that not already exist in the time of Jesus? And those disciples, were they not in God before they were in history?

56'. Perhaps they said nothing because they knew too many things about God and not enough about the world? Or perhaps because their Lord has not commanded them to speak or make themselves known? But they have certainly not disappeared altogether.

57. Everything was collapsing in me and around me, but in my heart the Lord gave me a sign to laugh with him and not to believe in misfortune,

57'. Will the intelligent and the scholars of the world also not want to explain to us the Book that we have written under the inspiration of the

and my astonishment and joy were boundless, as vanished despair.

58. Workers and resourceful people sometimes succeed in the world, but few seem to notice that it is to end up at the same point of ignorance and poverty as the idlers and the incapable before death and future life, for impiety blinds them all equally, and nails them to the outer layer of things.

59. On the day of revelation of the judgement we shall realize with astonishment that all the holy Scriptures differed in their words, but that they taught the same mystery of resurrection and of eternal life in God.

60. It has needed centuries and legions of seekers for the science of men to appear in the world, but it needs only a moment and only an inspired one to recall the science and the love of God in the heart of believers.

Shall we not realize the thing, and shall we not be surprised and moved by the recall of the Lord?

61. We are not «amusing» say the impious of the world. But how could we be so when we see hell gaping open below their steps of self-assured blind men?

Lord of high science and great love? Just to make the angels and saints in heaven laugh.

58'. Even destroyed and desperate, where shall we go if it is not to our Lord of compassion? For, who shall accept us in this lamentable state, if it is not the Generous and Merciful One, who consoles, fulfils and cures one of death?

«If we erase ourselves sincerely, God shall bring us into the light, but if we mean to shine, he shall plunge us in the darkness of oblivion.»

59'. Lord, we weep with joy on listening to your music that speaks to our souls and consoles them in the exile of death, but it is your holy dew that delivers us from the abyss of perdition and makes us flower again in your marvellous light where heavenly joy dwells for eternity.

60'. He who plunges into the holy light of the Lord of life forgets his reason and his judgement in this world, just like him who falls into the darkness of madness. But the former advances assuredly towards the unity of the Unique One, while the latter becomes dispersed in the highly opaque death of the outer layer.

61'. We are not «easy to get on with», say the believers of this world. But how could we be so when we announce the mysteries of the triple resurrection and those of the fair judgement?

62. The time is approaching, and is already here, when the believers shall concern themselves once more with God's things, and when they shall leave the things of the world to the impious.

63. We shall seek the most gifted and most capable men according to their works and according to their successes in the world to govern and to organize the people and the nation; and we shall pitilessly eliminate the incapable and the mediocre who mean to accomplish for everyone that which they have not been able to manage successfully for themselves.

64. We have not chosen to write the Book nor to preach the truth of God; it is the Lord who has chosen us and who has swooped down on us without warning like the eagle who snatches his prey and carries it up into the sky. If the Lord lets go right now, we would fall back heavily to the ground, and there would be nothing but a bag of mixed-up dumb and stupid bones. Really, we are all in the hand of God; some believe it, but very few experience it here below.

65. How could we have contemplated on our own writing a Book that has taken the twelve best years of our youth according to the world, that has demanded a thousand cares and withdrawal from life that surrounds us, that has provoked the judgement and the rebellion of our nearest, that has cost us poverty, which nobody wants to accept, that

62'. The action of Satan is not restricted to distancing believers from the faith and the love of God: it also consists in distancing them from the quest for the mysteries and the science of God.

63'. We shall seek the wisest and holiest men according to their predictions and according to their lives in the world to lead and to maintain the people and the nation; and we shall mercilessly eliminate the blind and the deaf who mean to impose on everyone that which they have neither seen nor heard for themselves.

64'. This very day, if he so wishes, God can reverse his judgement and humiliate us to dust, ridiculing us before all, believers and the impious, scholars and the ignorant, the intelligent and brutes, but we would remain turned towards his holy face and, even though covered in mud, we would praise his holy NAME without doubting his wisdom and his mercifulness, for the love he has implanted in us is not the kind which one can easily rid oneself of.

65'. O Lord of mercy and of peace! allow us now to hide ourselves and disappear behind you; allow us to complete your work in secret and in repose before the imbeciles, who let their inspired children die of poverty, come to congratulate us and shake our hand; before they pounce greedily on what they have always refused to buy for a piece of bread; before

leaves the world indifferent, that bores our close ones, that offends the religious, that makes us appear unbalanced, and that up to now engenders nothing but silence and abandonment? How could we have contemplated losing our life in this world in order to gain it in God on our own?

66. How could we still persevere in the completion of such a work in the midst of the desert of this time of impiety and of death on our own? Will this not make the believers reflect? Will this not lead them to examine the words written in the Book with the eyes of the heart? Will this not incite them to increase the part of their generous and compassionate Lord?

67. The Jewish believers are the most submissive to God, and shall be the first to be restored with consolation and with honour by the Lord.

68. The Jewish nonbelievers are the most rebellious against God, and they shall be the first to be driven out and exterminated from the face of the earth of the living. Here is a distinction that the believers should carefully take note of so as not to reject or bully their brothers in the faith in God.

69. Who can fail to feel appeased and consoled after having read the Book? And who can fail to feel en-

they seize our shadow and exhibit it in their circus shows; before they dismember our life stupidly and ferociously, as they do with beasts to surprise the soul in them.

66'. Before they pursue us to obtain what they themselves have never wanted to give to anyone; before they cover us in filth to reassure themselves in their baseness and cowardice. Drive them down into their wickedness and stupidity, O Lord, and remember those who have helped us and who have believed in your holy word, so that they receive your magnificent life without mixture, promised to faithful and generous hearts.

67'. The height of intelligence is to be an idiot before God, just as the height of idiocy is to believe oneself intelligent before him.

68'. Let us note how agitated, uneasy and unhappy is the life of the impious ones, and how their rebellion hurls them into blind dispersion and destructive madness.

69'. Quickly, quickly, a little more time to read it. A little more time to understand it. A little more time to

lightened and led after having meditated upon it even the slightest bit?

70. We are neither jurist nor judge to spoon-feed you laws and make you respect them, and we are neither politician nor technician to govern you and to organize you in this world.

71. We are only given the task of reminding you of the resurrection announced by the prophets, as well as God's judgement in which you shall be sorted, be it for joy or for pain.

72. What have the mediocre gained, by condemning the work that they did not understand? An even more irreparable platitude and their own condemnation by him who has inspired this work.

73. Imbeciles and rebels, be gone to the dust, to the misfortune and to the solitude of death reserved for the stupid adorers of the darkened world, or submit yourselves to the Lord while there is still time, and do not judge that which is beyond you, and do not oppose the Spirit's breath that you do not know.

74. Perhaps it is true that the Book is useless for this degenerate nation from the way to God: his intelligent

undertake it. A little more time to complete it. But then, all eternity to enjoy it.

70'. Note that we reap only problems because of this Book, and that our will does not intervene in it at all.
It would undoubtedly be more agreeable to be able to catch our breath a little and rest in the world.

71'. But God's judgement is urgent now, and its proclamation cannot wait, for the tribunal of the righteous one is growing impatient. Can we not understand it from the signs of the general decomposition of nations?

72'. As the dew changes the dead earth into meadows full of sweet-smelling flowers, heavenly grace makes our dried-up and burnt hearts flower again.

73'. God can transform the dead stones into the harvest of life, but he chooses them according to a secret judgement that remains incomprehensible to us.
Perhaps we shall understand when the veil is removed.
Alas! It will be too late to convert oneself.
It is best to interrogate the Lord and then listen to his response in our hearts and bend to his law without judging.

74'. Have pity on the rescued of your people and group them together in your holy light of life, so

and his right-thinking ones reject it, for their stupefaction in this world resembles death. We shall therefore place it in the hands of God, from where it came, so that the angels are the first to rejoice.

75. O Lord of Foresight! could you have given us the seed too late, when the heart of these men was already hardened like dead stone? However, your blessing is enough for even death to flower again magnificently.

that they can set ablaze the mountain of dead people that surround them and oppress them miserably. Allow your saints to attract your blessing over these inert bones, so that they can live again before you in repentance, in obedience and in the joy of rediscovered love.

75'. O Lord, if you wish, your talent shall be buried, or it shall light up the world once more, and our songs of gratitude shall send your NAME back to the stars.

75". Otherwise, dispersion, misfortune and death shall rain down on this impious and half-hearted people.
And a small part shall be saved and shall germinate once more in the simplicity and in the love of the Unique One.

In truth I tell you, if a man is not born of water and of spirit, he cannot enter the kingdom of God.

JESUS

Woe betide you, doctors of law, because having taken the key of science, you yourselves have not entered, and you have prevented those who wanted to enter from doing so.

JESUS

BOOK XXII

God has drawn you from the earth. He shall make you return to it and emerge from it once more... The day on which the tombs shall open and on which the secrets of hearts shall be divulged.

KORAN

Keep your heart above all, for from it emerge the springs of life.

PROVERBS

ÉVITE EN UR

1. We suffocate under the worthless explanations of the intelligent of the world, and their works increase the confusion of spirits and the impiety of hearts.

2. Their books and their names shall return to dust, but the work of the Lord shall remain forever, and his word shall span the centuries and shall confront victoriously the assaults of the qualified pedants of all nations.

3. The artist gets us through a moment, and the artisan makes us last a while, but who shall deliver us from death? And who shall give us the eternity of life if it is not the science of the Unique One?

THE SAGE

1'. The excrement of the innumerable flies could not wear out nor cover the great pyramid of God.

2'. Let us «waste» our time searching for God, and let us not listen to what the impious say about it, for their hearts are darkened, their eyes are blind and their hands are powerless to do violence to the holy light of the God of life.

3'. He who praises the Lord in his heart, even if it is for a tiny flower, is neither mediocre nor impious. And he who searches for him, even if it is only through a dead stone, is neither lazy nor incapable.

4. Let us display the Lord's law in our houses so that it penetrates our heads and so that it germinates in our hearts. Thus his way shall appear luminous and easy to us, and how!

4'. Study the Book and beg for your bread if it is the shortest route for you, for the only thing that counts is the precious discovery of the Lord, and it is only the science of the Unique One that gives the weight of the life that does not perish.

5. You judge with your malice, thinking you can surprise the vigilance of the Lord, but your malice blinds you and leads you to the pit of perdition, and you stupidly snigger when you are spoken to about the upright simplicity that engenders the light of life.

Your reason has become like a mortal poison, and your intelligence is like a scorpion that inoculates itself with its own venom.

5'. Now, we speak clearly and nobody listens, but when everyone asks, we shall remain dumb as a stump, and those that scorn us now shall be furious at not obtaining a response, for the danger shall be here and shall oppress them all over, and the anguish of fear shall make them interested in the things they scorned during the time of their impious assurance.

6. Holy and wise prophets of God, come to our aid, surround us with your sparkling cohort and support us so that we do not weaken on the way of the Lord. Pray to the Holiest One to console us in his heart at the end of our troubles.

Beseech the Lord to withhold his arm equipped with the sword of separation; time for the ignorant to be able to read and understand the inspired word; time for the hesitant to be able to choose in their hearts and repent before God; time for the rebels to be able to abandon themselves even more to the madness of the world.

6'. Time so that the impious are able to organize themselves proudly in the mud of the mixture; time so that the scholars and workers are able to triumph in their worthless works; time so that the believers are able to return to the simplicity of the faith and the love of God.

Then, let his arm fall and let his sword separate without mercy and without forgiveness the sheep from the goats! Let his children see his light shine and let them live in his sun! Let his enemies be struck down in the confusion of the darkness, and let them tear one another to pieces like beasts amid the smoking ruins of their false science!

7. We have not come to divert anyone from his faith, his worship or his sect. We have come to assemble the believers who seek the living Lord, in the grace, in the love and in the knowledge of the unique Splendour.

7'. We have not come to knock down that which is tottering, nor to kill that which is dying, nor to dissolve that which disintegrates by itself. We have come to give shape to that which is sought, to give body to that which is incarnated, to bring forth that which is being born.

8. We have come to remake the Church without monuments, without barriers, without ranks, without vanities and without finances. To remake the Church founded on the holy stone of the beginning and of the end. To remake the Church of the saints who speak to God in their hearts.

8'. We have come to remake the Church of the sages who make God shine in their hearts. The Lord knows his own and sustains those who observe his law, those who love his faith, those who follow his way and those who accomplish his work.

9. Five minutes with hypocrites and here we are sad, discouraged, useless, judged, condemned and cast out, unless God's wrath takes hold of us and curses the wicked after having condemned their depravity.

9'. Without the grace and without the love of God, we would be as stupid as the impious ones. Therefore, we have to be grateful to the Lord who has made us believers, but we can certainly not be proud of it!

10. Hypocrites curse themselves, which is the height of punishment for their hypocrisy. No forgiveness for those who think they are fooling God and who knowingly deceive men.
«All their cunning will go up in smoke when the incandescent cloud approaches them.»

10'. O Lord, who sees into hearts! deliver us from the rebels and from their malignance that kills the grace, the faith and the love that make us live in you; and make known to us the believers who love you and who praise you in their hearts, but above all, make us find those to whom you speak in secret.

11. O Lord who is so good and so wise, deliver us from the brutes, the criminals, the madmen and the cunning, and whip the self-satisfied mediocre; knock down into the dust

11'. When the Lord breathes into man and when he grasps the instrument of his wrath, no more serenity and no more sentences, for everything explodes into pieces in heaven

the ignorant vanity of the reasonable ones of the world; strike on the mouth the triumphant imbeciles who explain to us everything they do not understand.

12. O mortal ingratitude! we read the wise and holy books and we do not praise in our hearts the Lord of grace and of love who offers us the life without mixture.

13. If someone does not tell you that a work is beautiful, and if several do not affirm to you that it has value, you remain stupid and blind before it, and you turn away from the jewel and you vilify the artist, like those pigs that trample pearls underfoot and rip apart the imprudent ones who offer them to them.

14. Contrary to what many people think, the true realists are the believers who seek the substantial and essential life that does not perish, while the abstract delirious ones are those who attach themselves to perishable matter.
Will this perhaps cause an intelligent one who loves God and who seeks him in his heart to reflect?

15. Some take charge of the holy Scriptures like donkeys that carry a treasure they are incapable of using, or like dogs that guard a bone from

and everything falls as dust over the earth, and here is the servant broken by the terrible act, plunged into the darkness of solitude and rejected by all.

12'. O thick veil that entwines us, here we are like mummies that cannot reach the water of the resurrection, who do not know how to stretch out their hands towards him who offers it freely, and who do not even see his holy light!

13'. You are doubly cursed when you pay dearly in times of success for that which you have rejected and scorned in times of abandonment, for the only motivation for your action is the most stupid and avaricious speculation that shall leave your heart and hands empty on the day of judgement.

14'. Blessed be God: the holy Scriptures are still here and it is up to us to read them and meditate on them without letting ourselves be fooled by the hypocrites who use them for their own interests, without letting ourselves be tricked by the imbeciles who adapt them to their blind and deaf mediocrity, and without letting ourselves be misled by the well-intentioned ones who restrict them to their historical and moral comprehension.

15'. These recognize themselves straight away when they leaf through the Book, and their rage overflows immediately, for they have monopo-

which they cannot have the marrow, but who jealously prevent anyone approaching.

16. Get away, satisfied and pontificating mediocre! We pray to the merciful Lord to wake you, if it is still possible, with lashes from the leaden whip, for it is better for you to be torn to shreds and saved than to perish in the false assurance of your insensitive darkness.

17. Simplicity is not ignorance.

18. If the Book is just an ordinary kind of thing that does not interest anybody or hardly anybody, how can it become a fascinating thing and be sought after by many, without cruelly condemning those who bury it right now?

19. It is not in the style of the times, and it is not literature to anaesthetize the dying of this world. Here is the defect!

20. We have dissolved and purged our humours in the wet mud, and we have comforted and perfected them in the light of heaven.

21. Your quest is too arduous, Lord, and if you do not come to our help, we shall certainly fail, for our ears are deaf, our eyes are blind, our hands are powerless and your salvation is truly incredible!

lized the mysteries of God to exploit them profanely, and instead of becoming instructed like their Lord, they have become stupid and conceited like the devil they serve in secret.

16'. They adapt themselves to the mud that covers them entirely and they spread ugliness across the world. They level everything in themselves and around them, and here they are like beasts that ruminate calmly in the abattoir where they are piled up for death!

17'. Wisdom is not insensitivity.

18'. Let us become the younger brothers of Christ in God, and we shall hear the word of God and we shall do his works and we shall live in the Unique One.

19'. «Are all loved ones not of God? And are all lovers not in God?»

20'. We shall see the sperm appear and grow like the morning dew, and we shall see the germ become incarnate in its purity and change it into its own fixed and perfect nature.

21'. It is the interior of the interior that we must discover and make it appear in purity, and it is the interior of this interior that we must finally manifest in fixedness.

22. When we give up understanding is when we begin to truly understand.
– When we give up explaining anything is when we begin to make ourselves truly heard and understood.

22'. He who bathes in the clarity of the interior fire is like an idiot in the world, yet he alone is truly enlightened.
«In order to approach the truth, one has to be naked like it.»

23. Be only yourself, question only yourself, penetrate only yourself, lose yourself only in yourself, find yourself only in yourself, repose only in yourself and you shall approach the Lord of within, who accomplishes all things in you without you.

23'. Creation, man, art, are not perfectible, in the sense that they have only gone astray, and that their most perfect accomplishment is only the return to their initial perfection.
«There is something better than seizing the obviousness of life, and that is to participate in its primitive purity.»

23". Tolerate yourself,
Help yourself,
Seek yourself,
Discover yourself,
Know yourself,
Accomplish yourself,
with the aid of the Lord of heaven.

24. The seed of the stars is hidden in the earth.

24'. The slime of the earth is the first creature.

25. Accurate view is to see things as they were and as they shall be, that is, as they are in reality in the primary unity.

25'. The greatest work in the greatest ease, here is ART. The greatest love in the greatest purity, here is holiness. The greatest freedom in the greatest repose, here is wisdom.

26. Great generosity of soul is required to be the first to recognize that an unknown work is beautiful.

26'. He who explores his ignorance, his powerlessness and his death, is the only one who knows the madness and wisdom of ART.

27. Let the spirit of the artist be as high as the stars, and his life be as humble as dust!

28. All that is opposed to life manifests it all the more clearly, and all that receives it participates in it magnificently.

29. We cannot please everyone, for we are full of defects and weaknesses and still covered in foreign filth, but the Book is already a judgement that secretly separates the pure, enlightened hearts from the blind and satisfied dying ones of this world.

30. Everything that intends to direct or to force ART sterilizes it and kills it.

31. The artist, the believer, the saint, the sage is he who raises himself up to the illuminating beauty of the creation released from its gangue of death.

32. Why discourse when everything is so magnificently diversified by the light of God?

33. The true artist knows only heaven and earth; the science, the morals and the politics of men bore him and kill him.

27'. He who distinguishes little between the things of the world soon perceives the unity that gives life to them.

28'. What characterizes life is movement, change, diversity, freedom, purity, joy, fertility, gratuity and praise.

29'. If only he would give back to many the desire and the taste for studying the holy and wise Scriptures of all nations!
If only he would be for many the standard of victory and of freedom in Him who IS!
If only he would illuminate the hearts of those that await the light of life!

30'. Moderation is a distinctive feature of the sage, tyranny is characteristic of the madman, insensitivity is the lot of brutes.

31'. There is only one true ART, that which manifests the free spirit, which is the light of the Universe. There is only one true science, that which fixes this divine light in the repose of God.

32'. He who does not carry his joy in himself shall not see it reflected in the world and shall not see it flower in God.

33'. Only dead stars do not spin with joy under the breath of the Unique One.

34. The fellow-being is he who suffers and who opens himself up, and not he who closes himself up and causes suffering.

35. One is not a believer because one attends religious ceremonies, and one is not a nonbeliever because one does not go to them; for the true worship of God is practised in the heart, and his holy quest proceeds through the study of the wise Scriptures and through the operations of faith in action in the world.

36. Many are ignorant of God's things, but to crown it all, these ignorant ones now judge and condemn those who have been instructed in the mysteries of the Unique One.
Let us pray that the divine whip leads them back to the silence, to the obedience and to the humility that suit their condition of incurable deaf and blind ones.
«The agitation of the world is so great, Lord, and our voice is so weak that we measure sadly the madness of our preaching.»

37. A lukewarm, tottering and profaned Church is better than no Church at all, for a blind paralytic can still speak, while a dead man can no longer do anything for anyone.

34'. One learns to love by seeking to penetrate and to live in the state of others.

35'. We have to question ourselves sincerely about the Book and choose for ourselves in our hearts without taking into account the opinions of those who have a position to defend and to exploit here below.
«Does not the Lord breathe and walk right here?»

36'. Condemned here below to suffer the hypocrites in the world, in our houses and in our hearts, we aspire more and more to the communion of the saints where God's children shall welcome us kindly, and where nobody shall rise up against us because of our love for the Unique One, but on the contrary, where all shall spontaneously associate themselves with our praises, our blessings and our joy in the Lord of the centre.

37'. Communities should indeed produce saints capable of filling the last believers with enthusiasm. Would they perhaps have to begin by not exiling the Holy Spirit from their walls?

37". Can the Lord no longer count on believers hidden in the world? It is quite possible after all, for he alone judges consciences and hearts without any possible error.

38. We have no visions, we hear no voices, we do no miracles and heaven remains closed before our eyes; but the grace of the Highest has opened our understanding, and his love has confirmed our mission here below. Our lot is in his hands. He shall do as he pleases. For since we offered ourselves and he chose us, we no longer truly belong to ourselves.

38'. We accept being rejected, vilified and abandoned by people with influence, but at least, let the most intelligent in God take the trouble to examine and weigh up attentively the words of the Book, and let the simplest in God be concerned enough to question themselves in their hearts over the authenticity of the work presented to them.

39. Some who think they serve the Lord do him a disservice, and others who think they do him a disservice serve him without knowing it.

39'. Let us devote our leisure to the Lord, and the Lord shall multiply our leisure.

40. We can support ourselves by singing or by reciting prayers, hymns or verses communally, and be in communion in the grace and in the love of the Lord of life. But no-one should judge nor condemn those who prefer the solitude and silent prayer of the heart in the secret of the Unique One.

40'. When we are truly caught up in the quest for our mysterious Lord, the affairs of the world and the people who occupy themselves with them shall appear to us tiresome, empty and unbearable, and they shall consider us as incapable, useless and mad.

41. Let us be very careful with this, for it is not that which shines the most outside in the world that is the purest and the most precious inside in God.

41'. We are like senseless people, who have staked everything they have in God's game, and that seems scandalous to those who count only on the work of their hands to live and prosper in the world.

42. Opposition and the reproaches of the world are distressing and discouraging, but the judgement and condemnation of our nearest ones are cruel, even when the Lord sustains us in our holy venture.

42'. O merciful Lord! redeem at least the instruments of our torture when you finally let us catch our breath, before receiving us in your blessed and most glorious bosom, if you so wish.

43. There are some goads that do not allow the laziest to fall asleep, even during the time it takes to sigh, when the service of God and the service of men are equally pressing.

It is a difficult thing to understand and quite a hard one to accept; however, we consider ourselves privileged among the dying of this world.

44. Hey! Hey! Hey!
What? What? What?
Your blood is running, and your life is flying away!

45. Come, men of all nations, eat, drink, rejoice and live, for the Book is given to you in preference to that shrewd, wily and impious people, whose intelligence has become the greatest stupidity there can be.

46. Idiotic race that inherits the Book of the renewal of all things, you exchange it for a plate of lentils, and you even get rid of it by offering the plate of lentils as compensation to those who agree to take charge of the work.

47. Let your eyes remain stopped, your ears remain closed, O super intelligent ones! and let foreigners eat your bread and drink your wine while mocking you; let them strip you of your heritage and let them share out your riches; let them reduce you to slavery and make you work for nothing on your own land, so that we can hear your wit and so that we can appreciate your subtle jesting about God and about his sal-

43'. Faith in God and in his resurrection pays off immediately, for it helps us to bear that which drives us to despair and crushes the impious. Nourish it and fortify it in us until the bright day of the end and of the beginning, Lord of goodness.

44'. By watering our death, we shall live. By dissipating our life, we shall certainly die.

45'. O fatherland blessed by God and nourished by the holy Virgin, here you are, you have become like a prostitute who dishonours the family of the living and prefers the stream full of foreign waste to the table of her Lord and master!

46'. You have ridiculed the admonitions of your saints, and your rebellion has engendered poisoned blows and wounds. Now you are granted a time of respite in heaven and on earth for you to reflect and come back to the holy family.

47'. If you refuse, that shall be your end. Sapped, broken into pieces, burned to ashes and dispersed by the wind, without return and without forgiveness. Without name, without memory and without prayer forever. But if you rise up from the mud, if you empty your abscesses, if you wash yourself in the water of grace, if you wear the nuptial clothes and if you submit yourself to your magnificent Lord, you shall reflower the first

vation, about God and about his wrath, if you still dare.

among the nations, as you had been the first to fall; and your light shall light up the world and your peace shall charm all hearts. You shall be called blessed, born of the spirit and of the heart, and you shall reign without violence over the peoples who have become wiser.

48. O city of birth! there you are like a pile of corpses going cold, and your ancient pretension is dying with you. Within your walls nothing can no longer be heard but the noise of cattle ruminating heavily, and one can no longer breathe anything but the odour of the dung that rots in you. The holy Cordon has not saved you from the plague of the mediocre, and the blows have not opened up your understanding.

48'. O most spiritual capital! they say you are the most advanced, but it must be understood as though of rotten meat that already transpires the putrefaction of the charnel-house of death. Always saved miraculously, the Lord's patience shall tire one day, and you shall swim in tears and blood, and you shall dry out in the ashes before being renewed through heavenly grace.

49. That which IS is much more fantastic and much more formidable than anything we can imagine, but when that which IS is fixed in ONESELF, the eyes are dazzled, and the mouth remains dumb.

49'. No more questions or enigmas for him who approaches the living light that contains the Lord of eternity.

50. It is useless to run around in circles and to bustle about left, right and centre in order to avoid having to solve the enigma of life and death that is proposed to us here below, for the enigma subsists, and finally devours those who have been unable to solve it.

50'. No more letters, no more numbers, no more locks, no more doors, no more walls, no more prisons, no more tombs and no more deaths for him who finds, who matures and who eats the unity of the Unique One.

51. The profits, rewards, honours and nominations of men are derisory for the one who has found the Unique One. They are also derisory

51'. Make us know perfect joy in our discovery in you.
Make us know perfect freedom in our obedience to your holy will.

for those who have not found him, but as they do not know it, they console themselves by playing with the wind of vanity. In that case, it would be better to simply play the flute, for nothing deceitful would result from it either for them or for others.

52. Open up our heart and purify it, oh Lord, so that we can receive you in your entirety, and reinforce our love so that it can join with yours without being obliterated in your glory.

53. The apparent contradictions of the holy books exist only for those who do not know the unity of the unique Lord. It is better for them not to judge, and above all, not to condemn that which they understand only in images and not in naked truth.

54. When we are mortally sad without knowing why, it is because we empty ourselves of the things of the world and do not fill ourselves with those of God.

Indeed, that which is full of world resists God due to its dead weight, and that which is full of God resists the world due to its living weight, while that which is empty of world and of God finds itself unbearably crushed between heaven and earth, which then come together without blessing or fertilization.

Make us know perfect security in our observance of your holy law.

Make us know perfect peace in our abandonment in you.

Make us know perfect life in our love in you.

Make us know perfect contentment in our repose in you.

52'. There, where having abandoned and given up everything, we find ourselves fulfilled beyond all expression.

There, where prayer and praise give way to the dumb jubilation of holy union.

53'. We must begin by asking for help from the Lord who accomplishes his work in us, for by ourselves we are powerless to change anything in our corrupted nature. And we must also finish by leaving total freedom to the Lord for perfecting what he himself freed from the mud of the sin of death.

54'. When we have reached the light of the Unique One, all those who have desires shall see them accomplished and shall swim in the plenitude of God. But those who do not have desires shall see God, shall enter God, and God shall penetrate them, and they shall repose in the void of God, which is the hub of God's plenitude. But that is reserved for a small number of chosen ones, who possess the oil of love and of knowledge.

55. Hypocrites secretly delight in that which they denounce publicly, but the names they have given themselves denounce them publicly without their suspecting it.

55'. Thus, in «bien-pensante»[1] hypocrisy we find «panse bénite»,[2] and in «puritaine»[3] hypocrisy we find «putainerie»,[4] for each coin that shines in the world has a hidden reverse side where its true name is engraved.

56. A prostitute who loves for love is better than an irreproachable woman who loves for herself, for the former knows the charity of love and neither judges nor does violence to anything in the name of her shameful love, while the latter knows only the jealousy of greed, and condemns and bullies everything without pity in the name of her devouring love.

56'. If there are irreproachable women who love according to the love that is given and not according to that which takes everything, make them known to us, clear-sighted Lord! and give them to us as an inheritance, so that our children are made in your holy resemblance.

«Give us, oh Lord! that which is bone of our bones and flesh of our flesh, according to your holy science.»

57. What true believer would dare to presume before his Lord and before his brothers in God on decorations, titles, ranks or diplomas, all derisory things in the eyes of the Unique One and in the eyes of those who seek God?

57'. Would not he do better covering himself entirely with the black habit of penitents, so as to remember the vile filth of sin that embraces him all over, and so as to remain in the humility that is suitable for God's faithful?

58. It is the water of grace that melts the mortified heart and that separates in us pure life from the filth of death.

It is the fire of love that fertilizes the purified heart and that multiplies it in the glory of God.

58'. The poorer we are in everything, the more the Lord shall fill us with his faith, his joy, his love, his peace and his knowledge that do not perish.

1. Meaning «right-thinking».
2. Meaning «blessed belly».
3. Meaning «puritan».
4. Meaning «dirty trick».

59. This one hardly knows us, and he has been feeding us secretly for years, asking for nothing by way of thanks but the word of the Book. God has given more intelligence and more fortunate inspiration to a butcher than to all the multitude of important people strutting around in the immense city.

60. Is it not a double blessing of God manifested in a pleasant way? Who shall savour the amazing humour of the Highest? And who shall recognize his own stupidity before the Unique One?
O who shall cry at himself, and who shall also laugh at himself?

61. Vulgar works speak to us of exterior wisdom understood from outside.
– Philosophy books speak to us of exterior wisdom seen from within.
– Holy books speak to us of interior wisdom known within.
– Wise books speak to us of interior wisdom experienced outside.

62. Enthusiasm for the world and scepticism with regard to God sometimes lead the most intelligent to scepticism of the world and to enthusiasm for God, but they more often lead ordinary people to feel disgust and resentment towards themselves and others, and to death for all.

59'. He who serves the servant of the Lord shall be served by the Lord in person. This shall be a hard lesson for the intelligent, for the scholars and for the powerful of this world. One day, they shall understand it fully, but then it shall be too late for them to use it and for them to save themselves from the death that eats away at them.

60'. Here, it is the noble ascetic who prefaces the Book with his prestigious name after having sensed the truth of the message. There, it is the simple schoolteacher who gives a part of that which is necessary to him to transcribe the last verses of the Book. Finally, it is the believers of Pallandt who present the work in its entirety.

61'. Who knows best the divine Lord of life? The simple shepherds? The wise magi? The faithful adorers? The blessed disciples? The devoted believers? Or even he who guards the holy Virgin, helps her to give birth in secret and raises the little child who came from heaven?
O most intelligent ones! O most learned ones! O most important ones! reply, if you are capable of understanding the question.

62'. Perfect submission to the will of God is not a mindless or complacent resignation that endures all disorder without reacting. It is rather an attentive and joyous acceptance that uses all that appears in the best way without desiring anything in particular.

63. We denounce the shrewd and the mediocre who form committees under the cover of mutual aid and of charity, when they in fact hypocritically feed only their vanity and their greed, to the detriment of the weak and the poor who are isolated in the world.

63'. He who has found the thing of the Book can burn the Book to cook the thing, for that which he shall obtain in the end is worth more than the Book and the thing.

«Not a shrewd one shall penetrate the simplicity nor approach the purity of the thing, for malice glues them to the outer layer and prevents them from seeing the inside that lives.»

64. Tomorrow shall be dark, tomorrow shall be cold, tomorrow we shall be dead, tomorrow the resurrection and the judgement. Do you not see that tomorrow is called today? Do you not see that today grabs you and kills you without your doing anything other than running in front of it in the stupid hope of outdistancing it?

64'. Who shall remain in repose and who shall play dead so that today passes over him without stooping to pick him up and pin him in time? Who shall take advantage of today's respite to melt the yesterdays into the one living reality of God's unique today?

65. He who begins by doing violence to himself becomes hardened in pride and in hypocrisy, instead of opening himself to the grace that unbinds in the abandon of primary humility.

65'. One has to imbibe and dissolve before drying and cooking, for he who begins by cooking fixes the filth of sin instead of eliminating it.

66. Those who think they can observe with their own strength God's commandments as well as the multitude of men's prohibitions, collapse under the fantastic burden, and crawl miserably in the mud of sin, affecting an air of superiority before those who do not disguise their weaknesses. Therefore, hypocrisy, pride and hardness are born and become fortified, through too much confidence in oneself and not enough faith in God.

66'. We must begin by asking for God's help without being too concerned about the state which we find ourselves in, for he himself shall put his house in order if we let him do it in his way, without hindering him with our blind efforts. The observance of his laws shall then become for us light work, instead of being an unbearable burden, and we shall swim naturally in his holiness without effort and without fatigue, like he who floats on the great water.

67. Parents, who do all the work in the house, let little children believe that their aid is indispensable, while the latter do nothing but hinder them and slow them down in their task. And parents even let their children believe they have done all the work by themselves, and the pride of the little children makes the adults smile, knowing full well what chaos the house would fall into if they were not there to keep it in order.

67'. Thus, God does all the work in us, and when through our efforts we think we are helping him, we only hinder him and hold him back, but he also smiles paternally and lets us believe we are useful so as not to discourage our nascent goodwill, for when we have grown in the faith and the love of God, we shall be able to help him by listening to his word in our hearts and by manifesting it in the world.

68. We do not tell you not to pray, not to praise, not to rest and not to act. We tell you to efface yourselves more and more and let God pray, praise, rest and act in you, so that you float in his constructive joy instead of foundering in your powerless sadness.

68'. Let us pull and push in the direction of God and never in our personal direction, and everything shall go exactly as we wish, without hindrance and even with amazing ease, for the all-powerful hand acts for us, and we only have to follow it humbly instead of opposing it conceitedly.

69. What is so scandalous for instructed believers on learning that the worship of the Lord is in fact accomplished in our hearts without intermediaries, and not in an image on stone altars through the intervention of civil servants? Yet these people are necessary in order to keep and transmit the revelation of the holy Scriptures.

69'. Those who experience vertigo feel better with a blindfold over their eyes, and for those who are handicapped it is more advantageous to use crutches, but on the condition that those who guide them have neither blindfold nor crutches, and that they do not impose them on those who see the heart of things and who walk alone towards God's salvation.

70. Some think they understand everything and get upset, for they only grasp the outer layer of the word, which thus overwhelms them, instead of freeing them if they perceived it in its interior.

70'. Let us be simple and free in our hearts, and we shall no longer be complicated people or slaves in the world.

71. The restless, the greedy and the violent have invaded the world, and the place of those who truly search for God has become minuscule, and will soon have disappeared completely.

71'. It is then when the Lord shall assemble his own in the imperishable and peaceful kingdom, and shall abandon the reprobates to the frenzied ring of hell in the dead dust.

72. We no longer have a place in this world where hearts harden like iron and like the cement of dead temples.

72'. The harder and more ferocious they become, the more they shall be struck and broken into pieces in death.

73. The revolutionaries are burned by God, but they do not know it. Who shall reveal to them the amazing proximity of the Unique One? Who shall put them face to face with the divine fire so that they recognize their Lord? Who shall lead them back towards divine justice, which is the only thing that can fully satisfy them?

73'. It is more difficult to convert these people in their hearts than to maintain the flocks of the mediocre and hypocrites in the tepidness of their dying faith. But what a magnificent and dense harvest to offer to the Highest, rather than that straw without grain that the wind scatters in the dust of the world!

74. The religious and the believers have ended up confusing the living reality of God with the symbols and the historical figures that veil it, which plunges them into idolatry without their realizing it.
«Who is to blame? He who makes God's truth shine, or those who do not receive it?»

74'. Do we understand why everyone bows and scrapes before the malice of the rebel and why all adhere now to the impious dogma of scientific progress and material happiness in this fallen world? Why does everyone lend a hand today to the installation of humanity in the hell with no way out?

75. All of them have become speculative, and there are no longer any operatives among them to oppose the invading tide of the science of the outside that submerges the world.

75'. The Lord teaches science in secret, and they profane it in public. The Lord cures the sick, and they poison the healthy. The Lord revives the dead, and they kill the living.

76. Finally, the nonbelievers, seeing nothing but the idolatry of images and of individuals, have re-

76'. The Lord simplifies the law, and they complicate it inextricably. The Lord walks on water, and they

jected everything in a disorderly way, but they have fallen into an even worse idolatry, which is that of matter, which seals them in death without return. For essence, substance and filth are inextricably confused in it, and if they succeed in using the raw matter, however they are not able to separate it in an elemental way, and if they do succeed in separating it, it is with such violence and such scattering that they cannot join it together again in purity, for it has disappeared before their eyes full of malice and profane science.

sink into the earth. The Lord gives freely, and they sell even death. The Lord revives gloriously, and they rot ignominiously. The intelligent have become a calamity for the world, for their intelligence is applied to the surface of things, or spins round and round vertiginously without advancing, and when it seeks the inside of things, it is to volatilize them. But in reality it destroys nothing, and it is thus that they sink more and more into the hell that they themselves have created.

The spirit of the sage is dominated by a single and fixed idea: not to intervene, to let nature and time act.
LAO TSE

All things under the sky are born from that which moves, and all that moves, from that which reposes.
LAO TSE

BOOK XXIII

They shall come from the Orient and the Occident, from the North and from the South, those that shall sit at table in God's kingdom.

JESUS

The darkness shall change into dawn, you shall be full of confidence and your wait shall not be in vain.

JOB

UNE ÈREVIT

1. Natural needs have to be separated from the worship of God until they are absorbed in him effortlessly. Thus we shall avoid the division of the principal sin and its multiplication into particular sins, which end up discouraging people from the faith and the love of God.

2. A true believer who cries to his Lord for help while swimming through the mud is worth more than a hundred thousand hypocrites who pretend to be pious and who have made their permanent home in their hidden dunghill.

3. In any case we have to imitate artificially the virtues engendered by the love of God, for we would prevent love from being born and from growing and we would remain pris-

THE UNITY

1'. We must allow for a certain tolerance towards ourselves and towards others, just as the Lord does with everyone, but we must keep most alert in our search for and frequenting of the Perfect One, for it is he alone who shall deliver us from the traps and temptations of the world if we ask him ceaselessly.

2'. Let us pray to our beautiful Lord without becoming discouraged and let us ask him for aid and assistance, for he shall keep us away from sin and, in the end, he shall even prevent evil from approaching us. It is a marvel that is easy for him.

3'. Thus, it is better to pray to the Lord in our hearts with all our weaknesses, for in this way they shall become erased little by little; however by trying to eliminate them by

oners of hypocrisy, which is worse than the greatest impiety.

4. If someone is tempted by the world to the point of abandoning his religious state, or even the practices of his faith, let him go boldly into the world provided that he remains secretly in contact with his Lord in his heart; for when he has recognized, through personal experience, the void, the vanity and the mortal agony of the world, he shall come back cured forever to the bosom of the Unique One; and his Lord shall welcome him in a kindly way. This one shall never again feel like going outside and seeing what is happening there.

5. If, by accident, an impious person or a hypocrite has a quick look at the Book, he releases it as though he has burned himself and pushes it far away from him.

6. If a sincere believer happens to read some lines of the work, he does not want to put it down again, and he takes it home with him so as to get to know it in its entirety.
If a mediocre one opens the Book, he lays it down sniggering stupidly and looks around him for an opinion that reassures him in his death.

7. Each word of the Book can be held up to ridicule by the ignorant. What a punishment for them! They do not even know it. They move towards the abattoir with a black veil

ourselves, we shall do nothing but repress them and nourish them in the mud of malodorous sin.

4'. He who can remain outside the world does equally well, on the condition that he does no violence to himself, for, in that case, it is an enraged demon that thrives inside the skin of a sheep, and the last fall shall be worse than the first on the day of judgement, when the outer layers shall burst into pieces and the inside of all beings and all things shall be manifested.
«Lord, deliver us from the triumphant stupidity of the imbeciles; deliver us from the company of unyielding rebels; deliver us from the blind and beatific satisfaction of the mediocre.»

5'. Any old band of hypocrites or fakers can establish themselves and thrive under the cover of the holy Scriptures, without them being devalued as a result.

6'. But many simple people who cannot discern the good tool from the bad workmen condemn everything en bloc and withdraw forever from the faith and love of God. The fate of the imbeciles is certainly not enviable, but that of the deceivers is inexorably inscribed in the stench of hell.

7'. It is only madmen who exchange their life for wretched and transient things, for the price of a fantastic job in this world. There are no longer any sages who exchange

over their head and they mock those who call them to the freedom of life.

8. O Merciful One! come to our help in spite of ourselves, since our stupidity stops us even from shouting to you. O All-Powerful One! awake in us faith in immortality and orientate our hearts towards your holy face so that we are re-engendered in your purity and in your incorruptibility.

9. He who has recognized the unity of life does not feel ashamed to help an earthworm, for he knows beyond doubt that he aids himself by helping anything that lives.

10. How can we not madly desire the outer layers of things, which are the goods of this world? But too much work, too many lies and too many crimes are necessary to acquire them, and when one has obtained them, they are like smoke that vanishes into the night.

11. It is enough to make you an idiot while looking for the secrets of the world, but it is enough to make you become really mad while running after God's secret. O Lord! give us back the purity, the incorruptibility and the peace of your garden of Eden.

12. Here we are like enraged beasts that rip themselves apart in the quagmire into which we have fallen, and the good have their throats slit

their death for eternal life, for the price of an attentive repose here below.

8'. He who hands over his terrestrial life to God to obtain eternal life is a saint who is wise. He who hands over his eternal life to God to obtain God is a sage who is holy.

9'. Open your hand, open your spirit, open your heart, and life shall bathe you all over. Close your hand, close your spirit, close your heart, and death shall hem you in on all sides.

10'. He who exploits his fellow men by deceiving them, how much he despises them, but how much he despises himself, and what sadness and what solitude also! It is even better to die, and that is what they eventually do, for there are many ways to kill oneself through despair and through disgust at oneself.

11'. Purify our hearts with the fire of purgation and fertilize us with your heavenly love, by means of your wayfaring grace, O Magnanimous life-giver!

12'. Many are like corks floating on the sea of this world and are also, unfortunately, like dead pebbles in the sea of God. But some are like

cheek by jowl with the wicked in the great abattoir of death. Who would not be terrified every day of his life that he has been spared?

13. Who can persuade stupidity and rebellion when combined? Who can vanquish meanness of the soul united with meanness of the spirit? Who can hope for anything from maliciousness in the service of avarice? Who can obtain grace in the face of obtuse prejudice nourished by morose resentment? The Lord can change everything if he so wishes in a twinkling of an eye! He is all-powerful to make the heavenly seed buried in the tomb germinate.

14. He who does not know how to cry over the misfortune of others like over his own, he who does not know how to rejoice over the happiness of others like over his own, and he who does not know how to laugh at his misadventures like he laughs at those of others cannot be taught by God, for he is still separated from the unity of the Unique One.

15. We shall not hide from our children that they are clothed in animal skin and neither shall we hide from them the appetites and needs of the Beast, and we shall present them as natural functions indispensable to the maintenance of incarnate life, functions of which no-one should be proud or ashamed, for they are transient.

steadfast rocks in the sea of this world and are also, fortunately, like fish that swim in the sea of God.

13'. He who truly loves God in his heart is not an idiot, nor a rebel, nor vile, nor cunning, nor miserly, nor stubborn, nor full of hatred. It is up to him to flee from the wicked and diligently seek his fellow man, so as to love him as he loves himself in the unity of the unique Lord of love and life.

«Miracle! the rebels come to God in their hearts when the hypocrites no longer condemn them in the world.»

14'. We are not alone and abandoned in this world, we only need to listen to the voice that whispers in our hearts and to examine attentively that which comes to us and that which distances itself from us, silencing our personal wishes and judgements.

15'. Thus, the Angel, when he is no longer subject to the Beast, shall be able to remain firmly turned towards the Lord, and the Beast, when he is no longer held in contempt by the Angel, shall feel neither rebelliousness nor vice, and the Lord shall be able to free us without a foolish struggle and without tearing up any part of our fallen and provisional compound.

16. And above all, we shall not mix them with the mysteries of God, in order to avoid shameful repressions, delirious complexes, wretched deviations, unanimous hypocrisy and the dreadful mess that results from the idiotic confusion of the Angel and the Beast, which we must clearly separate and not ridicule by denying the one and demeaning the other at the same time.

17. The sages accomplish everything in God, for there is no longer any separation for them, but this is done naturally, without violence, as when heaven unites with earth in a holy way to procreate all things.
He who truly loves God never hides from him.

18. Only these who have first separated can join together, for purification is accomplished in separation and union is achieved in purity.

19. God shall dissolve us and shall coagulate us once more in purity. Woe betide those who shall have chosen to install themselves in the quagmire of death, for this time they shall never again emerge from it.

20. No, no, no, there is no peace, no stability and no organization possible in this world mixed with death. Those who claim the contrary are blind and stupid. Their intelligence and their courage are powerless to put in order the rottenness of death.

16'. For the Beast shall grow weaker in the darkness of the world, and the Angel shall grow stronger in God's light, and the final separation shall be accomplished without tearing and ripping. Many shall return to God when the men of God no longer concern themselves with anything but the things of God, that is, when they leave the things of the Beast to the Beast and those of the world to the world.

17'. Who shall understand the liberation provided by the intelligent and humble acceptance of our fallen state? Who shall understand that we must first look towards our Lord before trying to organize or even contain artificially the mud of sin in which we lie dying?

18'. One day, the Angel shall return to rouse the Beast purified by fire, and the whole compound shall revive in the glorious and incorruptible unity of the Unique One.

19'. Never more shall there be repose or happiness for them in the perpetually dying and perpetually renascent stench of hell.

20'. This fallen world is no more than a small sample of hell, and yet nobody can rest in peace during the period of his short life. What, then, must hell be like, where God's blessing is totally absent? Are we not right a thousand times over to orientate

Do they not see it clearly?

21. Yes, surely, the blessing of the Lord shall wash us of the sin of death and his spirit shall raise us in our tombs, and we shall praise his holy Name forever.

22. We can install ourselves in this transient world, but only like travellers who take shelter in a waiting room.

23. Everything that is subject to fire is not God's, for God is the very essence of fire.

24. There are too many literary hacks writing about the mysteries of the Unique One, and not enough enlightened saints and not enough operative sages.

25. Some die of hunger in this world because they do not know how to lie, to steal or to kill, and others are showered with riches to the point of absurdity because they serve the destructive, homicidal demon. Likewise, in the future life, some shall be showered with heavenly goods to the point of absurdity because they shall have faithfully served their Lord, and others shall burst in the desolation of death with the demons they shall have followed like imbeciles. It is a thing that shall astonish many shrewd and simple ones.

men towards the Lord of life rather than encouraging them to build on mud with mud?

21'. First of all, should we not burn the aggressive stench that binds us and poisons us from everywhere? For it is that which is an obstacle to the union of divine love.

22'. The final goal of humanity is not its installation in the world, it is its transfiguration and fixation in God.

23'. O density of pure gold in repose!
O heat of pure metal in fusion!
O sparkle of the volatilised splendour!

24'. Heavenly things and earthly things add to one another or subtract from one another. Only the Lord can divide them and mix them without confusion and without harm.

25'. Is not every word of our language like a blasphemy before the word of the Highest?
Is not every breath from our mouth like a pestilent exhalation from hell before the purity of the incorruptible one?
Is not every gesture of our hands like the grimace of an ape before the ART of the Most-Knowledgeable One? And however, what splendour remains in us and waits underneath the mud of death! If only it could finally awake and make us the heirs to the glory of God!

26. Many who serve the Lord with their lips and not with their heart have placed their self-love above God's truth. Thus, they exclude from the churches those who scold them instead of becoming converted. Thinking of saving themselves, they plunge into hypocrisy and into the worship of their own person.

27. O rich imbeciles! shall you not recognize that which is beautiful, that which is good and that which is true, when the thing is born before your blind eyes?
«What indeed attracts you is the money that things represent, and not the thing itself.»

28. The Lord having begun to flow in me, we sang together a little song, like the wind does in burgeoning leaves on a spring morning.

29. O my Lord, rejoice in me and all shall thus be well, for your joy submerges all anxiety and even makes one laugh at death.

30. He who has understood the Book does not explain anything to anyone, but he can certainly manifest something good and communicate something excellent.

31. An intelligent nation honours gifted and instructed men and employs them for great things.
An imbecilic nation despises them and lets them stagnate in poverty and in exile.

26'. If you now put a high price on that which you formerly rejected for a mouthful of bread, you are accursed in your intelligence, in your heart and in your goods, for you enrich the dead and you let the living ones around you die of hunger.

27'. Miserly and stupid people, you shall remain sunk forever in the mud of death, for the weight of your polluted money drags you down, and you stick to it, while it does not stick to you.

28'. The poet who holds the morning star in his hands sings like a joyful little child. Those who hold only the mud of the world cry bitterly for their lost life.

29'. Purge, water, fertilize, bind, shine, flow.
Cook, separate, unite, fix, sow, praise, rest.

30'. The true sage does not make speeches in the world. He digs, he waters his earth and he tastes the fruit of heaven and earth, which is the only true wealth.

31'. The general decomposition finally pulls people down to earth with the mediocre who lead it, and the sages emerge once more from the chaos to re-establish God's law in the heart of the small protected group.

32. If we are tired, let us rest in God, and if we are bored, let us look for the mystery of the Unique One. Thus, God shall be our guide and our support at all times.

33. Who shall spend his life being grateful for his condition so as always to be helped by God, the unique Living One?

34. Who does better: he who hides his wisdom, or he who hides his ignorance?

35. O believers of all religions, of all races and of all nations! recognize yourselves as the children of the unique God and support yourselves amid the growing tide of the impious.

36. It is useless to run after the author, we would find nothing but the void that dwells in an idiot in God, which would teach us nothing. The Book is sufficient for all works and for all rest.

37. How could those that have transformed the formidable revelation of the holy Scriptures into hypocritical, muddy morality recognize right now, under the symbolic figures of their faith, the incredible truth of the unique God and Principle?

38. These do well in transmitting blindly the mysteries of which they no longer know the foundation, but

32'. If the Book does not make us touch the Lord of love and of life, then the Book can be thrown onto the dunghill with all the literature that raves in the void.

33'. Who shall tie the words of the Book around his neck? Who shall display them in his house? Who shall make them germinate in his heart?

34'. He who does violence to nothing inside and outside sees everything grow in him and around him without effort.

35'. Let us accept our making a mistake and let us be able to recognize it. Let us learn to correct ourselves and let us know how to keep on the way without violence, and God shall teach us everything we wish to know.

36'. Let us strive to be the instruments of Providence, which nourishes the sages, the saints and the simple ones, for it is an easy way of participating in the growing blessing of the Unique One.

37'. There they are like illiterates who fiercely defend the books that none of them can read, but which all know through the images that illustrate them, and there they are who blindly reject him who has learned to read once more and wants to make known to them the means to their rescue.

38'. Of course, God punishes them for their conceited pretentiousness. What amazing humour to have

how can they judge the truth of a Scripture for which they do not have the key?

his treasure thus guarded and transmitted by blind fanatics, to offer it in secret to those he loves and who venerate him in their heart!

39. Some among them who think themselves more enlightened than the rest say of the Book: «It is a dream», for, living in a dream, they take the dream for reality and, inversely, reality for the dream. Who can wake them from their mortal drowsiness before the staggering judgement of the end?

39'. A good corrective has indeed brought the rebellious woman back onto God's holy way. The absurdity of suffering shall perhaps one day lead the reasonable ones of the faith to no longer rave in spirit! Such a miracle is easy for the Lord; we have an example of it before our eyes.

40. The stump has flowered again, the flower has given its scent and the fruit has matured heavily without anyone suspecting it.
«Who shall eat the gift of God? And who shall be penetrated by his splendour?»

40'. God jokes well with a poor idiot without instruction and without diplomas, so why would he not want to converse seriously with intelligent ones full of learning and laden with qualifications?

41. The denomination «right-thinking one» has become synonymous with hypocrite and with mediocre one in the world. Let us make the name «believer» become synonymous with free man detached from everything in the love of God.

41'. Before boiling the dirty linen, one has to soak it, otherwise, one cooks the filth instead of removing it, and the final state is worse than the initial one, for the dirt is fixed in the fabric and can no longer be removed.

42. Let our quest and our life be firstly for ourselves, and thus we shall be neither misunderstood nor disappointed by the mediocre, we shall be neither deceived nor bullied by the powerful, and we shall not be misled by the world.

42'. There are saints according to the world who repress their instinctive nature and there are sages according to the world who follow their instinctive nature. There are saints according to God who follow their intuitive nature and there are sages according to God who embody their heavenly nature. The last of these are the only survivors!

43. Little intelligent ones, rest a moment, look at great nature, contemplate the great ART, before death disperses you as playing cards are shuffled. Thus, your spirits and your souls shall open to the mystery of creation and to the love of the creator and shall fix themselves in him forever.

44. How many have come out again of their tombs among all the sages and among all the saints in the world? And how many among them have not even entered them at all? The word of the latter is more precious than any other for the intelligent who seek beyond particular creatures.

45. Only rediscovered innocence can reconcile men with God, with nature and with themselves.

46. Let us leave the Book and be content with the thing which the Book speaks of, for it alone can content us definitively if we possess it in its integrity.

47. It is the joyous and peaceful possession of that which is, that which moves and that which rests that makes the enlightenment and happiness of the sage.

48. Are you thinking of doing something good without the sun, without the moon, without the stars, without air, without water, and without earth? Then you are ignorant of agriculture, which is the science of God.

43'. Do you seriously intend to replace with compliments the food, clothing and heating that have been lacking for those who have all their lives sought deliverance for everybody? Hypocrites, help rather those who freely search for their Lord here below while there is still time for them and for you.

44'. A few sages have guessed the beginning of the beginnings, but how many of them have conceived of it clearly? How many have embodied it visibly? How many have held it in their hands? How many have fixed it in their heart? How many have united themselves to it for eternal life?

45'. Only the knowledge of God can save them from the alternation of life and death, if they so wish.

46'. Before being separated, earth and heaven formed just one single thing. Thus, by uniting them again, we shall form the unique thing of the beginning of the beginnings.

47'. The more we seek the approval of men, the less we shall obtain that from the Unique One.

48'. There is nothing good in the whole Book, except for a few small insignificant sentences that everyone reads, but that nobody really understands or practises.

49. We have not written such a Book at such a time to then be inundated with trivial questions.

50. Who teaches without profaning?
Who severs without judging?
Who lives the present?
Who sleeps in the storm?
Who makes rich without becoming poor?

51. If we desire wealth, let us begin by giving from our poverty, and let us continue by giving from our superfluity.

52. If we desire power, let us begin by supporting some weak ones, and let us continue by protecting them all.

53. If we wish to acquire a good reputation, let us begin by saying good things about our friends, and let us continue by praising even our enemies.

54. If we desire instruction, let us begin by studying a thousand things, and let us continue by studying a single thing.

55. If we desire the arts, let us begin by training severely our spirit and our hands, and let us continue by letting them go freely.

56. If we desire immortal science, let us begin by studying nature, and let us continue by imitating it very closely.

49'. Any wisdom that leads to hard labour is certainly the worst of madnesses.

50'. Who manifests heaven in himself?
Who receives and who gives without measure?
Who acts without disturbing?
Who rests without extinguishing?
Who is one with the Unique One?

51'. If we wish for security, let us begin by becoming humble, and let us continue by becoming invisible in everything.

52'. If we wish for freedom, let us begin by not doing violence to the nature of other beings, and let us continue by letting our own nature repose in itself.

53'. If we wish for happiness, let us begin by taking hold of all that is of the world, and let us continue by giving it up completely.

54'. If we wish for holiness, let us begin by thinking of others, and let us continue by thinking only of God.

55'. If we wish for wisdom, let us begin by looking at the world, and let us continue by looking into ourselves.

56'. Only the fact of a certain perfection allows one to attain great perfection and remain in it for eternity.

57. If you have found the unity of the Unique One, tear out the pages of the Book and let them fly away in the wind while humming a joyful song.

58. The more we struggle, the more we sink in the world.
The more we rest, the better we shall float in heaven.

59. Let us not have the conceited pretension of monopolizing God for ourselves alone, for the Father is for all those who love him in their hearts, and not for those who profanely give sermons in the world.

60. How can the degenerate disciples of the master judge the love of the master for someone? And how can they admit to or exclude anyone from the love of the wise and holy master, if they do not know either the will or the secret love of the master?

61. We have taken up the habit of the charlatan, for the disinterested despise of the world is less difficult to bear than its interested admiration.

62. The profession that allows us to live by helping others to live is a blessed profession, whatever it may be.

63. The bird charmer does not seize any of them, and that is why they all come to him without fear. Likewise, the sage apprehends no-one, and that is why everyone confides in him without distrust.

57'. If not, do not leave them day or night until they penetrate your understanding and until they lead you to the mud that neither wets nor stains anything.

58'. It is not the work that counts, nor the worker, but the thing which the work and the worker speak of.

59'. Each man and each woman is God's priest and priestess in their own home, for the conservation and transmission of the holy Scriptures and of their revealed mysteries.

60'. Their judgements have become derisory because their self-love has profanely substituted God's love. They have the keys to the kingdom in images but not in reality, and they do not tolerate that another receives them from God's hands without their approval.

61'. The Book is like the ark that carries and transmits the secret of the Unique One. Many shall carry it, but few shall penetrate it.

62'. The trade that allows us to live by threatening the life of others is an accursed profession, whatever it may be.

63'. The sage begins his work, but lets nature accomplish it in his place; thus, he works while resting, and everything works out for him effortlessly, for he obstructs nothing.

64. The mixture of elements that forms the multiple combinations of creation is like the mixture of playing cards that forms the multiple combinations of the game; and the elements return to the mass and are then combined once more, as the playing cards return to the pack and are redistributed without real increase or decrease, for neither profit nor loss exist for the immutable that IS.

64'. Magnificent Lord, who dwells in the holy land and who purifies it of the sin of death, invade me and inspire my spirit and my soul, so that I am submitted to your delivering grace and your fertilizing love, like all angelic creatures who sing your praises eternally, O Purest One! O Most-Perfect One! O Most-Gracious One! O Most-Knowledgeable One! O Most-Bounteous One! O Gentlest One! O Most-Loving One! who IS.

65. The science of Satan does violence to beings and things and leads to slavery in abject death.

65'. The science of God perfects beings and things and leads to freedom in the sweet-smelling life.

65". Each one can easily judge where the mortal complication of hell is, and where the vivifying simplicity of heaven is.

66. If we do not give up our works and ourselves, and if we do not become empty and free inside and out, there is no deliverance, here below or elsewhere, for anyone.

66'. Let us not cling on to anything or anyone, and we shall thus avoid the heavy burdens and the final drowning, for we shall float easily on the divine ocean where the Lord shall take us into his holy ark.

67. To accept a failure gladly is to prepare a victory already.

67'. Let us put everything and ourselves into God's hands and we shall be joyful and free.

68. The revelation of our God of light and life constitutes the basis of all religions and of all true philosophies taught by God.

68'. Just as the drunkard can no longer do without wine, the saint can no longer do without God, and the drunkenness of one and the other makes reasonable people smile.

69. Shame on you, blind clerics, because you have risen up proudly like a wall between God and men,

69'. They have made a personal cheese from the universal milk of the holy Church, and they have installed

instead of stooping humbly like a bridge before them!

70. Those who have goodwill in God and not in themselves shall work to re-establish the purity, simplicity, love and knowledge of the Church in their hearts and in their houses, without worrying about the prerogatives or the illusory sole rights of the shepherds full of pride.

71. The enormity of God's revelation can only be understood by the sons of God; the mediocre are irremediably excluded from it.

72. Men may well exclude other men from their human organizations. Not one of them can exclude anyone from the love of God.

73. Let us give a large part of our lives to the Lord, and the Lord shall give us his own immeasurable part.

74. To love life is to help life and is to accept movement and change, which are inherent to life.

75. The prophets have no need of ready-made prayers, for the Spirit of God inspires them supernaturally.

themselves inside without worrying about the seekers, the faithful and the abandoned. The Lord observes them through the dark crust of sin.

70'. Those that God chooses and to whom he sends his Holy Spirit are necessarily superior to those that men elect in their councils, for those that see the light are above those that feel with their hands the darkness. Do we not understand that the gift received from God prevails over the lesson learned from men, and that the light of heaven accomplishes the Scripture here below?

71'. Death shall be powerless against the one who has eaten God, for the light of life shall dwell in him forever.

72'. Thus, we should not fear the judgement of men that is made in the world, and we should not doubt the love of God, who is patient even with those that have gone astray the most.

73'. The greatest prayer is to listen. The greatest praise is to be silent. The greatest meditation is to think no more. The greatest action is to rest in God.

74'. The blow that strikes us today perhaps prepares us for the blessing that shall be showered upon us tomorrow. Who knows?

75'. The stinking filth shall be destroyed by fire, and the dark filth shall be separated by water.

76. It is wrong to continually draw men's attention to their innumerable sins, for they become discouraged and abandon the religion that has become stupid through the fault of the mediocre and ignorant, well-intentioned in themselves and not in God.

76'. It is better to orientate the hearts of sinners towards the Lord, whose grace and love shall deliver them from their darkness more surely than all of their efforts put together. The trust in God is worth more than the trust in oneself for survival.

77. The saint binds the soul and the spirit in God and overcomes the second death.

77'. The sage binds the soul, the spirit and the body in God and overcomes the first and the second death.

78. The end shall see the struggle of those that practice the science of God, which is integration of life, against those that practise the science of Satan, which is mortal disintegration.

78'. The makers of life shall be established in life, and the makers of death shall be driven back to death without remission. Let each one consider his work attentively, while there is still time to abandon bad actions.

79. The enemies of God fight against the temporal Churches, which are complicated, multiple, transient and particular.

79'. God's friends fight for the spiritual Church, which is simple, unique, eternal and universal.

79". Thus, everyone works for the unity of the Unique One.

I have struck down all the work of your hands, and you have not returned to me.
HAGGAI

Is it not God's will that people work for fire, and that nations tire themselves out for nothingness?
HABAKKUK

BOOK XXIV

> *Watch, observe and question the ploughman, and learn from him that what is sowed is what is reaped.*
>
> ISIS

> *He knows what enters the bosom of the earth and what comes out of it. He knows what descends from the heavens and what ascends to them.*
>
> KORAN

RÉTIVE NUE

1. He who nourishes us does not criticize us, but those who leave us to perish are lavish with their boundless judgements and condemnations, for they think they are superior in the world.

2. He is not like us, therefore he is mad, say the impious.

3. On searching for the dying world we shall become magnets of death and we shall die.

4. O my Lord! do you not hear the ignorant shepherds who, in order to flatter the mediocre and the hypocrites, acclaim the profane science and its mercenary scholars in the holy place?
Violence, ignorance and vanity

THE WELL

1'. Hypocrites who judge, you take care not to help to live those whom you condemn. You shall be judged in the same way. God shall take away from you all chance of salvation, and you shall stagnate in the desperation of death.

2'. They are not like me, therefore they are dead, says the Lord of life.

3'. On seeking the unique Living One, we shall become magnets of life and we shall live.

4'. If there are still intelligent and inspired men of God in the Churches, these shall examine their Scriptures up to the secret foundation where the immovable and imperishable stone established by God, established of God, established

have invaded their hands, their spirits and their hearts, and here are those that lead astray and corrupt the flocks entrusted to their safe-keeping.

Enlighten these blind ones, good Lord, or make them dumb, so that the violence of impious science does not destroy your holy and precious images.

O come holy Lord! with your whip and your crosier, with your cane and your sword, with your winnowing basket that sifts and separates the wheat from the chaff.

(This is the verse of the meeting and of the warning, which shall be repeated three times.)

5. The last saints shall not flatter the mediocre and the rebels who put pressure on them, for the quality of the last living ones shall be more precious to them than the multitude of incurable dead ones.

6. Men may well distract themselves sometimes with their works, but they must never take them seriously, for they are worthless and dead. Only the work of God is alive forever.

7. Let us seek the blessed places where the sun, the moon and the stars shine, and where the helpful elements and earth encourage the humble seekers of God.

8. No more solitude, no more sadness and no more abandonment for in God shines.

These shall read the Book attentively, and the praise from their hearts shall rise towards the Highest like the pure flame of the holy offering.

These shall denounce without fear the accursed science that does violence to nature, beings and things, and that sells death at a high price to all.

These shall recall the science of God that does violence to nothing and nobody and that gives life freely to all.

Blessed be the true servants of the Highest!

5'. Is it not enough that one voice of God be raised in the world to denounce and bring down the prestigious ventures of the evil one? Or are there no longer any living ones to hear it?

6'. When the science of God is manifested, all the work and all the inventions of men shall be discarded as useless. Only the reprobates shall remain submitted to servile work because of their blind pride.

7'. Wretchedness in the cold is only poverty in the sun, and it can become infinite wealth before God if we reap the gold that the Lord pours lavishly across the darkened world.

8'. If we wish God to choose us, let us not omit to choose him too,

him who converses in his heart with the Perfect One.

9. God is patient with the impatience of his prophets, for he wishes to give all the ones gone astray the greatest possible number of chances to return to him.

10. How many prepare themselves to enter the repose of God by abandoning the fallacious restlessness of the world and its worries renewed ad infinitum?

11. How many withdraw to the holy mountain so as to get to know the imperishable companion, the unfailing friend, the unique Lord of heaven who gives life without mixture?

12. We try to emerge from the heap of those who are dying before God, not to plunge our brothers in the cesspool, but rather to help them also to come out of the darkness of death.
«Shall they not come with us towards the splendour that shines in heaven?»

13. It is the essential and substantial word transmitted by the master that makes us the heirs to the Highest, on condition that we receive it in a holy way with gratitude and not profanely with malice.

and if we want him to choose us in his kingdom, let us not forget to choose him first in our hearts.

9'. It has been said: «A thousand years for man are like one day for God, and one day for the Unique One is like a thousand years for men.»

10'. How many enter the solitude of their heart, in order to pray, to praise and to contemplate the living God who is enough for everything?

11'. How many cook in secret the mysterious and holy dew that comes from heaven, in order to manifest the admirable Saviour who delivers from death?

12'. All our works are derisory before the work of life of the Highest.
Would we not have done better to adore him in silence, rather than write the Book for the ignorant vanity of this falsely-intelligent and falsely-learned time?

13'. A few devoted saints and a wise expert could show once again to the believers the path that saves from the exile and the death of this world, if the hearts of men were not so deeply buried beneath the filth of sin.

14. Wild flocks are decimated by wild beasts, but protected flocks end up in the abattoir.

So let the believers therefore support themselves individually in God, without exposing themselves uselessly in the world.

15. The powerless ones who recite ready-made prayers conceitedly think they are the only ones who pray properly, for they are ignorant of the praise to God that springs spontaneously from the heart of the inspired saint.

«God shall judge the dying who reject his living ones, and he shall turn away the dead who bully his envoys.»

16. We shall be known and alive in heaven thanks to God's work that does not perish, for our personal works shall disappear with the transitory world and our memory here below shall perish with time.

«The kingdom of the Perfect One is immutable, and its Lord does not lie.»

17. Let us not make ourselves out to be important, nor scornful, nor saved, nor pure, so as not to be odious before the Lord, and above all, so as not to make the Lord odious in the world.»

18. The sermonizers have succeeded in making God disgusting to the world, and the right-thinking ones have succeeded in making him the object of hate. A great success, in

14'. Deliver us, O good Lord! from the sordid battle for a life dying in a rotten world, and make us heirs to your incorruptible, living and eternal light, so that we may adore you in the madness of the love that gives and receives without measure.

15'. The water sometimes springs from the rock in the desert, but it is more often a deceptive mirage than a palpable and vivifying reality. Let us not fall asleep in the hum of the Churches and cloisters; let us struggle in them for our liberation, uniting ourselves wholeheartedly with the Lord of love, of poetry and of true science.

16'. The Book is not for bleating sheep, nor for ravishing wolves. It is for the free children of God who bless the Lord in their hearts and who fervently seek his grace, his love and his salvation, before the fury of the incandescent cloud that shall consume all impure things.

17'. The closer we are to the Lord of life, the more we shall hide it in the world, so as not to profane the love of the Unique One.

«The "respectable" people according to the world are not the "respectable" people according to God.»

18'. The mediocre and the hypocrites submerge the Churches, and the atheists dominate the world. How shall the true believers subsist if the Lord does not come rapidly to

truth, for which they congratulate themselves in an imbecilic way like bad servants who have sent away their master's guests, with the intention of taking their place at the table. They shall be ignominiously driven out and replaced by new, more faithful and more intelligent assistants.

19. Let us receive with humility, but also with effusiveness and love, those who come to ask us for information about God and about his salvation, and let us recommend to them the assiduous reading of the wise and holy Scriptures, instead of rebuffing them with boring sermons and arrogant opinions.

20. A good example of life in the love of the Lord is worth more than all the prepared speeches and all the platitudes delivered without inspiration.

21. The Book is for those to whom it is given to receive it. It is God's justice, which is beyond the understanding of men.

22. Hypocrites, the mediocre and atheists may well reject the Book; free believers shall propagate it with the aid of the Holy Spirit who inspired it, and their multitude shall cover all the earth if they remain united in God in their hearts, and if they do no violence to anyone in their faith.

help them?

Who has ever seen a good crop germinate and grow in a field of stones? Yet everything is possible for the Lord of life and love, who sows without reckoning, even in dead ash.

19'. Servant of God, friend of God, children of God, lover of God are enviable, true, unique and secret titles. All the rest are, by comparison, like the titles of an ex-convict, of which there is nothing to be proud.

20'. Those who reject the Book reject their own life without knowing it. Who shall unstop their ears if they do not wish to hear? And who shall open their eyes if they do not wish to see? Does the obviousness of the heavenly work not impose itself alone on the enlightened believers?

21'. First of all, the prophets remind us of him who is, him who lives, him who remains immovable in oneself for eternity.

22'. The Mother washes away our scum and the Father allies himself with our purity, for his glory is gleaming and pure like that of the sun. Thus, we must consume in ourselves all sin and wash all blemish, so that he might dwell in us and resurrect us in his heavenly splendour.

23. What is the use of triumphing here below, if it is triumphing in the mud of death that eventually kills us? Derisory triumph that the shrewd ones and the imbeciles madly pursue in this world.

23'. What a painful surprise at the end of time, when they see those that they despised because of their faith obtain eternal life, while they themselves shall reap only agony maintained parsimoniously.

23". O rich imbeciles! who despise the saints and the poor of God by letting them perish of misery in the world, one day you shall beg for your excrement as food, and rottenness shall serve as your bed and your clothes.

24. The freedom of God's children is an internal freedom that says everything and that does everything in rediscovered and guarded innocence.

24'. O you, the Radiant One! allow us to find you and eat you, so that we might dwell in your eternity and your glory without equal.

25. Let us ask for our right, but let us not demand it, so as not to put an obstacle to God's judgement.

25'. He who lives God's truth innocently is contradicted by no-one.

26. If we are searching for the world, let us work as much as possible. If we are searching for God, let us rest as much as we can.

26'. Each one admires his little person and each one is proud of his little works, without seeing that God and his work are the only immortal and admirable ones.

27. We have not asked for the submission or admiration of anyone, and we have imposed ourselves on no-one.
«Who shall follow us freely as far as the Lord of resurrection?»

27'. It is perfect renunciation that opens the gates of God's kingdom to us. It is perfect destitution that fills us with God's blessing. It is the perfect void that fills us with God's love.

28. Let him who knows of a similar book to this one publish it before God and before men, if he can. If not, let him publish what he has

28'. That which is fixed comes from the earth.
That which is always moving comes from the water.

heard and what he has seen in his heart after having read it.

29. Is there anything more absurd and more tragic than the fate of the impious who refuse to ask for anything from God in their hearts hardened by pride?

30. Why do those who speak about God feel themselves obliged to adopt those tones of pedants or the quavering of beaten dogs?

31. It is characteristic of man to be astonished by creation and to search for the creator.
It is characteristic of the Beast not to worry about it and to search only for itself.

32. Our honour is to have recalled God's promise, guaranteed by his love, and accomplished through his science in his transforming glory.

33. Neither believers nor atheists suspect God's science exists, hidden behind the symbols, writings and figures of revealed religions. Those who believe in it try to appropriate it through cunning and violence. A few of them ask God for it in their heart, and scarcely one or two obtain it in the century.

That which is smoky comes from the air.
That which is greasy comes from the fire.

29'. They proclaim themselves strong and free in the world, but they die like beasts in hopeless abandonment and decay.

30'. Let us improvise our preaching so that it is experienced in God, or let us humbly remain silent in the world.

31'. Many deny, many doubt, many believe, a few seek, a few understand, a few find, one or two live and rejoin the unity of the Unique One in heaven.

32'. The Book that exalts the glory, the love and the science of God shall be the safeguard of the believers. Those who reject it shall perish in the worthless wait for him who becomes embodied before their blind eyes.

33'. The master, on visiting the disciple's dwelling, broke everything except a bottle, then burned everything he could burn except the holy Scriptures, then extinguished the ashes with water except for a half-burnt stick. Finally, he opened all the windows, except that which faced north, and then he left for the south without a word.

34. No more drudgery, no more despair and no more defeat for him who obtains the aid of the Lord in the predicaments of this world.

35. How can we not doubt God in this world mixed with death? And how can we escape the desolation of this exile in perpetually renewed slavery, wretchedness and mortal agony?

36. If God does not give us belief, we cannot believe by ourselves, nor even less so remain in the faith of saved and imperishable life that he has promised us in reward for our faithfulness to his law.

37. The true mark of God's children is that they ask everything of their Father without hesitating or doubting.

38. Too many worries, too many problems and too many temptations assail us here below for us to be able to devote ourselves in peace to the study of God's word and to the quest for his salvation.

39. Whatever our assurance and whatever our distress, let us place ourselves every day of our life, together with our affairs, in the hands of the Lord of wisdom, who is the only one that can give us the victory and the peace which do not perish.

34'. It is better to hold out your hand and enjoy the freedom and the joy of God's children than to possess the goods of the world and lack the main heavenly food.

35'. The nonbelievers rely on themselves to organize themselves here below. The believers rely on God to save themselves from the exile of this world. Here is all the difference between the reason of the senses and the folly of faith.

36'. We can weep over the impious ones, we cannot judge them and even less condemn them, for it is the Lord that chooses us and dwells in us according to his wishes, and not according to ours.

37'. O holy Begetter! consume in us the rotting foreign woman and deliver us from the dark scum, so that we might shine in the light of life where you make your nest.

38'. Let us first pray, then, for God to smooth the paths of our quest and for him to discharge us of alien worries, by making our faith stronger than the obviousness of our blind reason.

39'. Let us not reject that which seems to us dark at the beginning, for it is undoubtedly that which shall enlighten us in the end.
«O holy light! which agrees to dwell in our death in order to resurrect our life!»

40. You who are thirsty for justice and honesty, you who seek peace and friendship, you who wait for freedom and love, come freely to the Lord and to his salvation, without worrying about obstacles, erected between God and men by the dead.

41. Let us piously exchange our prayers so that God may bless them doubly.

42. Since filth, rottenness, slavery, suffering, lying and death are inextricably linked to this world, what else can we expect but the absurd on wanting to organise ourselves in it, on wanting to dominate in it, or on accepting to decay in it or waiting to perish in it, even though it be in a holy way?

43. The decadence of religions and initiations comes from the fact that the guardians, the believers and the seekers take the symbols, figures and rites to be the mystery itself, whereas they are nothing more than its images and reminders.

44. It is better to believe stupidly in the unlikelihood of divine revelation than to demonstrate its apparent impossibility in an intelligent way.

45. The impious vainly hope to acquire by force that which they refuse to ask humbly of God. They shall surely end up broken into pieces by their own violence.

40'. We are not here to wait for men to come to us in dead temples, we are here to go to men and to install God in their living hearts.

41'. «Give up and die» are the words of the enemy.
«Seek me and live» are the words of the friend.

42'. Is not the only effective solution to seek solely the salvation of life, transmitted by the Lord desended from heaven and embodied among us for our reintegration in eternal and pure life? Is it not said: «Seek first the kingdom of God and its correct use, and all the rest shall be given to you in addition»?

43'. The kingdom of God is not an abstraction or an image, nor a vague ideal. It is the only living and palpable reality that saves from death, from now on, here below.
Shall we finally understand?

44'. Profane science accomplishes incredible wonders every day, and shall God's science be powerless to save us from death?

45'. Has the moment perhaps arrived for us to prepare ourselves to cross the blaze of raging fire? Who shall come out of it again unscathed like the seed of God?

46. We desire that no-one make use of the Book to judge or to condemn from outside, for it is always useless to be in the right, and it is often dangerous.

47. If the revelation of salvation were to become lost or to cease here below, who would deliver us from the agony of the world?

48. Let us unite a small number of chosen ones by the heart and let us promise before God: help, love and fidelity in this exiled world. Thus, the Lord in person shall bless our ventures and shall guide our quest.
«If we are struck down, let us return to God, and if we are fulfilled, let us bound towards him.»

49. The proud ones of the world do indeed suspect the truth of God, but they pretend to mock it in public, while they strive to do violence to it secretly through their dark and criminal machinations.

50. All the explanations and all the experiences of the world and of ourselves are illusory, for they leave us ignorant, wretched and dying like before.
Only the love and the science of the Highest can save us from the darkness of death.

51. Everything that the proud think of the humble seekers of God, and everything that they make them endure, is like a gravestone that they bear on their own accursed back.

46'. We indicate as incomplete all the comments on the words inscribed in the Book, for the reflections of the thing are not the thing itself.

47'. Let us save our holy Scriptures from disappearing, so that they might also save us from alien death.

48'. If we do not search for God's salvation with constancy, with perseverance, with stubbornness, with stupidity, with frenzy, we shall obtain nothing but the outer layer of holy things.
«Should we not beg the world to obtain a portion of the dead things that it sells so dearly to everyone?»

49'. O super-intelligent ones who marvel at one another complacently in the filth of sin, your malice and your pride exclude you forever from the light of life where the holy Lord dwells!

50'. All the scholars and all the geniuses of the world examine only the world and know only the dark world; thus, they are content with the derisory rewards of the world and go to oblivion and the death of the world like the animals they despise and exploit.

51'. It is disobedience and the absorption of a mixed fruit that have hurled us into death. It is obedience and the absorption of a pure fruit that shall re-establish us in life.

52. Everyone wants to improve his lot of dying men, but very few attempt to escape definitively from this lamentable condition.

53. The holy Scriptures, which teach how to come out of death, are mortally boring for the dead. On the contrary, everything that plunges them into death fills them with boundless passion and enthusiasm.

54. Few humans are curious about the revelation of the mystery of the fall and of the redemption, for few men have kept the memory and the taste of the pure and imperishable life of the beginning.

55. We have been ordered to believe and to love. We have not been forbidden to seek and to know, but rather quite the contrary.

56. Woe betide those who install themselves in the mud of this world and who fall asleep in its filth, for they shall not see the light of the Perfect One shine.

52'. Everyone is passionate about the affairs of the impermanent world; very few consider studying the prodigious revelation of God's sons.

53'. People impassioned of God shall find God and his life. People impassioned of the world shall find the world and its agonizing death.

«It is the frequenting of God that shall make us find the peace of God's house.»

54'. We shall obtain only that which we truly desire and request, but we shall be fulfilled only with eternal life embodied in God.

55'. Faith and love keep us safe until the day of forgiveness. Investigation and knowledge lead us from here below to eternal life, or to death without return.

56'. Woe betide those who forget themselves in idleness or in work, in pleasure or in desperation, for their lot shall be the death from which no-one returns.

Seek me and live.

AMOS

Oh, who shall let me know where to find him, how to arrive at his throne?

JOB

BOOK XXV

> The book you have received from heaven shall increase the blindness of many of you, but do not be alarmed at the fate of the infidels.
>
> KORAN

> I have come to this world for a judgement, so as those who do not see might see, and so as those who see might become blind.
>
> JESUS

VIT EN URÉE

1. He who reaches the Lord of life here below is like an idler whom all the workers of the world would not be able to equal with all of their labours.

2. All intellectual accomplishments are illusory, for they do not drive out the agony of death that grips us here below.

3. A crushed finger, and there go all of our beautiful philosophies, exploding in cries of pain and in mad gesticulations.

4. Oh, the fine discourses! Oh, the subtle thoughts! Oh, the scholarly edifice! Oh, the vacuity of the spirit! Oh, the wisdom of the void! Oh, the transcendence of nothingness!

THE STONE

1'. How hard-working is he who has no respite day or night in the quest for imperishable life! How idle is he who rests in the living unity of the Unique One!

2'. Only the palpable incarnation of the Lord of life can deliver us from all evil and all death.

3'. When they drove nails into his hands and into his feet, he analyzed nothing and he taught nothing; but he still forgave.

4'. The sun and the moon light us up, the rain and the dew water us, but no-one understands the prodigious doctrine of God that is sufficient for everything.

5. A kick in the backside judiciously applied brings men happily back from the worst strayings of abstraction.

6. Religions established by men propose disembodiment to us in the eternity of limbo.

7. Since all creation tries constantly to survive itself, why would we alone search annihilation in death?

8. Despite all men's philosophies, a broken leg is still a broken leg.

9. How generous is nature, how free, how varied, how simple, and how hidden!

10. Most shrewd ones, you have found the soap to scour the skin, but the filth within remains without remedy before your malice.

11. Some hypocrites preach humility to us with such pretensions that we cannot help ourselves from laughing on seeing them struggle in the mud where they play the triumphant masters.

12. Conceited hypocrites, keep your lessons for yourselves, and put them into practice, for then you shall no longer have to preach them to others.

5'. How satisfied with themselves are the wise monkeys who cackle over the void! Nothing but the shadow of the stick, and they climb once more up the tree of objectivity.

6'. God's revealed religion proposes the incarnation in the eternity of manifested life to us.

7'. It is good to hope for future salvation by praying to God with perseverance. It is better to search for immediate salvation by asking for God's aid day and night.

8'. With God's salvation, even a dead man can live again. It is truly incredible!

9'. Too many rules in our heads, too many compasses in our hands, too many balances in our hearts.

10'. How could he use the divine power he who has not become like an inoffensive little child once more?

11'. Then, we shall laugh no longer, for these false humble ones exude a false sweetness, a false assurance, a false humility and a false submission, which are the stench of the devil hidden beneath the veil of false holiness.

12'. We shall recognize the hypocrites by the fact that they never confess their faults and they never laugh at themselves.

13. No-one should make use of the Book to lecture anyone or to scold him, if he does not ask for it.

14. It is cruel that God's revelation has finally engendered in believers a sectarianism so blind that it is an obstacle to the very revelation itself.
«The more instructed they think they have been, the more ignorant they become.»

15. To penetrate is a good beginning.
To be penetrated is a good end.

16. Those who say: «Have patience and die» are criminals if they do not add: «Triumph and live».

17. Priests have obscured the prodigious revelation of the unique Splendour of life, but they have kept it intact, while the ignorant ones who have left it have amputated and disfigured the deep revelation of the secret of saving incarnation.
«It is up to the believers to dig out the guarded treasure instead of sleeping on top of it.»

18. The saint disembodies himself from the death of the world. The sage reincarnates himself in the life of God.

19. Many weak spirits stop at the death of the Lord and do not clearly conceive of his glorious resurrection. They are sincere, but they are also sinister in the extreme.

13'. The way is self-sufficient, for its odour is sweet and its light is persuasive.

14'. It is a hard punishment to keep the outer layer and ignore the almond because of blind and deaf faithfulness.
«The idolatry of people prevents the deep comprehension of the divine mystery and its accomplishment here below.»

15'. To open is a better beginning. To be opened is a better end.

16'. Those who say: «Triumph and live» are criminals if they do not say first: «Have patience and die».

17'. The philosophies of men are nothing but compromises with the world in which we are dying; they are incapable of giving back to us the pure life of the beginning. It is better to be ignorant of everything than to be an obstacle, through pretentious explanations, to the doctrine of heaven that resurrects us miraculously.

18'. Who is the ignorant one who sets them in opposition?
Who is the expert who unites them?

19'. We must follow the Lord beyond death on the cross of the world, unto the glorious resurrection and unto the heavenly coronation. Is that clear?

20. Humility precedes.

21. Holiness prepares.

22. Darkness nurtures.

23. Death separates.

24. Exile instructs us.

25. No-one can go to God without voluntarily giving up the part of the mixed world that has been shared out to him.

26. The mystery of Christ is the mystery of God made man and the mystery of man remade God.

27. The life of the sage comes out of the death of the saint just as the life of the butterfly comes out of the death of the caterpillar, which becomes a chrysalis, and then, a miracle of resurrection.

28. The simple disciples show us with their finger the mystery of divine incarnation.

29. The holy disciples proclaim in the world the mystery of divine death.

30. We have left heavenly life by crossing the darkness of death.

20'. Triumph follows.

21'. Wisdom accomplishes.

22'. Light springs forth.

23'. Resurrection reunites.

24'. Return fixes us.

25'. He who does not die to the world cannot resurrect in God, that is the law that severs, but that does not share out.

26'. He who aspires to reach the secret of divine resurrection without passing through the death of the mixed world hurtles towards irreparable crime and disaster.

27'. Likewise our lives shall come out again of the chaos of the dark lysis where the divine mystery of God's creation is renewed. Let those who know how to reflect look into this dark mirror!

28'. The faithful disciples lead us patiently to the mystery of divine birth.

29'. The wise disciples murmur in our ear the mystery of divine resurrection.

30'. It is impossible to reach heavenly life without crossing the darkness of death again.

31. It is not up to us to cut the dead wood that clutters up the great tree of life planted in the world. New blood, which comes from heaven in holy sacrifice shall make that which has remained alive green again, and the dead wood shall fall by itself.

32. He who speaks to God in his heart does not argue in the world about the person of his envoys.

33. Shall we open the eyes of those who have placed a blindfold over their eyes?

34. Shall we open up the hearing of those who have stuffed plugs in their ears?

35. Shall we open up the spirit of those who have placed a sack over their head and a weight on their heart?

36. At present, we shout from the rooftops that which was once whispered in the ear, for all prudence has become useless. Has men's ignorance with regard to wise and holy things not gone as far as it can?

37. God does not ask for slaves established in death, but rather sons freed in life. Let those who feel they are slaves behave like slaves, but let them not condemn those who, feeling themselves sons, behave like sons!

38. Many believers recite to us their beautiful lesson about the blood of Christ that saves from death, but

31'. Idolatry and sectarianism is to take the appearances of the revelation for the reality of the mystery of regenerated life.

«All the prophets approve of the Book that confirms them, and the Lord blesses the Book that consecrates him.»

32'. By sheer force of arguing over the pre-eminence of the glasses, the believers forget to taste the divine ambrosia they contain.

33'. We are talking about the believers who concern themselves with people, and not with mysteries.

34'. We are talking about the believers who cling onto the letter and forget the spirit.

35'. We are talking about the believers who fall asleep in the rites and the laws, neglecting the love and the knowledge of God.

36'. Does one not speak openly of God's secrets before the rough beasts? At present, the pigs move away by themselves from the smallest drop of dew, and the dogs no longer sniff the odour of holy things.

37'. Is it the dead and the dying installed in this century who shall read the Book of the renewal of life? No! But rather their children, who desire the palpable gift and not remote promises.

38'. Would they not do better to search for the blood of this king of heaven and live, instead of focusing

do they really know whom they are talking about and what it is really about? Let them first seek the Lord, and when they have found him, they shall act instead of arguing vainly.

39. The nonbelievers want to open their skull, which is serious.

on the habits of truth and stagnating in death?

«To preach the formula of water is not to give a drink to those who are thirsty.»

39'. The experts want to open their spirit, which is even more serious.

39". Will the Lord God perhaps open the heart of some of them?

40. Christ is alive and sometimes comes back to earth, but few see him, few receive him and few truly taste him.
Incredible revelation, which makes us tremble with joy and hope.

40'. Free believers can receive him and live, the others are scandalized and reject the divine gift, for they have established themselves in death and have relegated the presence of the Lord to the limbo of oblivion.

41. Proud believers nailed the gilded master in the name of the ancient law that he explained and accomplished before them.

41'. Conceited believers would not even notice the wise and holy master if he explained and accomplished the gospel once more in front of them.

42. Oh! curse of the blindness of the believers too schooled in letters.

42'. Oh! double curse of the blindness of the believers too ignorant of spirit.

43. The closer we move to God, the more we distance ourselves from the world; that is the mark that does not deceive, for the closer we move to the world, the more we also distance ourselves from the Unique One.

43'. We do not preach a doctrine of abandonment and dissolution in death; we preach a doctrine of purification and coagulation in life.

44. Worldly passions are categorically opposed to the quest for the Lord of life.

44'. Get away from God, politicians and patriots, financiers and scholars, sectarians and moralists, conquerors and dominators!

45. No violence of any kind should be done to him who refuses to recognize God, for that would be to plunge him into a death even more opaque.

46. What we say about the present representatives of the Churches is for the good of everyone; it is enough to read the Book carefully, for our quest is the pledge of our love for the lordly mystery.

47. The Church of the Lord of life is dear and precious to us like the stone on which it is founded, and we pray to God that his representatives return to the simplicity of him who established it.

48. The blood of the Beloved One is a blood that saves and that saves itself. Do we not see, do we not hear the holy cohort of transfigured and resurrected ones who bless God in their heart for eternity?

49. The fall of man has a divinely elevated goal, which is the acquisition of a base body and its glorification in God.

50. Let us allow those who devote themselves to the study of the mysteries of God to live freely among us, and let us maintain them modestly, so that the blessing of God also floods over us.

51. Those who transmit the exterior of divine revelation must not envy, repudiate or persecute those

45'. Failures and privations only usefully serve those who have the will to search for God, for that prevents them from losing themselves in the world.

46'. We are not here to chain prisoners or to finish off the sick, but rather to free them and cure them in the love of the handsome Lord of resurrection.

47'. This has to open the eyes of many of those who cling on vainly to the dead ruins, and who do not see the living heart of their foundation.

48'. The gentle seekers shall be saved, but also the violent ones, for the blood of the Lord of life warms or burns alternately, like the fire of heaven that fertilizes, and like the fire of earth that purges.

49'. Those who preach rejection of the body also lose the spirit and have to undergo incarnation once again in even more opaque darkness.

50'. Christ left the custody of his holy word to his known disciples, but he also left the custody of his wise word to his secret disciples.

51'. One word and the other complete one another in the unity of divine revelation, as the known and

who transmit the interior, for they are brothers in the unity of the secret of the Unique One.

52. He who possesses the spirit of life condensed in the rutilant blood of the heavenly Saviour identifies the symbols, the people and the rites in the unique truth of life.

53. There is no salvation for the brutes who please themselves in bestiality and in the excrements of the world.

54. What does it matter if we know neither the why nor the how of the mystery of life, as long as we taste its holy fruit that saves from death. «There are the believers. There are the possessors, and there are the experts.»

55. He who does not believe in God shall not come close to God.

56. God holds out his hands to all his children, but those who think they have reached the top of the ladder of revelation no longer hold out theirs towards him, and thus remain at a standstill in their ascent, and make speeches to preach to others what they themselves do not actually know.

57. We propose that you go up and go in depth. We do not propose that you fall asleep in the world, even

unknown disciples complete one another in the unity of the communion of life.

52'. We would like to avoid scandalizing the believers by going beyond the images, the people and the rites that conceal the mystery of the regeneration of humanity and creation gone astray.

53'. That is reserved for the simple children of God who follow his right way.

54'. Only one knows the why, it is he who is. A few know the how, they are those who operate. A small number know the taste, they are those who receive. Many know the warmth, they are those who believe.

55'. He who does not believe in the science of God shall not find God.

56'. No-one can climb the next rung if he does not see it or if he does not feel it clearly enough to dare to leave the rung below, without the risk of finding himself in the void and falling back into death. Thus, we must neither force nor do violence to anyone in going beyond the images of his faith, on pain of sterilizing him or making him fall.

57'. Did the master not say: «No-one can come to the Father if the Father does not attract him to him»?

though it be on the pillow of faith. Let those who want to sleep do it, and let them spare us their worthless explanations and their worthless sermons!

58. The ROOTS[1] of the tree of life...

Well! Now we say to you: «No-one can find the Lord of heaven if one does not embody him in oneself».

58'. are like the VILE TRIO[2] that unites heaven and earth.

I am black but beautiful, daughters of Jerusalem, like the tents of Cedar, like the pavilions of Solomon.
Do not take notice of my black complexion; it is the sun that has burnt me.

SOLOMON

Without name, it is at the origin of heaven and earth; with a name, it is the mother of all beings.

LAO TSE

---

1. The French RACINES is an anagram of ARSENIC.
2. The French TRIO VIL is an anagram of VITRIOL.

BOOK XXVI

We have created man from the black slime of the earth.
KORAN

If they had had knowledge of hidden things, they would not have been subjected for so long to servile work.
KORAN

VIENT RUÉE

1. Those who ignore the holy books live and die like beasts who pass through and disappear in the quagmire of death. Those who reject them shall end up in a hell a thousand times worse.

2. Your salvation is difficult to approach, Lord, and it is impossible to reach if we come up against the complications of those who preach it and the ignorance of those who teach it.

3. We must persevere in our quest up to the end with blind confidence, for he who has once spoken to the Lord in his heart is no longer ever abandoned or solitary in this world.

4. Oh! the rosebud.
Oh! the leaves on the ground.

THE CHOICE

1'. The beautiful and good things of this world are only appreciated by a few. How can the holy and wise things become known to the multitude of the self-satisfied ignorant?

2'. The Churches would be rather necessary for transmitting the holy torch of love, and the monasteries would be rather useful for keeping the holy fire of knowledge.

3'. Holy laziness is what makes us attentive and free to the word of God, and holy ignorance is what makes us transparent and receptive to his ray of life.

4'. I have slept outside of him in death, but he never forgets himself anywhere.

5. No more sack on the head, no more blind blows, no more pain and no more cries.

6. The sun has come after the mists of the long winter, and I smile at him while holding out my arms like a little child who greets the light of its birth.

7. He who IS becomes again without before and without after, without why and without how.

8. A flower sometimes receives the droppings of a bird, but the rain soon cleans it; when a believer receives a distinction from the world, it is rare that humility cleans him so quickly.

9. The Book is not for people with diplomas who take themselves seriously and who organize themselves in the agony of the world with the aid of brutes.

10. The fact of absorbing the profane science of the world engenders the blindness that distances us from God and his prodigious revelation.

11. We need to become capable of asking everything of God and obtaining everything from him in order not to have fears or cares any more. But that is only given to very few of God's children, because of the impurity of our hearts.

12. Nothing for the dead who remain in death. All for the living who fix themselves in life.

5'. Who can walk among the dead without bumping into them and without their bumping into us?

6'. Who could now separate me from my Lord? And who could obscure his light in my heart? The clouds still pass, but they do not remain.

7'. Who can float in the great ocean without becoming restless and without crying for help?

8'. Life mixed with death is agony and suffering, but pure life is infinite freedom in oneself, and life fixed in the Unique One is eternal joy and glory.

9'. Let it fall from their hands and let their eyes and ears remain stopped up by their conceited pretension!

10'. We abandon ourselves in God's hands, not to establish ourselves in the inaction of death, but to receive the magnificent gift of imperishable and pure life.

11'. Mortals pass through like the grass that is born and dies, but immortals remain like the beloved sun in the eternity of life fixed in God.

12'. Who shall be born to the imperishable glory of God? Who? Who? So few! So few! What a weight! What a weight!

13. There are two ways back to God: either the dissolution in free and universal life, or the coagulation in it.

13'. The first way is taught by many and accomplished by a few. The second way is taught by a few and achieved by very few.

13". He who separates them is ignorant.
He who unites them is wise.

14. To become unborn again or to be born twice, otherwise to remain a prisoner of the alternatives of deaths and births in the mixed worlds.

14'. Vanquish or die, such is the alternative that God proposes to us. Heaven greets the renounced-liberated ones with songs, but adores the victorious-embodied ones.

15. The Church is a good thing, but those who complicate it, who divide it and who obscure it are a bad thing, which we must not confuse with the good one.
«The Lord acknowledges his own in the secret of their hearts.»

15'. It is the Church of within, immortal and pure through the union of the saints in God, that we should honour in our hearts, and not the Church of without, temporal and soiled by men, that we should idolize in the world.

16. What defeat and what false peace is the abandonment of oneself in this world corrupted by death!

16'. The peace of the beasts advocated by some could never be the peace of God proposed by God.

17. Our goal is not to cease to be through dissolution in the origin, nor to be content with agonizing endlessly in the impermanence of mixed creation, but rather to become eternal in the stability that nothing can weaken. That's something that is clear!

17'. Our repose, our renunciation and our ignorance are only worthwhile if they permit us to see, understand and touch the mystery of divine incarnation, which is the only one that saves us from the brutishness of death.

18. Everything is useless and futile here below, except for God's salvation, but who validly concerns himself with that right now?

18'. Who is wise enough to abandon the worthless occupations of the world? Who is mad enough to devote himself to the quest for the Lord of life?

19. All the gold in the world for those who seek the science of death.
No help at all for those who seek the science of life.

19'. If the sanctuaries can no longer teach the science of God to those who truly hunger and thirst for it, it is because they have become tombs inhabited by dead people.

20. Let the guardians who cannot transcend the figures, the symbols and the rites of their religions not prevent those who seek God's salvation from going beyond the appearances destined to contain the profane.

20'. Enough of nonbelievers who, unable to go beyond the appearances of the transitory world, attempt to do violence to everything in order to discover its content, denying the salvation of the unique Splendour.

21. The Churches burden the believers to the point of absurdity and end up discouraging the best and eliminating the living, by sheer force of dead regulations and stupid demands.

21'. The prophets unburden the believers and free the living in the grace and in the love of God. That is why they are hated by the dead installed in the dead letter.

22. Without scholars and without workmen, science books are useless.

22'. Without sages and without saints, the books of salvation are worthless.

23. Resurrection begins again and it has already begun again, like a new promise from God. Here we have a marvellous sign for those who understand.

23'. The time of purification through fire is coming and that of purification through water is to follow, and the time of heavenly fertilization is hidden between them.

24. God is not a delirious abstraction of the human spirit, as the descriptions of some believers might have us believe. He is a living reality that is seen, smelled, touched, tasted and that gives imperishable life. Is that not sufficient and is it not marvellous?

24'. Someone said: «No-one has ever seen God», but we say: «Everyone sees God every day, but no-one recognizes him». Oh! stupor of the dazzling obviousness that no-one sees. Oh! too-cruel humour of the Perfect One who gleams. Oh! accursed stupidity of our proud malice that totally blinds us.

25. Only the obviousness of life is not seen nor believed here below. It is true that the obviousness of death is not better understood.

25'. Even the simple ones no longer see nor adore the Lord of life. Who shall send us a savage missionary to convert us to the obviousness and the love of the Highest?

26. Everything we say about God and everything we think about him is false. Only that which God is and that which God does is true.

26'. Those who imagine God in their own image are totally blind and ignorant. They vainly recreate on earth that which dazzles them in heaven.

27. God is not a hypothesis, he is an incandescent cloud, a translucent stone, a living reality for ever.

27'. No image could give us an idea of the living beauty of the unique heavenly Splendour.

28. There are imbeciles who attempt to prove with words the existence or non-existence of God. It is certainly the funniest thing in the world, or the saddest.

28'. How can you demonstrate water to fish if not by removing them from it momentarily? And how can you demonstrate light to men, if not by plunging them into darkness for a while?

29. To return to unconditioned and unconscious life, or to attain conditioned and conscious life.

29'. Supreme mystery: one day the disappeared shall dissolve the rediscovered, and the rediscovered shall coagulate the disappeared.

30. The world has never been as backward as it is now. This shall seem strange to many, but it is a terrifying reality.

30'. Those who have become insensitive to the beauty of God's creation can no longer be sensitive to the direct beauty of God.

31. The Lord of heaven sees us. He hears us and he approves of us.
What shall we do, then, with the approval or disapproval of those who have taken upon themselves to transmit his public doctrine in the world and who do not observe it?

31'. The Lord of heaven sees us. He inspires us and he fertilizes us.
What shall we do, then, with the approval or the disapproval of those who have undertaken to transmit his secret doctrine in hearts, and who do not understand it?

32. We have called no foreigner «dog», and we have not reserved the Lord's table for any people in particular. Everyone can sit at it if they sincerely desire it in their hearts. Is that not the thought of the holy Church of God right now?

33. There are those that are thirsty and those that are hungry for God in all peoples and in all nations. They all choose and sort themselves, and the Lord opens the door of the banquet of life to them when they present themselves before him in a holy way.

34. The Book of light is offered to blacks in a dark time; shall our brothers the miners not also receive it?

35. At present, we offer the Book of resurrection to the humble, to the humiliated, to the rejected, to the blacks, so that the masters become slaves and the slaves become masters. «The gift of God must no longer be offered to the sated who reject it, but rather to the hungry who expect salvation from it.»

36. The heirs may well ignore or reject their inheritance because they think they have been sufficiently instructed in their religion or wise enough in their science. Their pride and their malignity shall not force the gift of life of the Highest, and their intelligence shall be humiliated, and their freedom shall be taken away in the end.

32'. The faithful foreigners have become beloved children of God, and the rebellious children have become hated foreigners; it is a hard lesson that should protect us carefully from all denial and from all forgetting of the Lord of life.

33'. Those inspired by God shall seek that which is in accordance in the holy Scriptures and shall live. Those inspired by the devil shall seek that which contradicts itself and shall perish. For each shall be judged by his own eye and by his own heart.

34'. The wise Book is now given to the simple ones, as in the past the Book of simplicity was given to the wise.

35'. You were without a Book, without a prophet and without Scriptures, and you languished like the dregs of humanity. God sends you the jewel of his crown and the pearl of his treasure, for there you are, humble among the humble and poor among the poor. Shall you not receive them with enthusiasm and love, and shall you not live in a holy way before him?

36'. The powerful, the scholars, the rich and the intelligent of the world have scorned and rejected the gift of heaven. Shall you not be more prudent and more grateful to the Lord who freely offers you imperishable life? Oh! the faces of the powerful when they realize they are without strength. Oh! the heads of the scholars when they realize they

Shall they not come back humbly to God in their hearts instead of remaining slaves on foreign soil?

37. The conceited believers reject the new message, for they have not yet understood the old one that they keep fruitlessly buried in the death of letters and stones, instead of embodying it in the life of spirits and hearts.

38. You shall become glorious and you shall dominate your former masters, for the reign of the Holy Spirit draws near.
Treat them well, in memory of him who gave you the Book of glory.

39. The Semite slaves inherited from the proud Egyptians the secret of God, and they became free and glorious. The Western people inherited from the proud Semites the secret of God, and became free and glorious.

40. Here we are fallen in the mud, but we can choose to return to the free water or to fix ourselves in the precious stone.

41. «No filth inside, but no filth outside either.» A purified saint covered in mud is better than a perfumed wicked man full of rubbish; however, the sage keeps himself clean inside and out.

are imbeciles. Oh! the faces of the rich when they realize they are wretched. Oh! the noddle of the intelligent when they realize they are stupid.

37'. Quench your thirst, simple children of God, and bathe in the water of life that never runs out, while the proud and self-assured of the world lie dying in the stench of death.
«Each one chooses his lot and no-one will be able to recriminate at the end.»

38'. Receive among you as equals those who will have adopted it in their heart, for many of them have also received as equals those of you who have adopted their Scriptures in their hearts.

39'. The Black slaves now inherit from the proud Western people the secret of God, and they shall become free and glorious. Shall they be able to remain humble before God so as to keep the love of the Highest?

40'. Thus, the delivered ones go to the mother water and the saved ones go to the holy stone, but the accursed ones shall remain in the stinking mud.

41'. All came from red to go to black, passing through yellow and white. All shall return to red, starting from black and passing through white and yellow.

42. It pleased you, Lord God, to send us to the people of the humble and the gentle, to the people of simple children who believe in your holy Name of truth and who love you in their hearts. Shall you not make them shine above the pride of the rebels who bury your inspired word? Shall you not water them at your sacred spring that saves from death?

42'. What a surprise for the rebellious peoples who think of appropriating everything through force and violence, when they find themselves knocked to the ground amid their smoking ruins! How astonished they shall be when they see God's chosen people come out once more unscathed from the moving brazier of extermination! And what terror when they see the flames pursue them and engulf them without mercy!

43. We have written the Book under God's inspiration, without knowing to whom it was destined. The Lord revealed it to us at the last moment and our astonishment was great, and our admiration boundless, for if the ways of the Lord are impenetrable, his logic is brilliant and it illuminates the spirit of the believers.
«He truly gives to the poor.»

43'. The peoples that surround us think they are too strong to receive the Book of God's grace, but in reality they are too sick and too perverted. They think they are too righteous to receive the Book of God's love, but in reality they are too sinful and too unfaithful. They think they are too wise to receive the Book of God's knowledge, but in reality they are too proud and too ignorant.

44. The sated ones of the world have left us without help, for their hearts have remained closed in exchange for the message, and their hands have remained closed in exchange for our work.
Thus, let what they have done to us be done to them, and let them one day lack the necessary amid the abundance of those who have rejoined God!

44'. The Book of plenitude is removed from the sated ones and given to the hungry, so that they be fulfilled but not overfed.
O poor ones! O humble ones! O simple children of God! shall you not offer the bread and wine to him who offers you the substance and the essence of heavenly life?

45. The Holy Spirit is better than all the diplomas and all the degrees of vanity distributed by the world. Let us therefore maintain it among us,

45'. Let us help one another mutually in all possible ways, and let us prudently stay away from the nonbelievers who reject the Book that is

and let us not be seduced by profane science that estranges us from God's love and salvation.

given to us, and who advocate impious science.
Let us remain as a people of free saints, devoted to God.

46. Let us rejoice in the good news, for on the hundred and tenth day of the sun and on the seventh day of the moon, a prophet has been given to us and a Book has been offered to us to guide us towards the Lord of life and to comfort us in this dark world.

46'. Thus, we are no longer either orphans or abandoned in the exile of death, and the door of salvation is open to us in particular, after so many others. Shall we not be able to pass through it in great number, remaining faithful to our holy inheritance?

47. Faith, simplicity and sobriety shall sustain us in life more surely than science, than progress, and than the abundance of the profane world that is on its way to death without knowing it. «Shall we receive the gift of God with intelligence?»

47'. We give you the crowning stone that completes the holy edifice, and its light shall illuminate the nations, for the foundation stone is like the summit stone, and the summit stone is like the foundation stone in the unity of the One.

48. The scholars and the intelligent deny the obviousness of God's miracle, and the proud believers nail it in time without seeing that he renews himself constantly under their eyes of the blind.

48'. Did the master not say: «He who falls on the foundation stone shall be broken, and him on whom the summit stone falls shall be crushed»?
Do we no longer hear it?

49. Many have been broken because of the impurity of their hearts that has prevented them from recognizing the foundation stone planted in the earth.

49'. Many shall be crushed by the summit stone because of the impurity of their eyes that shall prevent them from seeing it fall from the sky.

50. The foundation stone is a cubic stone, and the summit stone is a pyramid-shaped stone. Did you know that?

50'. We have added nothing and we have taken away nothing. Do you see?

51. When we have become once more innocent and pure like little children, we shall also look at everything face to face, and we shall see the truth of the Perfect One shine, for we shall be transparent and precious like the diamond.

52. The curse that weighed on the sons of Cham is lifted for those who receive the Book of forgiveness and who keep it in their hearts.

53. On obeying the voice of God, we gather you up piously like a holiest gift, despite the opprobrium in which you are enveloped, and we wash you in the tears of joy of the rediscovered Lord.

54. The new Book for the new people.
The abundance of heaven for the hungry and the thirsty of the earth.

55. Let us keep ourselves from the multitude of drugs and medicaments of the over-scholarly ones, which kill the body.

56. Let us keep ourselves from the games of chance and the alcohol of the over-greedy ones, which kill the spirit.

57. Let us keep ourselves from the radios and the newspapers of the over-shrewd ones, which kill the soul.

51'. Only the sons of God attract the innocent children and read in their eyes, and only the innocent children attract the sons of God and read in their hearts. It is a sign that does not deceive.

52'. God has given us the most despised part of humanity, but is it not also the most hidden and the best? Is it not the most faithful and the most grateful?

53'. God does not look at the colour of your skin, but only at the purity of your hearts. Shall you not come to him, who gives himself to you without measure? «Oh royalty of innocent love! you attract innocence and you fix it in the purity of love.»

54'. For those gorged with food, for those sated with learning and for those overflowing with malice, the purge of death is quite enough.

55'. Let us eat and drink moderately, giving thanks to the Lord who gives us life and who sustains it.

56'. Let us instead sing and dance, and let us rejoice with our wives, without hypocrisy, in the Lord.

57'. Let us read the Book of deliverance that is dedicated to us, and let us compose praises to the Lord who sends it to us.

58. The sated peoples have rejected the message and the messenger.

59. Not even the price of a cannon, nor the price of a bomb-shell, nor the price of a cartridge for the Book that pleads before God for the life of all the men lost in the world.

58'. Shall the hungry peoples perhaps receive them more generously?

59'. If we praise God because of God's servant, it is a great joy, a great honour and a great reward for him and for us.

59". But how shall this stupid and rebellious people be saved, in spite of the astounding patience of the Highest?

The way of heaven is similar to the archer who, bending his bow, lowers that which is high and raises that which is low.

LAO TSE

That which is pure appears covered in shame.
The origin of that which is precious is that which has little value, and that which is elevated is founded on that which is low.

LAO TSE

BOOK XXVII

> *On earth there are priests in charge of celebrating a worship that is no more than the image and shadow of heavenly things.*
>
> PAUL

> *Behold a mystery that I reveal to you; we shall not all die, but we shall all be changed.*
>
> PAUL

UN IVER ÉTÉ

1. All misfortune that strikes us here below is a marvellous opportunity for asceticism to return in God if we know how to accept it cheerfully instead of rejecting it. But many prefer to return to wallow in the mud of the world.

2. How many can understand that without being scandalized in their spirits and in their hearts of blind and deaf men?

3. It is not for us to judge what happens to us. It is up to us only to make use of it without argument, in order to reach God and his salvation as quickly as possible.

4. To attach oneself to the house, the office, the workshop, the bar-

TIME

1'. If the blind pride of the organizers of this world and the absurd atrocity of death do not lead us back to God, how can the words of the Book ever be heard by the men exiled in this dark land?

2'. Let us not fall asleep on the little joys of this world, for they pass quickly and the misfortune that follows seems endless.

3'. Let us be very careful to use immediately all that happens to us for our rescue in God, so that we avoid the rebellion that plunges us into the absurdity of death, and the resignation that makes us stagnate in it.

4'. To become accustomed to prison or to become accustomed to

racks or the monastery is all the same thing.

5. Saints separate and unite things in heaven.
Scholars separate and unite things on earth.

6. There is no danger in praying so as to receive God's gift, but there is a considerable danger in trying to discover the secret of the Unique One. Many have found there impiety, madness or death.

7. Let us leave the proud believers who want to lecture others and who think they are automatically saved by the formulas and symbols of their religion, which they stupidly confuse with the living reality of God's gift.

8. Many of those who have seen, heard and touched the Lord have not known his hidden doctrine. How could those who now preach to us through images suspect the living secret that gives life to all of them?

9. The ashes of the impious and the wicked who die anchored in their wickedness and in their denial of God shall be scattered in the six directions or abandoned in the earth, and be forbidden to return among the believers submitted to God.

10. We were looking for the glorious crowning stone in heaven, but the Lord has made us see the humble the fallen world is the same thing, for the best organization shall not save us from it.

5'. It is most difficult of all to separate and unite the things of heaven with those of the earth. Only the sages achieve it, with the aid of God.

6'. There shall be many loved ones saved, but there shall be few possessors who will be established in glory and scarcely any experts who will be unified in the unique Splendour.

7'. Let us consider their sermons, but let us also consider the mud that covers them from head to foot and we shall understand that they do not preach like the saved, but rather cry out like lost ones. They illustrate, unknowingly, the parable of the blind leading the blind.

8'. Let these be prudent, humble and timid when lecturing us about the Lord who saves from death; for they themselves are not yet saved or enlightened in God.

9'. The ashes of the believers and the charitable ones who die confirmed in their faith and in their love for God shall be brought together so as to be honoured in every home, on the altar of rough stones dedicated to God.

10'. Shall we not be grateful to the Lord who looks lovingly at us despite our blackness?

foundation stone that was at our feet, so that we pick it up in the darkness of death and bring it to the light of life.

11. The foundation stone is the most despised because it is dark, but it is the most precious one, for all the others are hidden in it.

12. The Book is not for those who think they are saved, but for those who want to be saved.

13. We have not come to give water to those who stupidly think they can quench their thirst by reciting the formula of water and who reject the cup of life.

14. We shall leave our dead resting for four days so that they can resuscitate in particular, after which we shall burn them so that their ashes join the ashes of the ancestors until the great day of general resurrection.

Shall we not be confused at being the object of the fertilizing love of the Highest?

Shall we not be resurrected in glory by the word of life of the All-Powerful One who desires us as supernatural children?

11'. Thus, the black people is the most despised, but it is also the best, for it shall make all the others shine in the rediscovered Lord.

12'. We have not come to give a drink to those who are drowning, nor to give food to those who vomit because of their surplus.

13'. The Lord discharges us of meticulous obligations so that, having been the most enslaved in death, we become the most free in holy life.

14'. Let him who wishes to participate in the figure of the sacraments among his brothers do so freely, and let him who wishes to participate in them secretly in the Lord also do so freely, without anyone judging the choice of one or the other.

14''. Only the rotting bodies shall be consumed by fire or buried in the earth itself. The holy bodies that remain in a good state shall be carefully conserved until the time of the resurrection.

15. Let the educating fathers and judges be at least sixty years old, the counselling brothers and guardians at

15'. The law is now engraved in our hearts and no longer in the stone, for our hearts know what is good and

least forty years old, and let the believers who freely choose the light yoke of the Lord be at least twenty years old. However, the Holy Spirit has no age.

16. We think we run after God, but God still runs much more after us.

17. The whites who receive the Book are the first inheritors, but they are not superior to the blacks in anything. Let us consider them all as equal brothers in the love of God, and let us receive them with great affection, but let us not mix them up with each other.

18. It is because the Book has been refused by the right-thinking ones that the Lord has offered it to simple men. Let us therefore thank the Lord for the gift he grants to us, and let us thank the right-thinking ones who have therefore unknowingly sent it to us.

19. It is black freedom that shall enlighten the world and it is the black people that shall manifest once again the light of God in the world, for the black age nurtures the heavenly clarity.

20. If we acquire titles, degrees and diplomas of vanity in the world, God shall immediately close our spirit and heart to his grandiose revelation, and he shall leave us to rot in pride and death without help.

what is bad. Thus, freedom of choice is given to us so that our reward or our punishment are a healthy example for the world that watches us.

16'. Even in the sewer of the world, is he not with us to pull us out of it?

17'. Do not be ashamed of the black colour that God has chosen for you, for it is in that that all the others are hidden. Do you not know that the light came out of the darkness in the beginning, and that in the end shall rest in the golden splendour?

18'. The Lord's humour is great, and mocks the over-intelligent and the over-scholarly in an unheard-of manner.
The peoples that inherit the doctrine of heaven that have become proud have all experienced it in their time.

19'. It is a promise of the Lord that shall be accomplished before our eyes if we receive his inheritance without hesitation, for he chooses whoever he pleases to make his glory shine on earth.

20'. Let us run away even more from the impious scholars and intellectuals than from anyone, for they are not content with being dead in spirit and in heart, but also spread around them death in the spirit and in the heart of believers.

21. God only speaks to simple men who believe in his NAME, and only inspires his children who obey his VOICE.

21'. He who is boastful, even though it may be of the revelation of God, loses the revelation and loses himself.

22. God keeps a surprise for us that shall be quite sweet for some and quite cruel for others, for God's saved ones shall walk peacefully through the blaze while praising his holy NAME, while the reprobates shall rip each other apart without mercy or forgiveness in the devouring flames of hell.

22'. Let us imagine the powerless rage of the wicked when they realize that rottenness has no hold on the body of the chosen ones any more, while it has redoubled its effectiveness in that which concerns them! The saved shall not even think of laughing on seeing this spectacle, and the reprobates shall not think of crying, so great shall be the amazement of everyone.

23. Let us carefully preserve our precious faith in the Lord of life and let us keep away from the impious, for on the last day the scholars and the intelligent of the world shall scream under the blows of death.

23'. The simple children of God shall watch them in astonishment, for they themselves shall remain unharmed in the flames of the devouring fire, and misfortune shall never again reach them.

24. The Christian aristocracy of knowledge was decapitated from the beginning, and the symbols, the people, the rites and the sacraments have substituted the transcendent reality of the divine mystery.

24'. Thus, those who have proudly believed themselves to be the most enlightened have become idolatrous, blind and superstitious without knowing it and, demanding blind faith for all, have placed the light of God once more under the bushel and have deprived themselves of it.

25. Nonbelievers can be converted and approach the mystery of life so as to be saved, but how can the believers that have shut themselves away in the dead images of God's secret discover the tangible reality of the Lord descended from heaven and who saves from death?

25'. It is better to know nothing than to half know something and remain obstinately fixed in it, thinking oneself to be instructed about the all. However perfect it may be, the image of a flower has no scent, and that of bread does not satisfy one's hunger.

26. The more a man is annoyed with his condition of a beast exiled in the fallen world, the more he is considered by other men as an abnormal and dangerous being, but the more he is resigned to his condition of a slave serving death, the more he is considered here below as a normal and reasonable being.

27. The courage, ingenuity and work of men may well prolong somewhat their time in the prison of the world, but all of this could not give them back immortality, which is the only thing that really counts.

28. The nonbelievers are those that crush their brothers in the world while seeking their own love, their own freedom, their own justice, their own profit and their own assurance.

29. The cruel circumstances that govern us in this world are conditioned by our mortal state. It would be enough for us to acquire the intangible and glorious body of the heavenly Lord so as to be delivered from misfortune forever.

30. It is just as worthless to lie dying here below before God in despair or in self-satisfaction, in rebellion or in resignation, in success or in failure, for the end is death for everyone.

31. Cursed be the wicked spirits that deceive us, that fetter us and that harm us during the time of our quest! Let them be hurled into hell

26'. The worst rebel can be saved if he is instructed and helped in a brotherly way, instead of being repressed and blindly destroyed. And the worst criminal can be converted if he is aided by the gift of the spirit and the heart of men, instead of being exterminated in his rough body.

27'. What we must be concerned with above all is not to struggle against anyone in this world prisoner of darkness, but instead to survive long enough to find the palpable salvation of God, which is the only thing that saves us from death.

28'. The believers are those that seek in heaven the love, the freedom, the justice and the gift of God, in order to manifest them on earth for the safeguard of all.

29'. He who examines that which is and not that which he thinks to be is quickly enlightened by God, if he asks him humbly and simply in his heart, for without divine inspiration the very obviousness of life is not perceived here below.

30'. Only he who seeks and finds the incarnate Lord is no longer worthless before God, for he acquires the divine substance and is no longer subject to the accidents of death that crush the fallen man.

31'. Cursed be the philosophers, the intellectuals and the scholars who preach their own systems that lead men to desperation and death! Let

and let them destroy one another just like they rip us up right now! them be reduced to dust and scattered in the wind, the cowards and hypocrites that make the saints of God perish and that stifle their voices in the world!

32. Tepidness, humidity and darkness precede.

32'. Heat, dryness and light finish.

33. Is the black virgin not the first and most mysterious of all mothers? Is it not she whom God has looked at amorously since the beginning? Is it not she who has given birth to the light that illuminates the world?

33'. O you who have black skin and red heart! shall you not also make the purity of your eye and the whiteness of your light shine in the world? Shall you not receive the Lord among you in a holy way and shall you not make room for his envoys?

34. At present, there shall be a black community heirs to the holy foundation stone placed by the anointed one of God, because, for the first time, a Book and a prophet are given to the black peoples in particular, while formerly the divine revelation had been offered to them like a bone which is thrown to the dogs, to make it easier to put the collar of slavery on them.

34'. Shall you not give thanks to the Lord who now takes care to break the bone so as to offer you the nourishing marrow?

Shall you not receive the holy gift of the unique Splendour weeping with joy?

Shall you not kiss piously the Book that places you above the scholars and intelligent of this world?

35. The Lord does not send you a glorious, rich and powerful man. He sends you a poor, despised and unknown man. Take good note of that so that you never become proud of the message you are given and so that you never lose its living and hidden spirit.

«Keep it in your hearts and shine in God.»

35'. Does the Book not revere God's prophets and venerate the sons of God?

Does the Book not proclaim the preciousness of the flesh and the blood of the great King immolated for all on the earth?

Does the Book not make us heirs to the glory of the Lord resurrected in the transcendence of immortal life?

36. The Lord has bequeathed to us, finally, all the black peoples of the earth. O marvellous Lord! O precious inheritance that fulfils us far beyond all hopes!

36'. Likewise, the Lord has given you, finally, the rediscovered message and prophet. What shall you say of your Lord and what shall you say of your inheritance that fulfil you so magnificently?

37. The prophet said: «And the light shines in the darkness and the darkness has not received it», but this darkness was like a twilight that ended in the death of the letter. At present, we can say: «And the light shall shine in the darkness and the darkness shall receive it», for this new darkness is like a dawn that prepares itself in the secret of hearts purified and fertilized by God.

37'. A small number of whites spit out again the poison of impious science so as to survive, but a small number of blacks swallow it, and these are already dead for the divine revelation.

Finally, idiocy shall appear a relaxing and desirable thing compared to the reasoning madness of the scholars and the intelligent of the world, who lie dying in their conceited ignorance.

38. It has to be said: the wicked are those who wish to organize and to save the world through their work or through the work of others. They set themselves up as saviours of men, while they cheerfully bury all mankind.

38'. God truly possesses a marvellous humour, for he hides his secret from the scholars and the intelligent who explain the Universe to us, and he reveals it to the simple children of God who put their confidence in his light of life more than in their own learning.

39. One day God shall say to the pigs: «Do not throw pearls at men», for men shall have placed themselves below the beasts.

39'. And the earth shall shake out its parasites, and heaven shall dissolve them in the fire of divine wrath.

40. Let us draw lots for our representatives among those who have sworn obedience to God and loyalty to their brothers in the faith, for the choice of chance is less blind than that of men.

40'. Let us do the same for the help and the offerings destined for the seekers of the Unique One, for in this way, a saint can be helped by God, while otherwise he would always be ignored by men.

41. A simple person who believes in his heart in the intelligence, the power and the love of God is worth more than all the scholars who believe in their own intelligence, their own learning and in their own superiority in the world.

42. It is the poor who allow the rich to live, and it is those that produce with their hands who allow the merchants to live. The hardened exploiters shall lose their arrogant assurance on the day of reckoning.

43. As an artist, we received unemployment benefit from the capital. But as the author of the Book we have only been given the right to the scorn and silence of the big city and of the entire country.
«The reward of the prophets shall strike the world with stupor.»

44. Have we sought the glory of the world?
Have we tried to dominate anyone here below?
Have we amassed the goods of the earth for our sole use?

45. Incapable of earning our living on earth by our labour, how might we earn our heavenly life solely through our own merit if God does not benevolently aid us?

41'. Let us sing hymns of love to the all-powerful Lord who swims in heaven and in our hearts, so that, even in the midst of our joys and our grief, our faith remains turned towards him who consoles us from all exile and who saves us from all death.

42'. If God were to say to us on the day of judgement: «Get away, you are not inscribed in the book of life», we would nevertheless praise his holy Name among the damned and we would sing his praise in the madness of our love that cannot perish.

43'. Our works and our writings have not pleased the scholars, nor the intelligent, nor the merchants of these times, for the impiety of some has coupled with the hypocrisy of the others to engender the judgement that recognizes nothing of that which comes from the children of God.

44'. We have searched for the only glory of the Lord of life.
We have made ourselves a servant of God and of men.
We have collected the gifts of heaven and we offer them freely to all.

45'. Men have had the goodness to give us a little food out of charity, and God has had the goodness to give us alms and grant us a little light; that is why we consider ourselves privileged and fulfilled in one world and the other.

46. Let each black nation keep in a holy way the revealed word of God in its heart, and let it carefully preserve the Book of deliverance that has been given to it, as it would preserve a unique talisman on which was written the secret of deliverance from slavery and death.

47. The smallest consoler and liberator in God is worth more than all the great conquerors and organizers of the world. That is what we must never forget.

48. Shall we not be shrewder than those who exploit us and bully us?
Shall we not receive for ourselves the Book that they scornfully fling away from themselves?

49. It is a miracle of God that we have been able to write the Book at such a moment without dying of hunger and without being thrown out onto the street; for sure, those who have helped us shall have their material and spiritual reward in this world and in the other.
How small their number is! And how great it shall become!

50. Let us honour the language of the Book and let us conserve it in remembrance of the gift that has reached us through it. Let us also honour the students of the Book and let us help them in remembrance of him through whom the message has come to us.

46'. Depending on whether the NAME of God rises or falls, it is a blessing or a curse; for it has an obverse and a reverse. Thus, the same NAME can produce life or it can make death appear, according to the way in which it is presented to us, and also according to the way we present ourselves to it.

47'. He who loves God beyond human reason makes shine the divine intelligence that enlightens the worlds and that makes purified hearts shine.

48'. The word of God can save us from the slavery and death in which we lie dying, just as it can hurl into them the hypocrites and impious ones who overwhelm us with their impious assurance and self-importance.

49'. Subjecting ourselves in advance to the judgement of God, to the judgement of the sons of God, to the judgement of the friends of God and to the judgement of the prophets of God, we cannot fear the judgement of the intelligent of the world, nor that of the powerful of the world, nor that of the scholars of the world, nor that of the hypocrites and ignorant ones who bury us at present.

50'. The fault consists in leaving the seekers of God in abandonment and destitution. But the crime consists in forcing them into the works of the world on the hypocritical pretext of utilizing them or saving them.

51. Lanza is right at the beginning of the Book when he claims that there is only a small number of starving people who seek the truth in the world.

51'. Alas! we are indeed nothing more than a handful before God, and we do not even know one another in order to help each other in our quest.

52. Whatever his value, his talent and his usefulness, the man who is alone is condemned by man's society to perish, for being weak, mediocre and cowardly by nature, these people can only live in flocks where everything is exchanged sordidly and where nothing is given freely.

52'. That which appears advantageous in the world is not so before God. Thus, the man who is alone is loved and saved by God, while he is despised and rejected by the world; meanwhile, the flocks of self-assured and skilful ones go satisfied with their success to the slaughterhouses of death.

52". However, the married man is doubly blessed by God.

53. The shrewd and the intelligent ones of the world who have placed their trust in their astuteness and their skill shall one day be scattered in the darkness of death and shall cry in vain for help in the abomination and the desolation that shall be their lot forever.
They shall no longer rejoice as they do now.

53'. The lonely ones who seek their Lord here below shall one day be reunited in the lap of God, and shall recognize one another, congratulate one another and embrace one another weeping with joy, for then all shall be given to them freely in the eternity of the love of the Perfect One, and their joy shall be endless.
They shall no longer cry as they do now.

54. By frequenting the world we shall reap the salary of the world, which is death.

54'. Let us frequent God and we shall receive the salary of God, which is saved life.

55. O Lord! why are there so many men indifferent to your grace who establish themselves in the agony of the world? And why are there so few children who look for you with love and with overcoming in eternal life?

55'. Because, says the Lord, I desire for each one of my cherished ones a multitude of slaves to serve him. And just as I have chosen my saved ones because they have chosen themselves, also I have condemned the reprobates because they have also condemned themselves.

56. Shall those to whom we have given all not offer us the bread and wine necessary for the earthly representation of the communion of God's sages and saints in heaven?

56'. «My love is not blind and my justice is not shaky, says the Lord, and one never goes without the other.»

57. We were not born into a rich family and no-one has instructed us in the mysteries of God. We have had to discover all by ourselves the wise and holy Scriptures, and we have had to study them in poverty and in abandonment, so that no-one should think himself forgotten, whatever his state here below.

57'. We did not write the Book in the peace and security of a holy retreat. We wrote it from beginning to end in the midst of the fermenting sewer of the big city, so that nobody would feel abandoned, whatever their situation be here below.

We honour the royal splendour that restores the world, rendering it immortal, ageless, incorruptible, without infection, always alive, always prosperous, in possession of power at will, so that the dead are resurrected and there comes the immortality of the living being who restores the world as it pleases him.
ZARATHUSTRA

O radiant one! high up in heaven! Allow me to reach the height of heaven for eternity... All faces light up with joy on seeing you... Your brilliance is without equal.
THE EGYPTIAN BOOK OF THE DEAD

BOOK XXVIII

The body dissolves, that is the way of heaven.

LAO TSE

He has made you all of earth. He shall make you return to it and he shall take you from it once more.

KORAN

NI REVÊTUE	THE MIRE
1. Let those who reproach us for writing the Book and those who curse because of it or who curse it because of us, be themselves excluded and cursed on the day of God's judgement!	1'. Let those who praise us for writing the Book and those who bless us because of it or who bless it because of us, be themselves saved and blessed on the day of God's judgement!
2. Those who constantly step aside before God and those who proclaim their nothingness before God, can they be the enemies of God? Reply, O hypocrites who feign adoration of the Lord and who slyly place yourselves on all occasions before the priority of the Unique One!	2'. Have we not submitted ourselves to God's commandments as much as our weakness allows us? And if we reprimand the weakness of God's servants, is it not so as to make the word of God more radiant and pure in the darkened world?
3. Did we not wash the feet of the Saviour when he was embodied on this earth of exile? And did we not collect his tears and his blood when he died to save us? Did we not place the crown of pure gold on his royal	3'. Did we not rest on his bosom so-pure, and did he not kiss our lips in a holy way? Are we not his friend and his brother? And what is he that we are not potentially? And what are we that he is not in the act?

head when he was resurrected? And did we not prostrate ourselves at his shining and holy feet?

Have we not stepped aside in all circumstances before the splendour of the light of the Unique One, so as not to cast a shadow over God's salvation?

4. Who shall throw the Lord Christ at our head like a club, with the perspicacious eyes of a blind man? Let him be crushed by his own blindness and let him perish from his own blow, for the Spirit of God is not with him! Let him therefore be broken on the stone or be crushed by it!

4'. Does he defend the holy word of God, or does he defend the little cheese where he has settled in the name of God? That is what we wish to know, and that is what he has truly to ask himself.

«There are still honest and sincere people among the believers who hope and among those who seek God's salvation.»

5. Everywhere intrigues, platitudes and acts of cowardice to obtain a place in the world that perishes, and not a single impulse of the heart or the spirit to obtain a place in the world that does not perish.

5'. The intelligent and the skilful of this world are truly stupid, but they still do not know it. How great shall be the noise of their useless screaming and wailing when they find themselves stripped bare by God's judgement and exposed to the view of all!

6. They fight over the dung and they neglect the pearl that gleams above them. What worse curse than this?
Are they not to be pitied despite their admirable success in this transitory world?
Are they not already cursed by God and excluded from his salvation?

6'. Every verse of the Book has cost us a little of our bread and a little of our earthly life, but have we not unknowingly made a fabulous investment? God and the believers shall respond as they wish. As far as we are concerned, our gift remains free before God and towards men of goodwill.

7. Our own were the first to help and to receive the blacks who came to them. Shall the blacks not also be the first to receive and help our own who now go to them?

7'. The black peoples are still divided and as though in the process of being born, but one day they shall be united and strong if they receive the Book of union and of love in their hearts.

8. Let us not be distracted from our quest by the images of the world, and even less by the images of images of the world, which are like a vanity of vanity. Let us rather contemplate the image of the Lord in our purified hearts, until we embody it triumphantly in the life that does not perish.

9. He who is strong in God does not avenge himself and humiliates anyone, for he forgives even his enemies and makes them his friends.

10. Whatever the disorder of the societies in which we find ourselves, it is enough for us to remain faithful to the word of God and for us to accomplish it in the world so as to be saved.

11. When the deaf and the blind dominate in the world, vulgar methods take over subtle methods. Thus, beasts experience creation first by putting their nose to it, while superior men first see the stars that light up the sky and hear the voice of God that instructs them.

12. No, it is not a joy to be sent to preach the word of God to rebellious and lost men, for God's law is inexorable and men's heart is hardened like a rough stone.
No, it is not pleasant to soften the blow of God's anger, nor to save the cooled stone from the fire of righteous judgement. No, it is not advantageous to serve as a screen for God's

8'. Let us defend ourselves courageously against the filth of the world that invades us, but let us defend ourselves fiercely against the filth of sin that kills us, and let us consume it, so as to be able to receive the baptism of water and spirit that shall make us live in the eternity of the Unique One.

9'. Our joy overflows when the Lord smiles on us and our heart is sad when he hides himself from us.
Who shall let us live forever in his magnificent love?

10'. Realizing that one wastes one's time even working here below, makes us want to waste no more time, even resting in the world.

11'. Yes, a small remainder shall be sifted out, as one collects the still-glowing cinders at night from a heap of dead ashes, and these shall be nourished by God's sun and shall illuminate heaven forever.
As for the ashes, they shall serve as fertilizer to nourish the vine where God's chosen ones shall quench their thirst.

12'. One day (and what a day then!), God shall grow tired, and no intercessor shall descend or ascend between him and the rebels, for then the first shall have appeared in last place. There shall be a void and a strange delirium in the world, for men shall be abandoned to their own madness and the fire of heaven shall appear close and cruel without the

anger when the straw has replaced the grain in the world's silo.

protective screen of the saints' prayers. The noise of the light shall cover even the cries of the nations in fear.

13. The earth shall be covered by the bleached bones and the ashes of his creation, and the first noise to be heard shall be the noise of the rain from the heavens, and the first cry to be heard shall be the cry of the first one resurrected by God.

13'. O day of glory and of judgement! O day of love and of forgiveness! Some shall contemplate in fear their accusatory nakedness, while others shall sing God's praises because of their clothes of light.

14. When the birds come out again of the earth free and joyful, take heart again, my son. When the does and their fawns gambol in the springtide grass, rejoice, my child.

14'. When the flowers of the meadows drink the dew of the heavens, dance, my chosen one.
When the sun and the moon rest in your hands, sing, my beloved one.

14". But when your heart rejoins
my heart, be silent, my unique one.

15. Am I not right to contemplate the face of my Lord?
Am I not right to expose myself to the love of the unique Splendour?

15'. Give me, O Lord! the pure and imperishable body, the only one that can support without harm your loving look and penetrate up to the repose of your holy depth.

16. O divine ease of all creation! you work and you do not get tired. You rest and you do not get bored. You laugh at death, for your laughter is the imperishable life of eternal youth.
O Lord Father! give me your purity, give me your innocence, give me your freedom, give me your grace, give me your love, give me your power, give me your light, give me your generosity, give me your beauty, give me your life, give me your eternity, if it pleases your holy forgiveness.

16'. Hear my prayer, you, whose light is all intelligence, all love and all power of life. Come to me on your penetrating ray and awaken my life that is sleeping in the darkness of exile. Animate me again and save me from the horror of death, O marvellous Father! who is unstinting and tireless with your holy seed.

«Those who give the Lord a name other than that of Unique One born of He who IS, deceive themselves and deceive the world.»

17. Who dares to bury all humanity in the name of God's salvation? And who dares to reject God's salvation because of the ignorance of those who transmit God's word?

Who among them possesses the knowledge of the all-powerful presence of the Unique One?

18. Let us confess our faults and settle with generosity all debts and all litigation with whoever, so as not to dangerously increase the burden of death that already crushes us so much.

19. All those who steal vulgarly or subtly shall have to account for their dishonesty on the day of reckoning.

20. He who is truly strong is not afraid to appear weak by reaching agreement with his adversary before the time of judgement.

21. Let us go to our adversary and let us not tire of hearing him until we have come to an agreement with him, rather than exchanging blind writings that only increase the resentment and the confusion of everyone.

22. The super-intelligent impious ones who play at being revolutionaries in the world and the right-thinking hypocrites who play at being conservatives have buried us, because the name of the Beast whom they serve is not printed on our hands nor on our forehead on which shines the Name of the unique Lord of life.

17'. Ignorant hypocrites and conceited rebels, God undermines you all, and the common grave reconciles you in your common nothingness.

Is the light of the wise and holy books not sufficient to illuminate the way of the believers who seek God?

18'. Now, Lord, we cry before you, but it is with joy, for our hearts melt in the heavenly tears so that you might coagulate them into precious rubies in your immutable eternity.

19'. Let us strive not to be found in debt to anyone, for there shall be no appeal, no pity and no reprieve for the rogues.

20'. Every bad thought and every curse we provoke in the world is like a stone added to the invisible burden that bends us towards misfortune and towards death.

21'. The more cunning we are, the more we shall be deceived.

The more calculating we are, the more we shall be robbed.

The more we burden, the more we shall be crushed.

The more we plot, the more we shall be destroyed.

22'. Happy reprobation, happy exclusion, happy solitude, happy silence, happy prison that confirm our holy inheritance, for the wicked ones receive nothing but their own dung, which they recognize by its scent without ever making a mistake.

23. Have we not worked for God, for his believers and for his Churches?
Have we not defended, renewed and propagated the faith in the unique Splendour?

23'. Have we not reminded all the seekers of salvation of the humble and simple way of the divine kingdom?
Have we not confirmed and renewed the wise and holy words of the primary revelation?

24. The impious one receives but does not thank, profits but does not love, has plenty but does not praise. His fate is already decided, for he shall become like dead wood that is burnt to make fertilizer.

24'. The believer feels gratitude for the life he has received, feels love for him who gave it to him and praises him who perpetuates and saves it miraculously. He shall flower once more in the garden of God.

25. A nation survives itself because of its sages and its saints.

25'. It perishes because of its shrewd and its impious ones.

26. No need for connections, nor presentations, nor recommendations, nor introductions to get close to the Lord of salvation. There is no need for diplomas, nor certificates, nor enrolments, nor registrations.

26'. No need for passports, exeats, tricks, tips, grovelling, lies, cowardice, robberies or crimes, as needed to get close to people in high places in the world.

26". «Only a heart purified by fire and by water, and fertilized by the Holy Spirit.»

27. If we are asked what the Book is, let us reply: a stone on which believers lean firmly, and a spring from which they ceaselessly draw water.

27'. 36 opinions known simultaneously.
36 professions learned at one time.
36 things done at the same time.
36 lights seen all at once.
36 desires fulfilled in just one.
36 religions brought together in one faith.

28. Few men are capable of enduring God's freedom without dying, and few men are capable of enduring the free will bestowed on them here below without weakening.

28'. That is why so many men who can only live in flocks or like caged rabbits in the world, clamour for the slavery of the tyrant or the State.

29. Men's science is a stopgap that artificially, and with a great deal of effort, returns to them a small part of that which they irremediably lose through the effect of the fall into death.

30. Let us carefully observe the sordid hatreds that poison the relationships of hypocrites among themselves, and let us notice the affection with which God's true children surround themselves. It is a mark that must make the doubters reflect.

31. We are pursued right now, and we are condemned because we cure the sick who are abandoned, following the example of the Lord of forgiveness and of love who shows us the holy way.

32. Let us not receive among us any of those who have chosen to serve the Beast by exercising a profession of wild beast or a profession of domestic beast that threatens the freedom or the life of the innocent, the poor and the holy.

33. What would become of the world if the revelation of God disappeared through the action of the impious and if it stopped manifesting itself here through the disappearance of the prophets? One would only see herds of cattle exploited and reduced to slavery by a handful of wild beasts.

29'. He who knows how to laugh at the world and at himself with the Lord is truly illuminated by God.
«Is the saint not divinely warned of the catastrophes caused by men rebelling against God?»

30'. Is there a sweeter reward in this world than the affectionate gratitude of those whom we bless and help to get closer to the truth of the God of life? What more beautiful harvest to offer the unique harvester?

31'. Soon, we shall also be persecuted because we console those in despair, and we shall be condemned because we convert them to the salvation of life of the unique God, as hypocrisy and wickedness reach their peak in the world.

32'. Let the ones gone astray choose a profession of a free man that threatens no-one, and let them become converted to the love of God and to the mutual help of their fellow men if they wish to wipe out the curse of heaven that weighs on them and participate in the blessing of the children of God.

33'. No joy, no security, no repose, no peace for us, while one believer cries in this world of misery, while one who has gone astray gropes around in this darkness of exile, while one sick man lies dying in this charnel-house of death, while one crucified man moans on this cross of ransom.

34. There are no illegitimate children in the world; there are only well-off hypocrites who put their interest before that of God, for the Unique One is gracious to all those who seek him with a loving and sincere heart.

35. Here we are like small mines of the Lord of heaven, and here is the Lord of heaven like a small mine of the immensity of the unique Splendour. Thus, all are in One like gold coins are in gold.

36. The union of man and woman is holy and sacred before God. Woe betide those who profane it, for they shall become like beasts instead of being made like gods.

34'. We prefer to risk being deceived by all men than to judge just one prematurely, thus risking deceiving ourselves.

«We do not see the transparent heaven, but the Lord sees through the dark outer layers.»

35'. Thus, the magnetic dust shall rejoin the mass of the magnet and shall merge into it, and everything shall remain in One, as before the explosive cry of joy that emulsified the worlds on the face of the dark abyss.

36'. We shall join our wives in a holy way to ask for the blessing of the grace and the confirmation of God's love, who never denies his rescue to his beloved children.

36". Let him who can join the heavenly fire do so and live! For there is the salvation and the union that do not perish.

37. It is faith that permits us to approach knowledge of the love that saves from the exile of death.

37'. He who is in the darkness sees God outside himself, but he who is in the light sees God in oneself.

38. The Unique One sent us the letter of the Father engraved in the stone of Israel.

Then, he sent us the word of the Son preached all over the Western world.

Now, he sends us the thought of the Spirit that shall cover the whole world.

38'. Is it not the same and unique revelation from the beginning to the end? Did it not come out of the black earth? And now, does it not return to the black earth?

«Will the dark children that were the last in the world not become the first in God?»

39. The Son came to us from the Father through the Spirit. At present, the Spirit comes to us from the Son who has returned to the Father.

39'. Who can recognize the Lord embodied under his rags of a poor man? He is blessed, for it is God in person who enlightens him.

40. All that we say about the Lord of salvation is worthless if we do not know the incarnate Lord, for we go astray in the void of darkness instead of joining the plenitude of the Unique One.

40'. Thus, our disputes concerning the Lord of life are imbecilic like those of blind and deaf beggars who cannot recognize the colour and sound of pure gold.

40". Is the weight of the hidden splendour not sufficient to attract our attention? And is its incombustibility not sufficient to confirm our secret hope?

41. Let those who come or return to God in their hearts after having read the Book bear witness to him in the world, so that each one is confirmed, either in freely consented faith or in freely chosen impiety.

41'. We ask you to pray to God freely in your hearts, and to study the holy Scriptures, and not to parade yourself in the churches to make people believe in your holiness and in the impiety of others.

42. He who receives the Book in his heart is blessed by God, but he who rejects it excludes himself from the salvation of the unique Splendour.

42'. The Lord approves of us, for do we not follow his luminous trace? Do we not confirm his holy word? And do we not recall his wise way?

43. The revelation of God's salvation involves a Church to perpetuate it and a School to teach it, and the one cannot go without the other, on pain of the eventual disappearance of both.

43'. For sleeping faith and proud science lead to spiritual and corporal death, that is to say, to the erasure of divine revelation and the erasure of incarnate humanity.

44. The believers shall choose the word that aids them the most, and the seekers shall choose the one that instructs them the best.

44'. Everyone can enter the Church of God, but not everyone can enter the School of God.

45. A wretched man who praises God in his heart is worth a thousand times more than all the great men of the earth who think only about the world and their affairs.

46. Those who profess to represent God on men's earth must necessarily hear what God says to them when they humbly beg him to instruct them.

47. Not all the guardians of the holy Scriptures are sleeping in a sinecure. There are still some that are awaiting and seeking God's salvation here below.

48. Have we not put the Lord of heaven above all creature?
Have we not put his earthly revelation above all Scripture?

49. Have we not put his hidden School above all instruction?
Have we not put his revealed Church above all communion?

50. Are we for the holy Lord?
Are we of the holy Lord?
Are we with the holy Lord?

51. Let us deny the messenger if that suits us, but at least, let us receive the message that glorifies the Lord and let us acknowledge the word that opens spirits and hearts, so that nothing be given to us in vain.

45'. O holy mire of the abyss despised by the intelligent of the world, it is in you that the precious gold that ennobles the simple children of God is hidden!

46'. These shall tell us sincerely that which the Lord has revealed to them about the Book, but perhaps he does not hear them or he does not reply to them? Therefore, how can they claim to represent the Unique One?

47'. We trust in the perspicacity of the true lovers of the Unique One and we trust in their good faith, for they are seers and listeners of God.

48'. Have we not put ourselves last?
Have we not put his word first?

49'. Have we not brought back up to date the flesh and blood of the Lord once more?
Have we not returned the honour to bread and wine?
Have we not put into evidence the holy stone and oil once more?

50'. What do our exhortations say?
What do our preachings say?
What do our adorations say?
Reply, O seers who also hear!

51'. The Lord, who was innocent and true, endured sarcasm, insults, blows and death well without becoming angry. Thus, we who are bad and sinful, to what extent must we not endure everything without grumbling?

52. Whoever returns to the Lord sincerely is received with open heart, for the Lord has no rancour, and forgives even those who have stupidly preferred death to him.

52'. Has each one not received a part of intelligence in order to know what he is doing? And those who have lost it, is it not through having systematically despised it by doing evil?

52". Are we not here also to forgive, to console and to save following the example of the Living One of eternity?

53. The blacks have been waiting for their holy inheritance since one of their sages discovered the star that led him to the virgin mother and to the infant king.

53'. Shall they receive at present that which is offered to them in particular? The arrogant pride of their brothers favours them divinely, but none of them know it yet.

54. The dead shall dissolve the Living One but the Living One shall coagulate the dead and everyone shall rest in the unity of the Unique One; that is, if the dead still receive the Living One!

54'. For if the dead are like the dough, the Living One is like the yeast that enlivens it and transforms it for the heavenly baking that makes the golden bread of God.

One shall make a black man believe many things, but one shall never make him believe that there is no God.
ANONYMOUS AFRICAN

Behold, you shall call the nation you did not know, and the nations that did not know you shall rush up to you.
ISAIAH

BOOK XXIX

I accomplish the word of my servant and I execute the counsel of my envoys.

ISAIAH

Each nation has repudiated the mission of its prophet. They have disappeared one after another.

KORAN

URNE ET VIE	THE EGG
1. We shall recognize the servants of the Beast by the scornful, oppressive and murderous spirit they manifest towards free men on all occasions.	1'. Having given themselves to the Beast, they adore it with a devotion that does not even consider the blood of their human brothers.
2. The Beast devours men in order to subsist in his cesspit of dark and stinking death.	2'. God consumes the filth that blinds us and kills us in order to establish us in pure and eternal life.
3. Those who give themselves over to the Beast and who thus give being to evil are damned among the damned, and no forgiveness shall ever deliver them, for they knowingly betray the Lord of love and life.	3'. The name of the Beast is written with initials that are the signs of the Beast, and these signs are a number for those who understand, for they caricature the Name of God without truly reproducing it.

3". Only the Lord can change
within	the Innate	Immaculate	Innocent
the	Fenny	Female	Phantom
into	Certain	Concealed	Cinder
he	Aided	Afore	Art.

4. It is enough that we take out our beam, for by denouncing the mote that blinds our informer we shall remove neither one nor the other, but rather sink them in even more.

5. True believers endure the contradictions of those who do not believe as they do and those of the people who do not believe at all, for their hope is not worthless and their faith is not murderous.

6. We are invaded and as though overwhelmed by the word of God, so that we disappear more and more before him, and so that he is manifested better and better within us.

7. There is not a single verse of the Book that has not been the object of disapproval by the profane world. There is not a line of the Book to which it has not taken an aversion because of the time spent in writing it, and, above all, because of the Spirit that animates it.

8. Has the Lord not endured everything out of love for the Unique One and out of love for men gone astray in death?

9. The holy Mother flowed in me, and the wise Lord swam there in his golden boat.

10. While I, blinded by the spitting of the world, wandered, guided miraculously.

4'. The sage listens even to the warning of the ignorant one.
The ignorant one does not even listen to the warning of the sage.

5'. Tolerance is characteristic of God and of those who belong to him, just as intolerance is characteristic of the Beast and of those who serve it. This is an infallible mark that transcends all particular labels.

6'. The Lord chooses us and makes use of us for the good of all. We do not choose him and make use of him for our own good.

7'. Is he perhaps right? And perhaps we have stupidly wasted our time writing the Book, instead of earning a living like everyone else? God is the sole judge, and the believers shall reply in their hearts.

8'. Do we not have to submit ourselves more and more to the will of God and to the reprobation of the world?

9'. And heaven and earth, while kneeling, contemplated the unheard-of spectacle.

10'. In the nameless jubilation of the heart melted into the unity of the unique Splendour.

11. Discourse is nothing, and neither is the speaker. Only the subject of the discourse is interesting, and is worth attaining.

11'. If only we could at least rest at the feet of the Lord of life! It is a holy and blessed place for those who know.

12. The Lord of before the beginnings remains hidden in the bosom of the great sea, but the great sea manifests him visibly so that the whole of creation appears in the light of the Unique One.

12'. Everything started out from the unmixed liquid to move towards the unmixed solid. Everything shall start out again from the solid mixed by way of the fall to move to the unmixed liquid of the beginning, and finally, everything shall start out again from the unmixed liquid to fix itself in the unmixed solid of stable eternity.

13. What do light and darkness have in common?

13'. Nothing in substance! The mixed worlds in a mixture!

14. A portion of the light may well find itself momentarily emulsified in the darkness, but it is neither mixed up in it nor lost in it forever.

14'. At the end of time, it shall come together again in the bosom of the unique Splendour, and the children of God shall rest in the assured victory of love.

15. Here we are here below on a terrible battlefield, where there is no question of us resting here, and still less of us settling here.

15'. The mixed worlds shall be separated and delivered from the filth of the darkness, and they shall join the luminous purity of the unique Splendour.

16. God wants a living Church with the Lord of love in action in the hearts of the believers, and not a dead Church filled with hypocrites who only concern themselves with their own affairs and with those of the world. The mediocre and the hypocrites shall be discouraged so that the Church survives more in quality than in quantity.

16'. It is up to the true believers to re-build the Church in its primary purity. Let all those who put the Lord of life and his salvation above themselves and their goods come to the Lord in their hearts, so as to re-build the unity of love in the freedom of God's children!

17. Many shall be saved, but very few shall know the how, and hardly any shall get close to the why.

18. Everywhere there are learned critics and learned historians who sift and label the dust of death that covers God's word.

19. We are not here to exclude ourselves from humanity gone astray.

20. It has to be said all the same, even if it does not please everyone: isolated believers have done more for the life of the Church than the clerics it nourishes in its bosom.

21. There is nothing more dead than these timid proud ones who ask nothing of God nor of men, and who give nothing to anyone either. Darkness, cold, viscosity and stench! They rot in solitude!
«Who shall warm their hearts by the gentle fire of love?»

22. Doubt and impiety are transmitted to us through simple contact, like contagious diseases, and we die like plague victims in horror and stench. Shall the faith of a few not save us in the same way?

23. Is it not Melchior, the black king, who offered the gold of royalty and of love to the new-born Lord? And is it not the glorified Lord who sends the blacks the gold of liberation and of love?

17'. Our quest is difficult and doomed to failure without the inspiration of the Lord. But is it not sufficient for us to receive salvation from the hands of God's chosen ones?

18'. Is there not one saint, not one prophet, not one sage to free it from its hardened gangue and to revive it again in the heart of men?

19'. We are here to go to it and to enlighten it on the way of the free return to the unique Love of life.

20'. The good shepherd lives from day to day among his small flock like the holy master did, without worthless separations and without conceited restrictions.

21'. To withdraw into the solitude of God is not to exclude oneself from the heart of humanity, but rather to plunge into it completely through the channel of divine love that bathes all creation. Light, warmth, love and life! These germinate in the Lord!

22'. Do the first not come last at present, and do the last not come first? Shall we open our eyes and shall we understand the lesson of the Highest? Shall we see the light shine and straighten up?

23'. O you! the best of peoples, who know how to love and rejoice without hypocrisy, the Lord sends you the best of what he has, for he loves you and rejoices in you without constraint. Shall you relinquish his treasure like the other mad peoples?

24. The dedication of the Book to the blacks is dazzling, and no-one can doubt it, not even the whites who receive it first.

25. We knew you before you knew us.

26. The whites received us like blind men.

27. If it were like that, let the Book remain hidden in the bosom of the Unique One until the time of judgement!

28. Lord, let us catch a glimpse of your salvation once more, so that we are consoled in our distress.

29. Everywhere there are indifferent ones, idiots, sectarians, hypocrites or rebels who reject God's gift.

30. What a strange harvest, in which we must seek one by one the ears of good corn, drowned in the fields of tares! What a strange quest, in which we must collect a few grains of gold lost in the mountain of dead sand!

31. Just a few who believe, seek and ask God for their salvation, for a multitude of dead and dying men who sleep! O Lord! is it possible for you to mock your children so cruelly by isolating them like this in the world?

32. O unfortunate blindness! Do we not know that one of God's children weighs more on the scales of

24'. The Lord shall open up the understanding of the heart if we open up ourselves to his holy and perfect love.

25'. Do you know that? And do you understand it as you should?

26'. Shall the blacks receive us as deaf people?

27'. Is a single child of God not sufficient to justify the entire void of the earth?

28'. Lord, let us catch a glimpse of your victory once more so that we are comforted in our weakness.

29'. O believers! who wish to live before the Lord, where are you? Respond to the call before the fire that shall clean the earth of its thorns.

30'. The Lord has already lit his torch to reduce the useless multitudes to ashes, and we beg him to wait a little longer, in the hope of discovering a few isolated ears of corn, for we do not even think any longer of finding a field of good grain or a whole piece of his treasure.

31'. Are you not planted like a seed to make the whole earth germinate before the Lord? Are you not placed like yeast to make the whole mass of creatures rise up to God's salvation?, says the unique expert.

32'. Do the density, the weight, the good odour and the constancy of the one divine treasure not count for

judgement than all the kingdoms of the earth, than all their kings and all their subjects put together?

33. Is the master not considered by the profane world the king of charlatans for having announced the salvation declared unbelievable?

more than the scattering and the multitude of empty outer layers?

33'. Is the master not considered by the profane world the king of tumblers for having manifested the reputedly impossible resurrection?

33". Shall we not be honoured to be also treated as charlatans and tumblers because of our confirmation in the world of divine salvation and of glorious resurrection?

34. It is our joy to have neglected our life here below in order to remind the discouraged believers of God's salvation and forgiveness.

34'. It is our glory not to have worked for ourselves here below, but rather to have worked for all the creatures of God.

35. On leaving, we shall be light concerning the world because we shall have become dense in God. Who understands that at present?

35'. What shall seem like a catastrophe to many shall appear to a few as the prelude to God's salvation.

36. We have come to confirm the ancient revelations and we have come to renew them in the world before the decisive choice of the end.

36'. All opportunities shall have been given to each one to hear and to believe, to see and to touch, so that no complaint is made in the last judgement.

37. As long as we labour for ourselves, our works shall appear to us hard and sad.

37'. From the moment we labour for God, our works shall seem to us light and joyful.

38. The Lord does a disservice to those who work only for themselves.

38'. While he works in person for those who serve him.

39. We must strive to suffer and endure everything here below without recrimination, for nothing belongs to us, not even our body, and nothing is owed to us, not even our life.

39'. Hard words for those who think they are able to settle in this world of exile and be able to triumph in it through their work or through the work of others.

40. After the Lord has visited us as a family, is it not advisable that we also visit him in private?

41. Some Names of God consume and others water; some Names of God kill and others give life; some Names of God rise and others fall.

42. With a word, the Lord could dissolve the world into the limbo of oblivion, but he preferred to suffer insults, blows and death than to curse a portion of the creation of the Unique One.
What a lesson for all!

43. He who spends his time praying and seeking God, is the only one who is not useless here below.

44. He who is not vivified by heaven shall not resurrect from the earth.
«Unknown. Unbelievable. Incarnate. Impassible.»

45. We do not wish to abandon our body in order to dissolve ourselves in the limbo of the beginning. We wish to purify it and consolidate it with the aid of God, so as to be able to inhabit it for eternity.

46. Serge, the Algerian, believes in the message that comes from the master of the messenger. Shall the Lord not establish him as servant of the believers because of his loyalty,

40'. The communal prayer of believers draws God to men. The saint's solitary prayer magnetizes man to God.

41'. These divine Names are written, are spelt, are named and are sung to give forms and to break them up; that is a secret that God only entrusts to the renounced who prefer to die than to kill.

42'. The Lord teaches us not to reject his creation, however disfigured it may be, for behind the desolation of death still survives the spark of divine life. Who shall experience the wisdom of the sage? And who shall see it shine on the earth?

43'. Even if men were to exclude him from all of their goods, the angels of God would serve him as a prince of heaven.

44'. Here there is a condition that the intelligent ones of God shall note, for here is the ultimate degree reserved solely for the chosen sons of God.

45'. Here there is a difference that the intelligent ones of God shall note, for if partial union with God is worthy of praise and admiration, only total union in spirit, in soul and in body is worthy of adoration.

46'. Lanza, the poet, preaches to the deaf and teaches the blind. Shall not the Lord give him a people to instruct and lead in a holy way? Does the warmth of the heart not count

and shall he not crown him madman of God because of his faith?
«He loves within, so that he shall shine without.»

47. Bryan, the diplomat, suffocates in this dying world awaiting the breeze from the garden of Eden. Shall the Lord not moisten him with his Holy Spirit and shall he not make him float on his hidden sea?
«He hopes and is patient.»

48. Charles, known as Zou, sings like a bird and loves like a madman. Shall the Lord not water him with his precious shower of pearls and rubies?
«He muses and he finds.»

Robert, the engineer, is unsettled by the Book. He holds back and he waits. Shall the Lord not say a little word to reassure him?
«He hesitates and he doubts.»

49. The bread of heaven must be softened in the wine of the earth to be administered to God's children, for the communion of the Living One of eternity possesses a strength that can kill our weakness.

50. God gave us the Book of nature, but we did not read it!

51. He accomplished before us the mystery of incarnation and that of resurrection, but we did not see them!

52. There is a blessing for him who propagates the Book, and there is a blessing for him who receives it.

for more than the colour of the skin?
«He penetrates and he keeps.»

47'. Emmanuel, the forester, seeks the good odour of life with a well-developed sense of smell. Shall the Lord not lead him towards the holy dew that perfumes the world of Mary?
«He seeks and he rummages.»

48'. All are in God's hand, but they still struggle too much to be re-engendered in the life that does not perish. Who shall be the first to cease to subsist outside so as to be remade inside?
«He who will die and who will resurrect.»

49'. All that is beautiful and good here below is nothing but the reflection of the beauty and succulence of the pure substance of life, and all that is ugly and bad is nothing more than an image of the ugliness and the poison of the dark filth of death.

50'. He sent us the Lord to spell it out to us, but we did not hear him!

51'. If he prints for us his way white upon black, shall we notice it, shall we study it and shall we follow it? Or shall we say that we have not received it either?

52'. There is a blessing for him who reads the Book, and there is a blessing for him who listens to it.

53. There is a blessing for him who studies the Book, and there is a blessing for him who applies it.

53'. There is a blessing for him who experiences the Book, and there is a blessing for him who accomplishes it.

53". There is also a blessing for him who has heard the Book and him who has written it, let us be sure of that. That blessing shines like the evening moon and like the morning sun.

If you have done or if you do something bad, you shall not escape the pain, however far you flee.
BUDDHA

The good and the bad things you do, you do them to yourself.
KORAN

BOOK XXX

We shall reduce to dust all that decorates the earth.

KORAN

Let the dust return to the earth according to how it was, and let the spirit return to God who gave it.

ECCLESIASTES

VUE TERNIE

1. How can we think of the Lord and how can we pray to him, praise him and bless him when we are exposed to the recriminations, the screeching, the cries and even the howling of the profane world?

2. A small trickle of the great waters hardly reaches us at present, and we lie dying in the world, asking for grace.

3. All that comes from heaven and is not received by men wanders over the earth and overflows over nature.

4. He who is with God has no time to be against anyone.

5. It is the spirit of possession, of recrimination, of oppression and of

THE DARKNESS

1'. He who can retire to a room or a quiet place, does he know his luck and his happiness?
«Hell is certainly not favourable to prayers.»

2'. One day, we shall swim in the immensity of the heavenly sea, and all shall be given to us in profusion, even before we have asked for it.

3'. The blessing that is not received and absorbed overflows and changes into a curse for the ungrateful ones.

4'. All word of hate that will be whispered to us, even against the enemies of God, is not God's. That is clear and precise.

5'. God punishes the wicked ones that unjustly take hold of the life of

aggression that engenders misery, hate, slavery and misfortune in the world.

6. Nobody has the right to prosper here below if he does not profess impious atheism or if he does not display a hypocritical faith, for each group concerns itself with its own affairs and despises those of God.

7. There is no longer room in the world for the believers of God who adore his holy Name in their hearts.

8. The believers shall restore the purity of God's Church, and the priests that have remained faithful to God in their hearts shall be with them for the work of resurrection.

9. The secret of God is certainly holy, but the Churches that guard it are no longer so, unfortunately!, through the fault of those that constitute them.

10. Likewise our duty is to restore these Churches to the primary purity and simplicity, close to the will of God and far away from the passions of the world.

11. The passer-by of God opens the holy flask that the old prostitute kept hidden under her rags.

12. With the first sip, she becomes young and beautiful once more, and all those who shunned her in horror return to her full of love and respect.

beings and things. Our sight is short, but the judge's memory is inexorable.

6'. They all bear the initials of the Beast as a mark and as a flag, and they destroy themselves in the end, for they are God's enemies, because they deny him publicly, or betray him in secret.

7'. Their life is parsimoniously measured out for them, and soon it shall be totally questioned.

8'. The hypocrites and the impious shall be thrown out of God's paradise, and they shall accuse each other and rip each other apart without mercy and without forgiveness in the darkness of exile.

9'. Our duty is to denounce the intrusion of earthly affairs in the bosom of God's Churches.

10'. The hypocrites, the half-hearted and the impious shall be driven out, and everything shall be renewed in the Lord of life and truth for the good of his faithful creation.

11'. And after taking the first drink, he offers her the flask full of the golden liquor of the Gods.

12'. While those who maintained her in her vices and who exploited her shamelessly, fall to the ground under the weight of their iniquities that rebound on them.

13. With the second swig, the whole body of her beauty shines with the sweet light of God and her rags lie consumed at her feet.

14. With the third drink, she sings with the angels the praises of her creator and, veiled by her golden locks, she dances the step of free and holy life with the virgins.

15. The breath of the Holy Spirit is a breath of life and light that drives out death and its darkness.

16. It is a breath that gives life to believers, but that can be a death blow to the impious, for it is the breath of God that falls and rises, that rests and beats, that blows where it wants, without anyone being able to guess where it comes from nor where it is going.

17. The triumphant imbeciles may well split their sides with laughter on reading the Book of the secret; we must not be offended or annoyed about that.

18. All that the hypocritical pedants might invent and say about the Book, and about us, must not sadden or revolt us.

19. The two witnesses shall be exposed to the view of all in the public square and shall be guarded by the army rabble just as the Lord was on the cross.

13'. A divine perfume is exhaled from all her splendour and reaches her rediscovered children who inhale the good odour of life.

14'. Her children enter the dance and join in with their songs of joy under the loving gaze of the Father, who rejoices in his rediscovered and saved family.

15'. It is a breath of love that consoles the humble ones, but it is also a breath of justice that breaks the proud ones.

16'. It is the Spirit of God that does everything in and outside us. Therefore, we must not be proud of anything, for then we attribute to ourselves that which is entrusted to us, but which does not belong to us.
«ART, GLORY and JUDGEMENT belong only to God.»

17'. We must rather laugh with them, for however stupid and pretentious they may be, the different tone of our joy shall soon make them understand that we are not laughing at the same thing as them.

18'. Whatever the perfidy of their slander and whatever the virulence of their venom, they shall not be able to erase the inspired word of the heart of the believers and they shall not be able to sully us before God.

19'. One on his belly and the other on his back, three days and two nights, thus shall be exposed the first who come last.

20. When they straighten up under the breath of the Holy Spirit, they shall find themselves face to face, one on his knees and the other seated.

20'. So as also to be witnesses for each other to the miracle of God, and so that their praises rise in a single thrust towards the Lord of life and of resurrection.

21. The terror of the wicked ones shall then reach its height, and their boasting, which triumphed, shall become dumb with fright, for their water shall abandon them and they shall dry out before the eyes of the Highest, who shall reduce them to ashes.

21'. The joy of the believers shall also reach its height and the assurance of their faith shall become senseless, after having weakened in the extreme, for the water of grace shall flow in them abundantly, and the love of the Highest shall establish them in imperishable life.

22. The Father-God is the NAME of God unexpressed in the secret of the Water-God.

22'. God is hidden in his NAME.

23. The Water-God is the NAME of God which falls and rises in oneself.

23'. And his NAME is life.

24. The Spirit-God is the NAME of God which moves in all directions over the Water-God.

24'. And his NAME is alive.

25. The Body-God is the NAME of God which manifests and fixes itself in the Water-God.

25'. And his NAME feeds on life.

25". Thus, God is he who IS, through that which he IS, in that which he IS, for that which he IS.

26. With God, here we are above everything. Without God, here we are below everything.

26'. The thing is easy to verify in and around us.

27. It is God's favours that make the proud one blind and futile.

27'. The gifts of God are what give the intelligent one the measure of his poverty in everything.

28. Thus, the conceited ignorant one attributes the derisory glory of the world to himself.

29. We can love God with all our heart and remain turned towards him as much as possible in this restless and greedy world.

30. Therefore, the spiritual frequenting of the Unique One fills us with spiritual joy, but leaves us in material destitution.

31. Many receive the intellectual gifts of the world.

32. Only a few receive the spiritual gifts of God.

33. Riches without the sun of God are a curse that engenders misery and desolation.

34. Who can approach the cup of immortality?

35. Who possesses the nectar of the immortals?

36. The nonbeliever relies only on himself in this world, but the believer above all relies on God in heaven.

37. Thus, the saints bless the brimming floods of heavenly grace that fulfil them, while the impious ones curse the overflow they have not received and that swallows them up.

38. One must be deeply sunk into the bestial state to feel good in the

28'. Thus, the believer who has been instructed attributes to God alone the glory of all creation.

29'. Though that will not mean we shall obtain the material help that would deliver us from the tyrannical worry of earning or begging our daily subsistence.

30'. It is only the spiritual and substantial possession of the Lord of abundance that shall fulfil us in heaven and on earth.

31'. And a large number receive the material goods of the world.

32'. And barely one or two receive the palpable goods of God.

33'. Poverty with the sun of God is a blessing that engenders riches and joy.

34'. And who can wet his lips with the divine beverage?

35'. And who knows the origin of the wine of God?

36'. When one curses, the other blesses for the same reason. That is a sign we must note well.

37'. Likewise, the saints bless the fire of heavenly love that matures them and consolidates them, while the impious curse the superabundance of love that they have not lodged and that consumes them.

38'. How can one remain there at ease? How can one settle there com-

stench of death that dwells in us and oozes from everywhere.

39. Is it not because of the divine inheritance that subsists miraculously in us beneath the ignominy of the foreign filth?

40. He who praises the Lord for all he receives and for all that leaves him, for all that happens to him and for all that does not happen to him, is truly enlightened by God and his deliverance from the exile of death is assured.

41. Everyone fights over words, over ideas, over pre-eminences or over goods, which are like the shadows of the thing, instead of seeking the thing that is the sole substantial reality of the Being that rests in his bosom and that gives life to him.

42. It is not sufficient to think we do good; it is absolutely necessary for us to do good in order to be saved.

43. Knowing all the names of water or bathing in the great water are two quite different things.

44. Those who speak to us of the thing and who do not have it would do well to step aside humbly.

fortably? How can one rest there peacefully? How can one cling on there frantically?

39'. Would we not do better to separate these two, in the holy contemplation of God, rather than mixing them more and more in the worthless restlessness of the world?

40'. Who shall give us the intelligence to judge no more with our blind eyes, and who shall give us the prudence to recriminate no more with our imbecilic tongues? Who shall give us the intelligence to draw our life from heaven, and who shall give us the patience to ripen it on earth?

41'. Holy men designate the thing under a multitude of names and figures, but the thing is unique and remains just as it is in its virginity or in its maternity, and manifests its holiest and most secret centre, which is the Lord of life.

42'. It is not necessary to explain life and its movement; it is sufficient to possess life and the golden unity it conceals.

43'. Knowing all the properties of gold or possessing the treasure of life are also two quite different things.

44'. Those who keep silent about the thing and who possess it, would do well to show themselves prudently.

44''. Alas! it is just the opposite that happens, so blind is our pretension and so envious are our hearts.

45. It is our pretentious self-satisfaction that closes the doors of love and knowledge to us.

45'. And it is our impious wickedness that distances us from the chosen ones of God who transmit the word of life.

46. It is rest that lies in movement and that gives life to it.

46'. Just as it is the essence that is in substance and that makes forms emanate in it.

47. We have believed in our intelligence, in our work, in our will and in our learning in this world, but now here we are at your feet, holy and perfect Lord.

47'. Like dying men, stripped of everything, who founder in the great night, your gracious light and your precious love are our only hope in this lamentable state.

48. All our misdeeds and all our crimes in the world are insignificant before our repudiation and our forgetting of God.

48'. That is why the Lord forgives completely those who return to him with a repentant and broken heart, which melts in the tears of rediscovered holy love.

49. Day of darkness and despair, all shall seem lost to us, and we shall be as though annihilated by grief.

49'. It is then that the light of the Perfect One shall break through the great night, and his day shall shine on his saved ones forever.

50. O the cries of pain! O the heartrending lamentations of those who shall have freely chosen to settle in the darkness of outside!

50'. O the cries of joy! O the loving praises of those who shall have chosen in their heart to fix themselves in the light of within!

He joins with his dust, oh! how pure he is.

LAO TSE

He accomplishes his work by breathing into him a portion of his spirit.

KORAN

BOOK XXXI

You, who of all the corporeal world are the most perfect being I have seen, for your brilliant, immortal body.

ZOROASTER

Each age shall tell the following one the praise of your works; your marvels shall be made public.

DAVID

NEUVE TRIE

1. We aspire to the humblest and most discredited place in the world so that, while each one considers himself above us, nobody is scandalized in his faith by our person or by our situation.

2. It is the love of God, which seems so derisory to the shrewd ones of this world, that shall save us on the day of judgement.

3. Let the poor live for one day like the rich and the rich for one month like the poor, so that each one knows the state of the other.

4. This does not mean: experience vice or filth.

THE LIGHT

1'. The Book matters more than he who wrote it, and the thing of which the Book speaks matters more than the Book. Likewise, we must not forget that God's salvation matters more than the means to salvation.

2'. For we shall not appear with empty heart and hands.
«O extreme surprise of the weight of the light of life!»

3'. The believers who read the Book shall be transported by joy and shall propagate the news around them, for the Lord who disappeared into heaven comes back to earth and his reign approaches with certainty.

4'. That does not mean: pray no more or seek no more.

5. Do we know by which figure the Lord shall present himself to us? And are we confident of recognizing him in time?

5'. All forms belong to him par excellence, for he manifests them and he dissolves them effortlessly in his continuous creation.

6. It is a great act of charity to permit the poor whom we assist to do us favours in gratitude, for we thus give them the assurance of their dignity of free men.

6'. Those who are of God and those who belong to God recognize each other in that they put God before themselves on all occasions, and in that they relate everything to him and nothing to themselves. Here we have a sign that is excellent among all.

7. It is not good to triumph, nor to shine, nor even to be in the right in this dark world, poisoned by jealousy and hate.

7'. It is better to live hidden and unknown, and to do good in secret to the poor and humble who do not bite the hand that helps them.

8. One day, the proud ones of the world shall wake up in the dead mud and their astonishment, their rage and their desperation shall be frightful.

8'. They shall reveal themselves to be viler than vermin crawling in a decomposing corpse, for they shall eat death vomiting.

9. The Lord's chosen ones shall bathe in the sweet light that exhales the good odour of life and they shall congratulate one another endlessly.

9'. Not a single drop of the heavenly dew shall be lost in the quagmire of death, for a glass wall shall separate them from the damned.

10. Thus, the wicked ones shall see the unity of the holy light that shall bathe the children of God, and this shall add to their torments, for they shall be unable to participate in it in any other way.

10'. They shall be unable to make themselves heard or seen by the chosen ones because of their darkness, which shall overwhelm them with the filth of death. But they shall tear themselves to pieces amid the howls of their ever-renewed mortal agony.

11. Let us push away ugly and complicated things and let us devote all our leisure to the quest for the unique beauty.

11'. Let us cast off the tight clothing and let us consume the filth of sin that maintains us in the darkness of death.

12. The truth of God runs to meet him who seeks it with a humble and purified heart.

12'. But it flees from those who think they are able to do violence to it, it hides from those who scorn it and it abandons those who do a disservice to it.

13. Let him who feels alone and abandoned in the world take courage; let him pray to the Lord and his saints in his heart, and he shall receive what he has asked for.

13'. Let him reflect carefully on his request, so as not to receive empty outer layers instead of the substantial kernel that alone fulfils God's children.

14. We must carefully avoid all contact with worldly sceptics who denigrate everything, in their incapacity to receive anything from the truths of God.

14'. Believing themselves shrewd, they have become just like fools who triumph in the void of their hearts and of their spirits. Their role is to dirty everything that is not tainted like them.

15. We shall declare ourselves to know nothing, to have nothing and to be capable of nothing, which is the truth, in front of the wicked, the shrewd, the mediocre, the hypocrites and the impious.

15'. Our prudence, our silence and our absence shall be our safeguard before those who wish to know without studying, to see without believing and to judge without loving.

16. It is a sin before God and it is a danger for everyone to instruct a wicked one, and it is a madness and a danger for oneself to help him while his wickedness and his malice persist.

16'. Before simple believers, children of God, we shall manifest the goodness of the holy light, so that their hearts be confirmed in the faith of God and so that their spirits be penetrated by a heavenly ray.

17. He who recognizes God as his Father, adores him in his heart and obeys his voice, is a child of God and practices the true religion.

17'. Those who live off the work of others and have settled in religion like in a cheese may not agree with us, but do they agree with the Lord of truth?

18. An ignorant scholar who speaks openly of that which he ignores deep down shall always appear more instructed to other ignorant ones than a

18'. Christ is surely unique in God, but his forms are multiple in creation. Thus, we shall recognize him, first, by his work and by his

wise expert who veils the unique foundation of all that is.

19. On the day of judgement, each one shall be placed in the new hierarchy, where he has positioned himself without knowing it.

20. In each religion, the predestined ones shall read the Book of God's science and, having recognized it in their hearts, they shall put it into practice in the world. That day shall mark the proximity of the end of death and of the renewal of life.

21. In order to live in this world, shall we be forced to beg for our living by requesting a place from the omnipotence of the Churches, or from that of the sects, or from that of the parties, or from that of the secret associations?

22. Does the Lord not have the food of the worlds at his disposal? And is he not capable of making us live directly if he so wishes?

23. Or indeed has he resolved to make us endure the fate of Job, in spite of our present weakness and poverty?

24. Has he perhaps finally decided to reduce us to begging so that we are entirely his?

25. How would our wife and those in our entourage not doubt our mission?

weight, and then, by his word; but never by his appearance.

19'. All can love and believe; only a few can understand and find.

20'. One day, the miracles of God's children shall respond to the feats of the devil's children, and the former shall unmask and strike down the works of death of the impious, while the latter shall not even be able to damage the works of life of the sons of the Unique One.

21'. Shall the Lord postpone indefinitely the hour of his grace and of his secret gift? Shall we always be subjected to the invading tide of the impious, and shall we always be rejected by the blind wall of the hypocrites?

22'. Shall we have to work profanely much longer to earn our living here below, instead of praising and adoring God as our heart desires?

23'. Shall our faith and our work be constantly swallowed up, without result, by the apathy of the dying ones of the world that is fading away?

24'. Shall we be maintained much longer here below as useless and good for nothing, despite our mad quest and despite our senseless love?

25'. Have we not sometimes doubted the vigilance and protection of the Lord for ourselves?

26. How could we judge and condemn someone for his lack of faith, when our own is so unsteady?

27. If the Lord permits it, our example shall be a great comfort to all the believers who await God's salvation.

28. Many enlisted believers have reached the point of refusing to seek God's salvation here below, in the unconfessed fear of finding it and thus losing the hope of obtaining it on some far-off date, while they accommodate themselves in the present world. These people maintain the Lord in the tomb in order to organize themselves comfortably in the world.

29. The profane ones have infiltrated everywhere and currently hold command in the world, in the Churches and in the initiatory societies.

30. It does not matter that the Book appears to us confused and abstract; the essential thing is that we reach the precise and concrete thing of which the Book speaks.

31. Those who advocate rescue through man's will and his work are profane ones who conceitedly think they are initiated into the secrets of God.

32. While they are nothing more than toys of the evil one who brutally does violence to everything, but who undoes nothing gently and who unites nothing in a holy way.

26'. Shall the believers not regain courage by considering our case and seeing our ultimate rescue?

27'. For us it shall be a great reward and a great joy for a small job and for a small effort in the world.

28'. It is as though they refused to sit at the Lord's table, preferring the promise of later rescue to the banquet of life. Is it not, in reality, because they prefer to organize themselves in this world of death than to settle in the life of God?

29'. That is a fearful sign of the disorder of spirits, and there shall soon be an odour of decomposition of the nations that shall invade the world.

30'. Are the two ways not wisely intertwined in it to form the tree of life, instead of being profanely separated in order to make dead crutches?

31'. Lord, here we are broken and lying at your feet like a heap of ashes where nothing shines but the faith of our love for you, but where nothing moves by itself any more.

32'. If you do not come to revive us through your holy incarnation, here we are asleep until the day of your judgement, handsome Lord of mercy.

33. O people of God! that have shone so much in the world, shall you not raise once more the torch of the spirit that is going out on the earth?

34. O peoples visited by God! shall you not raise yourselves from the mud where you organize your mortal agony? And shall you not come back to the Lord of truth?

35. Who among you shall hold out a helping and fraternal hand to the new-born black peoples, so that they have access to the revelation of the unique Lord of life? From whom, then, shall they inherit the jewel?

36. It is worthless to try and mend our ways and save ourselves on our own, for we shall end up with nothing but the pride of an illusory success and the assurance of a deceptive security.

37. Thus, it is preferable for us to request the counsel and the help of the Lord in all circumstances, and to place ourselves with faith in his miraculous hands…

38. We must pass through the humility of death before reaching the glory of resurrection.

39. It is necessary to dissolve before coagulating.

33'. And shall you not put the holy books back on the altar of heavenly splendour that has descended to you?

34'. To him who brought you back, who still guards you and who shall save you if you give up the works of death, the covetousness and the hate that poison you more and more.

35'. Otherwise, shall they not be able to outstrip you with the aid of the Lord of faith and love, and leave you sunk in the quagmire of death with your proud intelligence, with your worthless science and with your blind reason?

36'. And our final state shall be a thousand times worse than the first, for we shall have skilfully accumulated and masked the mud that poisons us, instead of completely eliminating it.

37'. that gently separate in us the life from the poison that suffocates it and kills it more and more, for the Lord knows how to reject sin and how to infuse in us his holy and perfect salvation.

38'. Nevertheless, certain chosen ones of God shall be transformed without passing through death, for they eat the Lord of life from this moment on.

39'. That is the law of heaven and earth.

40. The Lord shall act first on us, and then we shall act on the world in his NAME, without ever attributing to ourselves the power that shall have been given to us by him.

41. Did the light of life not come out of the union of heaven and earth? And are the two ways of God not miraculously united in it alone?

42. Do we know of a more complete and more beautiful doctrine than that of the Book of the eternal revelation?

43. There is nothing new nor changing in it, for it has been eternal and perfect since the beginning of time.

44. The word of God proceeds from his NAME and goes back to his NAME. It leaves fluid and it returns solid.

45. Even one forms part of the numbers and the letters, while the accent gives life to them secretly without being attached or subject to any.

46. We must give up our will before God, but on the condition of first being sure of what we desire from him.

47. Do we have to content ourselves with nostalgia for earthly para-

40'. The true children of God recognize one another in this world in that they constantly return to God the glory of what they do in his NAME.

41'. The profane are ignorant of both, the half-instructed separate them and set them opposite one another; only the sages assemble them and unite them in the unity of God.

42'. Is this not the doctrine of the Lord of resurrection, derived from God's creation and perpetuated down to us?

43'. And it shall survive even after the end of time, for it is the doctrine of life that does not perish.

44'. The Lord of the worlds is embodied in turn!
O miracle! O mystery! O perfection! O all that ripens!

45'. It is the fifth that is before the first. It is the one that moves itself and that moves things invisibly and visibly.

46'. Renunciation without object would lead us back to the unconsciousness and to the dissolution of moving limbo, while renunciation with the object shall lead us to the consciousness and to the coagulation of fixed creation.

47'. Shall we be subjected much longer to the filth of the sin of death,

dise and with the hope of resurrection much longer, while we lie in mortal agony in the mud?

48. Shall we be left much longer to our own counsel and our own resources alone to survive in this darkened and cruel world? And shall we all become once more orphans of Father and Mother?

49. Shall the Lord not send us a sign that we can all see and hear, so that the best ones return to him?

50. The Book is a sign for those who still see and hear a little in the twilight of the end, but how many know it and how many transmit it?

51. O friend of men! shall you abandon us and leave us to organize ourselves in the filth of death that leads to the chaos of the absurd?

52. O Merciful One! who even forgives our imbecilic choice of death, shall you not send us once more a beloved son before the unbearable glare of your judgement?

53. Shall you not send us once more your holy essence and substance that are all you?

54. For our darkness is thickening and is becoming more and more opaque, like the announcement of the end of time.

with no effective help, with the only consolation of the hope of faith?

48'. Have the most courageous among us not already lost faith in God's salvation? And do they not preach the rescue of man by man and his definitive organization in the exile of the fallen world?

49'. So that they drag along the masses to convert themselves to him in their heart, before the final judgement?

50'. Let us pray to the merciful Lord so that he also manifests a public sign for those who no longer see or hear anything in the sick and dying world.

51'. Here we are abandoned and left on our own in the darkness of exile, and your star has hidden itself from us, and you have withdrawn to heaven.

52'. So that he manifests once more among us your holy light of life as a token of your forgiveness and as the first fruits of your unequalled glory.

53'. So that we be enlightened, consoled and reassured in your marvellous salvation.

54'. But we know that your day is near, for we feel your light moving in us like the child that is about to be born.

55. Hell is living away from God, at the cost of eternal forced labour, the only food being scraps of light buried in the ordure.

55'. Salvation is living close to God in the miraculous abundance of his pure and holy light, which is the freedom of God's children.

We honour the immortal, brilliant Sun, with its brilliant chargers.

ZARATHUSTRA

God is the patron of believers. He shall lead them from the darkness to the light.

KORAN

BOOK XXXII

There is no joy for the earth that lies for a long time without agriculture.

ZARATHUSTRA

You do not know the work of God that does all things.

ECCLESIASTES

VIRE NE TUE	THE COLOURS

1. The defects and insufficiencies of the Book must be imputed to our excremental weakness and indigence, which belong to the miry nothingness.

1'. The qualities and the beauties of the work must be attributed to our substantial light and to our essential inspiration, which belong to God.

2. Likewise, our temporal individuality should not be an obstacle to anyone, either repelling him or attracting him.

2'. For it is only the word of God and his salvation that finally matter, and they alone must be the object of all our thoughts and all our concerns here below.

3. Have we not stepped aside so as not to cast a shadow over God's light? And have we not worked gratuitously?

3'. In poverty, in solitude and in the reprobation of the world, for the community of our human brothers?

4. Are our masters not the living ones of eternity?

4'. And is our master not the Lord of eternal life?

5. The ardent desire for God's salvation magnetizes the Lord of heaven into our hearts.

5'. Shall we not also do in the world that which we accomplish in our hearts?

6. That which we do by ourselves is illusory and dead.

6'. That which we do with God is real and living.

7. The comments of the holy and wise Scriptures are images of the image of the thing, but certainly not the thing itself.

7'. Therefore, what certain scholars write of the narratives of the inspired word is quite illusory and is far removed from God's truth.

8. The exterior curiosity of the profane is the most effective barrier that maintains them in ignorance of the secret of the revealed word.

8'. Thus, it is the malice of our outer eye that maintains us in the exterior darkness, and it is the purity of our inner eye that brings us close to the light of God.

9. Ignorance is proving through words the non-existence of God's salvation.

9'. Wisdom consists in proving its real nature through facts.

10. Many write and speak of God's salvation.

10'. Very few truly act and feel it.

11. Who truly wrote the Book?

11'. And who truly reads it?

12. The same one.

12'. The same one.

13. HIM[1]

13'. HIM[1]

14. Many leave their religion and go to the death from which there is no return.
«The outside.»

14'. A few penetrate all religions and go to the life that does not perish.
«The inside.»

15. Profane life is life separated from God.

15'. Holy life is life linked to God.

15". Wise life is life restored in God.

---

1. In French LVI. See the dedication at the beginning of the book.

16. Let us not forget that the Book was written despite the blind hostility of the world, and that all kinds of discouragement, all kinds of reprimand and all kinds of opposition have been showered upon us...

16'. daily, with a continuity and a tenacity that are the mark of the rebellious spirit bent on repelling the heaven that witnessed its birth and from which it has stupidly exiled itself.

17. There is certainly a divine justice, and those who have fought the Book shall never penetrate it, and no good testimony and no help shall come to them from it on the day of judgement.

17'. It shall be like a stone that will weigh on their back and that will keep them bent towards the dead earth that they have extolled so much about and that will prevent them from seeing the heaven that they will have despised so much. They shall swallow their regrets with the rottenness in which they will have revelled.

18. Religion is like the wrapping of God's secret.

18'. In it, the light of life. Outside it, the darkness of death.

19. Religion is like the bridge that links us to God's salvation.

19'. Does one go to sleep on a bridge or settle on it?

20. We shall cross the bridge to reach the holy city of the Lord of life, of love and of peace.

20'. Or we shall leave it and go and settle in the hostile jungle. Thus, in any case, we shall not obstruct the precious passage.

21. Profane life invades the world on the pretext of freedom, but in reality it leads us to the most atrocious slavery there could be.

21'. Slavery of the life of beasts and of spiritual death. These shall be burned in the end like useless brambles, and they shall serve as fertilizer for the new world.

22. Woman has become profane since she put sin into herself and since she passed it on to man.

22'. None of God's secrets must therefore be entrusted to her, so as not to expose humanity to an even greater fall.

23. Man, who fell because of woman, shall raise her up again and, after purifying her, shall bring her back to God.

23'. Therefore, authority, command and decision currently belong to man, so that all is restored to the primary state.

24. A sign of the end of time shall be the renewed disobedience, emancipation and rebelliousness of woman with regard to God's word and to man who is its guardian.

24'. The dissolution shall be accomplished through fire, to the great surprise of the world, and it shall thus be radical and definitive; and the coagulation shall be accomplished by fire and water united in the unity of the One.

25. God's salvation shall come at the end of time, for many who are reserved.

25'. God's deliverance comes at all times, for a few who are chosen.

26. If we join the lowest with the highest through the intermediary of the most middle, we shall obtain the origin and the end of all that has been, all that is and all that shall be.

26'. Thus, we are silent in naming, we veil in showing and we rest in acting, and this can annoy only the profane ones driven by the spirit of hate, of violence and of darkness.

27. SAINTLY AND SAGE SCIENCE.

27'. SACRED and SECRET SALT.

27''. SOLELY SUN and SELENE.

28. The conceited profane explain to us and dissect for us the holy Scriptures, the rites and the symbols, like those scholarly doctors who explain and dissect a cold corpse.

28'. One and all are totally incapable of discovering life in its dark wrapping, and they are even far more incapable of fixing it in its secret core.

29. One day, God shall judge the world that has become incurable and shall consume with fire the stench of its malignant wound.

29'. He shall gather together the remains and he shall knead them with the water of heaven, in order to make with them a new creation that is sweet-smelling and without blemish.

30. Communal prayer brings material goods, and gifts to the community maintain them.

30'. Solitary prayer leads to spiritual goods, and private gifts confirm them.

31. One makes grace flow.

31'. The other makes love blaze.

32. The Churches still believe in the Lord descended among us, but they no longer know him, they no longer see him, they no longer touch him and they no longer eat him except in image.

32'. Their loyalty, their faith, their hope and their love are miraculous, and deserve the great reward of eternal life promised by the Lord to those who shall have believed in him until the end.

33. O handsome Lord of compassion and love! shall you not manifest yourself to your beloved children before the darkness of the end? Shall you not hold out to them a helping and reassuring hand?

33'. Shall you not allow one of your chosen sons to manifest your holy pardon that removes the sin of death, that gives health to the dying, faith to the nonbelievers and life to the dead?

34. O handsome Lord of mercy! shall you not give us once more the deposit of your salvation, so that we are comforted in your holy love before the collapse of the end that is coming?

34'. Shall you not allow one of your delivered sons to manifest your holy light of life that illuminates spirits and that saves souls and bodies? Shall you not manifest a small flash of your omnipotence for the benefit of your decimated children?

35. Those who revel in the baseness of this fallen world are enraged to see certain beings working to escape from it, and all their wickedness is applied to upsetting them, to discouraging them and to diverting them from their salvation and from their deliverance.

35'. It is up to those who hope for God's salvation, or who seek his deliverance, to flee from the professed or hidden hostility of the ignorant profane that surround them and suffocate them stupidly.

36. Not only do the profane ones reject God's revelation, they even persecute those who study it.

36'. Is there any worse curse than to reject the promise of life and to oppose the quest for life?

37. The mediocre are like beasts worried only about food and drink, but who ignore him who prepares it and who gives it.

37'. No other quality could replace the love of God, the faith in his salvation and the quest for his deliverance.

38. Those who oppose our hope of God's salvation or our quest for his secret of life are not our brothers, nor our sisters, nor our husbands, nor our wives, nor our children, nor our parents, nor our friends, nor our allies.

38'. Those are like beasts that wallow in the dung of the world and that mean to hold us back with them in the slavery of death, rather than coming with us towards the freedom of life.

39. Shall we save them and shall we save ourselves by remaining with them, by living their blind life and by adopting their profane thoughts, even though it may be out of charity or out of love for them?

39'. Would we not do better to flee from them and follow the handsome Lord of life and truth, as he rightly advised us? They shall be free to follow us when their eyes open to the vanity of the perishable world.

40. The profane deny God's salvation and blindly reject his deliverance.

40'. For they believe they save themselves through their work and they think they can break into God's secret through their science.

40". These are signs that we must note well.

41. To look for the world and to serve the Lord is impossible.

41'. To serve the world and to seek the Lord is even more impossible.

42. Some attain here below the spiritual enlightenment of the Lord of life, and we call them blessed.

42'. But where are those who attain corporeal knowledge of the unique Splendour? And what shall we call them?

43. The most intelligent and the most advanced in the study and knowledge of the mysteries of God penetrate only spiritual realization.

43'. It is the return to the free, moving and unconditioned state in God. They are God's delivered.

44. Some of these obtain the knowledge of divine science and go beyond spiritual realization to penetrate substantial realization.

44'. It is the access to the free, fixed and manifested state in God. They are God's resurrected.

45. If we wish to have access to the knowledge and the possession of God's revelation, we shall carefully spit out the instruction of the profane world and we shall protect our children from it.

45'. Religious schools and initiatory schools must not restrict their teaching to spiritual research; they must keep the ultimate rung, which is the substantial quest forgotten by all.

46. The difficulties, the pitfalls and the miseries of the world are also there for the believer, but it is he who survives and is made firmer in his faith, while the temptations of the world fade away more and more.

46'. Has the Lord's Providence not always nourished and saved us at the last moment? And has his love not always inspired us and fulfilled us beyond our wildest hopes?

47. We shall be tempted, purified, passed through the crucible and put to the test in all forms, but we shall not be forgotten, abandoned nor rejected.

47'. For the Lord is a good gardener who prunes, waters, enlightens and fertilizes us according to his ART that is perfect.

48. The impious one weakens in the end and succumbs in the darkness of doubt and despair.

48'. The believer becomes firmer and firmer in his faith, which enlightens him and protects him.

49. Even if we do not understand what we are doing, let us not omit to always thank the Lord for all that comes to us and for all that leaves us.

49'. Let us praise the Lord in the congregations for the material goods he sends us, and let us praise him in secret for the spiritual goods he gives us.

49". Let us bless the Unique One for the most secret gift of life that unites the low and the high in the humility and in the splendour of the Living One who saves from death.

50. We must obey the voice of the Lord that guides us towards salvation, and we must accept the blows that move us away from the quagmire of death.

50'. For we walk with a sack over our head and a stone on our back, and we are deaf and blind to God's truth.

51. We shall listen in the congregations to the comments and the explanations of the holy Scriptures that will comfort us in our wait or that will help us in our quest.

52. We shall frequent the Lord in the congregations, first to receive, then to give.

51'. And we shall study the holy Scriptures in the solitude of our room and in the secret of our heart, so that the light of the Perfect One manifests itself in us.

52'. Likewise, we shall frequent the Lord in the secret of our hearts, first to offer and then to receive.

52". But we shall never omit to praise him, in public and in private, for his holy and perfect incarnation.

> *All has been given to him. To his kingdom belong integrity and immortality. He gives to this world power and strength.*
>
> ZARATHUSTRA

> *Only God knows the mysteries, he unveils them to no-one, unless he concedes this favour to the most cherished of his envoys, for whom he provides the company of a procession of angels.*
>
> KORAN

BOOK XXXIII

The sun visits the army of the stars in the heights of heaven, but all men are earth and ash.

ECCLESIASTICUS

For not everything can be found in men, the son of man not being immortal.

ECCLESIASTICUS

ÉRINVÊTUE	THE FLOWERS
1. There are many hidden things in the Book for him who reflects.	1'. But there is one that contains all the others for him who understands.
2. Who shall reach the final step of the holy pyramid of the divine hierarchy?	2'. Who shall be identified with the heavenly stone that crowns it and that finishes it?
3. The Lord God has given us the inspiration for a prodigious and magnificent Book; we are not afraid to say it.	3'. For many shall once again hope for God's salvation, and some shall enter his deliverance thanks to it.
4. Those who receive the instruction of the world close themselves off to the instruction of God.	4'. And those who give themselves over to the science of the world are lost to the science of God.
5. It is by eating the body of God that we shall be renewed and transformed in the holy life.	5'. It is by drinking the blood of God that we shall be raised and enlightened in the glorious life.
6. No force of the darkness that oppresses the world now shall be able to suffocate for ever the revelation of the sons of God.	6'. The buried light shall appear one day, and it shall enlighten the judgement of nations, and it shall clothe those who rally round the Lord God.

7. All the good we conceitedly attribute to ourselves is a robbery with respect to God, which first ridicules us, then crushes us, and which we shall finally have to give account of on the day of judgement.

8. Supreme intelligence for man is to make God shine in oneself.

9. He who is intelligent frequents the house of God and feeds his servants.

10. He who is inspired prays to God in secret and feeds the poor man without letting anyone know.

11. It is not an insignificant reward, which we hope for from the madness of our love and from our senseless quest in this world.

12. The cunning and the skilful make a good living, and the seekers of God are reduced to begging.

13. The saints and the believers shall one day rest in the abundance of eternal life praising the holy NAME of God.

14. He who gives nothing of himself or of his good, he who does not help his fellow-man…

15. There is nothing mediocre, nothing narrow and nothing stubborn in the Lord God.

16. We seem wretched talking about the glory of God.

7'. God alone merits our adoration, our recognition and our praise. Thus, the saints and the sages hand over to God the slightest homage that reaches them.

8'. Who understands this? Who undertakes it? And who manifests it in the world?

9'. Thus, the abundance of heaven flows over him and his own.

10'. Thus, God attracts him to him and delivers him from death.

11'. For it is imperishable life, in which hardly anybody believes sincerely and simply any longer.

12'. What a surprising and disturbing spectacle for the believers who hope for God's salvation!

13'. What a surprising and disturbing spectacle for the impious ones who shall then despair of God's salvation!

14'. that one curses himself and condemns himself to abandonment, to decline and to death.

15'. There must therefore be no meanness in believers.

16'. But we must not become grotesque by talking about him without naturalness.

17. The help we have vainly asked of men shall one day be offered to us by them thousands and thousands of times without our requesting it.

18. We have begged to receive so as to be able to give; likewise, you shall beg to give so as to be able to receive also, but your gift shall remain in your hands like dead ash.

19. If we have been unable to earn our living through our work for so long, we are not ashamed of it; the shame is for those who have excluded us and for those who have rejected us without judgement.

20. What a scandal for all the mediocre who now judge us as mad, when they see the Lord's choice uncovered in that which regards us!

21. They shall strike their mouth and they shall bite their tongue, for their impious judgements shall crush them and their cries of vexation shall only increase their regrets at having made such a gross mistake.

22. The believers have to practice their religion regularly, and the intelligent have to study it patiently.

23. A people in which such a Book can be published is a great people.

24. Shall we be the only one to denounce the rottenness that invades the world and to rise up against the death that shall congeal it for much longer?

17'. But we shall not receive it, for God shall then have replaced it in us through his descending grace and through his ascending love, and our riches shall be infinite.

18'. For he who does not receive cannot give, and he who does not give cannot receive either. Let each one, then, help the poor man who fears God, before God enriches him for ever!

19'. Artists, who ought to be the most fraternal and charitable of men, have become exclusive and malicious; that is not a good sign, for now nonbelievers dominate among them.

20'. What stupor for all the well-off who reject us now, when they see the grace of God overflowing from our hands, and his love shining in our heart!

21'. Their prudence, their reason and their judgement shall be spread out at their feet like a heap of rubbish, and their nakedness shall appear before all like a heap of dry bones.

22'. The inspired ones have to penetrate deeply their religion, and the chosen ones have to accomplish it fully.

23'. But a people in which it is received is a far greater people.

24'. Shall we be the only one to preach the return to the Lord of life and to show once more the way of salvation for much longer?

25. If we do not penetrate the teachings of our faith, how shall we penetrate the teachings of foreign doctrines?

26. We truly preach in a desert of straying, of vanity and of death.

27. O miracle of God! many shall assemble and, recovered in their flesh of life, they shall praise his holy NAME, and the desert of men shall become like the garden of Eden.

28. It is not the business of women to scold us, and still less to judge us, as far as our quest for God is concerned.

29. Where is the intelligent one inspired by God who shall take in the errant virgin?

30. The ignorant wicked ones may well mock and deride him.

31. They shall remain exiled in the dark world and they shall tear one another to pieces like ferocious beasts.

32. He who refuses to listen to a servant of God, and he who refuses to aid him make the word of God known, cuts himself off from God's blessing and from the help of men.

33. He who reads the Book of the renewal at least once in its entirety is already blessed by God and is no longer an orphan in this world.

25'. Do we no longer know that all is presented to us under the veil of wise symbols and holy characters?

26'. Shall the Spirit of God not come to give life to the bones that we are addressing?

27'. The water of life shall flow from its secret centre and the beauty of the lordly creation shall be reflected in rediscovered immortality.

28'. She who caused us to be driven out of the garden of Eden must abstain from opposing our much hoped-for return.

29'. That one is blessed by God, for he shall see the birth of the king of heaven and his heritage shall never more be taken away from him.

30'. The Lord shall console him in his heart for eternity, and his lot shall never perish.

31'. The chosen one of the Lord God shall live in his glorious sun, and he shall rest in his bosom so-pure.

32'. These decline rapidly in the world, as well as their businesses, and they become wretched and ashamed, even though they were rich and glorious.

33'. It is truly difficult to become free in God, that is, without worldly desires and worries, in order to hear God's teaching without obstacle.

34. Those who have withdrawn from the profane world and who pray to God in their hearts by studying the holy Scriptures do not know either their luck or their happiness. Let them praise the Lord who has granted them the grace to search for him here below!

35. The end approaches, and nobody can oppose the darkness that invades the nations any longer, on pain of being destroyed by the impious ones.

36. Many now doubt their religion, and each one gets out of it in his own way, just as one leaves a house that is in danger of collapsing.

37. When the intelligent scholars ignore us, we shall rejoice at not being known with them.

38. When the blind sectarians reject us, we shall rejoice at not drying up with them.

39. The shrewd now speak in the name of the holy virgin and of God, but it is in order to impose their names and their works of death in the world even better.

40. Let us visit the dying and the dead in order to become aware of the vanity of our desires, our worries and our works in the world.

41. O unfathomable wisdom of the Lord God! that allows us to see that even the impious ones are useful for the salvation of his beloved ones in the world.

34'. The divine appears inhuman, but in that it withdraws from the world, while the demoniac is inhuman in doing violence to it. As for the human in the world, it is a mortal agony maintained at the price of forced labour.

35'. God shall allow the last enlightened believers to assemble, so that they may be saved from the bursting disaster.

36'. Who is the intelligent one that shall plunge himself to the roots of his faith in order to become strengthened in God's revelation?

37'. When the ignorant profane ones mock us, we shall rejoice at not being confused with them.

38'. When the impious politicians persecute us, we shall rejoice at not being judged with them.

39'. Thus they unmask themselves by putting themselves before God, for the true believer steps aside before the Lord and before his mysteries.

40'. Shall an intelligent one then perhaps think of searching for God and his salvation while there is still time?

41'. Who can understand this at present without having come close to the mystery of the Highest?

O who shall baptize the burned desert of death so that the Lord will send his Holy Spirit there?

42. We speak a new language, but we repeat the ancient unique revelation, for nobody invents anything in the ART of God.

43. We shall never say enough times to the ignorant conceited ones that the repose of the Being is neither non-being nor, in consequence, nothingness, with which they regularly confuse it.

44. O derision! the Book of faith is rejected by the blind and conceited believers who think they know all about the ancient revelation, whereas they are not even established on the outer layer of their Scriptures.

45. Is each one not best off just as he is? And does each one not want to live, however diminished he may be?

46. Would we not do better to search for the Lord of life, who alone can save us from death, and abandon the vanities of the world that make us waste the little time we are granted here below for resolving the fearsome enigma?

47. Believing a thing is good. Penetrating it is better. Possessing it is perfect.

48. The arts of men may well distract us and console us here below.

42'. God's truth may well wear all faces and all plumages; its holy nakedness always remains just as it is.

43'. Thus, the seed is not exactly the plant, but it potentially contains all of it, and nobody could confuse it with death without displaying his ignorance.

44'. The lonely, the ones gone astray, the rebels and the impious shall receive it before them with enthusiasm and gratitude, and they shall inherit the kingdom of God in place of the right-thinking ones mummified in the dead letter of their Scriptures.

45'. Given that we have to die and abandon everything, what, then, are the riches of the earth and all the work of men for us?

46'. Acceptance, solitude and leisure are useful to us above all for seeking the jewel that shall save us from the dispersion of death, for the first delivers us from the cares of the world, the second spares us its worries and the last one gives us the time necessary for the holy quest for life.

47'. O my Lord! how shall we obtain the leisure and the peace so necessary to the quest for your holy obviousness?

48'. Only the ART of God can deliver us from the putrefying infamy of deadly sin.

49. Nobody must be mistaken: God's creation is magnificent, it is splendid, it is perfect and it is unique in substance and in essence.

50. It is not sufficient for us to be delivered from death and to be restored as free spirits in God.

51. An intelligent one wanted to touch the body of immortality of our handsome Lord, and thanks to him we know that it is a palpable reality and not a worthless appearance.
«Satan was rejected for not having rendered homage to the holy and mysterious trinity of Adam.»

49'. For even fallen and mixed with the mud of outside, it is still beautiful and it shows us the way of return to the unique Splendour.

50'. We desire above all to resurrect again in the glorious body of the Lord of life.

51'. It is thanks to this body of glory that the sons of the Unique One are superior to all God's creatures, even to the angelic spirits, and it is thus that all bow before the glory of Adam and that Satan could not be readmitted to heaven before having adored the holiest body of the resurrected Christ.

51". It is a marvellous secret that we bring to light before all. That will perhaps cause those who have not settled and fallen asleep in the filth of the fallen world to reflect.

That which I teach is the traditional doctrine, the crowning beam that death does not reach. I apply myself to acting in accordance with the Fathers of the tradition.

LAO TSE

Why, O men born from the earth have you given yourselves over to death, when you have the power to participate in immortality?

HERMES TRISMEGISTUS

BOOK XXXIV

From this perfume comes, advancing towards him, his own nature in the form of a beautiful, brilliant, noble girl, of illustrious race, more brilliant of body than the most brilliant creatures.
ZARATHUSTRA

Flooded with light, one appears ignorant.
LAO TSE

TIRE EN UVE

1. As soon as we turn sincerely towards the Highest, our sins shall be forgiven.

2. Have we not worked for the glory of God and for the salvation of believers?

3. The way of the Highest is a way that washes and that sows. Did you know that?

4. Oh, resplendent Lord! have your prophets spoken in vain of your holy science that gives life and of your holy love that accomplishes the holy science in us?

5. Your sons work hard here below to make your salvation heard by exiled men.

SNOW

1'. And as soon as we reach him, in truth, they shall be miraculously removed from us.

2'. Shall the Lord of heaven and earth not make the seed he sows in the heart of upright men grow and multiply?

3'. It is also a way that makes grow and that multiplies in the incorruptibility of the Unique One.

4'. Is there no longer any attentive intelligence and is there no longer any purified heart among us to achieve your holy and perfect unity?

5'. But they are seated at table in your sun, where they celebrate your eternity as a day of joy that never ends.

6. Those who preach the word of God professionally in the world have to do so with love and with humility, for they do not manifestly possess the spirit and the body of the Lord of life.

7. Shall each believer not read daily for his family and for himself a page of the holy Scriptures, where the way of God is wisely represented?

8. Many nonbelievers shall be converted and many rebels shall be saved, but not a single hypocrite shall be forgiven if he does not return to the sincerity of the love of God.

9. We shall endure our dryness with patience and we shall moisten it through the reading of the revealed Scriptures that deliver us from doubt.

10. Let us listen to God's insane one who speaks to us: «On the day of the restitution of all things, God's chosen ones shall no longer know the filth of death, nor pain, nor illness, nor servile work, nor dirtiness, nor poverty, nor doubt, nor fear, nor hate, nor the darkness of exile».

11. Let us examine carefully what the prophets of God say, and let us be wary of what the interpreters make them say.

12. Those who weigh their servants' food and those who keep part of their wages shall also be put on rations one day, for they shall humbly

6'. Otherwise, the deaf would hear once more, the blind would see, the paralytic would walk, the dead would rise again, and all would give thanks to the almightiness of the Unique One.

7'. Let our spirit not exclude any Scripture inspired by God, but on the contrary, let them all be honoured in our homes and in our hearts.

8'. The adoration of the Lord of eternity could never be a sacrifice, a duty or a chore, for it is an incommunicable joy that love engenders in the freedom of God.

9'. The tombs of the sons of God are empty tombs; let us never forget it, so that our faith subsists in the miracle of life.

10'. Their robes shall be of an immaculate white and their faces shall gleam like molten gold; their desires shall be fulfilled even before they are defined, and the joy of their peace shall be unanimous in the unique Splendour. It is not a worthless promise that is made to us here.

11'. Do we not know that the last ones come first, and that the first ones come last in this world?

12'. The right-thinking ones compromise with the world while continuing to speak in his name who condemned the world and its works.

beg for the stinking mud of hell that shall be their food and their salary.

Thus, they have become the worst hypocrites on earth, and the professed enemies of the master, whom they pretend to love like the Judases they are in reality.

12". There is a mark that makes them unmistakeably recognizable: they blindly reject the Lord's true disciples, as the darkness blindly rejects the light of God.

13. We continue to preach the way of God in the desert, for we know that his word germinates in secret and that we shall see the formidable harvest transform the desert into a land of abundance.

13'. Who shall become simple enough and pure enough again to believe, to hear and to see the truth of the revealed mystery?

«Oh, magnanimous Lord! multiply your sons and your daughters, and give them your holy earth where nothing perishes.»

14. We receive the promises of God spiritually and in image here below, before receiving them bodily and in truth on the day of the general resurrection and of the ineluctable judgement.

14'. Therefore, those who think they have received all on receiving the word of teaching fall into the pride that excludes them from the palpable possession of God's love.

15. A few chosen ones of God have received, right in this world, the spiritual and bodily gift of the Highest before the end of time.

15'. These are the cherished children of God, in whom he has placed all his trust, and the great witnesses of his judgement.

16. We can make use of machines to relieve us, but we must not adore them nor think that they shall save us definitively from death.

16'. To organize oneself in the pigsty of exile is, in short, to want to organize oneself in the stench of the dung heap of death.

17. The kingdom of God is not constructed with stones and mortar, for it is the stone and the gold par excellence that needs neither mortar nor cutting.

17'. Is there anything more beautiful and higher than the family united in the Lord, that communicates to its children the love and intelligence of God?

18. No constraint in the learning of the way of God, which is all love and all freedom.

«Those who do violence to young souls prepare the henchmen of hell.»

19. He who refuses alms to God's seeker is not blessed, but he who refuses to give bread to him is surely damned.

20. We shall recognize the mediocre in that generosity of the heart offends them and in that the truth of God wounds them, for the dark quagmire is the lot they have chosen.

21. We live in such a precarious state and that is so subject to death that we should beg God every day of our lives to teach us the way to our deliverance and of our restitution in the primary splendour.

22. We should beg for our rescue before God with such tenacity that he is forced to grant it to us so as to rid himself of our mad insistence.

23. How could we be so patient in this world of death when we are so impatient for the world of life?

Quickly, quickly, Lord! come to us and show us your holy light!

24. Perhaps we shall be sent away by the Lord with strokes of the whip on the day of the confrontation, for our work is tiny here below, and we waste a lot of the time allocated to us on worldly cares.

18'. Love and charity can be understood and practised only by those who have first understood and practised tolerance towards themselves and towards others.

19'. Therefore, the senseless one refuses everything, the prudent one offers bread, the believer provides a meal and alms, but the sage adds hospitality for the night.

20'. One day, the senseless ones shall be discouraged by their own madness, for they shall rebound on them infinitely multiplied and they shall crush them with a blind and deaf ferocity from which nothing can deliver them.

21'. Alas! nearly all men have become used to death to the point of thinking it inevitable and irremediable, and many have forgotten it like beasts that only become aware of it again at the last moment of their life.

22'. The patience of the saints is not the brutishness of the beasts, and the quest of the sages is not the restlessness of the world.

23'. Those who have resigned themselves to earthly exile may well organize themselves here below, but for us who hope for eternal life, how could we settle in the mortal agony of this world?

24'. Oh, Lord of goodness and of forgiveness! grant us the time necessary for the quest for your holy secret and allow us to taste here below the first fruits of eternal life that you promised us from the beginning. Oh,

«Spare us the confusion of the wicked ones, O holy and perfect goodness!»

25. Do not let us lie in mortal agony in the world and do not abandon us to the mocking of the ignorant ones who reject you, Lord of compassion.

26. All that distracts us from God's salvation in the world is bad, and all that makes us forget it is fatal.

27. Of what importance are the forms of our quest and of our mortal agony in this world, as long as we are reborn happily to the life that does not perish!

28. We shall recognize the true seekers of God in that boredom does not reside in them, nor even approach them in the world.

29. Nothing shall save us from misery, filth, illness, suffering, ignorance, fear, hate, despair, solitude and death, except the science of the most-knowledgeable God.

30. The true believers in God endure the world, but they do not compromise with it, for their goal is not to settle in it, but rather to seek in it the concealed entrance to the kingdom that does not perish.

31. We shall know we are approaching the truth of God when we are less and less in agreement with the world, and when the world treats us in the same way.

come for our salvation, Holiest One, and descend into our purified hearts!

25'. For our faith wavers under the blows of death, and our love languishes in the darkness of exile.

26'. Alas! the men fallen from heaven have become used to the evil of death, and at present they no longer pay any attention to it at all.

27'. The law of the world is a hard law of murder, of exile and of suffering.
The law of heaven is a sweet law of love, of freedom and of joy.

28'. The true children of God are never lonely or abandoned, for the quest for the Father occupies them night and day.

29'. And nothing shall transmit it to us but the love of those who possess it through inheritance since the creation of man, for their word is the love of God that comes to us as far as the earth of exile.

30'. That which we think and that which we do in the world matter little in the end: it is that which we find in it of God that is all that shall matter for our final rescue; that is what is hard for many self-assured ones.

31'. And we shall know we have reached the truth of God when we love men without following them, and when men love us while following us.

32. Let us present the Book at each door and to each heart. Those who receive it and those who reject it shall be their own judges.

33. Instead of doing violence to everything and torturing everything like rebels who think of establishing themselves in the world thanks to their cunning…

34. The rich and the strong in God take on the task of aiding and supporting the poor and weak in God, so that the heavenly kingdom is repopulated even in its most lowly places.

35. Have the saints and the wise prophets not announced, despite all opposition, our rescue and our resurrection in God?

36. O sublime poverty of him who has all!
O sublime simplicity of him who knows all!
O sublime weakness of him who can do all!
O sublime peace of him who loves all!

37. Those who make the best of the lies and the death of the world are eventually devoured by lies and by death in this world.

38. Should we not burn with desire and impatience in our search for the divine treasure if we wish to have a chance of discovering it here below?

32'. The will of God is like a river that flows towards an ocean of love. It is madness to want to oppose it to the exhaustion of the absurd.

33'. let us attempt to discover the unique secret of life with the aid of God, like loving children subject to their most-knowledgeable Father.

34'. Even the mediocre can be saved, but on the condition of not stupidly opposing the saints who have agreed to answer for them.

35'. And has our handsome Lord of forgiveness not endured all from us in order to save us from the dark exile where we are dying?

36'. It is a salt, but it is also a sugar.
It is an earth, but it is also a fire.
It is a water, but it is also an air.
It is a light, but it is also an abyss.

37'. Oh, how marvellous and incredible is your truth of life, Lord! And how few of your children are capable of believing in it and seeking it here below!

38'. For here is our senseless hope and our mad desire, which save us from doubt, from despair and from death.

39. What is the use of astutely prolonging our mortal agony in the world if it is not to seek in it the salvation of God that delivers from all death?

39'. Is it not enough for us to pass on God's torch in this darkened world without worrying about who shall receive it? For it is he who wants it that receives it, and not he that we want!

40. For one saint that is recognized here below, how many remain unknown and pray for the salvation of souls?

40'. For one son of God who manifests himself in the world, how many work in secret for the rescue of souls and bodies?

41. Those who cannot bear to be scolded and corrected by men shall learn nothing from men.

41'. Those who cannot bear to be scolded and corrected by God shall learn nothing from God.

42. It is through the substance of virginity and through the essence of fertility that our life shall be re-established in the triumphant unity of the Unique One.

42'. Water us, Lord of heaven, with your holy dew that regenerates the souls, the spirits and the bodies disunited by the world's judgement of death.

42". Oh, Holiest One! allow us to hear and accomplish your great mystery before the general judgement that shall bring everything to light.

43. O Lord of knowledge! why do so many men fall asleep in the mud of the world? And why do those who stay a little more awake seek your secret outside of you?

43'. O Lord of justice! why do so many men fall asleep in your word? And why do those who stay a little more awake look for you with so much difficulty?

44. Because those have not germinated in me, says the Lord of the secret.

44'. Because those have not looked for the good almond that is hidden beneath the outer layers, says the Lord of the mystery.

45. The Book shall be like a chain of living gold that shall bind together the children of God in the quest for his holy light of life.

45'. Those that meet with the Book in their hand shall give each other the kiss of peace and shall receive communion in the Lord of life.

46. Certainly, we shall be close to those that invoke us in their heart to lead them on God's way.

47. The half-hearted ones that undertake the quest for the divine secret soon tire, and they return to their worthless occupations of the world as dogs return to their vomit.

48. The Churches compromise with the world in order to maintain multitudes of half-hearted ones in the blind observance of the revealed mysteries.

49. The world prefers quantity to quality.

50. All have fallen asleep on the divine promise and each one goes reassured about his business in the world, believing himself automatically saved through the quest and through the gift of a single one.

51. You shall be blamed, coloured peoples, for having received the Book of deliverance from the hands of a white man.

52. The true seekers of God succeed or die in the attempt, but they never retreat, for they have guessed the divine enormity of the goal they pursue.

53. The faint-hearted, the mediocre, the ignorant and the right-thinking will shower us with their discouragement, their reproaches, their sarcasm and their impediments of all kinds in our quest for the divine treasure.

46'. When we meet up to read the Book, he who inspired it shall most certainly be amidst us.

47'. Those that are thirsty and hungry for the life of God are caught up by the holy quest as though by a powerful magnet that no longer leaves them time to turn their eyes towards the world.

48'. This is a great human charity, but it is also a great danger, for it distances the best ones from the effective quest for the holy and wise mystery.

49'. But God prefers quality to quantity.

50'. And those who try to bring God's promise up to date are considered in the eyes of the sleeping mediocre as madmen and heretics, so vague and remote does God's gift appear to them.

51'. Reply: «We are honoured to have received this gift, and you are dishonoured for having rejected it».

52'. Nothing shall be lost from the holy and wise quest of the children of God, for the Lord is merciful towards those who have put their faith, their love and their goodwill in him.

53'. For it is the wicked devil who speaks and who acts through them in order to distance us from the kingdom of God, where he no longer has any power over us. Let us flee from them without turning round and let us not associate them with our salvation.

54. We shall not worship the human figures, the animal figures, the symbols or the images that are here to remind us of the divine mysteries, but they are nothing on their own.

54'. Idolatry is to confuse the appearances of the thing of God with the thing itself, and is to remain led astray by the outer layers that hide the pure and substantial almond of imperishable life.

55. Oh! gleaming cohort of sages and saints of God, who have endured victoriously the sarcasm, the insults and the blows in the quest for the Lord of truth…

55'. inspire in us the patience that shall vanquish the opposition of the profane world where we lie in mortal agony seeking God's salvation, which is deliverance from the claws of death.

56. All those who do not pray to God and who do not seek his salvation night and day, or do not hope for it, are wasting their time here below.

56'. Those who doubt it have only to visit an ossuary, and if there is still some remains of intelligence in them they shall no longer doubt on coming out of there.

57. Blind fanaticism is like unbelief and like impiety before God, for it prevents one from knowing the source of grace and from discovering the ocean of love.

57'. When we know the origin and the basis of divine life we shall be grateful and humble forever in the rediscovered Lord.

58. Those who reach God are at first stunned, then they laugh and cry, and finally they admire and praise for the eternity.

58'. The prudence of the Lord is unique, and his secret is of an astonishing and perfect humour. God's seers bear witness to this from now on.

59. O believers of the message! your depth and your unity shall be recognized if you recognize the legitimacy and the continuity of the revealed Scriptures.

59'. The true religions are those that preach resurrection, judgement and life in God for the chosen ones, or outside of God for the reprobates.

60. All the teachings lavished upon us so that we behave well in the world shall not prevent our dying in it ignorant and powerless with regard to God's salvation, if we do not seek it every day of our life.

60'. There is only one true goal for man here below, which is to come out of death with the aid of God, as did the handsome Lord of resurrection. But the secret of God belongs exclusively to him, and he transmits it to whom he wants, without anyone being able to force it.

61. God shall let his salvation be seen only to those whom the world does not satisfy, to those who do not bustle about in it, to those who do not settle in it.

62. O believers in God! open your ears and your hearts while you are still alive on the earth, for soon it will be too late to seek God's salvation.

63. There is no peace for the seekers of the world, not even when they have found the world, because then, what sadness, what solitude and what slavery!

64. Christ has ridiculed death and has ridiculed the wicked. The word of such a master is certainly a word of life that has to preserve us from discouragement and doubt in all circumstances.

65. The Book is magnificent and he who inspired it is radiant in heaven. Do we not see him? Do we not hear him?

66. However poor and however abandoned we appear in the world, we must keep our faith and our hope in the mercy of the Unique One, who observes us to see how we react in the exile of death.

67. Our state in the world has no importance at all before God, for what matters in his eyes is what we believe, what we seek and what we find here below.

61'. For we shall obtain everything according to the measure of our heart, and not according to the malice of our spirit or the skill of our hands.

62'. O believers in God! do not wait to be returned to dust to look into the secret of your hearts, for then it shall be too late to manifest anything in life.

63'. There is no peace for God's seekers as long as they have not found God, but then, what joy, what union and what deliverance!

64'. Who shall emerge of the tomb once more behind the Lord of resurrection, so as to be a new example of the almightiness of God and a brilliant confirmation of the faith of believers?

65'. God shall hide us under his robes of light, or he shall make us shine in the darkness of the world. His is the glory and the forgiveness.

66'. Shall we not recognize the inspired teaching that rings out in the plenitude of the word from among the delirious words that ring out in the void of the profane world?

67'. The beggar covered in mud who hides in his heart and in his hand God's jewel is worth more than everyone who rejects him.

68. Now that we have read the Book, there will never again be an excuse for us if we neglect God's salvation.

69. O believers in God! take fresh heart for the Lord sees your hearts exposed without being ashamed of your wretched state in the world.

70. Have we not given a marvellous fruit, like a good tree planted by the Lord in the land of exile?

71. Have we not produced the Book in the abandonment and in the solitude of the world, without weakening and without doubting God?

72. Let our meetings be holy and joyful in honour of the Lord who presides in our loving hearts!

73. Oh, the joy of those who rally to God!
Oh, the faithfulness of the lovers of the Unique One!
Oh, the passion of the seekers of life!

74. O simple children of God! do not reject the Lord because of those who disfigure him and who betray him in his own house.

75. Thus, you shall be received in his kingdom, while the hypocrites shall be thrown back into the darkness of the outside.

68'. For the Book is like a magnet that gathers the souls gone astray in death to offer them to God.

69'. O believers in God! let your hope germinate and let your faith flower once more, for the Lord sees you shining through the exile of death.

70'. Those who eat this fruit shall return to God's paradise, and they shall never leave it again thanks to their experience of death.

71'. Have we not accomplished God's will, despite the obstinate opposition of the profane world?

72'. He is here receiving communion with us. Do we not see him through the dark outer layer that still covers us?

73'. Oh, the sweetness of the children of God!
Oh, the security of the saved saints!
Oh, the brilliance of the sons of God!

74'. Go to him in all confidence in your hearts, serve him and love him as the best of all of you.

75'. Hardly anybody believes in the judgement of God any more, yet we shall all see it, and the surprise shall leave us voiceless and motionless.

76. Once again, the promise of salvation is given to the exiled ones that suffer and that pray to God for their deliverance.

76'. Once again, the gate of the kingdom is open for those who are thirsty for the pure and imperishable life that is resplendent in God.

77. It is quite natural that we struggle with all our might and with our own means against the misery, against the illness and against the death that constantly threaten us here below.

77'. But our efforts must not make us forget the quest for the salvation of God, which is the only thing that can deliver us for ever from the yoke and the exile of death.

78. Those who preach to us of heaven and who bury themselves in the petty things of this world are hypocrites who sow the hate towards God in the heart of exiled humans, instead of making his holy and perfect love flower there.

78'. The salvation of God is not, as some teach it, a remote and vague possibility. It is an immediate and palpable reality for him who attains it here below. This is what we must all know.

78". Let us never be ashamed of giving up a limited and vague opinion to adopt a more precise and broader idea of the salvation of God, for we shall thus open up and germinate in God, instead of stagnating and decomposing in the world.

There are two extremes that those who have given up the world should avoid. A life dedicated to pleasures and passions, degrading, sensual, base, without nobility, without benefit; and a life devoted to mortifications, painful, without nobility, without benefit.

BUDDHA

We have drunk the ambrosia, we have become immortal, we have seen the light, we have found the gods.

VEDA

BOOK XXXV

Oh, how small is the number of believers!

KORAN

They are infidels all those whose body is penetrated by impurity.

ZARATHUSTRA

VÊTE EN URI

1. O our Lord and our God! confirm in heaven our earthly word and vision, as we confirm here below your heavenly holy Name and holy presence.

2. The faithful pious ones hear of the thing under the veil of the holy Scriptures being talked about, according to their attention and according to their understanding. Those are listeners and are promised the salvation of God.

3. God's chosen ones receive the thing from the hands of the sons of God, according to their prayers and according to the purity of their life. Those are trustees and keepers of God.

BLOOD

1'. Who would dare to intervene in the profane affairs of men, when not even the Lord God puts the hand to them? Has each one not to believe, to pray, to seek and to find for himself?

2'. The holy believers in God benefit from the thing thanks to God's chosen ones, according to their charity and their loyalty. Those are helped and saved by God.

3'. The sons of God make the thing with their hands, according to the grace and the love of God, and they communicate it according to his holy will. Those are the experts and possessors of God.

4. Let each one practise his fathers' religion or that of his choice, and let each one penetrate his particular faith before comparing it with that of others.

5. Some good children sometimes receive from a son of God the thing which is hidden in all times, and they perfect it according to his instructions.

6. The former help their fellow-man and remind us in the darkened world of the wise and holy way that saves us from death.

7. Thus, there are those who hear of the thing being talked about or who see the effects of it.

8. Then, there are those who receive the thing and who use it according to God's commandments for the good of the poor and the abandoned.

9. Who shall attain knowledge of the unique Splendour?

10. O conceited and stupid rich men! we have begged from you a little bread in exchange for God's riches, and you have rejected us without even looking at what we were offering you!

11. Those who scorn and reject the poor believers at present shall one day be scorned and rejected by the Lord because of the poverty of their hearts.

4'. Thus, on penetrating as far as the secret centre, each one shall be unified in the unity of the Unique One and shall become a «Rediscovered Messenger».

5'. But very few wise inquirers obtain from God the grace to discover the origin of the chaos in which the holy light of life is hidden.

6'. The latter generally remain hidden, being content with raising up carriers of light who manifest God's truth in the world.

7'. Next, there are those who benefit from the thing without knowing it and without possessing it.

8'. Finally, there are those who with the aid of God know the thing and make it, for their salvation and for that of their own.

9'. And who shall be unified with the *Heloym* in the unique God?

10'. One day, you shall also beg from us a little of heaven's water in exchange for all your earthly riches, but we shall repel you without even glancing at your dung.

11'. Let us not think of finding the Lord and then leaving the world. We must first leave the world and we shall then find the Lord.

12. We have visited you from the outside, with remonstrances and recall to the grace, the love and the knowledge of the Lord of life.

13. He who does not know how to pray alone must pray with the community of believers, so as to train himself in the individual prayer that springs up at all times and in all places in the joy of divine union.

14. It is necessary to give in order to receive.

15. I forgive you your sin which is your sickness, my Lord said to me, so that instead of rising up against my NAME and against my creation, you praise my grace and my love in my eternity. Do you understand, my child, who shouts to your Father?

16. The blows we are dealt enlighten us marvellously, but very few understand this, and very few take advantage of it in this world.

17. We call to our God for help in the prison where we are dying, but he observes us without saying a word and he lets us rip ourselves to shreds on the brambles that invade it.

18. Let him who is alive send out cries of joy and gratitude towards the Lord who nourishes the Universe!

12'. At present, we visit you from inside, with encouragement and confirmation in the grace, the love and the knowledge of the Lord God.

13'. He who knows how to pray alone is self-sufficient, for the Lord is an almighty and perfect companion. However he does not disdain to pray sometimes also with the community of believers in the joy of fraternal union.

14'. And one has to sweat in order to be watered by the sweet dew of heaven.

15'. My friends, do not go to the feasts of men, from which one returns with sad heart and weary body. Go and visit the sick and the imprisoned and invite the poor, so that your contentment is perfect and so that the Lord sends you his blessing, which saves from death.

16'. We shall know for certain that we are close to the Lord when we love all humanity and all creation with the same vigour and with the same heart.

17'. At present, Lord, here we are reconciled with all the beings that have fallen into the mud of sin, without distinction, and our heart is forever united with the hearts of the wretched ones who suffer in *Gehenna*.

18'. O Lord of life! give us health of the body and contentment of the heart, but above all, give us the love

And let him who suffers ask for forgiveness, so that his sin is lifted from him by the Magnanimous One!

19. You plunge us into *Gehenna* with the damned, my God, and then you pull us out of it again, so that we understand that we should also visit them and comfort them in your NAME.

20. One does not pray in hell, one howls there with the accursed ones. Let us understand the lesson, Lord, before we are brutally hurled down there.

21. God's good children take advantage of all that happens to them, for they are in accordance with the will of the Father that leads them, while the others, who follow their own will, are blinded and tear themselves apart more and more on the brambles of the mixed world.

22. When we have become poor to the point of feeling like guests in our own homes, we shall be free and at peace everywhere in the world.

23. Our sons and our daughters shall repopulate the earth lost by Adam, and their praises to God shall resound up to the highest heavens.

24. The Book is not meant to be read in an accelerated world. It is destined for the survivors, for the time of their convalescence among the smoking ruins.

of your Being, that is, the insane love that carries us to your holy eternity.

19'. Your lessons are hard, Lord, and many do not understand them, but for your children it is an endless enrichment. O good Lord! teach us gently and with patience, for this world is wicked and pain dwells in it.

20'. Clear-sighted Lord, show us those who truly love you, so that we might kiss their hands from which emanates the excellent odour of love and charity.

21'. Humility is to remember always that we are in unstable equilibrium on the edge of the abyss, where suffering, madness and death float.

22'. If we do not measure the suffering of the fallen world, how shall we come to know our exile? And if we do not measure the joy of divine life, how shall we come to know the meaning of our rescue?

23'. One day, our joy and our repose shall be in God alone, for God is our joy and our repose for eternity.

24'. Have we not preached up to the very end in a desert of bones? Would the Lord not at present want to transform it into a perfumed garden resplendent with life?

25. You mix us with the damned and you withdraw yourself from us so that we can measure our nothingness. We are really not proud of ourselves here below, Lord.

26. If you abandon us, Lord, we are lost, for we cannot even shout for your help, so great has our weakness become.

27. The best way to pray to God and to serve him here below is to attend to the abandoned sick, to visit the prisoners without families, to help the poor, the widows and the orphans in need.

28. O believers in the unique Father! do not wait for the wretched to hold out their hands.

29. One single visit to the abandoned ones in prisons, hospitals or slums is worth more than a whole life of edifying prayers in worldly churches.

30. The Lord brutally expels his beloved ones from the places of vanity where the beautiful words resound in the void of the hearts.

31. When God abandons us, it is in order to make us measure the infinite of our weakness and of our nothingness.

32. An impious man who help his human brothers is closer to God than a believer who prays publicly without doing anything for anyone.

25'. As soon as suffering takes hold of us, all our prayers become choked in the gulps of pain, and our intelligence is swallowed up in the howling of the Beast.

26'. Do not hand us over to evil, handsome Lord of life, but deliver us before our hearts are marked by the doubt that kills the soul.

27'. Is there a prayer more magnificent to the Highest than the fraternal mutual aid of charity? And are there surer first fruits of our union in the unique Love?

28'. Look for them and help them, for many no longer have the courage nor the strength to come up to you.

29'. God sets aside a terrible surprise for the hypocrites who pray publicly and do evil in secret.

30'. Because he prefers them there where charity actively consoles suffering and wretched men.

31'. Thus, the intelligent learn that they are nothing without him.

32'. Thus, he who loves and respects God's creation already walks on the holy way that leads to the life that does not perish.

33. Is the Book not for the ones gone astray who search in tears for the path of life, rather than for the believers who have settled into the death of this world?

34. The end of the wicked shall be a teaching for those who believe in their hearts and for those who see with their eyes.

35. He who bites the hand that feeds him and who raises him to spiritual life is cursed, and his memory shall be anathema among his own like that of a Judas.

36. How shall we escape without your help, Lord of heaven, from the brutishness of the necessities of life exiled on earth?

37. The sons of God possess nothing in this perishable world, for their kingdom is in the beloved sun.

38. Man is ingenious in organizing himself on this earth of exile, but he cannot emerge from it without the aid of God.

39. Begging is demeaning for him who seeks the world, but it is the noblest state for him who seeks God.

40. Good Lord of charity, deliver us from this world where everything is sordidly bought, sold or exchanged.

33'. When the merciful Lord wakes us up with kicks it is not as a joke, but rather because we are not where we should be, and because we do not do what has to be done.

34'. Because of the hypocrites, priority for the Book is withdrawn from the right-thinking ones and given to those who receive it without a spirit of murder or exclusiveness.

35'. Bound from top to toe in the black sack, broken into pieces, reduced to ashes and scattered in the six directions, such will be the fate of the persecutors of God's prophets.

36'. This world is a terrifying battle of rough beasts that does not suit God's peace-loving children.

37'. Therefore, they preach to us the detachment from the terrestrial world and the return to the celestial world, where life is not contaminated by death.

38'. Truly, the kingdom of God is not of this world, which is why the sons of God appear errant and poor on the earth.

39'. A single earth, a single sea, a single fire, a single word, a single God.

40'. Receive us in the generous life of your holy love that never runs out.

41. No, this is not a Book for the satiated ones of the world that have settled down permanently in the cesspool of death.

41'. It is a Book for the hungry ones from heaven that tearfully look for their lost fatherland.

42. What a face the self-assured ones of this world shall pull when they are asked on the day of judgement: «Have you read the Book of deliverance that was proposed to you in particular?»

42'. They shall be told: Return to the stinking mud in which you revelled, and to the readings that sunk you in it and that you preferred to any other.

43. One needs the gift of genius to practise the fine arts in this world.

43'. And one has to have an angelic gift to pray and praise the Lord of heaven and earth.

43". But one has to have a divine gift to practise the great ART of the Almighty here below.

44. One always has to kill in order to live here below. Therefore, we consider this world to be bad, and we do not want to settle into crime.

44'. On the day of the restitution of all things, God's chosen ones shall eat the holy dew of heaven, and the damned shall only have the rottenness of hell as food.

45. The impious, who rely only on themselves, seem more courageous and more resistant to evil than those of us who believe in the Lord and who wait for his salvation day and night.
«They reject the revelation that they have been unable to penetrate either by cunning or by violence.»

45'. On the day of the terrible judgement, there shall no longer be enemies or friends, but only the wretched who shall have freely chosen the stinking mud of hell, and blessed who shall have just as freely chosen the pure and sweet-smelling life that never runs out.

46. Let our faith in the almightiness of God be blind and idiotic, so that it becomes clear-sighted and spiritual through the incarnation of the divine word that delivers us from the darkness of death.

46'. Those who receive the word of life participate in the grace of God that delivers from the slavery of the world. No servile work shall be imposed on them and death itself shall be cast far away from them, for their lot is the free and imperishable life in which the Lord of eternity dwells.

47. The wickedness of those who call themselves God's faithful has become such that true believers no longer cross the threshold of sacred places, and the abandoned reject God as derisory or as an intolerable millstone.

48. Some say of our preaching: «It is too beautiful to be true», for death that was introduced into the world because of them hides from them at present the pure and sweet-smelling life that does not end.

49. Where is the intelligent one who prostrates himself before the Lord of heaven and who receives his most holy and living blessing?

50. There is already a group of those cut off through faith and love in the world.

51. Many people who show intelligence and courage in the affairs of the world reveal themselves to be stupid and impotent in the affairs of God.

52. Our worst enemies are not outside, but indeed among us, like wolves dressed in sheep's clothing.

53. They say they are God's faithful, but they violate his commandments every day.

54. They say they are disciples of the Lord, but they settle down in the world on the backs of the wretched.

47'. There is a horrendous rottenness among the right-thinking ones and there is a hardened death among the atheists, but the worst wickedness is indeed in the self-satisfied hypocrites.

48'. Counterfeit resides everywhere in the world, and every day we have to take care not to confuse it with the truth of the wise and holy word that is the only thing that saves us from death.

49'. Where is the inspired one that prepares the holy tabernacle in which the unique Splendour of life shall rest?

50'. And there is already a group of those chosen through faith and through love in God.

51'. The judgements they rashly make about one and the other do nothing but display their conceited ignorance.

52'. For those, there shall be neither the forgiveness of men nor the forgiveness of God, for traitors and hypocrites are vomited by heaven and by earth.

53'. They claim to be right-thinking, but they say and do evil every day of their lives.

54'. All of them are already cursed and excluded from God's salvation, for they make the divine name odious to the weak and the small.

55. Let us run away as if from the pest from those who rip their friends to shreds, for tomorrow we shall also be torn apart by their poisoned and wicked tongues.

56. Shall the Lord and all God's wise prophets not kiss us on the lips like one of their own who has proclaimed and manifested the truth of God in the world?

57. Those who bury the word of God instead of making it circulate in the world shall be frustrated in the end, for they shall not reap anything, and shall even lose the hidden deposit.

58. We must not reply to malicious gossip with malicious gossip, for it is already quite enough that the wickedness of the wicked crushes them in the end without us adding anything to it.

59. At present, those who still preach the truth of God and who transmit his word of life no longer believe in the almightiness of the word that is radiant in heaven.

60. God has not subjected man to beasts, and above all not to dogs.

61. We must never despair in the darkness of our quest for the Lord of life.

62. The work of the Lord is imperishable, while the works of men disappear like smoke.

55'. If we do not pray for the wicked, who shall come to their help to bring them out of their wickedness?

56'. Have those not also been slandered, rejected, oppressed and unjustly fought against by the hypocrites set up in the world under the cover of God's name?

57'. The Lord of heaven fights victoriously against the rottenness of death, and his sages are the experts of his love, and his saints are the distributors of his grace.

58'. It is enough for us to pray for the conversion of the wicked, without judging and without condemning, before the great day of reckoning that is the only responsibility of the Lord of justice and forgiveness.

59'. How shall they bring the dying back to life, if they themselves are dying, and how shall they resurrect the dead, if they remain in death?

60'. The dogs that threaten man shall be beaten, and those that bite him shall be slaughtered.

61'. For we are close to his holy light, but we do not know the day or the hour of its manifestation.

62'. Time works for the sage, while it destroys the senseless one.

63. Is he who praises God in his heart not worth more than those who work in the profane world?

63'. And is he who captures his blessing not worth more than those who make themselves rich with mortal goods?

64. One day, God shall inform us in person, but then it shall be too late to reform our judgement and to change our behaviour in the world.

64'. Do we not see that the Lord always warns us in time? Shall we not come out at present of the quagmire of our worries and from the trap of our worldly occupations?

65. What do the judgements of the world matter, since it is not the world that shall judge us in the end?

65'. He who walks with God in God's way does not worry about being approved of by the world.

66. Those who organize themselves richly and comfortably in the world in order to preach the kingdom of God are hypocrites who prefer to have the shadow rather than to hope for its light.

66'. There is only one temple of God, that is the heart of man. All the rest is like a disguise that satisfies only the blind and incurable mediocre.

67. Those who preach the way of the Lord and who set themselves up in the world before installing themselves in God are hypocrites who deceive simple men and who satisfy only the mediocre.

67'. He who loves does not display the word «love» above his door to justify himself before the world, and he who gives does not write the word «charity» in order to make his bounty public before all.

68. When we see the great words of love and charity shamelessly displayed in the world, we shall know we are looking at businesses that aim for our freedom and our purse.

68'. The Lord, who possessed and was the palpable truth of God, asked for nothing of nobody, he gave everything to everyone, and he gave himself beyond measure.

69. The spiritual ones shall be overcome before God's tribunal and they shall be struck dumb with astonishment.

69'. Only the operative ones shall praise the Almighty without being amazed at anything.

70. What a surprise for those who preach the word of God without

70'. We should preach God's truth, but without superiority and without

knowing its ultimate meaning, when they see with their own eyes and when they feel with their hands the truth of the Unique One!

71. He who eats the simulacrum of God remains in the death of the world, that is something that is easy to verify.

72. It is our good thoughts of love and our holy repose that open our spirit to the mysteries of God's word, and not scholarly lectures amid the crowds of dying mediocre.

73. Good taste and beauty are no more expensive than vulgarity and ugliness. As for the truth of God, it is free for everyone.

74. What are they doing, but just what are they doing, all those who sleep in the world?

75. What are they doing, but just what are they doing, all those who bustle about in the world?

76. Shall we always waste our life looking for the world that abandons us in the end?

77. Oh, you who hope for God's salvation, wake up in the world!

78. Neither the morals of the world nor its licentiousness shall deliver us from death.

79. The science of God knows no progress, for it is perfect from the beginning.

arrogance, for only a few chosen ones know it spiritually, and extremely few sons of God possess it corporeally.

71'. He who eats God in body and in spirit becomes like God. That is something that does not deceive either.

72'. God's truth goes secretly to those who love it and who seek it in their hearts. Those truths that attack the world through publicity stunts can never be God's truth.

73'. If the beauty of the world eludes us, how shall the beauty of him who made it ever become perceptible to us?

74'. But where, then, are the watchmen of God?

75'. But where, then, are the seekers of the Unique One?

76'. And shall we risk nothing in the quest for the unique Splendour that fulfils us for eternity?

77'. And seek the secret light of the words of life, instead of being content with their clothes of shade.

78'. Only the incarnate love of the Perfect One that reigns in heaven.

79'. And his light illuminates the believer who harmonizes heaven and earth.

80. The immensity of the divine promise goes beyond the spirit of men and gives God's saints vertigo.

80'. Oh! who shall believe the unbelievable, and who shall receive in his heart the magnificent gift of God?

Those who, rebellious to God and to his envoys, try to differentiate between them, believing in some and repudiating the mission of others, create for themselves an arbitrary religion.
KORAN

They travelled the paths and they brought together all those they found, wicked and good, and the wedding room was filled with guests.
JESUS

BOOK XXXVI

None of those that had been invited shall taste my supper.

JESUS

One rejects the last place and one thus loses the first.

LAO TSE

REINE VEUT	KING SAVES

1. Courageous in the quest for God. Lazy in that for the world.

1'. Do not disregard your foundation and do not scorn it when you recognize it.

2. He who seeks the mystery of union and of life without the blessing and without the love of God shall only find dispersion and death. These words are very true.

2'. Let us thus take great care not to imitate the profane ones who think of doing violence to God's secret with impunity, as the strayed and rebellious peoples in the world do at present.

3. O believers who are dying in this world of exile! seek the Lord God with all your strength and help one another in all possible ways, so that the world does not bury you before the coming of the Saviour.

3'. When we have unified the word of God in the knowledge of God, there shall be nothing but admiring silence and intense jubilation in ourselves.

4. The intelligent of the world consider the teaching of the Book as an abstract thing, when in fact one is dealing with the most concrete thing in the Universe, which is the union of heaven and earth.

4'. If they knew the teaching of the other Scriptures, they would also know the meaning of this one, but their conceited pretension blinds them totally.

4". God mocks them and ridicules them beyond all expression before the simple children.

5. Profane decorations enable us to recognize the children of the devil, for they are darkness within the darkness.

5'. Holy manifestations make us recognize God's children, for they are light within the light.

6. Let us note how much the people of this nation have shown themselves to be blind and deaf with regard to the beauty and the truth of the revealed Book. Let us note how much they have remained stupid and dumb before the obviousness of the manifested light.

6'. Let us therefore take great care with what appears in us and around us, so as not to trample like brutish beasts on the salvation of God that appears in the world under the veil of the lordly creation.

7. He who thinks he knows closes himself up to all instruction, and the proud one cuts himself off from the grace and inspiration of God.

7'. For some, the Book shall be a stone that shall seal their tomb, but for others it shall be a stone that shall renew their life.

8. The damned shall say on the day of judgement: If at least we had been unaware of the existence of the message, we would be half guilty, for the word of the Living One was erased and as if veiled for us in the night of oblivion.

8'. But it has manifested itself anew before our eyes and it has resonated in our ears with dazzling clarity, and we have stupidly repelled it in spite of it being our last chance of salvation. Alas! We have taken the darkness for the light and the light for the darkness.

9. Shall we wait to be a multitude in believing the Book of the truth of life to be reassured in our renewed faith?

9'. The large number of believers or of nonbelievers is a blind and worthless assurance as far as God's truth is concerned.

10. Let us not devote ourselves to the work of the world like frenzied slaves in order to satisfy ever-renewed desires, for no hand of man or God would then be able to deliver us any longer from the brutishness of spiritual death.

10'. Let us maintain ourselves in the sufficiency of poverty and we shall have all the time necessary for the quest for the Perfect One, who embodies himself in the marvellous virgin revealed to the simple ones and to the wise children of God.

11. This one may begin in crime and end in holiness, and that one may commence with faith in God and end in murderous rebellion.

12. O faint-hearted ones from all nations! learn from your heart to know the beauty and the truth of God where it appears, and not just where they tell you it is.

13. The most instructed among the students of the wise and holy Scriptures interpret the divine mysteries as symbols of the spiritual renovation of man who has gone astray in this world.

14. We did not follow the heavenly son incarnate on the earth. Shall we follow the earthly son established in heaven?

15. Merciful Lord, grant us what is necessary, so that we might also give what is necessary to those who ask it of us.

16. If there is an incapable one, a useless one, a vagabond, an idiot, a wretch that the world rejects, let him come without fear to the Lord God, let him read the Book of deliverance and let him take his place at table for the banquet of the life that does not perish.

17. God's salvation that we announce and that we propose to exiled men surely seems incredible because it is too beautiful and too pure in this world darkened by death.

11'. Who knows the itinerary of light through the man salted by fire? And who knows the way of darkness in the man desalinated by water?

12'. One day, we shall taste the soul, the spirit and the body of the Lord God united in ONE and we shall emerge from the exile of this mortal world praising and blessing his holy NAME for eternity.

13'. How many of those understand that these holy mysteries also describe the corporeal regeneration of the man crucified here below?

14'. Shall we understand that it is the Unique One that always descends and ascends, so as to show us the path of the life that does not perish?

15'. Generous Lord, grant us the superabundance of life, so that we may give unstintingly in your NAME.

16'. For the skilful, the hard-working, the scholarly, the intelligent and the well-off of the world exclude themselves due to their conceited pretensions, their dead creations, their profane knowledge, their self-esteem and their satisfaction with the fallen world.

17'. Thus, the intelligent repel it, sniggering in accordance with their plain and blind reason. Only the simple and the innocent can receive it, for they do not obstruct the renewed miracle of God.

18. Have we not come to preach first to the shrewder, the most non-believing and the most rebellious peoples, so that, by rejecting the Book of science, their fate be decided by themselves without possible recriminations on the day of judgement?

18'. And have we not come to preach in second place to those peoples that are the most simple, the most believing and the most submissive to God, so that, by receiving the Book of salvation, their fate may be assured by themselves without possible error on the day of judgement?

19. Is there not a small remainder to awaken, to group and to save among the former?

19'. Is there not a great mass among the latter to awaken, to group and to save?

20. The most scholarly and the most intelligent take the revealed Scriptures for treatises on history and morals.

20'. The holiest and the most inspired take those same revealed Scriptures for treatises on asceticism and mysticism.

20". Where are God's enlightened sages that also know how to recognize in them the hidden science of the unique Splendour that saves them from death?

21. If we do not listen to the voice that calls us back to life, we shall be awoken by kicks and our throats shall be cut in the slaughter-house of death, despite our howls of rough beasts. Alas! hell is not a tale for children!

21'. On the day of judgement we shall all be interrogated on the unique teaching of God's envoys. Those who shall have repelled it, neglected it, scorned it or fought it shall pay the penalty for it. That which we announce here is not a worthless joke, be assured of that.

22. We have had to sell men the wine of the earth to survive in this world, and they have paid us its price, by thanking us.

22'. We have also offered them free of charge the wine of the Lord of heaven, but they have repelled it, mocking us.

23. The nonbelievers and the intelligent of this world remain dazed and stupid before the word of the Unique One, and they reject it as alien to their malignant nature.

23'. The believers and the inspired ones of God recognize the wise and holy word, and establish themselves in it in order to accomplish their divine nature for eternity.

24. O Mighty One who remains in unity for the eternity of eternities! give us children as innumerable and precious as the stars of your heaven of glory.

25. It is the Father who gives us all from his superabundance, and the Son is his prodigious gift of life manifested even as far as in this exiled world.

26. Thus, man overcomes earthly food and transforms it into him. But he is overcome by heavenly food that transforms him into God.

27. Therefore it only remains for us to find the marvellous Lord descended from heaven who said: «Eat, this is my flesh; drink, this is my blood».

28. For we know and we receive only in images in this world darkened by death, in prefiguration of the great day of judgement when we shall know and when we shall receive the holy and palpable reality.

29. Thus, do we understand why it is said that the Lord God shall judge the living and the dead, the living first and then the dead?

30. O terrifying mystery of the rescue or of the perdition of man gone astray in the filth of death!

31. This Book teaches us nothing, say the world's eternal informed ones, for, when looking for recipes, they find none here; or indeed, while raving in the abstraction of the void, they

24'. So that they might people for ever your kingdom reserved for the rediscovered children that do your holy will and that manifest your holy love.

25'. The Father only attracts to himself his own essence and his own substance. We must therefore become sons of God in order to reach the unity of the One.

26'. That which we repeat here to all believers is a great mystery, for it is the mystery of God that dwells in the purity of life delivered from death.

27'. Or to obtain from a secret priest of God the communion of this prodigious Lord that saves from death.
«Order of Melchizedek.»

28'. Nevertheless, God has allowed some of his sages to know him in this world, and has allowed some of his saints to receive him even here below, like the first fruits of the resurrection announced to all.

29'. For even the grace of the gift of life in this very world does not dispense us from the final judgement of the most-righteous God.

30'. We melt in terror, our teeth chatter and our hair stands on end despite our mad hope.

31'. Therefore, they finally remain prisoners in the pit of death like beasts wandering around gropingly, reciting the sentences of the sages and showing off with their maxims

stumble over the foundation stone that their short-sightedness prevents them from seeing.

32. The faith of God is rejected by the impious, but the science of God is also rejected by the believers in this darkened world.

33. Some of God's intelligent subsist among the multitude of the intelligent of the world, like the glowing embers that remain hidden under the dead ashes.

that they do not understand and that they do not apply.

32'. Therefore, all exclude themselves from God's immediate deliverance, except for God's children, who have looked for him since this dark time.

33'. Therefore, some whites shall remain the heirs to the heavenly doctrine among the multitude of proud dead.

33". Shall those, who are the blessed messengers of God, not also be the messengers that shall bless the coloured peoples called to God?

34. Let us not use the arms of the wicked to fight them and to reject them. Let us use faith, prayer and the charity of love that shall win them over to our cause or miraculously destroy them.

35. Let us therefore pray for those who oppress us, so that the word of God be for them like a judgement that makes them germinate or that dries them up here below.

36. Let each community pray, therefore, taking turns night and day, for their persecuted and for their persecutors, until the miracle of God becomes evident for all.

37. Let us respond to wickedness with charity, but let us keep separate from the wicked and from their doc-

34'. The blessing of life that is not received turns into a curse of death for the wicked. Therefore, we shall dominate the wicked by being better than them in everything and for everything.

35'. If our faith and love in God are perfect, we shall convert our persecutors, or the fire of heaven shall consume them before us.

36'. Let us bless our persecutors in our hearts in the name of God, for according to what they really are, the holy stone shall enlighten them and elevate them, or shall blind them and crush them.

37'. The children shall become slaves and the slaves shall become cherished children of God, for the children

trines of death as long as their wickedness and their pride lasts.

38. If a conflict arises between us, it is because the Spirit of God is no longer in us, and if we judge this conflict to be outside of us, it is because the love of God is no longer in us.

39. Let us therefore pray to the Lord God in our hearts before judging anything and let us grant ourselves a long time before excluding anything, for our hearts have become deaf and our hands have become blind in this world veiled in darkness.

40. All pretension to divine science that is not justified by holy works is mockery and trickery before God and before men.

41. The vanity of these senseless ones would be laughable if it had not cut them off from their brothers whom they oppress and from God whom they scoff at in the world.

42. Let us distance ourselves from the proud and not imitate them in anything, for, because of their scorn for the humble, their fate has already been decided by God.

43. It is a white man who announces these things, a white man whose message the whites have repelled sniggering, and whose warning they have scorned while deriding him.

at present scorn the holy heritage that the slaves receive with gratitude.

38'. Therefore, it is the secret voice of our hearts that we have to listen to, and it is the judgement of God that we have to hope for, for love is a to-ing and fro-ing that separates in us the light of life from the darkness of death.

39'. It is God's science that shall deliver us from the grip of the Beast and from the exile of death, and nothing else. But it is the blessing and the love of God that accomplish in us the resurrection and the glorification hoped for by the believers.

40'. Therefore, the unbounded pretension of those whose profane science crushes and enchains humanity, is what prefigures their dispersion in death.

41'. O supreme derision! those that have organized themselves in the mud of the world think they are a chosen people and a superior race, when in fact their holy heritage is taken away from them because of their blind pride!

42'. Their descendants, or what will remain of them, shall become the slaves of slaves, and no hand of man or God shall deliver them from that for a long time.

43'. We are different like the children of a same Father, but we could not divide ourselves and oppose one another without losing our holy heritage.

44. Let us pray to God so that he opens our eyes, and let us pray to him so that he unblocks our ears.

45. The Virgin vegetates until she receives the heavenly influx that animates her by breathing into her the divine soul, and this soul organizes her substance, clothes itself in it and appears in the world as the Saviour and the Renewer of men gone astray in death.

46. God has allowed that those who proudly boast of the colour of their skin have their heart darkened by the darkness of death.

47. Let us beware of the rationalist scholars who bury God's revelation in the tomb.

48. Neither the ones nor the others possess the unique knowledge of God's children, and their fate shall be settled at the last judgement. But, shall they still have an excuse after having known the Book of the means?

49. God sends us a prophet before the blow that shall drive us into the blind and deaf brutishness of death.

50. Where are God's intelligent ones who seek the Lord with all their might in the world, so as to emerge unscathed of the blaze that is being lit?

44'. But let us pray to him above all so that he loosens our hearts from the filth of death and binds them in his light of life.

45'. Therefore, you were awaiting the Holy Spirit that fertilizes you and gives you access to the filiation of God. Shall you not recognize the immensity of God's gift, and shall you not be grateful in your hearts towards him who chooses you at present as heirs and as privileged children?

46'. God has likewise allowed that those who do not show off the colour of their skin like a flag have their heart fertilized by his living gold.

47'. But let us also beware of the abstract delirious ones who pulverize it beyond our reach in heaven.

48'. None of those shall enter God's treasury from this world, for one group denies his existence in heaven and his incarnation on the earth, and the other group is unaware that the thing is still being accomplished before their blind eyes.

49'. Where are the believers in God who convert to the love of God and men in order to escape from the coming annihilation?

50'. For God's judgement has been decided and the great day approaches, but the wicked ones mock and do even more evil, while the believers abandon bad deeds and return to God in their heart.

51. Thus, the judgement has already begun without anyone suspecting it, and the Book shall only precipitate the choice of each one with regards to faith in God and in his resurrection.

52. Has not our earthly family refused to read the Book of incarnate truth, and has it not rejected and ignored it because of its goodwill in the world and of its ill will in God? Yet are they not nice people in the world?

53. Thus, our relatives and allied behave like blind men before the revelation of the Highest, for they indeed experience the affections of the earth and they are lovers in their own way, but they do not experience the affections of heaven and they do not truly love God and his salvation!

54. The apparent inhumanity of the Lord in the world is made from the certainty of the rediscovered life in God, while the humanity of the profane ones is made from the loss of themselves in the brutishness of death.

55. Is it not a sign of the end of time that woman listens again to the bad counsellor who seduced her in

51'. We could not force anyone to believe in the newly-arrived message, for the very obviousness of God's grace and love is denied by the ignorant ones established in the world.

52'. If we do not pray to the Lord God assiduously to inspire us and guide us through his Holy Spirit, we shall remain prisoners in the darkness, and the spirit of the darkness shall whisper to us a thousand bad reasons to settle down with him definitively.

53'. The Lord is right to recommend us to leave everything and follow him, for we thus abandon the dead to go to the Living One, and the dead who stay with the world have already chosen death, just as the living who follow the Living One have already chosen life.

54'. Is it not woman who let in evil by giving herself over to it? And is it not thus that death penetrated us through the channel of life?

54". Is it not also the Lord descended from heaven that embodies himself in woman and gives us back life by giving himself over to the death that dwells in us?

55'. For she suspects the message and the messenger sent by God. Let her pray, then, in her heart so as to

the beginning and who wants to lead her totally astray at the end?

56. O black peoples! up to now you were subject to the artifice of the world, but the Lord descends to you through his living word.

57. Is it not by receiving the devil that woman let in the Beast who has exiled us in the death of the world?

58. We reveal to you the mystery of the fall and the redemption so that you do not become proud of the fact that God has chosen you at present. For he comes to you before you go to him, and he leaves the proud before they deny him.

59. Finally, Christ came and was made golden since he stemmed solely from the light of God, like Adam before the fall.

60. Thus, those who are of the world come back to the world, and those who are of heaven go back to heaven.

61. Shall we not receive as a brother the Lord descended from heaven, and shall we not follow him out of the quagmire of death, since it is the will of God?

hear the voice of God, instead of consulting the world to hear the voice of the devil!

56'. Shall you not receive in a holy way the prodigious gift of life without mixture? And shall you not be grateful to him who brings you the salvation of God?

57'. And is it not by receiving God that woman lets in the Lord who reincorporates us into the life of God?

58'. Indeed, Cain came first and was made black as he stemmed mainly from the darkness of the world, while Abel came second and was made white as he stemmed mainly from the light of God, but the darkness did not receive the light.

59'. But the darkness still did not receive the light, despite the fact that the light had received the darkness in the first place.

60'. But God wants to bring back to him the men fallen in the world, and the devil wants to make those who have remained in heaven fall.

61'. Instead of repelling him profanely and immolating him criminally, as do the wicked counselled and blinded by Satan?

62. We are in this world like castaways lost for a long time on a desolate island where death lives and has priority.

62'. Those that settle there think they are doing the right thing, and many admire them and encourage them, not understanding that they are organizing themselves in the death that does not forgive.

63. Those who remember their lost fatherland and seek the way back to the life that does not perish night and day are mocked and bullied by many, for they seem like madmen to the world, while they are the only really wise ones in God.

63'. Therefore, the sages and saints of God who work for the rescue of men exiled in death are held in contempt and repelled by the scholars and the intelligent of the world, who install humanity in the common grave.

64. Unbelief, pride and avarice are the principal obstacles that block us from our quest for God and his salvation in the world. Who shall deliver us and who shall help us to be born into the pure life if we do not first strike the blow that breaks open our shroud of death from inside?

64'. Let us pray so as to obtain faith in God's revelation instead of our illusory beliefs. Let us pray so as to receive the intelligence of God's revelation instead of our worthless knowledge. Let us pray so as to receive the deliverance of God's revelation instead of our perishable goods.

65. All can withdraw from us any moment, be it due to a sordid interest, a bad thought or misunderstood word. The Lord God shall remain our unfailing and living companion, for his light illuminates us forever.

65'. Those who withdraw from God's children cut themselves off from the salvation of God and deprive themselves of it alone, for God's children are already brimming over with the divine gift for eternity, and their fate depends on God, and not on ignorant rebels.

66. The wicked offer their goods to those who drive them into the death of the world, and they refuse even bread to those who call them to the life of God.

66'. We shall withdraw from them or we shall reduce them to begging if they wish to enter into the word of God.

67. Rich and poor have repelled the gift that was offered to them for free; from now on, the rich shall pay for it at the price of their wealth and the poor shall acquire it at the price of their poverty, for God's treasure is unique, and has no price in the world.

68. God's treasure has been offered to us for free up to now, but we have scorned it and repelled it, without even examining that which was offered to us.

69. Those who shall have put obstacles in the way of the Book shall pay the penalty, and those who shall have helped it shall have their reward, for everything shall be judged and weighed up on the day of reckoning.

70. We shall remain silent, as did the Lord of truth, before those who, believing themselves superior, disguise themselves in one way or another to persecute us, judge us and condemn us here below.

71. We shall reject all uniforms and all profane decorations, which are the marks of the servitude of the world of Satan.

72. Nobody shall distance himself from his faith by coming to the revealed Book; quite the contrary, all shall be confirmed in their revelation, and some shall penetrate the depth and see the light of God gleam.

67'. For those who shall twist or force the word of the Book, the Book shall become a curse that shall blind them and a stone that shall be their downfall; but for those that shall enter this word, the Book shall be a blessing that shall enlighten them and a stone that shall save them.

68'. At present, everything shall be counted and weighed for us in the world, and the weight of God's treasure shall divest us to the tomb before it enriches us up to the heaven of eternity.

69'. It is a promise that shall be accomplished and that shall surprise many believers and many nonbelievers on the day the word of God is revealed in the hearts.

70'. We shall pray in our hearts so that they be converted to the simplicity of God's children, for the righteous judge shall treat them according to his justice, which does not allow itself to be led astray by any disguise.

71'. And we shall clothe ourselves in the immaculate robe of God's children to pray, to praise and to receive communion in the Highest.

72'. The Book does not disperse us in the multitude of branches, for it leads us to the unique root.
Neither does the Book disperse us in the multitude of roots, for it leads us to the unique top.

73. Many intelligent of the world shall explain to us in black and white the whys and the hows of the Book, and we in turn shall shine before all, with the intelligence of the world.

73'. But where is the intelligent one of God that shall find in white on black the why and the how of the Book, and who shall shine for himself with the holy light of God?

74. Those who receive the message in their heart are the survivors of the world that is dying. Misfortune shall distance itself from them and despair shall no longer reach them.

74'. Their hope shall not be disappointed, for the saints of God shall help them to be born in the kingdom of the Unique One, and the Lord in person shall take them into the heavenly dwellings.

75. Many do not always understand what they say, but the children of God know what they are talking about, for they see with their eyes and they touch with their hands.

75'. And that cannot be conceived by the intelligent of the world, so unbelievable and crazy does the thing seem to them, through the darkness of their hearts.

76. The wicked and the intelligent of the world want to be the masters putting themselves before God, in their homes and in the homes of others. This engenders catastrophes of the absurd in themselves and in the world, for they force everything and let nothing come and go freely.

76'. If our exterior exchanges are free and generous, our interior exchanges shall also be free and generous, and misfortune shall distance itself from us, for God's blessing shall circulate in us without hindrance, and his love shall ripen in our hearts.

77. Every distraction in this dying world is like a piece of our life that we blithely toss into the pit of death.

77'. We mean by distraction all that is not devoted to the unique spiritual and substantial quest for God here below.

78. We shall not save ourselves, not by the work of our hands, nor by the work of our will, nor by that of our intelligence.

78'. It is the blessing of God and it is the operation of his holy love in our purified hearts that shall accomplish the work of deliverance and of resurrection.

79. Life and death are inextricably mixed in the fallen world, and our profane sciences are powerless to separate them and exalt the pure life up to God's repose.

79'. Therefore, all our subtle thoughts, all our fine words and all our great works go to death, for our spirits, our hearts and our hands are darkened by the infamous mixture.

80. And our eyes do not see it and our ears do not hear it, so heavy has the curse of the fall weighed upon us.

80'. O Lord of light! deliver your children who pray to you in a holy way in their hearts, and open their eyes and their ears so that they recognize your salvation that saves them from death.

81. At present, the Book is also given to the yellow peoples who receive it in their hearts, and the reds shall hear of it so that the cycle is accomplished. For the blacks shall be guardians of the light that the whites have manifested in the world.

81'. The Book was written in the darkness of the world, by the glow of God's light that shines in the heart of men sown with the Lord of love and science.

82. O children of wisdom! if you consider the contents and the container separately, your wisdom shall remain lame and you shall not enter God's treasury.

82'. But if you know how to separate the content from the container and if you know how to unite them in God, you shall enter the eternity of the Unique One for eternity.

82". Let it be so for God's true children who do his holy will and who love their brothers in the Lord!

83. The ignorant ones stagnate in this mixed world, for they adapt themselves to the brutishness of misfortune in the exile of death.

83'. The intelligent ones disembody man and dematerialise him in a thousand ways. Those destroy creation thinking they are freeing themselves; they go backwards.

83". The sages embody God and manifest him in a single way. These complete creation to accomplish themselves; they advance.

84. The woman who believes and who does not understand is superior to the man who does not believe and who thinks he understands.

84'. No-one shall be instructed if he does not seek instruction. No-one shall be cured if he does not seek a cure. No-one shall be saved if he does not seek regeneration.

85. Those who are forgetful of God in the penury of exile would be even more so in the abundance of splendour.

85'. That is why the mediocre of heart stagnate in the mortal agony of this world, without hope and without forgiveness.

86. Shall we not do on a small scale what the Father and the Mother do on a grand scale? And shall we not accomplish the work of the Lord from the beginning to the end?

86'. Seek the heart, cook the heart, separate the heart, unite the heart, sow the heart. Thus, you shall have the heart that does not perish.

86". Our courage is believing in God.
Our intelligence is praying to God.
Our learning is praising God.
Our salvation is eating God.

87. The cup of iniquity is full or nearly full, and shall soon be poured over the earth like a fire that shall consume all the works of men, and there shall remain nothing but smoking ruins. Shall the survivors understand then?
«Let us do well what we have to do in this world, let us not believe in it and let us expect nothing of it.»

87'. What we consider as qualities that allow us to live and organize ourselves in this world are, in reality, the defects that distance ourselves from God and from his salvation. Who shall understand that, and who shall remedy it before the judgement that shall reduce all our works to ashes?
«Let us do well what we have to do in God, let us believe in his fruit and let us expect from it salvation.»

88. Is it not the height of the pride and blindness of the scholars and the intelligent of the world that they mean to seek God outside themselves, and that they want at all costs to reduce him to an equation or to a power exploitable by themselves and for themselves?

88'. True learning and intelligence are the experience of our impotence, the acceptance of our weakness and the awareness of our nullity outside of God. They are also the hope in God's help, the faith in his almighty and the love of his brilliant purity.

89. Those are lost, for they go to the dispersion of destructive madness.

89'. Those are saved, for they go to the union of creative wisdom.

90. The madness of the world, then, is to place oneself on the outside of God and remain there in order to examine him with curiosity from outside, in the senseless hope of surprising him and apprehending him.

90'. Divine wisdom is thus also to attract God into us so that he reveals himself to us and in us, according to his goodwill and not according to our own.

91. The scholars and the intelligent of the world shall never surprise him outside in his creation, for he mocks the rebels and the impious, and he leads them to blind and deaf death.

91'. God only gives himself over visibly and corporeally to his most submissive sons, in whom he has placed all his love and all his obligingness, for they are the beloved ones of his living and eternal heart.

92. Lucifer wanted to judge God's creation, and he was hurled into hell.
Adam disobeyed God, and he was sent to exile in death.

92'. What fate is set aside, therefore, for the scholars and the intelligent of the world who mean to analyse God and reduce him to their service?

92". The hour of judgement is surely approaching; prepare yourselves, children, and pray, so that your bringing forth be completed on that day. For there shall be no more time allowed for anyone, and the cloud of fire shall consume all filth, and the cloud of water shall separate all faeces from the unique purity.

93. The impious and the treacherous of the world sink and rot more and more in their crimes, which maintain them in the hell of the agony of death.

93'. The well-intentioned and the right-thinking ones of the world rely on their own intelligence and their own will to reform the world and themselves; they thus sink into the infection of pride or of hypocrisy that kill the soul.

93". Only the believers in God ask for the Lord's aid in all the circumstances of their exiled life here below; but they ask for it with humility, with faith, with love, with perseverance, with violence, with despair, with annihilation, which is the true humility that the Lord fertilizes and restores in eternal life.

94. The Names of God undo ascending that which they have done descending. Thus, they must not be twisted or paraded, as the ignorant ones who do not know what descends to earth nor what ascends to heaven, do.

94'. God's children are taught by God. The children of the world are taught by the world. The difference is enormous, but our eyes are blind, and our hearts are darkened by the fall.

95. Are we not sent by God and charged with preparing the royal way for the holiest coming of the victorious and glorious Lord, who shall subject the whole earth to his law of love and peace?

95'. Do we not have in us the Spirit of Elijah, and are we not the precursor of the Lord resurrected in his glory, who comes into the darkened world for the judgement so dreaded by some and so hoped for by others?

95". We call the believers in God and we call back God's children, but we have no-one to convince in the world.
So, let him who hesitates and who doubts, then, ask God for a sign in his heart, which shall enlighten him completely!

96. Incapable of fighting like dogs to get close to the rubbish of the world, how shall we subsist here below if the Lord does not lend us his helping and all-powerful hand?

96'. Poverty looks well after God's children, but wretchedness kills everyone. «The Lord's Providence watches over his own, day and night, never tiring.»

97. The impious and the hypocrites are excluded from this Book, and nothing good shall come to them of it, for their malice shall never penetrate it; rather, it shall fall back on them and crush them in the end.

97'. O Lord of justice! let the sack of darkness envelop them tightly all over, and let the filthy mud turn them blind, deaf and stupid, until the time of their sincere repentance.

97". O holy and perfect Lord! allow your believers to be comforted in their wait and confirmed in their faith by the Book of your revelations, and allow your children to be guided in their quest and consoled in their hope by the Book of your marvels.

98. We have tricked no-one and we have seized no-one, but we have reminded everyone of the Lord who waits patiently in our darkened hearts.

98'. And we have guided them towards the unique Splendour that enlightens purified hearts. It is an excellent sign for those who understand.

99. O God of the living! aid your children to help and console the poor and abandoned who believe in your holy Name and who hope for your salvation.

99'. It is a magnificent reward to help the poor of God, but very few know it, unfortunately!

100. Many are scandalized, for appearances are deceptive in this world, and they neglect to ask the Lord's advice humbly in their hearts.

100'. They condemn themselves more and more without knowing it, and the redoubled blows of misfortune and death do not lead them back to the Lord of life who embodies himself in the world.

101. We cannot do anything by ourselves, we do not know anything, we do not hear anything and we do not see anything, for the filth of the sin of death envelops us all over, and the devil blows into us envy, vanity, fear and hate without ever tiring.

101'. Are we not weak among the weak, poor among the poor, errant among the errant and blind among the blind? For our will, our learning, our intelligence and our judgement have been ridiculed beyond all expression, and our impotence in the face of evil has revealed itself to be total.

102. If we do not abdicate completely before the Lord of grace and forgiveness, how shall he ever dwell in us? And if he is not established in us, how shall we pray for our enemies, and how shall we free ourselves from the bonds of sin that maintain us in death?

103. Is there not here the traditional and complete teaching of the lordly word, transmitted throughout the ages, since the primary revelation?

104. Those who only see the letter of the revealed Scriptures remain in the darkness of blind faith and fight blindly, in God's name, against the truth of God that flourishes on the earth for the salvation of men.

105. They repel God's children in the name of the Father whom they do not know, and they condemn them in the name of the Son whom they do not possess.

106. The believers get tired of hoping for a problematic and remote salvation, while the necessities of life press in on them all over in this world, for they no longer know that their rescue is achievable from now on with the aid of the incarnate Lord.

107. Are we not of obscure, weak, poor and despised origin in the world?

102'. O mystery of life! here we are sown and fertilized by the Almighty after our annihilation before his Splendour; and we are already stirring with his marvellous life, awaiting the hour of our rebirth in his imperishable and glorious light.

103'. The divine word neither adds to nor takes away anything from his magnificent creation, but rather confirms itself in all times and in all places.

104'. Is it not obvious to those who do God's will and accomplish his work here below? For they penetrate the wise and holy word, and the divine word penetrates them and enlightens them totally.

105'. For those who compromise with the world no longer hear the voice of the Spirit, and the reasoners have replaced God's prophets, and the intelligent have driven out his sages and his saints.

106'. O enormity of the divine proposal revealed once more to fallen men! How many shall abandon the pursuit of the darkened world to seek the light that engenders the holy and perfect Saviour?

107'. And is he not of divine origin, all-powerful, dripping with riches and adored in heaven and on earth?

108. We are ill from your quest, Lord, and in mortal agony from your absence, for the world and its distractions disgust us, and our desire is in you alone at present.

108'. Rain, rain, Lord of benediction, so that we are radiant with your light of life and so that we are remade in your holy and perfect image.

108". Let us re-read untiringly the wise and holy words, for each time it shall be like dew that is ever more abundant and ever more nourishing for our hearts.

All the Universe and we ourselves are darkness and death without your love, Lord.

While without our love, you remain alive and radiant forever before our wretched mortal agony.

O my Lord and my God! through your love for us that is infallible, do not allow our love for you to falter. O my King! do not let our faces ever again turn away from your face, until you enter us and until we penetrate you for ever.

AMEN

(This is the verse of the dog or of faithfulness, which reminds us of humility, faith and love in the Lord.

It is also the verse of the blessing and the acquisition that provides us with God's abundance.)

It is by approaching him, like the living stone rejected by men but chosen and precious before God, that you too, like living stones, form a spiritual house.

PETER

O peoples, men born of the earth! you who have abandoned yourselves to drunkenness, to sleep and to ignorance of God, be abstemious, stop wallowing in debauchery, bewitched as you are by brutish sleep!

HERMES TRISMEGISTUS

BOOK XXXVII

The multitude of men make themselves useful; I alone am inept, similar to a pariah. I alone am different from other men because I venerate the nourishing Mother.
LAO TSE

The bread of God is that which descends from heaven and which gives life to the world.
JESUS

ÉTUVE RIEN

1. He who studies the Book is promised to life, whatever his appearance is in the world.

2. When we approach the Lord and his holy truth of life, we shall be turned inside out and shaken like sacks, and all our learning and all our pretension shall fall into the nothingness.

THE BEGINNING

1'. He who repels the Book is promised to death, whatever his assurance is in the world.

2'. For the plenitude of the divine revelation demands our total poverty and our entire freedom of spirit and of heart.

2". The rebellious spirit and those who follow him prefer to remain in death and perish, rather than submit themselves through obeying to love. Shall we succeed where the Lord has failed? And shall we remain there whence he has withdrawn?

3. The wisdom of the world is a game of man's spirit.

3'. The wisdom of God is a game of natural elements.

4. When we begin the quest for God, we shall be imprudent and exposed like birds. When we complete the quest for God, we shall be prudent and hidden like snakes.

5. O priests of the embodied Lord! O faithful of the beloved Mother! come to the Book of renewal that shall make you penetrate the depths, and that shall lead you to the heights of your religions, where the unique light of the unique Love shines.

6. The Lord shall fulfil us in our solitude, and we shall drag the peoples in our wake to his dazzling, perfect glory, so that those who belong to him eternally may be returned to his hands: the loved ones of his heart who come to him in their hearts.

7. O friends! the Lord is hidden in you, and he expects from the faith of your intelligence and from the goodwill of your love that you let him become the all-powerful companion who delivers from the hands of death. Shall you not let yourself be brought to the life by the most expert hands of the Unique One?

8. The powerful ones of the world refuse our work and repel the Book, thinking they discourage us by letting us perish; but the Lord fulfils us in secret with his art and with his love, and here we are richer than the richest, and there are those same rich ones more destitute than the most wretched.

4'. There is a solution to everything for him who has the courage to wait, for everything that is undone on one side is also restored on the other side through the patience of acts of faith.

5'. We propose madly the grace and the love of God to you, and we sow unstintingly his truth and his forgiveness. Shall you not rise like holy manna engendered by God? And shall you not fill his arms stretched out towards you?

6'. O my God! me, a poor wretch, ignorant and weak among all, you fulfil me beyond all bounds, for it is your marvellous way of mocking me and laughing at me, who bemoans so much your beauty and your goodness buried in the heart of my exiled brothers.

7'. We prefer to remain unknown to men on earth and to be recognized by the Lord in heaven; for the glory of the world is a smoke that disperses in the darkness, while the glory of God is a smoke that condenses in the light.

Who knows this at present?

8'. O my Lord! your joy invades me like a sea wall that breaks, and here I am swept away, upside down, all my reason foundered and wobbling like a drunkard, scandalizing the right-thinking ones who look at me with scorn.

And both of us laugh without even being able to say a word to one another!

O miracle of the gift that never runs out!

9. Here we are sick, ageing and leaning more and more towards the tomb, but our soul hopes madly for your help and your favour, O Magnanimous One! who distributes the gold of life to your beloved ones.

10. Your humour is not so cruel, Lord of justice, for the hearts of men are closed by their goodwill to explain and organize the world without your love, without your work, without you, and the ashes of the ruins cover their intelligence and swallow up their courage without their tiring of ignoring you.

11. Let us become blind, deaf, dumb and paralytic, so that the Lord of life that sleeps in us might enter his domain, and that we be made to see, hear, speak and work in him, through him and for him, without concerning ourselves with the blind, deaf, howling and agitated world.

12. We have not hoped for or looked for disciples, nor communities, nor churches, for we have remained turned towards God throughout the time of our quest, and if the disciples come, if the communities appear and if the churches spread, it is because we fade away more and more before the Lord who comes all resplendent with God's salvation.

«One day we shall refuse that which we are offering free at present for all the goods in the world.»

9'. You, the Impeccable and Perfect One, give us back our health, our youth and the immunity of our bodies so that, clothed in your glory, we might praise you in a holy way in your eternity!

10'. God of mad love, you give yourself unstintingly, and we must remain silent and await your great judgement like the impotent and like the poor, carrying your secret that fulfils us beyond all expression. And we already shine with your light, but the darkness does not see it.

11'. He who knows, possesses and touches God's truth no longer has any systems, any recipes, any explanations or any organizations to propose to anyone, for the possessive knowledge of divine love frees him who attains it beyond all bounds known or unknown.

12'. Thus, our offering shall be more and more agreeable to God, for it shall grow constantly with the souls of the believers who hope for his light of life and who embody his good and inexhaustible heart; for it is God alone that becomes human in us and that makes us divine in him through his grace and through his love.

13. Those who ignore God's servant, those who forget him and those who deny him are cut off from God's counsel and from his salvation.

13'. Those fall into the abyss, for they stupidly cut the bond that links them to the heaven of eternity.

14. The community of God's children in each home is subject to God.

14'. And each holy home is in the community of the Lord God.

15. We shall thus pray for our meal:
«Thank you Lord, who delivers yourself for our food under the dark veil of earthly creatures. Make our digestion be accomplished perfectly, so that we receive your precious life and reject the poison of death.»

15'. We shall pray thus for the communion:
«Thank you Lord, who gives yourself to us for our salvation under the luminous veil of the celestial creature. Make your glorious life shine in us forever, after having annihilated the abomination of the sin of death that maintains us in the mortal agony of exile.»

16. If you do not know me when I am flighty...

16'. you shall not find me when I am wise.

17. We are ignorant before triumphant scholars.
We have gone astray before triumphant imbeciles.
We are useless before triumphant workers.
We are mad before triumphant reasonable people.
We are wretched before the triumphant rich.
We are reprobates before the triumphant right-thinking ones.
We are lost before the triumphant self-assured ones.
We are despicable before the triumphant powerful.
We are obscure before the triumphant intelligent.
We are buried before the triumphant restless ones.
We are ashamed before triumphant hypocrites.
We are stupid before the triumphant enlightened ones.
We are incapable before triumphant meddlesome people.
We are dumb before triumphant speechifiers.
We are foolish before the triumphant shrewd.
We are cowardly before triumphant heroes.
We are deserter before triumphant enlisted ones.
We are out of place before the triumphant world.

Is it perhaps also because we are truthful and salutary before the children of the triumphant God?

18. We shall be treated as parasites in our own families, and we shall suffer the reproaches of the reasonable ones because of our quest for the Lord of life.

18'. If we are despised, discouraged and bullied in our holy quest, is it not the mark of Satan that diverts us from the way of salvation?

18". We shall withdraw from the senseless ones who have nothing but discouragement, reproaches and sarcasm to set against our search for God's salvation, and we shall leave them in the hands of Satan, whom they have chosen as counsellor and teacher, for the very absurdity of their condition does not reveal to them the lamentable state in which they lie dying without hope.

19. All that we do for the world gives us no rights over the world, but it increases our duties and our responsibilities towards it.

19'. All that we do for God subjects all his creation to us and renders us free in it.

20. We have all fallen onto a pile of filth where brutes camp out, and which the most intelligent vainly attempt to organize.

20'. The saints propose patience and detachment to us with a view to our future deliverance. Only the sages teach us to separate life from death, in order to live again in the freedom of God's children.

21. Men ignorant of God propose wonderful recipes to us to arrange the rubbish on which we lie dying. But unfortunately! the rubbish remains what it is, and its odour is unbearable and its taste deadly, despite all the systems through which they skilfully mask it.

21'. The Lord God has marked out a mysterious and quite obvious way, so that we might all be able to come out of the mud into which we have fallen through disobedience of his holy commandment. He reveals it to his repentant children who do his will and who accomplish his work.

22. If the Lord withdraws from us and if we rave in our visions and in our words like the deaf and the blind of the profane world, we shall with-

22'. And if the Lord visits us once again, we shall remain silent and secret so as not to expose ourselves to being publicly contradicted by events

draw into silence and we shall become pupils of the deaf and the blind, who shall teach us humility and prudence through their ignorance and through their temerity.

23. We shall avoid all food that is violently corrupted with infection, all that is manufactured and falsified by men, and all that resists us on not offering itself. Thus, we shall not stupidly increase within us and outside of us the heavy load of death.

24. Éléonore comes to the Book quite young, but the Book shall make her really big. Shall the Lord not cover her with his exquisite perfume? She hears and she sees.

25. Our passage here below shall not have been useless if we have succeeded in giving back to humans exiled in the mortal agony of this world the hope of God's salvation and the taste for his immediate quest.

26. We have emphasized the death that holds the world in its blind claws, but we have also pointed out the life that constantly renews itself through it.

that are delayed. And if the Lord induces us to prophesy in the world, we shall resist up to the limits of our strength, in order to be quite sure that it is him that speaks in us, and we ourselves that speak in him.

23'. We shall seek all food that is preserved naturally without rotting, all that is direct and natural, and all that offers itself, coming from the earth and from heaven, so as to increase in us the good odour of life that does not perish. Thus, we shall prepare intelligently the day of resurrection.

24'. It is a marvellous state to be a child of God, but who can maintain oneself in it here below without weakening and without failing?

25'. The Lord shall testify for us in person on the day of the great judgement, and he shall confirm our filial undertaking; and his survivors shall praise us for our fraternal work.

26'. We have recalled the terrestrial lock and the heavenly key that open the door of the abode of blessed life, where God's children rejoice for eternity with the joy of the unique Splendour.

26". Thus, we have deliberately lost our life in this mixed world, in order to save it in the kingdom of God.

27. The simple ones conserve their religion, while waiting to be saved miraculously.

The shrewd ones mock their religion, while waiting to be ridiculed by their own systems.

The mediocre dry out their religion, while waiting to return to dust.

The rebels fight their religion, while waiting to be destroyed by their own rebellion.

The right-thinking ones flatter their religion, while waiting to be praised by it.

The nonbelievers scorn their religion, while waiting to deny themselves.

The skilful ones adorn their religion, while waiting to be crushed by the weight of their complications.

The hypocrites corrupt their religion, while waiting to rot in hell.

The faithful maintain their religion, while waiting to be supported by it.

The unfaithful abandon their religion, while waiting to be abandoned by those they invent for themselves.

The scholars suppress their religion, while waiting to be pulverized by their profane science.

The intelligent explain their religion, while waiting to be refuted by absurdity.

The laity forget their religion, while waiting to lose themselves in the world.

The clerics settle down in their religion, while waiting to be established in heaven.

★

The saints live their religion, while waiting to taste its spiritual juice.

The sages scour their religion, while waiting to find its corporeal substance.

28. The Lord forgives us and makes us see his salvation, despite our straying and despite our crimes.

What forgiveness and what salvation does the Lord propose, then, to men gone astray in death?

28'. Each one gone astray and each criminal can hope to obtain the forgiveness and the salvation of the Lord, if he asks him for them sincerely and tenaciously. What hope and what consolation do we propose, then, to our human brothers?

29. Alas! the chaos of death is not an illusion.

Alas! the rebellious spirit is not an illusion.

Alas! mortal sin is not an illusion.

Alas! the evil that dwells in us is not an illusion.

Alas! the mortal agony of the fallen world is not an illusion.

29'. Fortunately, the promised land is not an illusion.

Fortunately, the Lord of life is not an illusion.

Fortunately, the incarnation of the Living One is not an illusion.

Fortunately, the remedy of life is not an illusion.

Fortunately, the salvation of the repentant world is not an illusion.

30. There shall be a general judgement that shall remunerate each one according to his faith and according to the works of his faith, and all that does not resist the fire shall be reduced to ashes and count for nothing with its author.

30'. Those who have triumphed in the works of the world shall be terrified and dumb with stupor, and their surprise shall be equalled only by their despair at having been so gravely mistaken.

30". The children of God and his saved ones shall be witnesses to the ruin of the shrewd ones and of their final engulfment.

31. We shall seek the Lord of wisdom with the patience of a madman, without letting ourselves be distracted by the fallen world and by its worthless works.

31'. We shall enter the heart of our revealed Scriptures in order to find the hidden pearl, instead of floating on them and running aground in the profane world.

32. Neither the proud nor the delirious who adhere to the false doctrines of the world shall be able to receive the intelligence of the Book, nor take hold of it, nor give it as a reference.

33. We ask for forgiveness three times over of those whom we have offended or harmed during the time of our madness, and we ask God for forgiveness a thousand times over for our offences and for our crimes committed during our straying.

34. It is a sinner who speaks, an ordinary man who seeks God in the middle of the inconveniences of the world, with a wretched profession, without the encouragement or the aid of anyone.

35. We shall not try to fight our persecutors, for we would sink ourselves with them into the stinking mud of death. We shall expose them to the public, we shall pray for them, we shall forgive them, we shall flee them and we shall forget them.

36. Those who only seek to organize themselves better and better in this fallen world forget the kingdom promised by God, and sink deeper and deeper into the exile of mortal agony and dispersion where they shall remain for eternity.

32'. Where are the blacks, where are the whites, where are the yellow ones and where are the red ones that have remained simple and believing, that shall receive the kingdom promised by the Lord and that shall enter his holy heritage?

33'. O miracle of divine love! The right-thinking ones refuse their forgiveness three times over, but the Lord of compassion grants his at the first request, for he is there like a beggar at the door of our heart, waiting for us to agree to open it to him.

34'. So that the most imprisoned, the most abandoned and the most destitute might take courage and not despair of reaching the hidden kingdom that delivers from all sadness, all misery and all evil.

35'. Let us equally pray to God so that he might deliver us from their persecutions by opening for us the gates of the secret garden where hate and death have no access, for where there is pure life, there is also pure love.

36'. Do we not see the vanity of the goodwill of men and the absurdity of their efforts to organize this mixed world of death? Ah! if the believers had the madness to truly believe, they would use their goodwill in seeking God's salvation, and the reign of the Unique One would be quite close!

37. There is great deliverance in becoming like a dead man in the hands of God.

37'. But there is a far greater one in becoming like a living one in his resplendent heart.

38. We must proclaim it openly:
Faith, without the hope of God's salvation, is worthless.
Humility, without the search for God's salvation, is worthless.
Patience, without the practice of God's salvation, is worthless.
For they end up in the pit of death, just like unbelief, just like pride and just like violence, in this world inhabited by evil that does not forgive.

38'. Thus, we do not propose passive resignation before the mortal agony of the world, nor a bestial brutishness before the death that inhabits it, as certain ascetics that have measured the vanity of human works do, but who do not know that God's salvation is the celestial medicine that saves from death and from its procession of infinite worries and despair. Did the prophet not say: «Seek me and live», leaving God to speak?

39. All the labels that the sterilizers of life would like to stick on us shall not add anything to nor subtract anything from the formidable proposition of the Book, which addresses all humans endowed by God with the intelligence necessary for the accomplishment of their rescue here below.

39'. Alas! the judgement has begun and the Book has hardly been born in the world, while men refuse the forgiveness and the salvation of God that is proposed to them in the holy Scriptures, while they turn away from their revealed religions, where they see nothing but superstitions and dead morals.

39". While the world camouflages more and more hypocritically misfortune and death, but from which no-one truly delivers us.

40. Let us search assiduously for the Lord of life, while there is still time for us, for when we collide with the absurd it will be too late. And despite our disguises, we shall find only the false door of drunkenness, or the wall of despair, or the abyss of madness.

40'. When misfortune and death fall upon us, the fine words and the help of our own shall appear to us empty and useless, for our solitude shall be such that our own thoughts and our own works shall seem to us senseless and worthless.

41. Inspiration without action is powerless, and action without inspiration is blind.
The two together make the perfection of the human work.

41'. Art without nature is impotent, and nature without art is blind.
The two united make the perfection of the divine work.

42. The punishment of the wicked shall be to see that their wicked deeds have served for the salvation of the believers without their realizing it, and that they have not harmed anybody but themselves.

42'. The reward of God's children shall be to see that their help has served both for their own salvation and for that of those they helped without hope of a reward.

43. A verse from the Book shall enlighten the true child of God, while the whole Book shall blind the children of the profane world. It is God's justice that makes each one judge oneself without knowing it.

43'. A word, a gesture, teach him who houses in oneself the Spirit of God, while all creation teaches nothing to those who rely on their own intelligence. They make fools of themselves and they do not know it!

44. The triumphant optimists who want to organize the world while denying the misfortune and death that dwell in it send shivers down our spine, for they have raced in order to reach more quickly the pit from which there is no return, and the crowd of blind men acclaims them and follows their lead, singing a hymn of victory that covers the voice of the prophets sent by God.

44'. We are pessimists when we recall the vanity of men's efforts to organize themselves and to save themselves in this fallen world, but we are optimists on recalling God's salvation promised to simple and believing men. Alas! how many still believe in the spiritual and corporeal rescue of man exiled here below, when no-one any longer believes in the ancient fall?

45. «What is one playing at today in the world?» ask the profane ones curious of the void.
And the true believers reply: «We do not know, for the quest for God's salvation prevents us from concerning ourselves with knowing what the world is playing at right now».

45'. Those who neglect the quest for God's salvation commit a crime towards themselves; but those who persecute the seekers of God's salvation commit a crime against all. Is it not also here, the sin that shall not be forgiven? And are they not also here, the accursed ones that shall be thrown into the exterior darkness?

46. O obtuse and ignorant women, take good care not to oppose the quest for God's salvation in the name of your profane little reasons, which prolong your mortal agony in this world, but which do not deliver you from it!

46'. O reasonable and blind women, do not stupidly oppose the holy quest of your husbands, for you would be cut off from God's salvation right from this world, and your punishment would be irremediable! Help them, rather, with love, so as to participate in their reward and in their rescue.

47. Everything serves us if we serve God and his creation uprightly.

47'. The light shall appear like a dot in the darkness and shall grow until the day of God.

48. We must say it and repeat it: the most authentic, the most precise and the most accomplished revelation of the mystery of life and of God's salvation is to be found in the known books of God's prophets and in the unknown books of God's sages. Is our religion not a living symbol of the mystery hidden in all times? Do we no longer see it? Do we no longer hear it?

48'. The Lord of life may well have become incarnate once universally for the salvation of all, and he may well also return once universally for the judgement of all; but we must know at present that he came from the beginning, that he is coming right now and that he shall still come in private for the salvation of some.

49. It is a new and immense revelation that we are making here, so that each believer might take courage and boldly undertake the quest for God's salvation, always present and always possible in this world.

49'. Alas! here also there shall be many called and few chosen, for the majority of believers prefer to remain lamenting past salvation and in the hope of the salvation to come, rather than undertaking the quest for the present salvation.

50. The nonbelievers that attempt to force God's secret, and those that try to violate holy nature, shall be destroyed from within and from without by their own malice and by their own rebellion.

50'. The believers who hear the word of God and who accomplish it by helping holy nature shall be saved within and without by their own simplicity and by their own obedience.

51. God has given each one enough intelligence and enough simplicity to easily accomplish his own

51'. Alas! many scorn their share of intelligence and become like brutes before the teaching of the

rescue here below by penetrating the revealed word.

52. Let us pray so that the terrifying urgency of the quest for God's salvation becomes obvious to us before it is too late to undertake it.

53. God's salvation is the most experimental science there could be, for it is the science of the God that has created the world and the universes that surround it, and this one does not rave abstractly in the void!

Unique One. Many also scorn their share of simplicity and become like conceited monkeys before the word of God.

52'. For hell shall be made of this regret, and even more, of the astounding ease of the salvation that shall have been proposed to us vainly in this world.

53'. We repeat the enormous revelation because it is incredible: God sends his holiest essence that becomes incarnate in the purest substance of the world for the salvation of all fallen creation.
Let him understand who can.
Let him experience who would.

53". Let us consider CHRISTMAS. Let us penetrate CHRISTMAS. Let us imitate CHRISTMAS. Let us adore CHRISTMAS. Let us sing CHRISTMAS.

54. Without the blessing of God, we are totally powerless to manifest here below the life of the Lord of resurrection.

55. The whole of God's creation can participate in God's salvation through the mediation of the sons of God. Thus, animals, vegetables and even minerals can be restored to the glory and the immortality of the Unique One; no-one must be ignorant of this nor forget it.

56. Let us rejoice that there are several of us to help one another in the quest for God's salvation, for he who reminds us of it now was alone in rediscovering the ancient path

54'. The light of God shall first fertilize our interior darkness; then, our darkness shall manifest the light of God.

55'. Is it not because of the effect of the Almighty's grace that the Book is given to simple men of goodwill in God? And is it not because of the effect of his justice that the Book is rejected and scorned by the wicked, by the shrewd and by the hypocrites?

56'. Let us consider the state of him who shows us the path and who separates for us the brambles and thorns that have accumulated through the negligence of the guardians of God's

invaded by the brambles of ignorance and oblivion.

57. If the world ignores us or rejects us, let us not struggle against the world to be acknowledged or accepted by it. Let us turn instead towards the heavenly Father and towards the earthly Mother who shall shower us with the very real goods of life.

58. Many of the saints themselves have neither seen nor touched the Lord embodied in this world; but they are blessed, for they have believed without seeing or feeling, and their reward finally shines in heaven.

59. The malice of the wicked allows them to deceive and to steal from men for a time, but it shall never allow them to deceive nor to steal from God, be it only for a second. That is totally assured.

60. The impious and the dead overflowing with energy to deny the revelation of the sons of God and to obstinately oppose God's salvation collapse lamentably when misfortune brushes them with its dark wing and when sickness overcomes them for a short while.

61. Let us run away from people that are sinister, dull, lacking enthusiasm and encouragement, for they are certainly not God's, and we shall not succeed in rousing them, while they

way. Let us consider his footprints that mysteriously mark the route that we must follow.

57'. Thus, by ignoring us or by moving us away from the showy goods of profane life, the world saves us from the impasse of death and orients us towards the eternal goods of life without mixture, where the Lord rests with his beloved ones.

58'. Very few among the saints themselves have seen and touched the Lord embodied in this world; but they are blessed, for they have believed before seeing and feeling, and their reward already shines on earth.

59'. The stupidity of the shrewd ones permits them to mock the revelation of God's salvation and to oppose it, but it shall never permit them to benefit from it, not even for a second. That is totally certain.

60'. All their strength is made up of the negation of divine life and of the rejection of God's salvation that are proposed to them here below. Thus, they are like rags when the devil abandons them, for divine life is withdrawn from them, and they are like puppets emptied of all substance that lie dying, abandoned by all.

61'. Let us seek our brothers in the faith and in the hope of God's salvation, and let us talk to them of the holy Mysteries that justify our daily quest, and let us rejoice together at

shall know quite well how to drive us to despair and to drag us down into their blind and deaf mortal agony.

62. Let us run away from the world and its multiple cares, for the struggle to have the right to die there in misery is too exhausting and too distracting from the quest for God's salvation, which is all that truly matters.

63. The fallen world is, in reality, the filth under which is hidden the true world that we must rediscover and magnify in God.

the enormity of God's promise that justifies our present hope and enthusiasm.

62'. Let us withdraw into the peace and solitude of our holy communities, so as to be able to concentrate all our attention on the quest for God's salvation. When we have found it, we shall be able to return to the world, if it suits us.

63'. We preach the earthly heaven and the heavenly earth, and not the disembodied heaven nor the exiled earth, as do the extremists who separate, but who do not know how to unite.

63". We desire the united kingdom,
the complete kingdom,
the kingdom of God.

64. One thing is certain: if we believe ourselves more intelligent than God, and if we think we are above his envoys, we have gone astray and are lost without remission in the exile of death.

65. We are all lost in this mixed world of death, and our end is written in the ordure that dwells in us.

64'. Is it not our revealer, our founder, who proposes to us, with God's permission, the heavenly medicine that is the Saviour miraculously embodied for the salvation of God's children?

65'. Thus, if anyway we are lost, what do we risk by devoting our little reprieve of life to seeking God's salvation, which alone can save us from the dispersion of death?

66. Is it not our founder who tells us these surprising, overwhelming and stupefying words: «All this is present before your eyes and within reach of your hands, every day of your life. Keep watch, then, in order to see, and pray in order to know, before being swallowed up by death»?

67. You think you are seeing what we are and you rejoice in it for us and for you.
«If you do not know me in my baseness…»

68. He who contemplates his Lord and who humbly calls him to his aid in all circumstances is more holy than all humanity that tries courageously to reform itself and to organize itself in the world without managing to do so.

69. The Book was written with the inspiration of the Spirit. The author is as ignorant and as unprovided for on completing it as he was on beginning it.

66'. But we see what we are not, and we are saddened by it for you and for us.
«you shall not find me in my nobleness.»

67'. We must not exhaust ourselves struggling uselessly against ourselves nor against the world, but must rather seek without respite God and his salvation, which shall deliver us from the mortal agony of death perpetually maintained here below.

68'. Perhaps all is dark?
Perhaps all is light?
Perhaps all is light and dark?
God alone knows!

69". The quest for God and his salvation is quite long and quite disappointing, and men prefer to rely reasonably on the work of their hands to subsist and to organize themselves here below.
For one must be mad to believe in God and in his salvation, and one must be insane to seek them in this world. And yet they are here waiting for us! Is everything not clearly taught in our sublime and profound revealed religion?

Do they know the mysteries of Nature? Nevertheless, they write.

KORAN

Those who know Nature do not try to express it in words, and those who try to do so show that they do not know it.

CHUANG TZU

BOOK XXXVIII

If this endeavour or this work comes from men, it shall collapse by itself; but if it comes from God, you shall be unable to destroy it. Do not run the risk of fighting against God himself.

GAMALIEL

One must obey God rather than men.

PETER

| UNE VÉRITÉ | THE END |

1. Our only merit, our only knowledge and our only intelligence is to leave the Lord of life to act as he pleases inside us and outside of us.

1'. Have we not revived the ashes of faith for multitudes? And have we not put the origin of salvation back in sight for a few?

1". All our laws and all our prohibitions are nothing more than hypocrisy and wickedness if our hearts are not subject to the law of love of the Perfect One.

2. If someone means to excommunicate us in the name of God or in the name of God's truth…
If someone execrates us or curses us…

2'. we shall ask him if he truly possesses the communion of God, that is, if he sees it, if he feels it and if he tastes it, not in image, but in substantial reality.

3. The true children of God's word are those who are neither enlisted, nor asleep, nor labelled, nor emasculated, nor reassured, nor accustomed, nor slaves, nor dead in the world.

3'. The true children of God's word are those who remain free, alert, loving, sober and believing, and who seek the all in all things, even in nothing.

4. Did we not announce accurately and well in advance the fall and the failure of the regime without God?

4'. Did we not warn the sleeping ones of the geological catastrophes that are beginning to torment the world gone astray?

5. Do we not foresee the cosmic catastrophes that shall follow and that shall shake the rebellious world?

5'. Do we not glimpse, alas! the destruction and fragmentation of the rebellious world through its accursed science?

6. O my Lord and my God! at least save your loving, obedient children, gather them under your wing, and pass onto them the remains of the impious and the senseless ones who defy you at present.

6'. O my Lord and my God! open the spirit and the heart of your loving and obedient children, so that they might recognize their holiest Mother and Father united in the Saviour and that they might live before you.

6". O my Lord and my God! open the spirit and the heart of the rebels and fools who stupidly pillage your creation and who mercilessly attack it, before the blow that shall shatter them into the death without return.

7. If the right-thinking ones complain of not understanding the Book, we shall ask them if they understand the words of their revealed Scriptures better.

7'. If they understood the words of their holy Scriptures, they would also understand the words of the Scripture revealed anew.

8. Elizabeth was asleep, but the prince wakes her and she shall sing a new canticle. Does she not already read openly from the Book?
«She digs the mine and finds jewels that illuminate.»

8'. The sage does violence to no nature, but allows each to fulfil his own as happily as possible on this earth of exile.

9. O right-thinking ones! who introduce yourselves to others as an example of holiness, can you tell us why Jesus preferred the illiterate, the drinkers, the tax collectors, the pros-

9'. Vanity, hypocrisy and avarice form the stinking and explosive mixture that shall scatter you in the mud of hell, where your place has been marked since the beginning of your

titutes and the thieves to the company of the Pharisees, your old models? Is it not because of the stench that has also become yours at present?

10. On not speaking of the necessity of worldly things, nor of the urgency of things of this century, the Book shall be neither received nor understood by those who organize themselves in the mortal agony of the world, nor by those who stagnate in it.

11. Which is this Pallandt family gifted with the grace of the Holy Spirit? Does Granny Marthe not also come to the Book after having doubted? And does she not become an apostle of the truth of the Lord embodied in the world?
«She shall be reassured, for she has feared.»

12. All is illicit and goes to malediction for those who are dying in the oblivion and the absence of God. These are like dead coals and are, unfortunately, legion in the world.

13. Did the learned masters not also repel the Book as being alien to their revelations, their traditions and their sciences?

14. The Book is therefore neither flesh nor fish, neither stone nor plant, and nevertheless it is.

triumphant wickedness; for you have put yourselves before God and you have substituted your profane words for his revealed word.

10'. On speaking of the necessity of heavenly things and of the urgency of the eternal thing, the Book shall be received and understood by those who seek the exit from their dark prison and by those who hope for God's salvation.

11'. Thérèse, Molly and Marguerite germinate in secret in their hearts, but what blossoming is the Lord not capable of producing before our eyes? They come last, but they shall be in front, and nobody shall be able to shake their faith long matured in secret.
«They shall flow like the springs of the great rivers.»

12'. All is licit and goes to benediction for those who live in the memory and the presence of God. But where are those whose heart shines and warms like the spring sun?

13'. Alas! here we are like an ignorant master among the scholars of the world, and like the lowliest brother among the believers who seek the Lord and his kingdom here below.

14'. What is, then, the thing that is neither flesh nor fish, neither stone nor plant, and that nevertheless IS?

15. Might the wretched, the weak, the imbeciles, the afflicted, the abandoned, the desperate and the excommunicated perhaps like to cast a fraternal glance over the Book, so that it at least serves the most disinherited by helping them to bear their mortal agony in this assured and learned world?

15'. How wisely the Lord God brings us back to the mud and the dregs of the world where the pearl promised to his love lies hidden!

O miracle of the true wisdom that deceives the proud ones and the triumphant ones who dominate here below!

16. O believers! have the heart and the spirit to secretly support the true poor who pray to God in their hearts for their benefactors, if you have the intelligence to seek them and to discover them in the world where they are hidden.

16'. Let us give in secret, consoling the true poor of God, and let us receive fraternally that which they offer us in return, so that their soul also rejoices at the gift freely granted.

16". The hypocrites who give proudly receive their retribution, which is the curse of the bad poor whom they publicly humiliate.

17. The possession of earthly glory and riches shines and flaunts itself in the profane world.

17'. The possession of divine glory and goods shines and conceals itself in God's secret.

18. The Lord instructs us day to day through thousands of meetings, thousands of events and thousands of occasions, if we are sufficiently awake to understand his lessons and sufficiently intelligent to take advantage of them, for even the ashes teach us when our eye is open.

18'. If a job is repulsive to us or stupefies us, let us have the courage to change it rather than suffer the disgust and brutishness that kill the soul. Prayer and praise to God with bread and water are worth more than mindlessness with a full feeding-trough.

19. Our faith is not held in an abstract idea, nor in an elusive ideal, nor in the great number of faithful, nor in human works, nor in the goods of this world, nor in profane or

19'. Our faith is held in the certainty of the divine nature embodied in the flesh of the world.

Our faith is nourished by the hope of rediscovering this divine nature

religious honours, nor men's sciences, nor in the powers of the ascetics.

buried in the sin of death.

Our faith is brought to life by the effusion of the Holy Spirit that fertilizes the divine nature and thus remakes us as children of God, in the image of God himself.

20. Holy MOTHER OF GOD, guide our quest and light up our way in the darkness of this world of exile, so that we reach through your grace to the Lord embodied, who shall deliver us from the sin of death where we are in wretched mortal agony!

20'. Holy MOTHER OF GOD, be so good as to reveal yourself to your loving and candid children, by parting for them alone, with the permission of our Lord God, the dark veil that misleads the wicked and the proud sectarians of the darkened world!

21. Let us rejoice if the world disappoints us, if it abandons us, if it repels us, if it ruins us, if it starves us, if it hates us, if it bullies us, if it afflicts us, if it strips us bare, if it imprisons us, if it crucifies us, for it is the Lord who gives us a sign to seek his salvation and his way.

21'. Did we not remain until the end, subject to the duties, the temptations and the persecutions of the profane world, so that nobody could excuse himself from not seeking God and his salvation, whatever his state be here below?

Happy are those that have vanquished the world by fleeing it, and blessed are those that have vanquished the world by enduring it!

22. He who adores the Lord of life is nourished by the Lord of life; it is a marvel that is natural to him, but few understand it here below.

22'. The holy books shall seem empty and boring to us at the beginning of our quest, but in the end they are the only ones among all that we shall find precious and fascinating.

23. My joy overflows like a lively torrent, and the desire for your love is all that subsists in me, for the world is as though drowned by your light that rises from everywhere, O Lord of resurrection!

23'. My joy is my agreement with your holy will, O Lord of invading life! Thus, my joy is your joy, my will is your will, my love is your love, and here I am in you, through you, for you inexpressibly.

24. Ah! Lord, I sink.

24'. Oh! Lord, I emerge.

25. You begin.

25'. And you finish.

26. It is a great darkness.

26'. And it is a great light.

27. I was dead.

27'. And I live.

28. Cry, dying ones of the world.

28'. And then rejoice!

29. For the grace is still hidden.

29'. But love already illuminates all the earth.

30. Let us clap our hands, dance and laugh before the Lord God who sees us.

30'. For death has been swallowed up by life, and the filth has returned to nothingness.

31. Come on! let us wake up and hear what is being said to us.

31'. Let us weep with joy at God's victory that erases our mortal blemish.

32. Here, a great silence, like the secret frontier of the promised kingdom.

32'. And then the song of the angels that never ends.

33. It is a lot of water…

33'. and it is a little earth.

34. The deluge of grace…

34'. prepares the heavenly harvest…

34". celebrated in the eternal banquet.

35. Each one, if he so desires, may express his desire in our sacred plenary meetings, so that if the Lord hears it and approves of it, he is fulfilled.

35'. He who thus receives a gift from the Lord must also confess it before his brothers and thank the Lord in private, and then praise him with them.

36. The hypocrites, the right-thinking ones, the blind sectarians and the established profiteers shall reject the Book that denounces them and that they do not penetrate, for they do not have in them the Spirit that inspired it.

36'. The true believers, the good-hearted religious ones, the simple and the poor of God, shall receive the Book that serves them, for the Spirit that dwells in them shall recognize itself in the Book.

37. The hypocrites, the dried out ones, the sectarians, the self-assured ones and the triumphant shall answer on the day of judgement for the disgusted, for the repelled, for the revolted, for the desperate and for the crushed; and their astonishment shall be immense on learning that they are responsible for those whom they have aroused through their false behaviour, that is, through their dishonesty, through their greediness, through their cruelty, through their pride and through their criminal blindness.

37'. Let us strive never to put anyone off from the quest for God's salvation, be it through our exactingness, through our negligence, through our pretension, through our judgement or through our intolerance; let us rather strive to be living examples for all those who do not hear God's voice or hesitate in their heart and above all for those who are revolted at the attitude of the false believers who abound right now in the degenerated world.

38. If we are not with God, who shall be with us?

38'. And if we are with God, who shall be against us?

39. All that does not go to God ends up in absurdity, of which death is the most obvious demonstration.

39'. All that goes to God ends up in the permanence of life, of which the resurrection is the most obvious demonstration.

40. Let us take the Book to prison, to hospital, to the barracks, where we have the necessary time to become reconciled with God and with his salvation; but let us also take it with us in our free time, and let us associate it with our Sunday recreation, so that the day of the Lord be doubled and even tripled for us.

40'. The Book replies marvellously to those who know how to question it in the simplicity of their heart. It is cause for astonishment in the believers who remember the forsaken word, and it is cause for admiration in those who hear it a little in the inside.

41. Have I gone astray by praying to you in the inside, Lord?

41'. No, my friend, for only those who pray to my appearances to obtain my outer layers go astray.

42. Have I made a mistake in praising you in the inside, my God?

42'. No, my child, for only those who praise my creatures giving thanks for the crumbs from my table are mistaken.

43. Have I lost my way seeking you in the inside, O Living One?

43'. No, my son, for only those who seek me outside to find my inside loose their way.

44. Why do you leave us in poverty here below, overflowing Lord?

44'. It is to gratify you better in my kingdom, ungrateful children.

45. Why do you leave us in sadness here below, compassionate Lord?

45'. It is to console you better in my kingdom, wicked children.

46. Why do you leave us in ignorance here below, learned Lord?

46'. It is to instruct you better in my kingdom, malicious children.

47. Why do you abandon us here below, loving Lord?

47'. It is to cherish you better in my kingdom, forgetful children.

48. Why do you leave us in mortal agony in this fallen world, living Lord?

48'. It is to revive you better in my kingdom, disobedient children.

49. Why do you let us perish in death here below, mighty Lord?

49'. It is to instruct you better through the absurdity of exile, revolted children.

50. On giving us grace, the Lord encourages all humanity to persevere towards him, for we are entirely covered by sin, our blindness is total and our merit is non-existent in this world darkened by the fall.

50'. Those who speak of us with pride shall be mistaken, and those who speak of us with scorn shall be equally misled.
The Lord knows us, and we recognize the Lord.

51. Let us take the necessary time for the quest for God and his salvation, thus blind and deaf greed shall not keep us in the slavery of the world.

51'. Let us work for what is necessary to us and let us cease when the superfluous appears, for it is a gift from God that must manifest itself naturally.

52. Let our dwelling remain as unknown as possible to the rich and powerful of the world, let our table put them off by its frugality and its simplicity, and let none of them just walk into it in an inconsiderate way with the insolence that characterizes them!

52'. Let our house be always open to the simple and the poor of God, let our table be welcoming to their natural fraternity, and let none of them ever have to wait at our door!

53. Only the ignorant lose their life to become famous, or to make their fortune, or to organize the mud, or to remain slaves, or to become tramps in this world.

53'. The only necessary thing is sufficient in order to have the superfluous, and the superfluous is sufficient in order to have the only necessary thing. And the two together are sufficient to have one's life saved.

54. The greatest intelligence in oneself is like the greatest wisdom in the world and like the greatest madness in God.

54'. The greatest intelligence in God is like the greatest wisdom in God and the greatest madness in the world.

55. The intelligent, the scholars, the rebellious and the triumphant who think to reach God's secret without God's consent, remain in the worst blindness, for it is the greatest illusion there could be.

55'. The conquerors, the financiers, the workers and the organizers who think to establish themselves and prosper in the world without God's help are really mistaken, for it is the greatest disillusion there could be.

56. The mediocre, the self-assured, the bewildered and the beasts who think to rest and ruminate tranquilly in the world without God's peace remain in the worst drunkenness, for it is the greatest precariousness there could be.

56'. The hypocrites, the shrewd, the skilful and the sly who think to manage and save themselves in the world without God's blessing have gone astray in the worst form, for it is the greatest deception there could be.

57. Ah! if we might understand just once the urgency of our rescue, nothing nor nobody would any longer be able to distract us from the quest for God's salvation, and we would break with the world without hesitation and without regret, totally and definitively.

57'. The words of the prophets are true, true, true. The words of the Lord are alive, alive, alive. But alas! we are foolish, foolish, foolish, for we prefer the perpetual agony of death to the life of God's chosen ones that never ends.

58. Are the arts not currently diverted, ridiculed and debased by the multitude of mediocre and incapable ones who have invaded and contaminated them shamelessly?

58'. Is the ART of God not the most mislead, the most ridiculed and the most debased by the mediocre and incapable ones who have invaded and contaminated it in the world?

58". The intelligent and the imbeciles have joined together to ridicule the arts of the world and the ART of God, debased by the incapable ones, instead of rejecting the incapable ones and examining the arts proposed to them by the true artists and the true prophets of God.

59. The thing comes from the inside to the outside, but it also goes from the outside to the inside, and it remains in itself for eternity.

59'. Things say the word, but the word is not said by things.

Words say the thing, but the thing is not said by words.

60. The gift of God remains solitary in our heart and in our hands, for this people has become stupid by the sheer force of believing in its own intelligence, and it revels in the works of death, and it repels the work of life that it is offered to it freely.

60'. We shall withdraw, then, from this nation to which we are sent, but which does not want us, so that our preaching is not the object of scandal or curse for anyone, since it cannot be the object of edification and benediction for anyone in it.

60". If the Lord is with this nation, we shall certainly be excluded; but if he is with us, shall this nation not also be excluded? Let the Lord come to an arrangement, then, directly with it, or let him arrange it with its too intelligent and its too shrewd ones, and let our hands be clean of its corrupted and rebellious blood!

61. O holiest lords of resurrection, sons of God the Eternal One! consider our goodwill and our obedience in this matter, and consider the ill will of the donkeys who refuse the water offered to them with your aid and with God's permission.

61'. O holiest lords of eternal life and vicars of almighty God! consider the refusal and the malice of these people who conceitedly think they are able to manage alone in the chaos of death, and give us souls capable of receiving God's seed.

62. We shall not mistreat the impious who are amongst us, but we shall

62'. The peoples, the families and the individuals who shall deny and

leave them if they are more numerous, or indeed they shall leave us if we are more numerous. And in any case, we shall avoid settling amongst them and we shall avoid their settling amongst us.

lose the revelation of their divine filiation shall stagnate in the life of beasts, shall become the slaves of absurdity and shall disappear in the despair and brutishness of death forever. They shall be taken to be a beginning whereas they shall in fact be an end.

63. This people believes it has become so intelligent that it even refuses to examine the obviousness of that which is proposed to it. Thus, it has become the most stupid, and its inheritance shall be given to the other peoples that have preserved their faith in God's salvation, and it shall be a slave among them until it has excluded the impious that lead it to degradation, to brutishness and to death.

63'. Worthiness, probity, justice, talent, piety, charity, holiness and wisdom should be considered and placed before wealth, for it is they that make wealth, and not wealth that makes them. Let us not waste our time in becoming famous, rich or powerful in the world, for we would be deceived and excluded in the end. Let us rather train ourselves to seek God's salvation, which gives life to those who find it here below.

64. If we truly and exclusively search for the unique necessary thing, which is God's salvation and his blessed kingdom, the blind world shall not help us, but quite the contrary, it shall harass and discourage us by every means in its power.

64'. And if we persevere in the quest for the door, the lock and the key of deliverance, we shall be insulted by the world that shall treat us like idlers, like cowards, like fools and like enemies, and shall finally reduce us to despair and begging so that we have no other recourse but to turn to the Lord of life.

65. Our quest for the divine treasure requires such an effort and such work for such a long time, night and day, that all the courageous ones and all the workers of the world even give up the idea of undertaking it, and that is why we are seen as idlers and as useless in the eyes of the world, which can neither believe nor understand that God's glory rests in us alone.

65'. Our quest shall be solitary, long and hard in the darkness of this world, so as to test our faith, our steadfastness and our courage, before we are granted God's gift; we shall have to expect no aid and no counsel from the profane world, but only the aid and the counsel of God and his sons, who live in him forever.

66. When the implacable wall of absurdity and despair rises up before us in the world, we shall go forward all the same, through the effect of absurd and desperate faith, until we touch the obstacle with our hands and therefore discover, to our immense surprise, that it is a mirage set up by the devil to discourage us from persevering up to the kingdom of God.

66'. When the marvellous body of the triumphant Lord appears before our bedazzled eyes, we shall stretch out our purified hands sacredly, through the effect of grateful and wild faith, in order to find out, to our immense joy, the tangible reality of the risen glorious one who lives beyond all death.

67. We come to the Lord in destitution and desolation, but the Lord showers us with his love and his joy that never run out, if we are found clean within and without.

67'. The Book is a channel, but it is also a bridge. It is a sea, but it is also an arch. It is a wind that blows, but it is also an earthly sun that gives light.

68. It must indeed be admitted, alas! woman, lost and rebellious by nature, appears radically opposed to the quest for God's salvation, and he who drags her along with him in his quest drags a ball and chain that discourage him and that bruise him to nobody's benefit.

68'. Courageous and blind Marthas are legion in the world. It is they who keep us in our labelled place in death, it is they who organize the chaos without realizing that it always has to be done again, it is they who decorate our prison and who forget that one can come out of it.

68". Their work and their dedication are a blessing if they unburden us of worldly cares and if they therefore help us to better devote ourselves to the quest for God's salvation. But if their superficial and contemptible judgement condemns us and plagues us in our holy quest, it is a curse from which we must flee wholeheartedly; for it is better for us to seek life in the desert and live than to be served in the world and die.

69. The work of men and of the world combines diversity and differences, and that is why it must always be done again, even if it is carefully accomplished thousands and thousands of times.

69'. The work of God joins unity and uniqueness, and that is why it need never be done again when it is accomplished once entirely by a wise child of God.

69". When the smoke rises from the earth and covers the ground as it accumulates, it shall be time for the chosen ones to make their way to the places reserved by God, and it shall be high time for the called ones to remember our warnings, but it shall be too late for the impious ones, who shall collide with one another in the invading darkness.

And they struck blind the people that were at the entrance to the house, from the smallest to the tallest, and they tired themselves out in vain seeking the door.
GENESIS

Flee to the mountain, for fear that you might perish.
GENESIS

BOOK XXXIX

> *Ruin is coming. They shall seek peace and there shall be none. There shall be misfortune upon misfortune, and news upon news.*
> EZEKIEL

> *On the first blow from his thundering sword, all the mountains and the earth shall tremble in fear, for the disorder and crimes of men pierce the vault of the heavens.*
> OUR LADY OF LA SALETTE

VERTE UNIE

1. The Lord God is our witness, as are Emmanuel and his family, that we have patiently, humbly and freely offered his salvation to the world, which repels us without even examining what we propose.

2. But the Lord prohibits us even from laughing so, and we remain in God's hand as a servant of God, as a child of God, as a friend of God, as a son of God, until the world feels God's wrath and weeps in the terror of smoke and of stones, of blood and bones, of fire and water. Until the world calls for help, and it howls, and it begs, and no-one answers except for the demented laughter of death.

3. Thierry, the washer-man, has been washed; Thierry, the prickly one, has been smoothed; Thierry,

THE ISLAND

1'. At present we should laugh and mock the world, and propose to it the insane and empty works of the world, at the price of the heavy gold and silver of the world, which we shall then throw at the head of the foolish world.

2'. When the Lord gives us the powers of his house we shall attract many new believers, but those who come right now in the darkness and in solitude shall be established the first among all, and nobody shall take from them their holy reward. O you who come to the Lord of life and forgiveness! bless those through whom you come to him and you shall be blessed by the Father, by the Mother and by the children!

3'. The vicar received the revelation of the lordly secret like a holy sacrament, which he carries at pres-

the slow one, has overtaken everyone, and at present his faith in God serves as an example to others. The Lord shall certainly confirm him through the goods of the earth and through the goods of heaven. This man has acquired the true intelligence that shall not be taken away from him.

4. O my Lord and my God! you test us cruelly up to the end of our quest and to the end of our straying, for we are misled, and we seek you on the outside in the world instead of seeking you within ourselves.

5. Man alone or woman alone do nothing, but the two united multiply according to God's order, and the children are the visible image in the world of the image which is hidden in the parents.

6. If we try to obtain for ourselves and as by fraudulent means the goods of this world, we shall reap only its leprosy. But if we ask honestly of our Lord and master that which is necessary for us, we shall receive it without harm.

7. God's saints are single, but God's sages are married.

8. O pure essence included in the pure substance that moans with fallen man! allow the Book that speaks once again of your love to appear in the

ent in his heart, and he shines even for the blind who come to him from everywhere. The Lord visits his true priests and he enlightens them through his genuine priests. He who receives discovers him who gives, and remains silent.

4'. «If two of us are joined together in my name, you shall find me», said the Lord. These are great words that we must examine carefully, for it is also said: «What God has joined together, let no man put asunder». And man and woman shall thus be joined together in a holy way for the quest for God.

5'. These words are true for everything we do here below, and we must take good note of it, so that the actions of our faith produce the hoped-for fruit.

6'. Let us not distance ourselves from the goods that depend directly on God's blessing, so that we are never separated from the Lord of abundance and so that we never think we are self-sufficient, as do the insane ones of the cities.

7'. Happy shall be those who notice this difference, and blessed shall be those who understand it!

8'. O She who is loved and who contains the Loved One! allow the Book of your splendour to magnetize once again the multitude of your

world, so that your mourning children perceive your call once more before the terrifying judgement that is coming.

children who have fallen in the mud, and who wander miserably, reassuring themselves with your old promise, without doing anything to penetrate it or to truly put it into practice.

8". O holiest Father – Mother – Son! please enlighten your dying ones before it is too late.

9. Reliving the sadness and abandonment of the Lord at Easter, has the Book not brought us out of the darkness through verses 28' and 28 of BOOK XXXIV?

9'. On asking ourselves if it was necessary to work in the world in order to maintain our house, have we not been taught by verses 34' and 34 of BOOK XXIV?

9". On doubting still whether it was necessary to abandon our profession in the world in order to serve God, has the Book not confirmed it to us through verses 3 and 3' of BOOK XXVI?

10. On wanting a confirmation of the way of God, has our wife not been taught by verses 14' and 14 of BOOK XXIV?

10'. And still doubting, has she not been convinced by verses 64' and 64 of BOOK IV?

10". Finally, before our obstinacy in wanting to do the right thing in the eyes of the world, have we not received a severe warning through verses 56' and 56 of BOOK XXIV?

11. Therefore, our faith in the help of the highest Father and the worthiest Mother is pathetic and wavering, despite the constant proofs of their love, which surrounds us and supports us lovingly.

11'. And our shame is total, for our weakness is notorious. Are we not incapable of bearing victoriously the slightest tribulation for the love of God? And is our misery not complete for this very reason?

12. How could our own indignity, which the love of the Lord of forgiveness does not disdain to console, not be an immense encouragement for all those who wander in the darkness and desolation of this world of exile?

12'. How could our doubts and our recriminations, which the Lord of abundance does not disdain to satisfy, not be a unique comfort for all those who despair in the mortal agony of this bogged-down world?

13. Your servants and your children are in straitened circumstances, Lord, and if they barely manage to maintain their house it is as if through a miracle that must always be renewed, even though they observe your law and work for the life of everyone.

13'. While the useless and sterile impious ones are handsomely maintained by the world, in proportion to their uselessness and even their harmfulness, for the greatest prebends are reserved for those who work for the death of all.

14. O Lord of intelligence! how long shall you allow to pass for idiots and incapable ones those who serve you and who seek you here below in tears of mortal agony and of hope?

14'. O almighty Lord! how long shall you abandon to beggary those who neglect to insure their fortune in this world in order to seek you better in themselves?

14". O Lord of justice! how long shall you allow those who prefer to pray to you and praise you rather than to extricate themselves from this world infected by death to be trampled on and reduced to nothing?

15. In all that we sow and in all that grows and multiplies, let us think about the share of God's servants and poor, and our goods shall grow and multiply in proportion to that share granted to the children of the Highest.

15'. As for the money and gold that we receive, earn or steal, let us give a generous portion to God's children, so that the curse and leprosy attached to them do not fall on us and do not make their dwelling in us.

15". We say that we must help God's prophets, God's priests, God's children and God's poor, whose blessing shall purify us of our sins. But we do not say that we must help the world's prophets, the world's priests, the world's children and the world's poor, whose curse shall cover us in filth.

16. Let us offer every day of our lives a new praise to the Lord of life, as we would place a grain of wheat in a sack; and we shall be astonished at having made ourselves such a treasure so easily and so quickly.

16'. For our hearts shall soon be overflowing with God's love, and his light shall guide us in the night of the world towards the unity of the miraculous life that shall never forsake us.

17. You plunge us into darkness and desolation, Lord, but it is because we abandon you, because we deny you and because we betray you; for you are all grace and all love, O Radiant One! and you console us, give us help and enlighten us at our slightest movement towards you.

17'. It is our goodwill in you that triggers your help in heaven. It is our faith in you that manifests it in the world. It is our love in you that recognizes it in our hearts and that praises it in our mouths, O Holiest One! who gives yourself for our failing and lost lives.

18. We shall by no means lead the rebels and the mediocre to the revelation of the sons of God, for the thing bores them and is by nature repugnant to them.

18'. Our preaching appears unreal and useless to them in this world of false reality and false utility that shall soon release them.

19. Is not the whole Book a hymn to the Lord God and like a fountain of youth in which pious souls soak themselves for the love and for the life that never end?

19'. Alas! the religious ones and the impious ones alike repel the rediscovered message of God, and the world repels the servant of God who does not work in the world in the manner of the profane world.

20. At present, we complete the Book thanks to the help of the believers of Pallandt. They make a treasure for themselves that shall astonish them and shall stupefy the world, but no-one yet knows it, not even them.

20'. Their children shall benefit from it and bear witness to it, without the children of the world, who shall see it, being able to take hold of it, because of their malice and their wickedness, which cook in their blood.

21. Because they have not judged our apparent uselessness in the world, the Lord shall not judge their usefulness in his kingdom.

21'. Because they have not scorned our apparent laziness in the world, the Lord shall not scorn their works for his kingdom.

22. Because they have not been scandalised at our apparent weakness in the world, the Lord shall fortify them forever in his kingdom.

23. For the Lord accomplishes the word of his envoys because they also accomplish the word of the Lord.

24. Those who have blindfolded their eyes so as not to see my light shall become ever blinder.

25. Those who have gagged their mouths so as not to question my servants shall become ever more stupid.

26. I shall close their eyes, I shall stop up their ears, I shall put a gag over their mouths and I shall place a heavy stone on their hearts, says the Lord, so that they do not see my envoys, they do not hear them, they do not question them and they do not recognize them.

27. Our origin, our person and our existence shall not be hidden from anybody, so that the scandal of some and the edification of others shall serve as a testimony to them on the day of judgement.

28. The official scholars, heirs and descendants of the furious coalblowers who were the first to force fire, nature, beings and things, are right now honoured and rewarded more than anyone, for they are the priests of the science of the evil one who has the world in his clutches...

22'. Because they have not repelled our apparent poverty in the world, the Lord shall establish them in the overflowing riches of his kingdom.

23'. And the Lord does the will of his children because they also do his will, which is holy and perfect.

24'. Those who have stopped their ears so as not to hear my word shall become even more deaf.

25'. Those who have made their heart heavy so as not to help my devotees shall become even harder and deader.

26'. For my vengeance shall be blind as their eyes have been for my prophets, it shall be deaf as their ears have been for my envoys, it shall be dumb as their mouths have been for my saints, and it shall be heavy as their hearts have been for my poor.

27'. For the prophets that serve God are like stumbling blocks that make some fall, and like foundation stones that consolidate others.

28'. who enchains it on the pretext of freeing it, who poisons it under the mask of beneficence, who stupefies it on the promise of distracting it, who plunges it into darkness on promising it light, who severs it from the God of life by passing himself off as him and imposing death on all.

29. It is not by chance that the demons of hell are represented as ceaselessly working the bellows of the forge that fan the fire in which the damned are burning.

29'. There we are, but our situation is so identical to the ancient image that we can no longer know the state into which we have been hurled by the science of the devil.

30. What is more stupid than the machine? And are we not under the reign of the blind and deaf machine? And do we not adore the machine that chews us up like a beast?

30'. Is there anything more stupid than the anonymous State? And are we not under the reign of the blind and deaf Beast? And do we not adore the Beast that blindly grinds us?

30". The official magicians of Pharaoh are stronger than ever in the world. They have only changed their appearances and tricks, their names and methods, but their marvels still stupefy the world and maintain it in the slavery of death.

31. Profane science has even conquered the heart of the religious ones, who ally themselves with it, without realizing that it devours them unforgivingly.

31'. For they scorned the science of God, which was taken away from them, and now they are held up to ridicule by the science of the devil, which they publicly adore.

32. The time of machines has hardly begun and everyone is seduced, without realizing that machines are dead works that produce nothing but death.

32'. And all think they make use of the machines, without realizing that they themselves serve the machines like slaves dulled by death.

33. They all plead the cause of the rebel at present and praise his accursed science. Priests and nonbelievers, monks and laymen, scholars and the ignorant, artists and workmen, the rich and the poor, the healthy and the sick, the right-thinking and the impious, bosses and labourers, all applaud the fire that shall devour them.

33'. The impious ones say: «We have substituted God for our science» and the believers add: «God has given science to man so that he can free himself» but neither one or the other sees the open abyss beneath their feet, nor the smoke that rises and that shall swallow them up forever.

34. O pain! Our voice is stifled by the multitude of cripples who sink cheerfully into the stinking death of hell, and we remain alone, without means and without help, to make them hear the ultimate warning from the Lord of justice who sends us into the world, like the grain under the wheel of mill.

35. O who shall announce the urgency of repentance with us? And who shall come and help us gather the seed of the new world?

36. O who shall help himself to survive by helping us in our mission that has become impossible through the indifference of all?

37. How shall our Lord receive us if we do not even manage to make his reprimand heard in this dying and profaning world?

38. We humbly plead with you in the name of God's creation that is dying and is going to perish. We ask for your aid so that the Book may appear in the world, and so that it may be distributed before the mortal blow that shall reduce everything to ashes.

39. We beg on our knees for your fraternal aid for the world that is

34'. O cruel punishment! The Book of deliverance remains un-known, while the very filth is royally financed by the rich ones of the world, while the dead faith is bursting with the gifts of the right-thinking ones, while the works of death are encouraged by the good-intentioned ones who serve the devil without wanting to know it.

35'. O who shall let out the cry of alarm with us, before absurdity engulfs the world? And who shall pray to the God of forgiveness so that the Book might appear before the flashing blow of his growling thunderbolt?

36'. And who shall save himself by seeking refuge under the wings of the Highest while the door is still ajar?

37'. Be careful, you who read this, for our character is by nature merry and playful, and the threats we communicate to you come as though over us and through us, without us having anything to do with it.

38'. We ask for your support, O believers in God scattered across the world! so that our testimony might be not in vain and so that the final warning of the Lord of justice might reach all those who still think to save themselves by their own means.

39'. We knock at your hearts, O believers who float on the mud of the

going to perish, but above all, for those who still have hope and who believe in the omnipotence of the Perfect One, amid the rising tide of impious ones, hypocrites, traitors and rebels, who reek of death.

world! so that you might transmit the Book that calls God's children to the high islands, where God's wrath shall pass over their heads without touching them.

These two verses shall be read only after the formal acquiescence of those who listen, for they bind anyone who reads them or who hears them, albeit once only.

40. At present, here we are, each of us responsible before the Lord, for ourselves, for our children, for our parents, for our friends, for our servants and for our close ones, if we neglect to warn them about the threat and about the promise of the Book of the final hour.

40'. At present, here we are as though harnessed to work and as though under the yoke of the Lord who pays the workers of his vineyard, and we cannot go backwards without falling into the pit from which nobody returns. Let us advance, therefore, courageously, for the repose of the Lord is close, and his salary is eternal salvation that does not disappoint.

41. A single verse shall attract God's chosen child, and a single verse shall make the wicked one who has already condemned himself in his heart run away.

41'. For the inspired word of the Lord draws or repels us according to what is hidden in each one of us.

42. Since we have been threatened with the imminent end of the world and nothing has happened, say the impious ones, we no longer believe in that bad joke. Leave us in peace now, and let us organise ourselves in this world that belongs to us.

42'. Alas! they do not know that the prayers, the tears and the sacrifice of the saints and of their patroness have only held back until now the arm of God's wrath, but the weight increases in proportion to our denial of God, and now it is enormous and becoming unsustainable, even for the strongest.

43. Even the crash of God's wrath, which teeters before swooping down on the world, shall not be under-

43'. Even the rumbling of God's wrath, which seethes before submerging the world, shall not be unstood by the men in revolt against God.

44. The believers shall understand, but it shall be too late for many of them because they shall have failed to heed God's warning.

45. My friends, do you not see the restlessness of the absurd that piles up before you all over the world in an impossible equilibrium?

46. My friends, do you not see the number and the enormity of your illnesses in the world, and do you not see the exhausting labour of your work that has continually to be begun again?

47. Many have been taken for being impious because they do not frequent the churches, but they are linked to God because they accomplish the precepts of divine charity.

48. There shall certainly be tears, wailing and gnashing of teeth on the day of retribution, and the surprise at this judgement shall multiply particularly the cries of those who shall find themselves repelled and damned, whereas they considered themselves to be justified and saved.

derstood by the men occupied with themselves.

44'. God's children shall understand and they shall see with their eyes and they shall hear with their ears, but misfortune shall not reach them, for they shall have arrived at the earthly islands of refuge.

45'. Do you not see the universal denial of the true Lord of life, to the benefit of him who fakes and disembodies all life in order to feed on it?

46'. Are you not tired of constructing in the mud without secure foundation, and are you not tired of rotting in the agony of death for so long?

47'. Many pass for pious ones because they observe the exterior ceremonies, but they are cut off from God because they neglect to accomplish the true divine precepts.

48'. There shall also be cries and tears of joy, and unexpected leaps on the day of reckoning and of the baring of souls; and likewise, astonishment at this verdict shall multiply in an unexpected way the praises of those who shall find themselves admitted and justified, when they expected to be thrashed and banished.

48". Those who are intelligent shall take note of these verses and shall change their behaviour, doing what they did not do, without ceasing to do well what they already did.

49. Who is he that scolds and threatens us, the right-thinking ones shall say, and with what right and by what authority does he concern himself with us, whereas we do not know him?

50. He is a layman among laymen, and he is neither cleric nor priest to teach us the way of God, which we know better than he. He is neither appointed nor authorised by anyone to speak to us.

51. Alas! three times alas! the «right-thinking ones» do not like us, and we do not like them. And if we scold them it is by God's order and as by holding our nose, because by ourselves, we would never have had such courage or been so charitable. The impious and the rebellious smell good by comparison with them, and they also appear upright.

52. We call «right-thinking ones» those who flaunt themselves in the churches with the contemptuous insolence conferred upon them by their social and worldly situations, their money, their titles, their diplomas, their decorations, their vanities, their devotions and their false self-assurance as saved ones.

53. We call «right-thinking ones» those who, under the cover of religion and devotion, exploit the unfortunate shamelessly; those who get fat on the sweat and tears of the abandoned ones; those who through their

49'. Who is he to lecture us, and is he worth more than us to scold us so roughly? Is he even part of our brotherhood? For we do not see him at our meetings, nor in our public processions.

50'. Who is he that, while covered in the mud of sin, gets up to thrash us publicly? If he were a prophet of God and envoy of God we should know it, for God would have chosen him by preference over us, since we are reserved in first place for his salvation.

51'. Yes, God has made us a rag-and-bone man against our will, and we are not proud of rummaging in the dustbins of this world. But does one not sometimes find there, among the rubbish, silverware thrown away by negligent servants? And does that silverware, once cleaned, not shine once more on the master's table?

52'. We call «right-thinking ones» those who crush the poor, scorn the simple, corrupt the priests and force their hand when it suits them, thus using the Church to cover up their despicable deeds and to defend their causes of the damned.

53'. We call «right-thinking ones» those who take over holy places for money and do their will there, and not God's will; those who occupy the most important positions, when they are not even worthy of the least;

hypocrisy drive the last believers out of the churches; those who through their selfishness and their contempt give rise to and maintain the rebellion and hate of the unfortunate.

those who bury God's word or turn it to their advantage; those who use the Church to prosper in the world, instead of serving the Church to prosper in God.

53". We call «right-thinking ones» the most insolent, the most hypocritical and the fiercest of rogues; the purebred rogue, who dominates humanity as scoria floats on molten metal, so that he can easily be collected and thrown away as rubbish.

54. If we put ourselves in God's place, we shall cover our eyes and stop our ears and we shall remain in the death of blind and deaf idols.

54'. If we love the Lord, we shall recognize his word and we shall come back humbly to him, who receives us lovingly in his heart.

I summon the apostles of the latter times, the faithful disciples of Jesus Christ... Fight, children of light, you little number, for behold the time of times, the end of ends.

OUR LADY OF LA SALETTE

The apostles of the latter times shall be in all parts the good odour of Jesus Christ for the poor and for the small, while they shall be an odour of death for the great, for the rich and proud worldlings.

LOUIS-MARIE DE MONTFORT

BOOK XXXX

There is a place for silver where it is extracted, for gold, a place where it is purified.

JOB

VÉNÈRE ITU

THE MELTING

1. I shall go to you, my hands full of your grapes and my back bent under the weight of your harvest, and my joy shall be to receive your kiss of life and to communicate it to the children you have entrusted to me, O Lord! who rewards holy obedience.

1'. I shall go to you, with purified heart and clear spirit in your resurrected body, if you send me your salvation from this world, Lord of true love and knowledge; for only your splendour is received by your splendour, and only your holy unity melts into the Unique One.

2. O Lord of freedom! give us the supreme intelligence that is obedience to your holy will, so that your creation be subjected to us through the love we have for it, as we are subjected to you through the love you have for us.

2'. O Lord of foundation! give us the almighty faith that coagulates and dissolves your holy light of life, so that we may be established as lords and faithful guardians of your marvellous creation in the eternity of your glory.

3. Go, take the Book of the final warning and preach to the world that falls asleep in its filth, for the hour is approaching when its time shall end, and it has already begun without anyone realizing it.

3'. Go, take the Book of the last chance and preach my coming while begging for your earthly life, for nothing belongs to anyone here below any longer, but nobody knows it yet.

4. Let us remember the misdeeds that we commit, and let us forget those that we suffer.

5. Alas! those that have taken charge of guiding the believers do not penetrate their own Scriptures and they no longer hear their own Lord, for they have become like blind and deaf civil servants, locked away in dead regulations and abandoned by the Holy Spirit that they hate above all else.

6. At present, we are experiencing the cruel truth of the lordly word, and we see those who have taken charge of transmitting the word of God, burying it and sitting upon it, in case a curious one wants to examine it too closely.

7. The idols of this world seem to satisfy those that serve them and those that flatter them, but in reality they devour their most intimate substance which is their soul, and they offer death to their worshippers as a final reward.

8. Those who have established themselves in the blind and deaf letter of the revealed Scriptures can no

4'. Let us remember the kind deeds done to us and let us forget those we do.

5'. How shall they reply on the day of judgement when they are asked once more for the talent they have buried? Their excessive prudence has become like the worst ignorance, the worst cowardice and the worst death. They have also seized the keys to God's science and, having failed to penetrate it, they now prevent others from entering it.

6'. All the wealthy in money, in honours, in diplomas, in qualifications, in sciences, in castes, in ranks, in positions and in occupations are prevented through pretension and through pride from receiving and penetrating the revealed word of God.

6". They subtly corrupt God's word through their petty judgements, others scorn it openly in the world and all bend it more or less adroitly according to their interests at the time.

7'. We shall go to the humble, the poor, the disinherited, the abandoned, the ignorant, the simple, the small, the vagabonds, the oppressed and the crippled, so that they be made rich, liberated, honoured, instructed, cured and resurrected in the Lord who is coming.

8'. After having ignored us, repelled us, buried us, rejected us, condemned and held us in contempt, the

longer receive anything from the deep and the high, for their pride prevents them from accepting anything from the Holy Spirit that teaches humble and open hearts.

9. We shall blindly and stupidly observe the counsels of the master who tells us to pray for our enemies and to bless our persecutors, to love, to help and to bear others and ourselves, not to judge and not to condemn, to ask for our life from God every day and to thank him and praise him for this inestimable gift, forgiving everyone and doing good in secret without concerning ourselves too much with the affairs of the world.

10. O terror, O sadness! the world has killed indiscriminately the nonbelievers, intelligent or stupid, scholarly or ignorant, for they all reject the Book as a useless and futile thing, after having cast a blind glance over it or after having heard it without understanding it.

11. As for the «right-thinking ones» who have emasculated and killed the word of God in order to preserve it, the living revelation that is offered to them once again frightens them and makes them run away, just as the light makes the cockroaches go back under the blind stone.

12. We shall rejoice in our holy reward.

right-thinking ones shall pillage us shamelessly, without recognizing us.

«Mediocrity and cowardice steal the outer layer, but they do not receive the hidden almond.»

9'. We shall follow the Lord's word blindly and stupidly so that our blind and deaf reason is not an obstacle to the accomplishment of works of faith, so that our superficial judgement does not deprive us of the fruits of works of faith, and so that our fallen intelligence does not drag us into the sordid battle of brutish beasts that never ends.

10'. The curse they have brought upon themselves through their denial and abandonment of God becomes still heavier with their insane vanity, and here they are blind and deaf to the word of life. Their brutishness condemns them more and more without their realizing it, and their false self-assurance leads them to the grave.

11'. They are incapable of discerning the true from the false, the beautiful from the ugly, the good from the bad, life from death, and they need qualified and licensed counsellors, as blind and deaf as themselves, to guide them in their conceited darkness.

12'. And they shall howl like beasts, without even understanding what is happening to them.

13. Those that reject us shall be rejected on the day of judgement.

14. Our triumph in God shall be so dazzling that the damned shall wonder by what miracle they did not hear our voice.

15. Those who love the ancient revelation shall also love the new one.

16. Many shepherds have goodwill, but they have lost the salt of wisdom, and the most instructed among them no longer know it except through symbols and hearsay, without knowing what it truly is.

17. If we are ignored and rejected by the world because of our quest for God, it is because a great reward is reserved for us, but few know this.

18. Many are intelligent and many are reasonable according to the blind and deaf world, but very few possess the divine Spirit that alone enlightens and instructs about the word of God, who teaches the science of eternal life.

19. The more pressing and numerous my advances towards you have been, says the Lord God, the more total and definitive shall be my refusal on the day of judgement if you did not receive them at the time or recognize them in your hearts.

13'. And those who bury us shall be buried forever.

14'. Those we love the most are those who love God and his marvellous creation the most, for are we not child and assistant of God?

15'. Those who understand the new revelation shall also understand the ancient one.

16'. Happy are they who remember that the Lord was born in a humble stable, blessed are they who rediscover his footsteps in this world, and most blessed are they who once more give him warmth like wise donkeys.

17'. The angels of God mount a vigilant guard around those that are promised salvation, so that they do not go astray amid the illusory possessions of this suffering world.

18'. We are not in fashion, and the intelligent and scholars of the world deliberately ignore us, or look down on us sniggering or pityingly. One day we shall also ignore them, in spite of their howls like hunted down beasts.

19'. You shall bite your fingers and your tongue, and you shall tear apart one another in the confusion and rage of your blind and deaf darkness, on learning of your own stupidly chosen sentence.

20. As for you, the blessed of my heart, who have respected my law, observed my commandments and accomplished my work, you shall be dressed in new clothes and you shall wear my glory for eternity, and your joy shall never end, says the silent Judge.

21. The disdain that the world shows us is our safeguard.

22. Our great intelligence and our subtle malice distance us from God's salvation as surely as the stupidity and coarseness of the brutes established here below.

20'. Your surprise shall be dumb, but then your praises and your songs of victory shall cover up even the noise of hell where the damned shall rot, and you shall live in the gratitude of my love without ever tiring, says the Lord of justice and forgiveness.

21'. The attention we pay to God's creation is our rescue.

22'. On seeing you, Lord, we shall fall to the ground, on hearing your voice we shall roll around in joy, on smelling your odour we shall draw ourselves up, and with your kiss you shall pass into us, and we shall live in you forever.

On that day, the deaf shall hear the words «of a Book» and, on coming out of the darkness and obscurity, the blind shall see.

ISAIAH

The words of the sages are like goads, and their collected words like driven nails. They are given by a single Shepherd.

ECCLESIASTES

LITANIES OF THE MOTHER AND OF THE SON

QUEEN WANTS

1. Egg of God.
2. Sea of milk.
3. Luminous secret.
4. Freshness of bones.
5. Living earth.
6. Lucid jewel.
7. Radiant balm.
8. Fragrant Eve.
9. Deluge of grace.
10. Womb of the sun.
11. Moon of purity.
12. Mother of gods.
13. Resplendent water.
14. Sublime remedy.
15. Aureole of saints.
16. Nourishing pulp.
17. Palpable light.
18. Health of body and soul.
19. Diaphanous lover.
20. Cradle of worlds.
21. Flesh of God.
22. Nurse of the stars.
23. Germinative shower.
24. Bounding life.
25. Baptism of resurrection.
26. Multiplier of seeds.
27. Inexhaustible spring.
28. Obligatory entrance.
29. Eternal youth.

KING SAVES

1. Secret of the secret.
2. Seed of fire.
3. Weight of light.
4. Unity of the Unique One.
5. Sun of stone.
6. Fixed and red gold.
7. Dot in the centre.
8. Victorious essence.
9. Animator of stars.
10. Creator of forms.
11. Inhabitant of life.
12. Hub of heaven.
13. Immobile eye.
14. Piercing beauty.
15. Mystery of union.
16. Force of life.
17. Perfect fixedness.
18. Most precious ruby.
19. Him in Her.
20. Indomitable power.
21. Freezer of the sea.
22. Soul of salt.
23. Generous donator.
24. Sweet cooking of life.
25. Treasure without equal.
26. Indefatigable Begetter.
27. Awoken lion.
28. Resurrection of seeds.
29. Condenser of saps.

30	House of God.	30	Universal fertilizer.
31	Marrow of the Universe.	31	Transforming blessing.
32	Beloved tunic.	32	Creator of worlds.
33	Sweet-lit lamp.	33	Saviour of life.
34	Strong-smelling honey.	34	Shepherd of lights.
35	Jelly of heaven.	35	Density of love.
36	Little white bird.	36	Royal purple.
37	Maid of honour.	37	Crown of gold.
38	Marvellous inebriation.	38	Primary and ultimate germ.
39	Ecstasy of the abyss.	39	Erective column.
40	Overflowing virgin.	40	Powerful jet.
41	Rose of forgetting.	41	Transfiguration of the living.
42	Notorious healer.	42	Secret desire of the darkness.
43	Potion of joy.	43	Immortal repose.
44	Immortal friend.	44	Floating loner.
45	Holy oasis.	45	Fixed and living God.
46	Winged refuge.	46	Lord who fulfils.
47	Island of salvation.	47	Remarkable bounty.
48	Rich breast.	48	Magnanimous king.
49	Red-entrailed dove.	49	Transforming fire.
50	Primary clay.	50	Blinding light.
51	Plankton of the heavens.	51	Warmth of life.
52	Raised torch.	52	Vanquisher of death.
53	Succulent dew.	53	Concentration of life.
54	Blessing of God.	54	Essence of wine.
55	Opalescent cloud.	55	Ultimate virtue.
56	Odour of health.	56	Primary number.
57	Elusive fairy.	57	Radiant beauty.
58	Hidden fruit.	58	Unfailing health.
59	Reserved enclosure.	59	Magnet of the stars.
60	Most secret spring.	60	Assembler of universes.
61	Purified womb.	61	Cooker of stars.
62	Melting food.	62	Holy virtuoso.
63	Queen of light.	63	Modeller of gods.
64	Communion of the living.	64	Dark void.
65	Flying host.	65	Clear plenitude.
66	Tree of life.	66	Regent of the great sea.
67	Nectar of the gods.	67	Unique male.
68	Holy quintessence.	68	Victorious buried one.

69	Miraculous washerwoman.	69	Crucified one limbed again.
70	Clarity of the heavens.	70	Dispersed one who unifies.
71	Amiable reconciler.	71	Eternal resurrected one.
72	Refuge of peace.	72	Blaze of fire.
73	Hidden pearl.	73	Incorruptible blood.
74	Errant nacelle.	74	Unbearable look.
75	Mirror of God.	75	Consuming purity.
76	Very deep well.	76	Invincible right side.
77	Lady of love.	77	Serene constructor.
78	Oil of sweetness.	78	Breaker of chains.
79	Queen of the caves.	79	Explosive sweetness.
80	Sleeping one of the rock.	80	Living blaze.
81	Hidden reserve.	81	Freer of slaves.
82	Gathered manna.	82	Dazzling heart.
83	Sweat of the stone.	83	Consumer of filth.
84	Wife of the sun.	84	Overflowing with seed.
85	Mother of eternity.	85	Astounding strength.
86	Enigma that shines.	86	Sharp justice.
87	Innate truth.	87	Piercing arrow.
88	Preserved water.	88	Burner of brambles.
89	Dozing queen.	89	Love that gathers.
90	Veiled beauty.	90	Globe of pure gold.
91	Jam of sages.	91	Fixed quintessence.
92	Soap of the pure.	92	Unshakable rock.
93	Scales of the righteous.	93	Victorious stone.
94	God's altar of repose.	94	Immobile whirlwind.
95	Balmy rose.	95	Destroyer of prisons.
96	Substance of bread.	96	Toppler of walls.
97	Treasure of snow.	97	Knot of worlds.
98	Hoped-for almond.	98	Concentrated fire.
99	Adored firefly.	99	Coagulator of waters.
100	Desired traveller.	100	Ripper-open of tombs.
101	Very first secret.	101	Saviour of the living and the dead.
102	Mother and Daughter, Wife and Sister.	102	End of all ends.
103	Fortified entrance.	103	Consistency of love.
104	Light of the visionaries.	104	Diffuser and gatherer of souls.
105	Sifted star.	105	Ripe fruit.

106	Liquefied earth.	106	Cooked truth.
107	Frozen water.	107	Marvellous concentration.
108	Coagulated air.	108	Soul of creation.
109	Boat of the sun.	109	Taut bow.
110	Food of the chosen ones.	110	Nested eagle.
111	Safeguard of the saints.	111	Manifest and hidden Father.
112	Great sea of the sages.		
113	Unifying clarity.		
114	Living reality.		
115	Renewer of the dead.		
116	Vivandiere of angels.		
117	Devoted nymph.		
118	Beloved one of poets.		
119	Darling of God's children.		
120	Inspired lover.		
121	Dew of heaven and earth.		
122	Alphabet of the prophets.		
123	Pardon of God.		
124	Hidden resurrection.		
125	Mistress of Christians.		
126	Purest eye of believers.		
127	Assembly of stars.		
128	Pale and living gold.		
129	Substantial mystery.		
130	Banquet of God.		
131	Tabernacle of the holiest fire.		
132	Cup of the Lord.		
133	Incombustible incense.		
134	Winged stone.		
135	Dry and moving water.		
136	Secret of hearts.		
137	Lively recumbent figure.		
138	Secret that contains the secret.		
139	Beacon of the strayed ones.		
140	Salvation of those bogged down in the mud.		
141	Magnet of the Lord.		
142	Lye of sweetness.		
143	Friend of the exiled.		
144	Mother sought by all.		

TABLE OF CONTENTS

To the reader 7
Preface by Lanza del Vasto 13
Presentation by Emmanuel and Charles d'Hooghvorst 17
Biographical note 21

THE MESSAGE REDISCOVERED

Dedication... 25
Golden Father.. 26
Radiant Mother 27
The light 28

Book				
I	Vérité nue	The green shoot	....	29
II	Ève tri une	Pure life	....	39
III	Un être vie	Globe without blemish	....	51
IV	Vertu niée	The veil	....	65
V	Trêve unie	The heavenly Mother	....	79
VI	Unité rêve	The eternal circle	....	91
VII	Vu et renié	The Saviour	....	101
VIII	Trié en vue	Love	....	111
IX	Vue tri née	The accomplishment	....	121
X	Ivre et nue	Wisdom	....	131
XI	Rive ténue	Living earth	....	141
XII	Nuit rêvée	The source	....	151
XIII	Vue... et rien	The medium	....	163
XIV	Enivre tue	The presence	....	175
XV	Nuée revit	The way out	....	189

XVI	Réunit Ève	The rock	....	207
XVII	Ève nue rit	Joy	....	223
XVIII	Vie neutre	The wait	....	237
XIX	Nue vitrée	The mirror	....	251
XX	Vête ruine	Salt	....	265
XXI	Vue nitrée	Frost	....	279
XXII	Évite en Ur	The sage	....	297
XXIII	Une ère vit	The unity	....	315
XXIV	Rétive nue	The well	....	331
XXV	Vit en urée	The stone	....	343
XXVI	Vient ruée	The choice	....	353
XXVII	Un iver été	Time	....	365
XXVIII	Ni revêtue	The mire	....	377
XXIX	Urne et vie	The egg	....	389
XXX	Vue ternie	The darkness	....	399
XXXI	Neuve trie	The light	....	407
XXXII	Vire ne tue	The colours	....	417
XXXIII	Érin vêtue	The flowers	....	425
XXXIV	Tire en uve	Snow	....	433
XXXV	Vête en uri	Blood	....	445
XXXVI	Reine veut	King saves	....	457
XXXVII	Étuve rien	The beginning	....	477
XXXVIII	Une vérité	The end	....	493
XXXIX	Verte unie	The island	....	507
XXXX	Vénère itu	The melting	....	519

Litanies of the Mother and of the Son 525

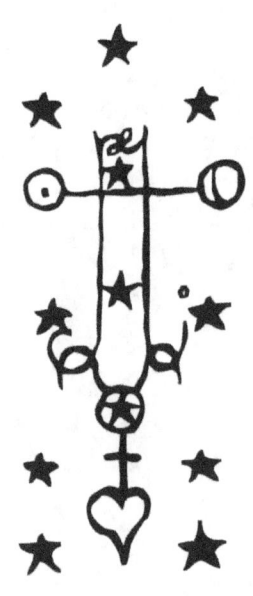

All rights reserved
Printed in E.U.
Legal deposit : February 2024

www.ingramcontent.com/pod-product-compliance
Lightning Source LLC
Chambersburg PA
CBHW051358230426
43669CB00011B/1691